How It Feels to Be Free

How It Feels to Be Free

Black Women Entertainers and the Civil Rights Movement

RUTH FELDSTEIN

OXFORD
UNIVERSITY PRESS

OXFORD
UNIVERSITY PRESS

Oxford University Press is a department of the University of Oxford.
It furthers the University's objective of excellence in research,
scholarship, and education by publishing worldwide.

Oxford   New York

Auckland   Cape Town   Dar es Salaam   Hong Kong   Karachi
Kuala Lumpur   Madrid   Melbourne   Mexico City   Nairobi
New Delhi   Shanghai   Taipei   Toronto

With offices in

Argentina   Austria   Brazil   Chile   Czech Republic   France   Greece
Guatemala   Hungary   Italy   Japan   Poland   Portugal   Singapore
South Korea   Switzerland   Thailand   Turkey   Ukraine   Vietnam

Oxford is a registered trade mark of Oxford University Press
in the UK and certain other countries.

Published in the United States of America by
Oxford University Press
198 Madison Avenue, New York, NY 10016

Parts of this book have been adapted from "'I Don't Trust You Anymore': Nina Simone, Culture,
and Black Activism in the 1960s," *Journal of American History*, March 2005, Volume 91, Number 4:
1349–1379, by permission of Oxford University Press, and "Screening Antiapartheid: Miriam Makeba,
'Come Back, Africa' and the Transnational Circulation of Black Culture and Politics," *Feminist Studies*,
Volume 39, Number 1 (2013): 12–39. Reprinted by permission of the publisher, Feminist Studies, Inc.

Library of Congress Cataloging-in-Publication Data
Feldstein, Ruth, 1965–
How it feels to be free : black women entertainers and the civil rights movement / Ruth Feldstein.
pages   cm
Includes bibliographical references and index.
ISBN 978-0-19-531403-8 (alk. paper)
1. African American women political activists—History—20th century.
2. African American women entertainers—Political activity—History—20th century.
3. Performing arts—Political aspects—United States—20th century.
4. African Americans—Music—Political aspects—History—20th century.
5. African Americans—Civil rights—History—20th century.
6. United States—Race relations—History—20th century. I. Title.
E185.86.F4342   2013
323.1196'073—dc23   2013019878

1 3 5 7 9 8 6 4 2

Printed in the United States of America
on acid-free paper

To Asa, Sara, Max, and Elizabeth

Contents

How It Feels to Be Free

Introduction

PERFORMING CIVIL RIGHTS

Overture

When Lena Horne walked into an elegant apartment in midtown Manhattan to meet with attorney general Robert Kennedy on May 24, 1963, she did more than join in solidarity with black Americans. She crossed into a new chapter in her own evolving activism. Horne might have been invited to the Kennedy family's New York home because of her celebrity status, but she left it feeling quite changed. At least, that is how she described this experience in her autobiography *Lena*, published two years later.[1]

The unusual gathering was the result of conversations that Robert Kennedy and African American writer James Baldwin had been having about dramatic events unfolding in Birmingham, Alabama. For weeks, African Americans in Birmingham had staged massive nonviolent protests and demonstrations to desegregate public facilities, and for weeks, the city's commissioner Bull Connor, state troopers, and other white supporters of segregation had responded with violence. Footage of protesters—including children—facing beatings, hoses, and dogs appeared on televisions around the country and in newspapers across the world. Bombs had exploded in the home of Martin Luther King Jr.'s brother and at the hotel headquarters for the Southern Christian Leadership Conference (SCLC). In this atmosphere, the attorney general wanted to reaffirm the administration's commitment to civil rights in the company of influential African Americans. But he also wanted those influential African Americans to consider what role they might play in de-escalating the situation, and how they could counter the rising militancy among masses of protesters in Birmingham and in other cities that might be wracked by related scenes of violence. Baldwin, most famous at that point for *The Fire Next Time*, two essays written in the form of letters that shot to the top of bestseller lists and "sounded a warning and a hope" about race relations, reached out primarily to intellectuals and entertainers. In addition to Horne, the delegation he convened included singer and film star Harry Belafonte, psychologist Kenneth Clark, Lorraine Hansberry, author of the award-winning play *A Raisin in the Sun*, and younger organizers from civil rights organizations.[2]

The meeting did not go as Kennedy hoped. After hors d'oeuvres and small talk, he explained how important it was for African Americans to support the administration and steer away from the kind of radical protest he associated with Malcolm X. Jerome Smith, a 23-year-old activist with the Congress of Racial Equality (CORE), refused to acquiesce to Kennedy's perspective. Smith was a veteran of the Freedom Rides, a 1961 campaign to desegregate interstate buses during which pro-segregation whites severely beat black and white activists and bombed buses. For much of their journey, Freedom Riders had received limited support from government officials. Sitting in the Kennedy apartment alongside celebrities from Hollywood, Broadway, and Washington, D.C., Smith named the deep frustration that many African Americans were experiencing and their unwillingness, two years later, to wait for small steps on the part of the administration. He would never fight for the United States, he said; even being in the same room with Kennedy and having a conversation that he felt was oriented around accommodation made him want to throw up. Some of the celebrities supported Smith's perspective—Hansberry walked out when Kennedy sought to dismiss what Smith said as unpatriotic—and any common ground was hard to find amidst threats of vomiting and countercharges of disloyalty.[3]

The Curtain Rises

From the mid-1950s into the early 1960s, activism that had been evident for decades among African Americans escalated into more visible and sustained struggles for black freedom. It is difficult to date when the civil rights movement started, and in fact, the word *movement* is itself potentially misleading given how many strands were braided together in struggles for black freedom that developed over a long period of time and across regional and national boundaries. The familiar opposition between nonviolent interracial activism ostensibly based in the South and separatist radicalism ostensibly based in the North does not begin to capture what was in reality overlapping sets of strategies and organizers. In varied coalitions, "ordinary" people with no prior connection to social movements, as well as leaders and grassroots activists, all generated activism that was energizing and mutually reinforcing, affecting people across generations and borders.[4]

Culture was a key battleground in the civil rights movement. Had that not been the case, Robert Kennedy would never have taken comedian Dick Gregory's advice to meet with Baldwin, Horne, and other black celebrities. In 1962, Lorraine Hansberry issued a "challenge to artists." She declared that people who worked in the entertainment and culture industries needed to "paint," "sing," and "write" about civil rights.[5] While many artists, singers, and writers would heed Hansberry's call in the years to come, many other performers were already involved in struggles for black freedom, and had been for some time.

There were those who chose to affiliate directly and publicly. Harry Belafonte's hit songs such as "Day-O" and "Jamaica Farewell" did not speak directly to civil rights issues in the ways that "We Shall Overcome" did. But at least from the time of the Montgomery Bus Boycott in 1956 onward, he performed on behalf of civil rights organizations, raised funds from other entertainers, strategized with full-time organizers, and provided essential financial support for events and for Martin Luther King Jr. personally. As an activist-entertainer, Belafonte and others, including Dick Gregory and actors Ossie Davis and Ruby Dee, put their popularity on the line by consistently identifying with black activism in the 1960s. The SNCC Freedom Singers were protesters and performers; they used music and song (with titles like "Fighting for My Rights" and "I Love Your Dog, I Love My Dog") to carry their explicit message of protest from the jails in Albany, Georgia, in 1961 to the Newport Folk Festival in 1963, fundraising and educating along the way. As Freedom Singer member, scholar, and activist Bernice Johnson Reagon subsequently observed, civil rights freedom struggles revealed "culture to be not luxury, not leisure, not entertainment, but the lifeblood of a community."[6]

Other entertainers supported black freedom struggles in less direct ways. Sam Cooke, for example, sang that "a change is going to come" in his 1964 song by that name, but did not identify with or perform on behalf of civil rights organizations. Another singer, Martha Reeves, repeatedly claimed that she had never intended "Dancing in the Street" to have anything to do with the violence that occurred in numerous Northern cities after the song's release in 1964. "My Lord, it was a party song," she later said. Still, Reeves could not control the ways that many consumers made sense of the song as having everything to do with black urban protest.[7] With a spectrum of involvement and performance strategies, these and many other entertainers helped to make the civil rights movement meaningful to people around the world. A multitude of people never marched or boycotted, but they encountered and responded to the politics of black activism when they listened to certain music, bought particular albums, or watched certain films and television shows.[8]

Into the Spotlight

Lena Horne and five younger women performers—South African folk singer Miriam Makeba, jazz vocalist and pianist Nina Simone, jazz vocalist and film actress Abbey Lincoln, and stage, film, and television actresses Diahann Carroll and Cicely Tyson—were among those entertainers who became prominent in the overlapping worlds of civil rights politics and entertainment. *How It Feels to Be Free* tells the story of this cohort of black women entertainers, and the ways that they developed interrelated performance strategies and political positions during a long and multifaceted civil rights movement. All six women used their status as celebrities to support black activism and all six played with gender roles as they performed black womanhood in new and distinct ways.[9] In their public performances and their political protests—and crucially in myriad instances when the lines between those blurred—they drew attention to unequal relationships between blacks and whites *and* to relationships between men and women. As a result, even when they were part of larger groups of activist-entertainers who connected popular culture and racial politics, these women also stood out. Whether they were at a jazz club in Greenwich Village or on a movie set in Hollywood, performing before a live television audience or at an international music festival in France, Horne, Makeba, Simone, Lincoln, Carroll, and Tyson drew attention to the fact that they were women and black. In all sorts of ways, they insisted that the liberation they desired could not separate race from sex.[10]

   The contributions that Horne, Makeba, Simone, Lincoln, Carroll, and Tyson made to black activism also affected another transformative social movement: second-wave feminism. These women did not necessarily call themselves feminists. But they offered critiques and demands that became central tenets of feminism generally and of black feminism specifically.[11]

With some good reason, many people associate women's liberation with white women, but these black women performers shift attention beyond famous markers like publication of Betty Friedan's *The Feminine Mystique* in 1963 or protests and (mythical) bra burnings at the Miss America pageant in 1968. In the late 1950s, Abbey Lincoln rejected comparisons between herself and Marilyn Monroe and rejected a route toward celebrity based on tight-fitting and revealing gowns. A few years later, Nina Simone sang about the rage of a black woman domestic in her remake of "Pirate Jenny." Black women entertainers' politicized performances suggest that a concern with gender politics did not necessarily develop out of or after concerns with racial politics, precisely because they were among those who addressed issues of race and gender and, often, class at the same time.[12]

With fans around the world and ties to different countries, these six black women performers, and their activism on- and offstage, had international dimensions. They traveled extensively and were able to export ideas about black protest and gender at the same time that the people they met and the experiences they had outside of the United States had an impact on the choices that they made domestically. Through their work as entertainers, popular culture and civil rights together crossed borders, affording consumers opportunities for pleasure and commitment.[13]

Lena Horne, from the start of her career in the 1930s into the 1960s, and Miriam Makeba, Nina Simone, Abbey Lincoln, Diahann Carroll, and Cicely Tyson from the late 1950s onward all worked hard to control their public images. But people loved to talk and write about famous stars and celebrity culture, and these women set into motion widespread conversations among critics, fans, and activists that they could not always control. Their political significance developed out of the cultural work they did and their efforts at self-representation, as well as the ways that fans and critics reacted to them and produced them as celebrities. The music the women sang, the records they sold, and the films and television shows in which they appeared were not direct extensions of preexisting political organizing or ideologies and were not mirrors that simply reflected back entrenched black activism. Miriam Makeba's "The Click Song," for instance, did not at first glance seem to be political in any way. However, her encounters with audiences when she performed this celebratory melody transformed the literal meaning of the lyrics. Performances and reactions to these performances together shaped dialogues about race relations and gender. These, in turn, contributed to shifting expectations about freedom for black Americans and about relations between the sexes.[14]

In short, *How It Feels to Be Free* suggests that a fuller understanding of black activism and feminism requires expanding the realm of political activity. Ministers, marches, activist leaders, grassroots organizers, and legislation were all important to the way that civil right politics became relevant to ordinary Americans and non-Americans outside of political organizations, but so too was a global mass culture in which these black women played a crucial role. The ways in which they came to "perform civil rights"—the ways that their on- and offstage appearances and reactions to these appearances, became ground on which both performers and audiences made sense of black activism—helped constitute the political history of this period.

The Cast

Horne, Makeba, Simone, Lincoln, Carroll, and Tyson were hardly the only ones to "perform civil rights," and this was by no means a monolithic group. The women's backgrounds, political commitments, performance styles, and fans diverged considerably. Miriam Makeba hailed from a small town outside of Johannesburg, South Africa, and Abbey Lincoln was born in Chicago; Diahann Carroll sang on Broadway, in nightclubs, and on the *Ed Sullivan* show, while Cicely Tyson never sang at all in these years.[15] When Lena Horne attended the March on Washington in 1963, she was 46 years old and had long been associated with Hollywood glamour. By contrast, Nina Simone, nearly 20 years younger than Horne, was known by the early 1960s for her fiery songs opposing racial discrimination. She rarely performed on television, never appeared in a Hollywood film, and was associated with militant black radical politics; some whites admit to having been frightened of her in the 1960s. The women's careers traversed television and film, jazz and pop music, the National Association for the Advancement of Colored People (NAACP) and the Black Panthers, Selma and South Africa.

Alongside these and other differences these six women shared a great deal. They were all famous around the world. All had some relationship with organized movements for racial equality. Their careers nurtured and were nurtured by black activism, and they took risks when they chose to participate in struggles for black freedom and to straddle the worlds of culture and politics. Further, all six were part of circles of New York–based activist-entertainers, offering a window into the significance of women to the city's subcultures of activists and artists.[16]

Perhaps of greatest importance, their performances inspired more than critical acclaim and commercial success. These were women who moved their fans—who got them on their feet and brought them to tears. To see Lena Horne in her first moments on screen as the sexy temptress Georgia Brown, in the all-black cast film *Cabin in the Sky* (1943), emerge from a tiled bathroom in a silk robe into a bedroom decorated with ribbons, lingerie, mirrors, and other luxuries; to see her then powder her face, remove her robe to reveal a lace bra from the back, and then dress in a skirt and polka dot midriff tied up inches above her navel and liberally perfume herself, is to witness what was compelling about Horne as a new kind of black female celebrity. To listen to Nina Simone sing "Mississippi Goddam" is to hear talent, self-control, and emotion; to feel power and rage; and to sense politics in motion. This is not a celebratory story of linear progress. But to watch and listen to all of these women is to witness transformations in American society more broadly, and to experience the overlapping emotional and political impact that they had. When New Jersey governor Chris Christie lowered the flag to half-mast to mark the 2012 death of singer Whitney Houston, and when mourners celebrated her as a patriot and as a star, they affirmed these transformations—even as they were also implicitly acknowledging the ongoing struggles many black women performers have faced.

How It Feels to Be Free is not a collective biography or a comprehensive overview of six careers or personal lives. It focuses on particular episodes and select periods in each woman's professional life as a way to explore shared conversations and concerns across this loosely connected cohort. Taken together, these episodes illuminate four related issues: the multiple ways that cultural production mattered to black activism; the transnational and domestic dimensions of black politics and culture; the simultaneous development of black activism and feminism; and the significance of gender and popular culture to canonical memories of the civil rights movement that continue to circulate today.[17] Ultimately, this book explores how black women entertainers made sense of, supported, developed, critiqued, and disseminated black activism in cultural work that may at times have seemed to be "just" entertainment. As they did so, it argues, they also helped to remake meanings of black womanhood.

"Exactly Who She Is": Lena Horne Across Decades

Lena Horne stands out in this group. By the time she wrote her autobiography *Lena* and described the meeting she attended with Robert Kennedy, Horne was an international celebrity whose career had already spanned three decades. She was associated with a series of firsts, such as integrating

big band music when she toured with the previously all-white Charlie Bar-
net Band in 1940, to name just one. *Lena* began with her birth in 1917 and
chronicled key events in her professional life: how she began dancing professionally in Harlem's Cotton Club in 1933, how her singing career blos-
somed over the course of the 1930s, as she toured with Noble Sissle's
Society Orchestra and in nightclubs. The book was a "who's who" of the
people she met—Richard Wright, Joe Louis, Billie Holiday, Vincente Min-
nelli, Ava Gardner, Humphrey Bogart—during her stints at Barney
Josephson's Café Society Downtown in the 1930s and, after 1941, in Hollywood. She offered details about her movie career and how she had
appeared in some eleven films in the 1940s. Mostly this was in the role of
singer who was marginal to the main story, but in two all-black cast films
released in 1943, Horne played the lead: as the performer Selina Rogers in
Stormy Weather and as Georgia Brown in *Cabin in the Sky*.[18]

Yet Horne emphasized her politicization and activism on behalf of civil
rights between 1963 and 1965 as *the* definitive turning point in her life,
and she portrayed the meeting with Kennedy as both a climax and a
trigger. It was an emotionally significant event, she explained, because the
young activist Jerome Smith, the "soul of the meeting," took "us back to
the common dirt of our existence and rubbed our noses in it." As a result,
despite Kennedy's goals, nobody wanted to be "logical and reasonable and
patient" and nobody cared, she said, "about expressions of good will." This
encounter was a catalyst, according to *Lena*, because subsequently Horne
participated in a concert sponsored by the Student Nonviolent Coordinating Committee (SNCC) in New York and flew to Jackson, Mississippi,
to sing at a rally alongside NAACP leader Medgar Evers. Horne emphasized the impact Evers had on her and her horror and rage when she heard
about his murder in June just a week after she had been with him in Mississippi. She also described her decision to record new songs that had to
do with African American struggles for freedom and to perform and speak
on behalf of SNCC, the SCLC, the National Council of Negro Women
(NCNW), and other civil rights organizations.[19]

This autobiography was just one source among many that created a
before-and-after arc about Lena Horne. In *Lena* and in other accounts,
Horne suggested that prior to the 1960s, she had merely been a "good
little symbol." Black leaders "spent a lot of time telling me to be on my best
behavior," Horne recalled, and she had complied—so much so that she
"was ice," according to one critic. The "after" part of the story, which accelerated following the meeting with Kennedy, showed an ascent. Specifically

as a result of her activism she "was awake again." When she sang her new civil rights-oriented songs, Horne wrote in the last sentences of *Lena*: "I was really home at last. . . . [H]ome to my race and my people." Fans and critics agreed, and in the 1960s, an established consensus across lines of race developed about the famous Lena Horne: in the 1940s she had been a "cold, hard, professional, stylized, mannered, taut and tense singer of sophistication," as one journalist put it. In the 1960s she became "absolutely joyful" and "determined to be exactly who she is."[20]

If, like many movies that begin with older characters and then flash back to their younger selves, the tape of Lena Horne's life is rewound, the 1940s look very different indeed. In this period, Lena Horne carved out a unique position for herself as a politicized black female entertainer. Twenty years before she sat with Robert Kennedy and James Baldwin in New York, or stood alongside Medgar Evers in Jackson, her friends and allies ranged from Walter White, executive director of the NAACP in the 1940s, to Paul Robeson, the left-oriented and deeply politically engaged entertainer. Her activism, like her fans, crossed numerous divides.

Horne's family was anchored in the black bourgeoisie of the early twentieth century, a world in which manners, hard work, and racial uplift were watchwords. Dignified behavior was considered, along with organizing, a vehicle through which to improve race relations. This lineage was evident in Horne's allies and activism and was also apparent in the ways that white and black critics reacted to her. In 1947, a critic from the *New York Post* geographically located her as part of a black elite when he commended the "pretty Negro actress and singer" as a "hardworking gal from Chauncey Street." Horne's musical repertoire, one that relied more on popular songs and nightclub ballads than on jazz or blues music associated with poorer African American migrants to the north, reinforced ideas about her respectability. In Hollywood, Walter White counted on Horne as an ally in his efforts to "have broadened the roles in which Negroes are presented in the moving pictures," as Eleanor Roosevelt put it, in a letter supporting this campaign.[21]

At the same time, in the 1940s, Horne not only adhered to a code in which ladylike and respectable behavior was the way to prove that African Americans deserved inclusion. She also wrote columns, joined organizations, and gave interviews and speeches supporting desegregation and progressive candidates. Among those she endorsed were Benjamin Davis, a prominent African American politician and communist activist who represented Harlem, and Henry Wallace, who ran in the presidential election of 1948 as the Progressive Party candidate. Despite Walter White's admonitions that Horne dress conservatively and not be "too" outspoken, she associated with the left, and named class- and race-based inequities that African Americans faced. "Tired and overworked as she may be," according to a 1947 article about the "real Lena Horne" in *Ebony*, "she rarely turns down a request to appear at a benefit, a mass meeting or a party to speak out against race hate, for housing and veterans needs, against with-hunters."[22]

Lena Horne was thus never content to remain just a lady and was never seen only in that light either. As a performer, she rejected definitions of black women as either sexualized Jezebels or as caretaking and subordinate Mammies. These were powerful and historically entrenched images that had boxed in all black women and had limited the options for black women performers for over a century. Two stories that circulated widely in the 1940s and that Horne recycled 20 years later in *Lena* captured how she stood out: In one, Horne, in 1941, became the first African American woman to sign a contract with a major Hollywood studio, one in which MGM executives acceded to her demand that she not play any maids on film. This deal was the "biggest news in recent years," wrote one observer in the black press.[23] The second occurred in 1943, when Horne was one of many celebrities who entertained American soldiers under the auspices of the United Services Organization (USO). At a base in Arkansas, she learned that prisoners of war would have better seats to one of her shows than African American servicemen. She voiced objections to the local NAACP and the next day gave a performance exclusively for black soldiers. Even then, Nazi prisoners of war "crowded in" (according to one account). Horne again insisted that they be excluded. When the U.S. military denied her request, Horne stopped touring with the USO. She continued to entertain American soldiers, but she funded and organized her trips independently.[24]

"Glamorous" was the word that critics, black and white, consistently used to describe Lena Horne.[25] It was *the* attribute through which Horne carved out a space for herself in the 1940s as what might be called a respectable sex symbol. Horne stood out as a performer not just because of her talent or her beauty (though both were notable and much commented on), but because she represented herself as a distinctly modern black female performer, one who was sexual and respectable, who was desirable yet also unattainable. Known as the "first black pinup girl," Horne claimed the right of African American men to look at her as a glamorous

FIGURE O.I Lena Horne singing next to pianist Silky Hendricks of the 299th Ground Force Band, during a war bond tour performance in 1945.

(Ralph Crane/Time Life Pictures/Getty Images)

sex symbol. In her confrontation with the American military, she asserted her right as a black woman to be the object of their gaze and their rights as soldiers/citizens to desire her. For an African American female entertainer to claim—and be granted access—to the category of "sex symbol" and the designation "radiantly beautiful" was significant because for centuries whites had implicitly and explicitly defined "beauty" as a value that excluded black women. At the same time, Horne countered the centuries-old assumption that black women were inherently available objects of white male sexual desire.[26]

Even a scene that did not appear in *Cabin in the Sky*—of the fictional Georgia Brown in a bubble bath, with bare shoulders swaying as she sings "Ain't It the Truth"—attested to Horne's unique status. It became common knowledge that censors eliminated this scene prior to the film's official release. While the incident was surely evidence for the combination of racism and sexism that limited black women in the entertainment industry and the power that angry local calls for censorship could have, it also suggested that for all of the sexual appeal Horne had, she was a star who could not be seen in too compromising a position. "She never has had a bubble bath in her life, except for movie purposes," noted journalist Frank Nugent, adding that the Georgia Brown version of Lena Horne was "strictly a movie creation."[27] That Horne was challenging assumptions about black women was clear at the time; with Lena Horne, "we have," in the words of the then-popular periodical *Negro Digest*, "the most powerful of all social weapons: glamour."[28]

Why, then, did Lena Horne conclude that if the meeting with Robert Kennedy had "any value," it was "to impress on Mr. Kennedy the depth of the feelings that Negroes not directly involved" with politics had?[29] Why and how did she count herself among the politically uninvolved when her work—onstage and off—had significant political meaning, for all African Americans and especially for African American women? And why did she describe herself as having represented blackness in all of the wrong ways earlier in time?

Horne was profoundly influenced by a "younger generation" of activist-entertainers who "made this revolution," as she put it in 1965, and by the debates about culture, politics, and meanings of race and blackness that were swirling around her in New York from the late 1950s onward. In 1957, Horne had the starring role in the Broadway show *Jamaica*. During this year and a half of "heaven," the woman who was an "institution," according to *Jamaica* costar Ossie Davis, lived in Manhattan and befriended

FIGURE 0.2 Lucifer Jr. (Rex Ingram) urges the glamorous Georgia Brown (Lena Horne) to "mosey over" to see—and seduce—Little Joe (Eddie Anderson) in the 1943 film *Cabin in the Sky*.
(Academy of Motion Picture Arts and Sciences)

many "young modern kids," in and out of show business. She associated the younger people she met with "activism" and with "new techniques for dealing" with problems that they encountered on and off stage. Horne concluded that "a new generation was taking over." And she was deeply impressed.[30] It was from this vantage point that she regarded her meeting with Robert Kennedy as a turning point and came to the conclusion that her earlier self did not meet the criteria for appropriate or authentic expressions of blackness and activism.[31]

As Horne grappled with the work that a younger generation was doing, younger women performers, in turn, grappled with her legacy and ongoing presence. In direct and indirect ways, Miriam Makeba, Nina Simone, Abbey Lincoln, Diahann Carroll, and Cicely Tyson encountered the long shadow that Lena Horne cast as an icon of black female glamour and felt the impact of Horne's decades of celebrity. Like Horne, they developed performance strategies and political positions; like Horne, they were deeply concerned with how they could (or could not) represent themselves. Horne was involved as an activist-entertainer in the '60s at the same time

that she was a foundational figure to whom younger black women entertainers were consistently compared. The five younger stars looked to Lena
Horne as a model, alternatively as what to be and what not to be.

Setting the Stage

All six of these women drew on a rich tradition of black women performers
who for centuries had used entertainment to resist racist and sexual stereotypes. In her study of race and performance in the nineteenth century,
scholar Daphne Brooks explains how historically black women performers
could have a significant impact because they evoked an "insurgent power"
that exceeded the ways that audiences tried to define them as primitive
and as sexualized objects.[32] Black women entertainers reached even larger
audiences by the early twentieth century when networks of transportation
and communication improved and mass culture industries like radio,
records, and film flourished. Singer, dancer, and actress Aida Overton
Walker was perhaps the first black woman entertainer associated with this
era of mass culture; consumers in the United States and in England celebrated her as the "Queen of the Cakewalk"—a dance routine with roots in
slavery that featured women in elegant dress and inventive body movements that she popularized in the early 1900s. Forty years before Horne's
contract with MGM and declarations that "she's nobody's Mammy,"
Walker refused to appear on stage in plantation-era garb.[33]

Many black women performers experienced success and significant
exploitation simultaneously. In the 1910s and '20s, for example, blues
singers like Gertrude "Ma" Rainey and Bessie Smith had crossover appeal
among black and white consumers of "race records." They sang about
issues of importance to black women—men who mistreated them, the
pleasures of good sex, and the challenges that working-class African
American migrants from the rural South faced in the urban North. Fans
were captivated, even as many whites associated them with sexual promis-
cuity, deviance, and racial inferiority, and even as women performers
faced widespread discrimination in the record business and in daily life.
In the United States and then in France, the American-born singer and
dancer Josephine Baker, know in the 1920s for the "Danse sauvage" and
her costume—a skirt of artificial bananas—found ways to capitalize on
associations between black women and primitive sexuality to garner international fame and offer new aesthetic styles. She was able to use, if not
free herself from, associations as the quintessential black exotic woman.[34]

Hollywood films offered performers unprecedented visibility and potential mass appeal, but posed challenges to black women who had so little control over the modes of production. In the 1930s, Ethel Waters, Hattie McDaniel, Fredi Washington, Louise Beavers, and other ambitious and talented black women found ways to work in this white-dominated and segregated industry. They did not have many choices about the kinds of roles they played, but they infused what seemed to be stereotypical parts of black servants or "tragic mulattas" with a combination of dignity, humor, and unforgettable personal style. McDaniel's "Mammy" in *Gone with the Wind*, for example, was a landmark performance for which she became, in 1939, the first African American woman to receive an Oscar. Facing criticism from prominent African Americans like NAACP executive director Walter White for perpetuating negative stereotypes, she retorted, "Why should I complain about making seven thousand dollars a week playing a maid? If I didn't, I'd be making seven dollars a week actually being one!" This story is in all likelihood apocryphal. Yet it persists and continues to resonate because it attests to the ways that black women in the entertainment industry who made money and inspired pride among African American fans could still face criticism for the ways that they represented black women.[35]

McDaniel and others sought to undermine images of black women as subordinate Mammies by performing their own version of subordination on screen. Still other women in this era, such as pianists and singers like Hazel Scott and Marian Anderson, achieved acclaim when they gained access to arenas associated with elite culture—the Metropolitan Opera House, Carnegie Hall, and the Juilliard School, for example. Composer Mary Lou Williams, with her religious jazz music, reached St. Patrick's Cathedral. Gospel singer and guitarist Rosetta Tharpe fused church-based gospel music with early rock 'n' roll and rejected the dichotomy between sacred and secular, much to the delight of her fans in the 1930s and 1940s. These and other black women performers built careers in mass culture and in high culture. They insisted on their talent and relevance and defied prevailing expectations of what black women could do and what spaces they should occupy as performers. Sometimes their covert challenges became overt. In 1939, when white members of the Daughters of the American Revolution blocked singer Marian Anderson from performing at Constitution Hall in Washington, D.C., she instead gave a free and much publicized outdoor concert at the Lincoln Memorial. With supporters who included First Lady Eleanor Roosevelt, Anderson used her concert to counter the discrimination that the DAR endorsed.[36]

The women of *How It Feels to Be Free* extended this history when they engaged politically through culture and performance, but also took advantage of changes in the music, film, and television industries to define themselves as doing something new. It was no coincidence that black activism accelerated in the post–World War II years at the same time that mass consumer culture industries also proliferated. Culture became increasingly critical in the postwar fight for civil rights for several reasons. Activists relied on newer commodities like television (and older venues like the press and radio) to disseminate images and news about political protests, despite resistance from whites in these industries. In addition to concrete physical connections between technologies of popular culture and political organizing, participating in a vibrant consumer culture and enjoying entertainment were among the ways that African Americans asserted their rights as citizens.[37] Protesters might demand, for example, the right to buy tickets at a movie theater, to sit in good seats once they had tickets, and to see themselves accurately represented on screen. Their claims exposed the interconnections between race and political representation, and between cultural representations and economics. Many black activists were committed to reshaping identities as well as power relations and laws. As African Americans reconsidered meanings of blackness in their public lives, in personal relationships, and in seemingly apolitical leisure activities, popular culture assumed added relevance. It was an arena in which they carved out new meanings of identity and renegotiated power relations. This was true for those who struggled for creative control in culture industries as well as for black consumers.[38]

Horne, Makeba, Simone, Lincoln, Carroll, and Tyson tended to encounter two sets of reactions to their work. The first had to do with the veracity of what they said, sang about, performed, or looked like. Was it real? Was it accurate? In other words, were they representing blackness, on-screen, on stage, or in song in a way that was *authentic*? Of course, as the example of McDaniel in *Gone With the Wind* makes clear, the definition of authenticity was fraught; many white audiences concluded that "Mammy" was an accurate representation of racial subordination in the antebellum era, whereas some African American critics and fans (even those who objected vociferously to the film) saw a smart and outspoken fictional character who talked back to the whites she ostensibly served and who was usually right in her assessments of them.[39] Although authenticity itself was a moving target, it persisted as a barometer on which to evaluate black performers. A second related recurring question was whether black women performers succeeded because of or in spite of race. Was Miriam Makeba a great folk singer whose talent transcended national and racial boundaries, or was she a great South African black woman singer? Was the television sitcom *Julia*, in 1968, a landmark because its heroine, played by Diahann Carroll, was a black woman, or because the series deemed the race of that heroine unimportant? This tension between universalism and racial particularity had a long history and affected male entertainers as well. But as with questions about authenticity, it became increasingly relevant to black women entertainers in the civil rights era as advocates of black power and black cultural nationalism argued that black cultural autonomy was an essential political strategy. Debates about authenticity and universalism moved from the background to the foreground and would have specific implications for black women.[40]

The five younger performers—Makeba, Simone, Lincoln, Carroll, and Tyson—all lived and worked in New York in the late 1950s. They participated in Greenwich Village and Harlem subcultures around which activism and cultural experimentation coalesced. From those subcultures, they built for themselves national and international reputations. Although these were the same neighborhoods where Horne had started her career 20 years earlier, the scene in which this generation met each other and others felt remarkably different. Chapter 1 explores the sense of excitement and possibility among black entertainer-activists in the late 1950s.

South African singer Miriam Makeba first arrived in the United States in 1958 and made the country her home for the next decade. Her songs from this period rarely mentioned the apartheid regime that officially exiled her in 1961, and for several years after her arrival, she seldom discussed or sang about racial politics in any explicit way. Yet, as chapter 2 suggests, through her popularity among white and black audiences, she educated American consumers about apartheid and antiapartheid activism, and gestured toward the connections between civil rights in South Africa and in the United States. Her performance strategies as a black woman from South Africa had repercussions for women internationally and for the development of both black power and second-wave feminism.

Nina Simone embraced in her music and in her offstage persona a confrontational style and overt political statements that her good friend Makeba mostly avoided. Chapter 3 explores how the Southern-born classical pianist became a recording artist who forged black cultural nationalism through songs in the early 1960s and how she made female power an important component of her demands for racial equality and pride. To do so, Simone also drew on her experiences in Europe and Africa and on the ideas about Africa that were evident in the United States, partially as the result of entertainers like Makeba.

By 1968, several years after passage of landmark civil rights legislation, and as urban unrest, black power activism, and an ethos of "black is beautiful" became more widespread, mainstream Hollywood films and television turned to the subject of race relations with greater regularity and apparent comfort. Chapter 4 asks what impact this shift had on black women entertainers and what role they played in it by focusing on two mainstream productions—the Hollywood film *For Love of Ivy*, starring Abbey Lincoln as a maid to a white family, and the television series *Julia*, starring Diahann Carroll as a widowed nurse and mother. Abbey Lincoln's trajectory was particularly significant because she was known as a politicized jazz vocalist when she got this part as a black domestic; as such, *For Love of Ivy* sheds light on how women performers' prior political commitments affected the production and reception of mainstream productions, and suggests how complicated and multifaceted "resistance" might be in that context.

Cicely Tyson had been acting since the late 1950s but became a superstar in the early 1970s, with award-winning roles in the film *Sounder* (1972), the television special *The Autobiography of Miss Jane Pittman* (1974), and the first television blockbuster miniseries, *Roots* (1976). All three productions focused on aspects of African American history; all three celebrated a limited type of black resistance; and all three suggested that the right kind of resistance and activism had yielded success and freedom. Chapter 5 looks at the significance of Tyson to this process of history making and memory making in popular culture. As Tyson soared to international stardom, she insisted that it was important to portray black women as dignified and respectable. Through her heroines from the past she emerged as a star who reinforced the sense that traditional gender relations were a precondition to successful black activism. Her work also set that activism firmly in the past. Indeed, when *Roots* aired in 1976, it seemed to signal that a distinctly American civil rights movement was no longer needed.

Of course, black activism was neither over nor not needed in the 1970s. But the political and social climate that nourished these women early in their careers, and the interracial subcultures in Harlem and Greenwich Village where their lives had first intersected and flourished, were no longer as vibrant. The book concludes by looking at the lives of these six black women entertainers in the 1970s and beyond, and gestures back to reconsider them as part of networks that had developed decades earlier. The recent deaths of Simone, Makeba, Horne, and Lincoln have reminded new audiences of the tremendous contributions that they and other performing women have made. But posthumous narratives often continue to isolate each one and obscure the vital communities of women whose members performed civil rights and, in the process, questioned the relationship between culture and politics and changed meanings of black womanhood.

How It Feels to Be Free brings women entertainers and their contributions center stage to histories of civil rights and the rise of feminism. In 1969, six years after he had called upon black celebrities to meet with Robert Kennedy, James Baldwin offered an elegy to his close friend, playwright Lorraine Hansberry. Baldwin recalled that many people were "unable to believe, apparently, that a really serious intention could be contained in so glamorous a frame."[41] As with Hansberry, it is time to take seriously these women, their definitions of glamour, and the work that they did.

I

"The World Was on Fire"

MAKING NEW YORK CITY SUBCULTURES

BETWEEN 1956 AND 1959, five aspiring black women entertainers arrived in New York City, and quickly delighted a growing number of critics and fans. Miriam Makeba, Nina Simone, Abbey Lincoln, Diahann Carroll, and Cicely Tyson would leave their mark, individually and collectively, on audiences around the world. They were part of that "new generation" of young entertainers that so impressed Lena Horne in 1957 when she made the city her permanent home for the first time in over a decade.[1]

Makeba, Simone, Lincoln, Carroll, and Tyson got their start amidst a prevailing sense among black artists in New York that entertainment, cultural innovation, and a politics of black emancipation could reinforce each other—in what seemed to them to be unprecedented ways. It felt like "the world was on fire," as Maya Angelou put it, evoking an era when artists, entertainers, and intellectuals with very different personal and performance styles, class and regional backgrounds, and political perspectives came together in one city. She recalled one night when Abbey Lincoln was singing in the Village, Malcolm X was speaking in Harlem, and Congolese independence leader and prime minister Patrice Lumumba was attending meetings at the United Nations; with those choices, who could know where to go, Angelou wondered. Uptown or downtown, in nightclubs or apartments, "I found myself surrounded by people who were revolutionaries," said South African expatriate and trumpeter Hugh Masekela, describing Manhattan shortly after his arrival in 1960. "Whether they were African or American artists or activists, it all seemed to come together magically at that moment."[2] To better understand the impact Makeba, Simone, Lincoln, Carroll, and Tyson had and the choices that they made about how to perform black womanhood over the course of their careers, one needs to envision the worlds they moved into—how they made the most of this unique time and place and what obstacles they encountered in this moment of apparent promise.

AFRICAN AMERICANS IN New York organized widely in the post–World War II years despite efforts on the part of the government to suppress anyone or anything associated with the left in the inaugural decade of the Cold War. Hoping to extend the coalitions of the New Deal era and the gains made during the war, black New Yorkers resisted workplace discrimination in unions and unfair housing policies in neighborhood groups. Members of the Nation of Islam, grassroots community organizations, and the NAACP all mobilized against police brutality and called for reforms in the criminal justice system. Those involved with the Consumers Protective Committee and other organizations protested against businesses that discriminated against African American consumers.[3] Thus, well before many white Americans talked about a civil rights "movement," New Yorkers who cared about civil rights were active and ideologically diverse. Well before black power became a phrase with a great deal of currency, black power perspectives were taking shape and circulating in organizations and in cultural commodities coming out of New York. And well before Larry Neal wrote, in a 1969 manifesto, that the black arts movement sought "to link, in a highly conscious manner, art and politics in order to assist in the liberation of black people," black writers and performers were crafting strategies to represent blackness in politically relevant ways that captured the complexity and vitality of their lives and identities through culture.[4]

By the mid-1950s, New Yorkers who cared about equality and black liberation felt more hopeful and energized than they had in the immediate postwar years when Cold War pressures had been more pervasive. In the short span from May 1954 to December 1955, the Supreme Court issued the landmark *Brown v. Board of Education* Supreme Court ruling; the Senate officially censured Senator Joseph McCarthy; a rising star in the Nation of Islam, 30-year-old Malcolm X, assumed leadership of the 116th Street Mosque No. 7 in Harlem; the Afro-Asian Conference in Bandung, Indonesia, prominently brought together twenty-nine countries to affirm nonalignment, anticolonialism, and antiracism; and African Americans in Montgomery began a bus boycott, reluctantly led by a young minister named Martin Luther King Jr. These were just some of the events—in the city, the country, and across the world—that contributed to the tremendous sense of potential that percolated in and out of organizations, including among black musicians, writers, actors, artists, and intellectuals in New York who cared about cultural creativity and racial equality.[5] Maya Angelou, James Baldwin, Harry Belafonte, Alice Childress, Ossie

Davis, Ruby Dee, Lonne Elder, Lorraine Hansberry, LeRoi Jones (later Amiri Baraka), John Killens, Hugh Masekela, Julian Mayfield, Odetta, Sidney Poitier, Max Roach, Sonia Sanchez, Diana Sands—these were just some of the many New York–based playwrights, poets, actors, and musicians, along with Horne, Makeba, Simone, Carroll, Lincoln and Tyson, who contributed and responded to a sense of intertwined political and cultural vibrancy.

Many black entertainers, artists, musicians, and writers who took a stand against racial discrimination assumed that white supremacy was more than an American problem and regarded black culture as having ties to Africa and the United States. Some engaged in their creative work with the decolonization struggles and independence movements in Africa and Asia, and these investments contributed to a sense of energy and cultural innovation in the United States.[6] Hansberry, for example, started writing the play *Les Blancs*, set in the imaginary African country of Zatembe and critical of European colonialism in Africa, in 1960. That same year, Max Roach and Oscar Brown Jr.'s collaborative album of jazz music, *We Insist! The Freedom Now Suite*, offered a historical overview from slavery to contemporary freedom struggles in the United States and Africa, and Randy Weston and Melba Liston composed *Uhuru Afrika*, an album that celebrated African independence movements.[7]

The United Nations reinforced exchanges across borders. African diplomats from newly independent countries argued for freedom at the U.N. and went to their temporary homes in New York, creating opportunities for social interactions and political dialogue between African Americans and non-Americans of color. Maya Angelou took time away from her work at the New York office of the Southern Christian Leadership Conference (SCLC), where she was preparing for a benefit performance at Carnegie Hall, to hear Vusumzi Make and Oliver Tambo, South African representatives of the Pan-African Congress and the African National Congress, speak at the home of African American writer John Oliver Killens. South African–born Miriam Makeba lived with a Namibian activist and his American wife for several months when she first came to the United States. Organizations like the American Society for African Culture (AMSAC), the NAACP, and the Urban League organized dinners and social events for African dignitaries that provided occasions for contact between diplomats from abroad and African American organizers, intellectuals, and entertainers.[8] These and many other ordinary encounters in restaurants, apartment buildings, and jazz clubs reinforced a global perspective on race relations.

The United Nations was also a launching pad for celebrations and for protests—an international political theater of sorts. Black Americans in New York participated enthusiastically in parades and motorcades in Harlem welcoming visitors to New York and to the United Nations, including one for Ghana's prime minister, Kwame Nkrumah, in 1958 and for Cuba's Fidel Castro in 1960. "Blacks on the street absorbed more political education on these occasions than they had from any lesson since the Great Depression," said African American attorney Conrad Lynn, recalling the jubilant reception for Castro at the Hotel Theresa in Harlem. The crowds were far less jubilant in February 1961, when several hundred people, including Abbey Lincoln and a group of black women writers and performers that called themselves the Cultural Association of Women of African Heritage, staged a rally outside of the United Nations to protest the murder of Congo prime minister Patrice Lumumba. A smaller group went inside the U.N. to make their voices heard at the Security Council meeting where Adlai Stevenson announced Lumumba's death. In addition to spreading word about the upcoming rally at a Harlem bookstore, Lincoln and the other women spent an afternoon sewing black armbands and veils for protesters to wear as a symbol of their mourning.[9]

Seemingly apolitical interactions between performers could also foster transnational connections. Trumpeter Hugh Masekela arrived in New York (via London) from his native South Africa in 1960, thanks in part to support he received from Harry Belafonte. On his first night in the country, the 21-year-old, who had inherited Louie Armstrong's hand-me-down trumpet in Johannesburg, went to the Jazz Gallery in the Village to see Dizzy Gillespie and Thelonius Monk. Gillespie greeted Masekela "like a long-lost brother" and told him "how glad he was that I had finally gotten out of that apartheid hellhole"; later that evening, the two trumpet players went to the Five Spot, where Charles Mingus was playing and where they might meet Max Roach. In another instance, several weeks after singer Miriam Makeba arrived in the United States from her native South Africa, actress Cicely Tyson was preparing for a role on television as a young pregnant African woman. She sought advice from Makeba about how to play the part accurately. Her new friend's response to the question, "How does a pregnant African woman behave?" was "A pregnant woman is a pregnant woman!'" Socially, culturally, and politically, then, New York was a crossroads at which people, and meanings of blackness and representation, intersected.[10]

It was in this milieu that these five young women—Miriam Makeba, Nina Simone, Abbey Lincoln, Diahann Carroll, and Cicely Tyson—either literally arrived in New York or arrived professionally as part of New York–based circles of activist entertainers. Tyson and Carroll were native New Yorkers, while Simone, Lincoln, and Makeba were part of larger migrations of African Americans to cities and of Africans to the United States. Like Lena Horne, all five women traveled around the country and the world to perform, and Manhattan was not consistently their primary residence. In the early 1960s, the integrated Westchester suburb of Mt. Vernon was home to Nina Simone (as it was for Ossie Davis and Ruby Dee, and Sidney Poitier); during their brief marriage, Miriam Makeba and Hugh Masekela were neighbors of Dizzy Gillespie in Englewood, New Jersey. But the city remained their hub, as they moved between Harlem and the celebrated bohemianism of Greenwich Village, making stops along the way to perform at midtown venues like Carnegie Hall and Lincoln Center, the noted "saloon for sophisticates," the Blue Angel Club on East Fifty-Second Street, and the elegant Persian Room at the Plaza Hotel.[11]

Harlem was the "new black Rome of the African Diaspora" in the late 1940s, said Ossie Davis, and the area retained its status as an intellectual, cultural, and political center for black life in the following decade. Harlem's Minton's Playhouse was a club where bebop musicians held jam sessions in the '40s and where new jazz music continued to thrive. At the Apollo Theater, audiences could watch the same show from noon until midnight for $1. *Freedom*, the newspaper founded by Paul Robeson, came out of Harlem during its short run from 1951 to 1955, and when *Freedom* became *Freedomways* in 1961, its ties to Harlem and to a black cultural left persisted.[12] Abbey Lincoln and Max Roach made Harlem their home when they first lived together and then married; their penthouse was headquarters for the black women who helped organize the protests at the United Nations against the 1961 assassination of Patrice Lumumba.[13]

Lorraine Hansberry would have liked to live in Harlem, but it was "too damn crowded," she explained. Second to Harlem in appeal was Greenwich Village. In 1960, after Nina Simone received a $10,000 royalty check for her first two albums (*Little Girl Blue* and *Nina Simone and Her Friends*) and had a hit album (*Nina Simone at Town Hall*), she promptly moved to a spacious twelfth-floor apartment on 103rd Street and bought a new Mercedes convertible, which she eagerly drove to the Village. There, Simone explained, with the "artistic and intellectual crowd," she found "the audience that was the first to pick up on me in a really big way."[14]

The Village was home to jazz clubs and cabarets like the Village Gate, the Village Vanguard, the Bitter End—a favorite for folk music fans—and

Stanley's Bar, the meeting place of choice for black activists who lived in the neighborhood. It was in the Village and the Lower East Side that a nascent black arts movement developed, centered around literary organizations like On Guard for Freedom (founded in 1960 by Calvin Hicks, with support from Leroi Jones) and Umbra (founded in 1962). Miriam Makeba lived in the Village when she first came to the United States; so too did Carroll, Hansberry, and black arts movement playwright Lonne Elder (who would write the screenplay for the film *Sounder* in 1973). Shortly after Diahann Carroll and her husband, white music producer Monte Kay, moved to the area in 1956, Carroll befriended next door neighbor Miles Davis, learning both about his music and what he meant when he asked for some "sugar." Racial discrimination and threats of violence were part of daily life for many blacks in the Village. Further, while the area's sexual subcultures were a source of appeal to some residents and visitors, Miriam Makeba expressed more than a little ambivalence about the neighborhood's associations with non-normative sexuality when she recalled being "harassed" by local women who "because of my short hair . . . must have thought I was a lesbian."[15] But charged encounters and prejudices did not lessen the appeal of paying relatively low rent and the thrill of being on the cutting edge.

Above all, Harlem and the Village offered performers, especially those who were younger and just starting out, a sense that they were not alone, that they belonged to communities in which activism and entertainment intermingled. As Nina Simone recalled, the Village Gate was a wonderful place to be in the late 1950s because "politics was mixed in with so much of what went on . . . that I remember it now as two sides of the same coin, politics and jazz."[16] Simone's nostalgic musings echo those of many others. Together, black entertainers talked politics and auditioned. They collaborated and read each other's work, discussing fiction, drama, photography, and poetry. They went to clubs, listened to new music, and attended events and meetings sponsored by many different organizations, including the Harlem Writers Guild (HWG), AMSAC, and the SCLC, to name just a few. The HWG was a left-oriented writers group that had ties to the Popular Front and included former Communist Party members, while the CIA-supported AMSAC, committed to disseminating culture from Africa, had much more of a Cold War anticommunist orientation and the SCLC was a Southern-based civil rights group in which African American ministers played prominent roles.[17] Despite distinct agendas, at events that all three and many other organizations sponsored in New York, there was a synergy between antiracist culture and politics. In the words of actress Ruby Dee, this "was a time of giving birth and of getting born into a wider concept of ourselves as actors, and into a heightened sense of art and the Struggle as inseparable bedmates."[18]

More established and successful black stars and relative newcomers who were usually younger often worked and socialized together. They shared much in common: All but a lucky few experienced some degree of financial insecurity despite the good reviews that they might receive. Miriam Makeba babysat when she moved to New York. Nina Simone, like many other black women migrants to New York, worked as a domestic for a white family between gigs at New York nightclubs until the gap between critical acclaim and economic security narrowed. Cicely Tyson nearly gave up on show business altogether because she could not support herself; her good friend Sidney Poitier, persuaded her to hang on a bit longer.[19]

Community did not imply or require consensus, with regard to politics or aesthetics. In 1957, for example, Harry Belafonte rejected Otto Preminger's offer to star in the film version of *Porgy and Bess* because he felt that the film's story about poor blacks on "catfish row" was denigrating to African Americans. But his close friend and fellow activist Sidney Poitier accepted the role. While Miles Davis performed at a benefit concert at Carnegie Hall in 1961 to support the African Research Foundation, Max Roach demonstrated on that same stage because he thought the ARF had connections to the CIA and, by extension, to colonialism.[20] Generational divides, too, could matter a great deal or not at all within subsets of communities. A contingent of male performers and writers, including Belafonte, Poitier, Ossie Davis, Leroi Jones (later Amiri Baraka), Harold Cruse, and John Oliver Killens, served in segregated army units during World War II and described that experience as formative; Belafonte and Davis each recalled reading W. E. B. Dubois during their army service, and the tremendous impact that had on their developing left-wing, antiracist, and anti-imperialist politics.[21] A younger generation often had fewer direct links to the left-oriented cultural and political activism of the World War II years, and some had not thought much about racial politics. When she first got to New York, Nina Simone "laughed at the political jokes at the Village Gate," but did not fully appreciate them, and "I wasn't [at that point] taking the trouble to educate myself in an organized way." Hansberry, on the other hand, Simone's good friend, peer, and godmother to her daughter, was immersed in what Simone called "the bigger picture."[22]

Interracialism and radical black politics and culture were not mutually exclusive, and entertainer-activists often built communities that crossed lines of race. African American poet Lorenzo Thomas recalled "a kind of integrated society that did not seem to exist elsewhere" among poets living in the Lower East Side, even as black poets increasingly asserted the importance of blackness to their poetry and called themselves nationalists. Set in the Village, the 1959 film *Shadows* focused on three African American siblings and the relationships they have with each other and with white peers. With his handheld cameras and improvised dialogue, independent white filmmaker John Cassavetes "established the beginning of a very tentative reevaluation of the Negro image [on screen]," according to one black critic, "since some interracialism was taken for granted in the plot."[23] This ethos was evident in public and private life. Interracial marriage was rarely free of stress, critics, or costs, but it did become less furtive. Lena Horne and Lennie Hayton, a white Jewish musician, had married in France in 1947, and they chose to keep their marriage a secret for three years and lived in Europe for long stretches to avoid controversy. By the late 1950s, Harry Belafonte, Diahann Carroll, Lorraine Hansberry, Leroi Jones, and Nina Simone were among those whose marriages to white spouses received some public scrutiny, but whose relationships did not derail or define their careers.[24] Black activist-entertainers in New York participated, sometimes simultaneously, in what scholar James Smethurst describes as "three distinct, though often intersecting spheres: an interracial (though sometimes coded as essentially 'white'), culturally radical bohemia; an interracial Left political milieu; and a 'black' and generally Left nationalist subculture." Nina Simone put it more simply: describing the "jazz scene," the "folk crowd," and the "beat poets, weird writers and artistic drunks" in the Village, she emphasized that "the whole thing was multi-racial and integrated."[25]

Alongside this considerable diversity, a cross-section of black public figures in New York's worlds of culture and entertainment had certain commitments in common: to challenge the restrictions of Cold War McCarthyism *and* the racial status quo, and to issue these challenges through innovative cultural production and not just traditional movement organizing. Above all, a range of black activist entertainers based in New York worked to participate in creative and independent politicized subcultures and in the booming postwar mass culture industries of music, film, and television. Looking back on these years, Nina Simone recalled that there was a "hunger," as she put it, "to be the first one to discover what was

FIGURE I.I Nina Simone (center) met with (from left to right) Chuck McDew, Lorraine Hansberry, Theodore Bikel, and James Forman at Bikel's Greenwich Village apartment in 1963; they joined in what the *New York Amsterdam News* referred to as an "impromptu song session."

(Courtesy of *New York Amsterdam News*)

coming next," and the excitement of being around people who "understood something special was happening, that it was an extraordinary time."[26]

MANY PERFORMERS AND consumers found that "something special" in music. Discrimination was a reality in the industry—and black women faced racial and gender discrimination—but there were some points of entry for them. It was in the jazz clubs of Greenwich Village that Abbey Lincoln, Nina Simone, and Miriam Makeba caught the attention of music critics and fans in the late 1950s. Their backgrounds varied, and they meshed music and politics in disparate ways. Yet all three made a commitment to black freedom struggles and were able to move from one genre of music to another in ways that made it hard for critics to classify or define them. They were by no means the only successful vocalists, male or female, who moved between jazz, blues, folk, and classical music. Nor were they alone, at a time when civil rights organizations actively recruited celebrities, in choosing to perform in support of civil rights groups. But they were among a generally smaller group of black women to be part of a critical discourse about jazz as art and jazz as politics.[27]

Abbey Lincoln had several names before she moved to New York in 1956. Born in Chicago in 1930 and raised in Michigan as Anna Marie Wooldridge, she "knew that I was going to be a singer" by the time she was working at a Honolulu nightclub in the early 1950s. The woman whom a critic in *Variety* described as a "sultry dish with a lissome figure" had considerable success at Los Angeles nightclubs—first as Gaby Wooldridge, and then, because the Moulin Rouge nightclub owners encouraged her to have a "French" and sexier name, as Gaby Lee. She became known as a "sepia Marilyn Monroe" as the result of a small part in the film *The Girl Can't Help It* (1956), wearing a dress that Monroe once wore. Lincoln seemed to be on a path similar to that of Lena Horne—as a glamorous object of desire and successful nightclub singer.[28] But the transplanted New Yorker had already started to undergo another transformation. She renamed herself Abbey Lincoln and claimed new types of music and new ways of representing herself as a black woman. Within a year of moving to Harlem, Lincoln made her debut at the Village Vanguard, perhaps the premier jazz club in the heart of the Village. Critics praised her "arrival" as a jazz singer. By the late 1950s, Lincoln, now married to jazz drummer and composer Max Roach, abandoned sexy sheath dresses and straightened hair, and rejected images of herself as the glamorous "girl in the Marilyn Monroe dress." She was singing traditional and more experimental jazz vocals that drew on African American poets and African American themes. In her music and lyrics, and in interviews, she identified herself in terms of black nationalism.[29]

In 1959, Lincoln released the album *Abbey Is Blue*. This was her fourth album in as many years, and the first in which she wrote lyrics that directly addressed the black freedom movement. In the song "Let Up," she wondered when life's many frustrations would ease for black people; in "Afro Blue" (with lyrics by Oscar Brown), Lincoln affirmed African Americans' ties to Africa ("a land my soul is from"), and the beauty of blackness. Moreover, critics wrote about her and this album in the ways that she had reconstructed herself: as a jazz singer who was committed as a woman to black freedom struggles. As Lincoln explained in the liner notes to her 1961 album *Straight Ahead*, in part as the result of her relationship and musical collaborations with Max Roach, she had realized "how wonderful

FIGURE 1.2 Abbey Lincoln in the film *The Girl Can't Help It* (1956); she became known as the "sepia Marilyn Monroe" because Monroe had once worn that same dress.

(Gilles Petard/Redfirns/Getty Images)

it is to be a black woman." Elaborating further, she noted: "I gained insight into the kind of individuality that *was* mine and needed bringing out. And I decided I would not again sing anything that wasn't meaningful to me."[30]

Nina Simone was born Eunice Waymon in 1933 in the small town of Tryon, North Carolina. Her mother was a housekeeper by day and a Methodist minister at night; her father worked mostly as a handyman.

Simone started playing piano when she was three years old and was soon the pianist at her mother's church. As a result of local fundraising efforts on the part of whites and blacks in her town, she began studying classical music with a white teacher at age five. After high school, Simone continued her classical studies at the Juilliard School in New York City. She planned to go from Juilliard to the Curtis Institute of Music in Philadelphia, in the hopes of becoming what she thought would be the first African American classical pianist. Simone was devastated when the Curtis Institute rejected her in 1951. She assumed that the rejection was based on her race.[31]

Several years later, tired of giving piano lessons and in need of money to continue her classical training, Simone started to play popular music at an Atlantic City nightclub. Under pressure from her boss, she also sang, and then began to write her own music and lyrics. Simone's first popular hit came in 1958 with a ballad-like recording of George Gershwin's celebrated "I Loves You Porgy," which reached number 2 on the R&B charts and the top 20 on *Billboard*. Within months of moving to Manhattan in 1958, the 25- year-old classical pianist turned singer with one album out (*Little Girl Blue*), had performed at New York City Town Hall and at the Village Gate.[32] One critic suggested that "the greatest compliments could only be understatements of her talent." Simone was not at this point writing and singing directly about black activism, but *Ebony* had already called her a "singularly arresting figure who insists on going her own way," and her compelling stage presence drew in and captivated audiences. As Simone became more involved with circles of activists and activist-entertainers, the content of her music and her looks started to change. She would not remain a "cocktail and supper club performer," as one critic described her early years, for long.[33]

Less than a year after Simone moved from Philadelphia to New York, in December 1959, a 26-year-old South African singer, Miriam Makeba, landed in New York's Idlewild Airport (renamed Kennedy Airport four years later). Within ten days, she had her American debut on *The Steve Allen* television show before a live audience in Los Angeles and a television audience of sixty million viewers. Makeba then returned to New York for her first appearance at the Village Vanguard, where Harry Belafonte, Sidney Poitier, Nina Simone, Diahann Carroll, Duke Ellington, and Miles Davis shared a table in front. Reviews were effusive. She "interpreted both dialect tunes and jazz standards with a finesse that heralded the appearance of a new star," wrote a critic in *Look* magazine.[34]

Born outside of Johannesburg in the segregated Prospect Township in 1932, Miriam Makeba was raised in an extended family network. Her mother, known among blacks as an isangoma—a healer—did domestic work in the homes of whites and sold home-brewed beer to supplement her income. It was illegal for South African blacks to drink alcohol, however, and authorities jailed her mother, along with the infant Makeba, for six months. As a child, Makeba went to an all-black school and sang in the school chorus. Her life changed dramatically in 1948, when she turned sixteen. Under the leadership of Daniel Malan and the Nationalist Party, apartheid became the official law of the land in South Africa. In the aftermath of this election, long-entrenched practices of white supremacy escalated and were institutionalized and economic conditions worsened almost immediately for South African blacks.[35]

By the early 1950s, Makeba was committing more time and energy to music and to a life as a professional performer. She was a key member in successful bands, including the Cuban Brothers, the Manhattan Brothers, and as lead singer for the all-woman group the Skylarks; she also had starring roles in the all-black musical variety shows that were popular in South Africa and neighboring countries and in the jazz opera *King Kong* that toured throughout the continent. Most western audiences did not learn about Makeba, a celebrity throughout Africa, until after she had appeared in an anti-apartheid film, *Come Back, Africa*. Lionel Rogosin, a white New Yorker and independent filmmaker, covertly made the film in South Africa in 1958. He smuggled *Come Back, Africa* out of the country and to the Venice Film Festival in August 1959, and helped Makeba leave South Africa to join him there. In London after the festival, Makeba met Harry Belafonte, who was struck by her talent and presence on stage. Belafonte and Rogosin supported her move to the United States, where Belafonte became both her mentor and collaborator.[36]

Miriam Makeba, Nina Simone, and Abbey Lincoln were three talented women who made their way to New York's thriving music scene at a moment when the city was central to the production of politically inflected culture. While their styles and self-definitions varied, and only Lincoln fully embraced and was comfortable with the label jazz singer, all three vocalists helped forge a jazz scene in which music was simultaneously an innovative art form, a popular commodity, and increasingly, a strand in larger political interventions that would be named the civil rights and black power movements. These were years when musicians, producers, consumers, and critics of jazz engaged in sometimes acrimonious debates about the "appropriate" role of politics in jazz, about racial discrimination in the industry, and about the relationship between jazz and high culture, on the one hand, and a seemingly ever-encroaching mass culture, on the other.[37] In the late 1950s, Abbey Lincoln participated actively in these debates, commenting directly on American race relations, apartheid, and decolonization efforts in Africa, and claiming jazz as an arena in which to do so. She politicized her performances sooner and more forcefully than did Nina Simone, who would move in that direction by the early 1960s, or Miriam Makeba, who clung to the position that she was just an entertainer and made her political views known in less direct ways.

The postwar jazz scene in New York had origins in the 1940s when musicians like Dizzy Gillespie, Charlie Parker, Max Roach, and others jammed at the Minton Street Playhouse in Harlem, performed at the Onyx Club on Fifty-Second Street, and forged the style that became known by 1944 as bebop. Black musicians rarely agreed on the cultural or political implications of bebop, but this multiplicity suggested that the music issued intertwined cultural and political challenges, and that amidst the wartime demands for greater economic and political equity, black musicians demanded that they be taken seriously as artists. Dizzy Gillespie rejected an explicit equation between music and politics when he explained that they never said "Let's play eight bars of protest." But he still saw himself and others in the "vanguard of social change."[38]

This "vanguard" was larger, more multifaceted, political, and informed by a transnational racial cosmopolitanism by the mid-1950s. The Charles Mingus Jazz Workshop, for instance, which opened at the Café Bohemia in New York in October 1955, featured Mingus with other musicians interested in dissonant musical and improvisational styles that defied categorization. In the famous and controversial "Fables of Faubus" (1959), Mingus mocked Orval Faubus, the Arkansas governor who became famous—and infamous—for his stand against integration during the school crisis at Central High in Little Rock in 1957. The Columbia record company objected to "Fables," and Mingus could not record the song with lyrics until 1960. Even before "Fables of Faubus," however, Mingus had released "Work Song" and the "Haitian Fight Song," songs whose titles made political statements about race relations in and out of the United States.[39]

Two events that occurred within months of each other further galvanized musicians. On February 1, 1960, sit-ins began in Greensboro, North Carolina, and on March 21, white South African authorities in Sharpeville shot and killed 69 peaceful black protesters, mostly in the back, and wounded nearly 200 others. Mingus wrote "Prayer for Passive Resistance" shortly after sit-ins spread to American cities and towns throughout the South, and as many Americans expressed horror about what had come to be known as the Sharpeville massacre. The album *We Insist! The Freedom Now Suite* included vocals by Lincoln, who used screams and other techniques to transform her voice into what critics regarded as a political weapon; the song "Tears for Johannesburg" directly evoked the violence in Sharpeville. Initially, Max Roach had planned for the album to mark the 100th anniversary of the emancipation proclamation. Instead, he released *We Insist!*, with its photo of three black male protesters sitting at a lunch counter on the cover, to support the sit-ins and the larger movement that protesters in Greensboro had provoked. The first public performance of songs from the album took place in January 1961 at the Village Gate, at a fundraising event for the Congress of Racial Equality (CORE).[40]

By the end of the 1950s and early '60s—when Lincoln was deeply involved in musical activism and communities of politicized jazz musicians, when Makeba's career in the United States as a black woman exiled from South Africa took off, and when Simone was earning rave reviews and making the shift from supper club singer to a performer who "had to take politics seriously"—music fans could choose from an array of styles and genres. They could listen to recently released recordings by Makeba, Simone, or Lincoln, or other women vocalists like Mahalia Jackson, Dinah Washington, and Ella Fitzgerald; some might opt instead for composer Melba Liston and Randy Weston's *Uhuru Afrika*, Sonny Rollins's *The Freedom Suite*, or Nigerian drummer Michael Babtunde Olatunji's *Drums of Passion*.[41] They could alternate between these and other recordings by musicians invested in black freedom struggles or inspired by events in Africa, and more commercial productions. In its first year, Motown, the record company that Berry Gordy founded in Detroit in 1959, had numerous hits, including Barrett Strong's "Money (That's What I Want)," and the Miracles' "Shop Around," which reached the top spot on *Billboard*'s R&B charts. Harry Belafonte's album *Harry Belafonte—Calypso* was the first platinum album to sell one million copies in one year and pushed both Elvis and Frank Sinatra off the charts in 1956. Folk music was experiencing its own dramatic revival. Folk singer Odetta's first solo albums, *Odetta Sings Ballads and Blues* and *At the Gate of Horn*, released in 1956 and 1957, influenced singers and fans, black and white.[42] These developments in music, from jazz to rhythm and blues, and from Motown to calypso, helped accelerate the pace of black activism within and beyond

New York. Here was music that expressed and contributed to new demands and new hopes among blacks as cultural producers and consumers.[43]

Miriam Makeba, Nina Simone, and Abbey Lincoln were among the black women who inserted themselves into these politicized musical sub-cultures and into conversations about music and racial politics in which men and ideas about black masculinity had dominated. For years, black male musicians had challenged widespread assumptions among whites that because of their skin color, they were "natural" entertainers. Since the 1940s, they had done so by laying claim to musical virtuosity. Charlie Parker, Dizzie Gillespie, Thelonius Monk, and others associated with the development of bebop positioned themselves as highly skilled modernist artists who honed their craft and scorned popular entertainment. But in their efforts to resist racial stereotypes of black entertainers, they implic-itly equated cultural creativity with masculinity and forged an ethos of African American musical virtuosity that had everything to do with gen-der. Despite the actual presence of women musicians, including Mary Lou Williams and Melba Liston, to name two, the vision of bebop, and of jazz more generally, as a hip alternative to the mainstream depended on an implied equation between the music and certain expressions of black masculinity. White audiences especially regarded these styles of masculin-ity as evidence for what was countercultural and oppositional about jazz. Gendered meanings of jazz infused the music with an avant-garde radi-calism and with associations to a modernist universal high culture. Both sets of associations seemed to preclude women.[44] These dynamics and the accompanying marginalization of women persisted into the 1960s, as consumers and producers increasingly invested jazz with political mean-ings. For instance, a roundtable panel discussion on "jazz and revolu-tionary black nationalism" that appeared in the publication *Jazz* over the course of fourteen issues, did not include a single woman.[45]

In obvious and sometimes less obvious ways, Makeba, Simone, and Lincoln alternatively used their music, lyrics, and their self-presentations on- and offstage to disentangle masculinity from the political radicalism with which jazz was associated. This process included engaging with and challenging the expectation that black women in public needed to be respectable and ladylike to prove their worth. Racial uplift and the values with which Lena Horne and her family were associated—and the tightrope between respectability and sexuality on which the glamorous Horne had balanced in the 1940s—were not preconditions to making their voices heard. Instead, alongside music and lyrics, they used accessories of fashion and style to remake meanings of glamour and black female sexuality in ways that had little to do with cabarets, pinup girls, and all-black cast films. Still, like Horne, all three younger singers challenged the overlapping sexualization and subordination of black women performers. And like Horne, who maintained sometimes unpopular political commitments and personal loyalties into the 1950s—to Paul Robeson, for example—even as she worked to expand her professional visibility and audience base, Lincoln, Simone, and Makeba took risks when they made political commitments, and also did what they could to advance their own careers.[46]

These risks were very real, and their efforts came at a cost. Abbey Lincoln both succeeded and struggled precisely because she invested in racial politics as an outspoken black woman jazz singer. She achieved acclaim, but critics targeted her because of the commitments she made as a black woman to politicized jazz and to black freedom. Simone, too, faced criticism and threats of censorship when she wrote and performed songs that challenged white Americans and denounced interracialism. Despite all three women entertainers' efforts to control their representations, many Americans, black and white, continued to define them, Makeba especially, in relation to the prominent men in their lives. Even with these and other limitations, Miriam Makeba, Nina Simone, and Abbey Lincoln contributed to and succeeded in a politicized and popular musical world that was centered in New York in the late 1950s and early '60s, and reverberated around the world.

THE BLEECKER STREET Theater was blocks away from the Village Vanguard. This proximity was a boon given that music was only one form of expressive culture that energized politicized subcultures of black entertainers and their audiences in late 1950s New York. Diahann Carroll, Cicely Tyson, Miriam Makeba, and, later in the decade, Lincoln, were among those who counted on a combination of media outlets. Although Miriam Makeba was first and foremost a singer, her popularity in the United States depended on her appearance in a single, 86-minute, independently produced film and was accelerated further by her numerous television appearances. As they pursued varied opportunities in off-Broadway theaters, nightclubs, writers' workshops, fledgling and established television shows, art house–oriented independent films, and Hollywood studios, Carroll, Tyson, and Makeba also crossed the borders between what many people associated with avant-garde and "quality" culture and the commercial mainstream.[47] All of these venues could provide a source of income and a site of activism for black artists, and be a source of pleasure and politics for fans. All of these venues could also be stages on which black women made inroads, on the one hand, and encountered both racial prejudice and gender discrimination, on the other.

Born in Harlem in 1935 and named Carol Diahann Johnson, Carroll moved to the "middle class safety of Yonkers" when she was a teenager. Even before the move, though, her family was one of the "haves" in a neighborhood of "have-nots"—with a "shiny new Chrysler" and a family-owned brownstone. The recipient of a Metropolitan Opera scholarship, Carroll began voice and music lessons when she was ten years old; she was modeling and had won a television talent show even before she graduated from the High School of Music and Art in Manhattan. In the early 1950s, Carroll left college to divide her time between studying music, acting classes, and performing. Initially, finding a stage required long trips to hotels in the Catskills and small towns along the East Coast where people "had never seen a black person before." Soon, though, she had gigs in more prestigious urban nightspots.[48]

Success came to Carroll quickly. She landed a role in a Broadway play, the Truman Capote-Harold Arlen musical *House of Flowers*, in 1954; she played small parts in films—*Carmen Jones* (1954) and *Porgy and Bess* (1959); and she performed at numerous high-end Manhattan nightclubs and on television, which yielded several records. This "entertainer of the year," who moved from hotel bars to theater, film, and television, was a "quadruple threat," according to one critic.[49] In 1961, Carroll costarred in *Paris Blues*, a movie about two expatriate jazz musicians (played by Paul Newman and Sidney Poitier) and their romances with American women (played by Joanne Woodward and Carroll), filmed on location in Paris. The following year, as the lead in the Broadway musical, *No Strings*, she won a Tony award. "What more can a girl ask for?" asked the *Chicago Defender* critic. The young woman who performed in the United States, Cairo, Havana, and Paris was "an entertainer of international import," according to a critic for the *New York Daily News*.[50] As a chic nightclub singer with an elaborate wardrobe and with roots in the black middle class, the light-skinned Carroll, far more than Lincoln, Simone, or Makeba, relied on Lena Horne's legacy and performance strategies.

Like Carroll, Cicely Tyson got her start in Harlem, but otherwise their class backgrounds and their routes to show business diverged. Born in 1933 to working-class West Indian parents, Tyson never considered a

FIGURE I.3 Diahann Carroll, circa 1960, as her stage, film, and recording career ascended.

(Hulton Archive/Getty Images)

career in acting or show business when she was a child; how could she have, she would later ask journalists, when her devout mother believed that movies "were evil."[51] Working as a secretary after high school, Tyson made her way to acting via modeling: "from the typing pool to an Emmy," as *People* magazine put it in 1974. Once Tyson was smitten with acting, she never looked back. She spoke of an epiphany-like experience that motivated her to study with prominent coaches like Paul Mann and to commit herself to representing blackness in particular ways.[52]

Tyson first made a name for herself as a dramatic actress. With just a few small but well-received roles in film, television, and stage behind her, the "first-class performer" went on to win two consecutive Vernon Rice Awards for outstanding achievement in off-Broadway theater, in 1961 and 1962. Soon after that she got a part on the television drama *East Side, West Side*, and was one of the few black women in a regular series. But critical acclaim did not translate into consistent work or commercial appeal, and until the 1970s, Tyson had stretches when she worked very little.[53]

Tyson and Carroll worked alongside African American actors in black left-wing–oriented theater and in more mainstream dramas and musicals. Some of their fellow cast members had performed for years in small theaters in Harlem and the Village before the blockbuster success of *A Raisin in the Sun* in 1959. Lorraine Hansberry's fictional account of a working-class black family in Chicago won the prestigious New York Drama Critics Circle Award in 1959 and ran for two years on Broadway.[54] *Raisin's* critical and commercial success in New York and in national tours with several casts made the entire notion of black theater more viable. In concrete terms, the play created more jobs for black actors on stage; its ripple effects also contributed to opportunities in film and television. In more elusive but equally relevant ways, *Raisin* offered a "powerful surge of encouragement" to black performers and "made everything possible," said Ossie Davis, who assumed the male lead after Sidney Poitier.[55] The combined casts of *Raisin, The Blacks*, and other off Broadway and Broadway productions in which Tyson and Carroll had roles—among them *Moon on a Rainbow Shawl, Tiger, Tiger Burning Black*, and *No Strings*—included Claudia McNeil, Diana Sands, Roscoe Lee Brown, Pearl Bailey, James Earl Jones, Maya Angelou, Louis Gossett Jr., Juanita Hall, Billie Dee Williams, and Alvin Ailey. Hollywood films like *Carmen Jones* and *Porgy and Bess*, in which Carroll appeared, also provided a showcase for black entertainment and were a stepping stone for cast members. Many, like Tyson and Carroll, achieved even greater popularity and commercial success in Hollywood films and television subsequently. But they could not have done so had they not, in the late 1950s and early '60s, moved between commercial and less commercial venues and benefited from the energy and cross-fertilizations between politicized and more mainstream productions.

Tyson, particularly, shared off-Broadway stages with actors who embraced an activist avant-garde sensibility and a global perspective on race

and colonialism. Many others tapped into that mood and absorbed cosmopolitan perspectives from the content of the plays. In 1961, for example,
Tyson's first award-winning role was as Virtue in the off-Broadway production of *The Blacks*. A controversial drama by French avant-garde playwright Jean Genet, *The Blacks* was structured around a play-within-a-play
format. The all-black cast reenacted the rape and murder of a white woman
in a mock trial before white oppressors (black actors in white masks), who
ultimately reveal themselves as "just" actors. Steeped in French anticolonialist discourse, *The Blacks*, recalled one participant, "was delicious to
our taste" because of its confrontational political content and relevance.
James Earl Jones later reminisced that until he was in *The Blacks*, he felt
"fairly free of racial conflict and frustration"; working on this play, however, required him to "walk through the hatred, distrust, and disaffections
that can split blacks and whites." On "that small New York stage," said
another of the actors, "we reflected the real-life confrontations that were
occurring daily in America's streets. . . . Blacks did sneer behind their
masks at the rulers they both loathed and envied. We would throw off the
white yoke which dragged us down into an eternal genuflection."[56] The
play became a "fixture" at the St. Mark's Playhouse. During its three-plus-
year run in the Village that included 1,400 performances, black actors
wrestled with the contradiction that white audiences might flock to see
them address controversial issues on stage, but resist thinking about race
and power relations in their own lives.[57]

In this densely politicized atmosphere, Tyson focused on acting as a
craft. Unlike Abbey Lincoln, she made no public statements about race
relations domestically or abroad, and she avoided arguments on the set
that others had about racial politics, colonialism, or commercial culture.
"Cicely, delicate and black-rose beautiful, was serious and aloof" during
rehearsals for *The Blacks*, recalled one fellow-cast member. As friendships
and cliques developed among the cast and crew, "she sat in the rear of the
theater, her small head bent into the manuscript, saving her warmth for
the character and her smiles for the stage."[58] Tyson was committed to representing blackness on stage with accuracy and with dignity. Her desire
and ability to do so apart from organizations of politicized African Americans were evident at this early moment in her career and would prevail in
her careful choice of roles for years to come.

"You need film," Diahann Carroll's agent (and then-husband) Monte
Kay told her in 1959, as he urged the Tony award-winning performer to be
less selective and to accept a small part in the movie version of *Porgy and*

Bess. Carroll was initially reluctant. She knew that Dorothy Dandridge and Sidney Poitier were the rare full-fledged Hollywood celebrities; they had appeared in studio films designed to attract white audiences in large numbers and both received Oscar nominations (Dandridge for *Carmen Jones* in 1954, and Poitier for *Lilies of the Field* in 1964, which he won). But after a brief spurt of "social problem" films in the late 1940s that took up questions of discrimination, most leaders in an industry weakened by the blacklist and the ascendance of television anointed as stars just a handful of black actors and tended to avoid controversial topics having to do with race relations. As a result, there continued to be limited opportunities for African Americans in film in the late 1950s, mostly as "extras" with only "bit parts," according to Carroll.[59] Moreover, as had been the case for Lena Horne and other black actors who had worked in Hollywood 15 years earlier, those parts continued to offer a narrow range in terms of character development.

When filmmakers did risk raising the topic of racial politics, they did so cautiously. Hansberry rewrote *Raisin* for its film adaptation in 1960, but industry insiders at Columbia rejected new scenes that might alienate white audiences or be potentially "racially provocative."[60] Martin Ritt, a white director who had been blacklisted in the 1950s and whose ties to an antiracist left dated back to the 1930s, made *Paris, Blues,* in which Carroll starred, in 1961. The film sanitized its themes of political commitment and race when the expatriate white jazz musician (Newman), who must choose between romantic love and musical genius, drove the narrative forward. A parallel storyline about the African American jazz musician (Poitier), who must choose between fighting for civil rights and romance in the United States (with the character played by Carroll) versus a life in Paris relatively free of prejudice, became somewhat tangential. Even more, the film suppressed its initial evocation of a potential interracial romance between the characters played by Paul Newman and Diahann Carroll.[61] Limitations in the quantity and quality of parts available to black women in Hollywood films meant that Cicely Tyson waited years between roles in film dramas and depended on opportunities in New York; for Carroll, these limitations meant that she needed to intersperse her work in Hollywood with nightclub performances in New York and around the world to remain in the public eye.

Roles in less commercial and independent films that directors made and distributed beyond the Hollywood studio system could provide alternatives. As with New York–based and black-oriented theater, international

film festivals and art house movie theaters contributed to changing relationships between "art" and mass culture, and between culture and racial
politics in the late 1950s. It was in these settings that Americans and Europeans first saw the anti-apartheid film *Come Back, Africa*, and from which
Miriam Makeba extended her fan base and catapulted herself to international fame. Similarly, *Nothing but a Man* was a low-budget, black-and-white
film that two independent filmmakers shot in 1963 and had an award-
winning debut at the Venice Film Festival. It was Abbey Lincoln's first
major role in a film. A few years later, she costarred in a romantic comedy
alongside Sidney Poitier.[62]

Both international film festivals and small art house movie theaters
were essentially products of the postwar era. The Venice Film Festival,
which had the patronage of Mussolini from its inception in 1932 until
1940, was revived in 1946 after a wartime hiatus; 1946 also marked the
first festivals in Cannes and Locarno. By the late 1950s, international film
festivals had spread to San Francisco, London, and Moscow. Their primary audiences at this time were the press, producers, distributors, and
others in the industry, and one goal was to convey the sense that movies
were art and not simply escapist or entertaining mass culture. And yet,
film festivals produced distinct commercial advantages for the films that
its arbiters labeled as quality.[63]

Films screened at international festivals and then at smaller art house
movie theaters in New York and other urban centers in the United States
were similar to jazz music in that they tended to appeal to younger audiences with left-oriented politics or self-styled avant-garde preferences, and
to older, college-educated, largely white, and self-declared elite fans. These
were the consumers who were most interested in spending time and
money to see films that were on the commercial margins, often imported,
associated with quality high culture, and, potentially, with political significance. While overall movie attendance was declining by the early 1960s,
art houses in the United States grew, from fewer than 100 such theaters
in 1950 to over 600 by the mid-1960s.[64] When Lionel Rogosin, the native
New Yorker who directed *Come Back, Africa*, returned to the United States
from Venice and had difficulty finding a commercial distributor for his
film, he decided to become an independent exhibitor. In February 1960,
he leased the Bleecker Street Theater in the heart of Greenwich Village, an
"intimate (250-seat)" space, noted the *New York Times*, where he screened
Come Back, Africa to "small but steadily growing audiences" over the
course of several weeks.[65] By distributing his film independently and first

screening it in the Village, a neighborhood hospitable to nonmainstream popular culture, Rogosin narrowed his initial target audience, but also freed himself from constraints about how to depict race relations that others in the world of more commercial moviemaking faced.

Television in its last gasp of a "golden age" was yet another arena that provided new opportunities as well as challenges to young black women performers like Carroll, Tyson, and Makeba. Regardless of the realities of discrimination in the music industry, and in the jazz world in particular, both whites and blacks assumed the presence and excellence of black performers, whereas opportunities for black entertainers were more limited in television.[66] As was the case with Hollywood films, whiteness remained the norm, or the ostensibly universal standard from which each black performer departed. Because definitions of desirable femininity remained tied largely to middle-class white women, black women faced additional constraints.

The work that Miriam Makeba and Cicely Tyson did on television in the late 1950s into the early 1960s stood out. From her very first performance on television's popular *The Steve Allen Show* on, Makeba made such appearances an important part of her persona in the United States. In certain respects, she followed in the footsteps of her mentor, Harry Belafonte. Belafonte had first appeared on American television in 1955; by 1957, after the release of the album *Calypso*, he generally received $50,000 for each guest appearance. The special *Tonight with Harry Belafonte*, broadcast on CBS in 1959, earned him an Emmy award, another first for a black entertainer.[67] Over the years, Belafonte and Makeba, individually and together, appeared on variety shows with some regularity.[68] Makeba, along with Diahann Carroll, Lena Horne, and Abbey Lincoln, earlier in her career, capitalized on the fact that top-rated television variety shows like *The Steve Allen Show*, *The Ed Sullivan Show*, and Johnny Carson's *The Tonight Show* tended to be more hospitable to black entertainers than were dramatic series—as long as the hosts remained white men. Makeba used musical numbers on popular variety shows particularly effectively to build bridges between the art house audiences of *Come Back, Africa* and television audiences in homes throughout the country.[69]

It was difficult for black women to parlay television appearances into greater success or power because the creative control that Belafonte acquired on television in the late 1950s was exceptional.[70] After the Broadway show *Jamaica* opened, Steve Allen introduced as his guest the "exciting, glamorous, Lena Horne" as a star who had "gotten right to the top in every single phase of show business there is, movies, and records, radio, television, and now the stage." But what Horne really wanted—a television show of her own to host—remained an elusive goal.[71] Many black performers faced a "wall of frustration," according to one reporter in 1955, as they confronted a television industry that would only "throw them a bone from time to time." Even though many television writers in these years considered themselves to be personally opposed to racism, advertisers who either supported segregation or wanted the support of white Southern consumers avoided storylines that included black people or problems of prejudice. In fact, television's short history was tied to a politics of racial exclusion. In 1950, when NBC cancelled activist-entertainer Paul Robeson's appearance on *Today with Mrs. Roosevelt*, in which he had been scheduled to participate in a discussion about "the Negro in politics," he became the first American, white or black, to be exiled from the industry. *The Nat King Cole Show* seemed far less controversial and generated support from black stars when it premiered in 1956. However, it went off the air after a 64-week run, largely because of objections from Southern affiliates and a lack of national sponsors. The NAACP formed a committee to press radio and television industries to provide more opportunities for black Americans in the mid-1950s, but a decade later, *Billboard* magazine still reported that only a "limited" number of black entertainers received "star treatment" on network television.[72]

Tyson's early years in show business further illuminate the potential—and potential pitfalls—of television for black women. In 1963, she joined the cast of *East Side, West Side*, a new dramatic series set in New York and made by New Yorkers. The show revolved around social workers and urban life. Tyson's character, Jane Foster, worked alongside the progressive white social worker Neil Brock (played by George C. Scott). Although she was officially his secretary, they collaborated with each other and with Frieda Hechlinger (Elizabeth Wilson), Brock's white female boss, to address social problems common to city dwellers of any race and class. These included, as producers David Susskind and Daniel Melnick explained to Roy Wilkins, executive director of the NAACP, "mental illness, juvenile delinquency, unemployment, racial prejudice, gambling, slum clearance, and mental retardation." Several episodes confronted discrimination in the urban North head-on. In "Who Do You Kill?," shot in Harlem, Brock and Jane try to help an impoverished and loving African American couple whose baby dies as the result of a rat bite. There is little that the social workers can do, however, and the script cast an unsparing look at discrimination in the labor force and at "slumlords" in a segregated housing market, while also sympathizing with the black father's rage.[73]

Convinced of the show's quality and commercial viability, a critic in *Variety* observed that with *East Side, West Side,* "for the first time, the 'winds of change' marking the Negro protest movement in this country, won a dramatic outing on a network." Producer David Susskind declared that the show was "achieving total integration with total reality" because "a

FIGURE 1.4 Cicely Tyson in 1963 as Jane Foster in the critically acclaimed but short-lived television series *East Side, West Side.*

(CBS Photo Archive/Getty Images)

substantial and dedicated part" of New York City social workers and their staff were, in fact, "Negroes." The *New York Times* concluded that the series offered evidence for the ways that "the vigorous campaign to put more Negroes in front of television cameras" had "produced impressive results."[74] Thus, the production and content of the show reflected a desire among New York–based writers, producers, and actors for innovative and politically engaged quality programming. Just a year later, though, Susskind noted that Southern affiliates objected to the show for reasons directly related to Tyson and race—because a "Negro actress was an integrated member" of the cast, whose character was a competent worker and had "frequent disputes with her white co-star." While it is difficult to track such charges statistically and disagreements among network executives and the producers also weakened *East Side, West Side*, CBS employees acknowledged that some Southern affiliates would not carry the show; unlike the films from the 1940s in which Horne had appeared only to sing, in brief scenes that could then be cut for theaters in the South, Tyson was an essential part of the dramatic narrative in many episodes. Resistance to her contributed to the show's low ratings. The network cancelled the award-winning drama after just one year.[75]

Diahann Carroll, Cicely Tyson, and Miriam Makeba moved from one venue to another because they were excited by an atmosphere that valued innovation and by new opportunities, and also because they felt that they could not afford—professionally or economically—not to. Carroll had an "agent, a personal manager, and a rehearsal pianist" before she was 20 years old; she modeled, sang, and practiced daily with a vocal coach and drama teacher because she knew that as a black woman, she could not count on any one type of entertainment venue.[76] Amidst the numerous ups and occasional downs in the early years of their careers, all three women worked to reach audiences that crossed lines of race and class, at the same time that they also performed on smaller stages, on the cultural margins, and in politicized subcultures with more targeted niche audiences and broader parameters for representing and talking about race. The extent to which they visibly engaged with racial politics varied, as it did for black women vocalists. The content of *The Blacks* and *East Side, West Side*, for instance, put Tyson at the center of conversations about race and anticolonialism, and about race and housing discrimination in the urban North, even when she was not directly involved with organizations that took on these topics. Whereas *Paris, Blues* offered a depoliticized look at two African Americans wrestling with their commitments to civil rights—a story in which questions of romance trumped questions about politics—even as Carroll would soon be hosting fundraisers in her own home to support the Student Nonviolent Coordinating Committee (SNCC).[77] But on all of these stages, black women acquired skills and practiced tactics they would use for years to come.

FOR ALL FIVE young black women entertainers, building a career as a performer was an uneasy process despite the sense of excitement and possibility that they experienced living in New York City in this period. That Nina Simone, Abbey Lincoln, Miriam Makeba, Diahann Carroll, and Cicely Tyson wanted and were able to establish themselves professionally in different industries highlights their ambition and talent, as well as the changes in the politics of racial representation that the communities of which they were a part helped set into motion. That they all, at some point in these years, experienced discrimination based on their race and gender highlights how precarious their successes were. Finally, that they pursued the varied opportunities they did highlights the degree to which they negotiated their political commitments and willingness to resist the racial status quo with their professional aspirations. The specific ways that each woman was involved in a complex process of self-fashioning—and the stakes and the political work this self-fashioning did—will be explored in subsequent chapters. But the New York City subcultures in which they socialized and performed, and from which they built their careers, played an important part in the choices that they would make thereafter.

As noted, American audiences were first able to see the anti-apartheid film *Come Back, Africa* in 1960 at the Bleecker Street Theater in Greenwich Village. The film played there at the same time that Miriam Makeba was singing at the nearby Village Vanguard, with its associations to an interracial and politicized avant-garde, when she also had engagements at the Blue Angel, a more upscale club known for its chic and mostly white audiences, and shortly after her appearance on *The Steve Allen Show*. Connecting the dots between these places helps to locate Makeba and her fans, and the worlds that she and other black women entertainers inhabited—spatially, culturally, and politically. One night, Makeba was walking home to her apartment in the Village after meeting Sara Vaughan at the Waldorf Hotel's Empire Room. She passed the Bleecker Street Theater and saw her own name emblazoned above. "I cannot believe it when I see the marquee: 'COME BACK AFRICA, STARRING MIRIAM

MAKEBA.' I am surprised because I am only in the movie for three minutes. . . . But I am happy if my name will bring people into the theater, because the documentary is an important look at the terrible conditions we live in at home."[78] Makeba was right: Her presence in the film had brought people into theaters. What she might not have been able to anticipate was what that would mean for how Americans made sense of apartheid, Africa, and black women across continents.

2

"Africa's Musical Ambassador"

MIRIAM MAKEBA AND THE "VOICE OF AFRICA" IN THE UNITED STATES

IN DECEMBER 1959, Miriam Makeba stepped onto the stage for her opening at the Village Vanguard wearing a simple strapless Indian silk dress of green and blue, with a cape draped over one shoulder. Swaying her body back and forth in the smoky club into which an interracial crowd of 300 people had jammed, she performed, in her clear soprano, a set that included a Xhosa wedding tune, a Zulu ballad, and a Yiddish folk song. She could "feel [her] emotion reaching out" to the crowd and could sense their response to her, she later recalled. Only the clap of applause at the end, which felt like "thunder," could break the intense emotional connection between herself and the audience. Makeba's experience—from her repertoire to her appearance to performance style—could not have been more different from Lena Horne's. Almost 20 years earlier, Horne had made a name for herself singing popular standards like Cole Porter's "Let's Do It" dressed in a long, tight gown with a plunging neckline and glittery spaghetti straps in front of all-white audiences at upscale New York City cabarets. The neckline did not keep critics in the 1940s from remarking on Horne's restraint and onstage aloofness, and the distance she worked to establish from her audiences; the "chocolate cream chanteuse," noted *Time*, "eschews the barrel-house manner, claws no walls" and performed with "seductive reserve."[1]

From Miriam Makeba's first weeks in the United States, Americans seized on all that seemed new, exciting, and different about her. Critics hailed the "African tribeswoman" as a welcome "import from South Africa." Harry Belafonte could not offer Makeba enough praise. "She is easily," he observed in *Newsweek*, a month after Makeba's arrival, "the most revolutionary new talent to appear in any medium in the last decade."[2] Of course, Belafonte was hardly a neutral observer. The star that *Look* magazine dubbed the "first Negro matinee idol in our entertainment industry" was enthusiastic about Makeba since they had met in London. He was there for his first European concert tour and to tape a television Christmas special for BBC-TV, and she had traveled to the city from the Venice Film Festival where *Come Back, Africa* had premiered. "Miss Makeba," Belafonte said after he had seen her in the anti-apartheid film and a live performance, and then arranged a personal introduction, "I am an admirer of yours." Belafonte was among those who helped facilitate Makeba's travel to the United States after she had been waiting six months for a visa, and he handled the logistics of her initial American performances. "Big Brother," as Makeba called Belafonte, was midwife, of sorts, to her career in the United States. The duo toured and recorded together, and as Makeba became known "as the first South African Negro to become an internationally popular performer," she did so explicitly as "Belafonte's protégé."[3]

For nearly ten years after her American debut, Miriam Makeba was based in New York and was a high-powered star in the United States and abroad. Her albums were critical and commercial successes. In 1962, she sang at a birthday celebration for President Kennedy, who offered his "personal appreciation" for her "contribution of time and talent." In 1963 and in 1964, Makeba testified before the United Nations Committee on apartheid; in 1965, she and Belafonte won a Grammy Award—the first ever conferred on a South African performer—for the album *An Evening with Belafonte/Makeba*. Her hit song released in 1967, "Pata Pata," went to the top 5 on the charts; translated into many languages, it became an international success.[4]

Nonetheless, Makeba's days of stardom in the United States were numbered. "Stokely Takes a Bride" announced the press in April 1968, and with that news, her status plummeted even more abruptly than it had risen. Stokely Carmichael, a longtime organizer in the Student Nonviolent Coordinating Committee (SNCC), publicly called for "black power" in June 1966, several months after establishing the Lowndes County Freedom Organization, a third party in Alabama that was committed to increasing voter registration and with a black panther as its symbol. Even though black power perspectives calling for social, political, economic, and cultural transformations in race relations had been evident for some time, he helped transform a phrase with a long history into a seemingly new idea, one that "stirred up a storm in and out of the civil rights movement," noted Edwin Newman, host of *Meet the Press*, in 1966. By the time Makeba and Carmichael wed, he had left SNCC to work with the California-based

Black Panther Party and had spent much of the previous year traveling around the world speaking about his global vision of black power. Carmichael was both enormously popular and enormously polarizing. Friends and foes alike regarded him as the voice of black power, or the "young man behind an angry message," as African American photographer Gordon Parks put it in a profile for *Esquire*. Within months of the wedding, many of Makeba's recording and performing contracts were cancelled. The FBI had tracked Carmichael for some time, and Makeba faced similar surveillance as well as diminished professional opportunities. The couple moved to Guinea in 1968.[5]

During the years between her American debut and her marriage, Miriam Makeba repeatedly insisted that she was "no diplomat, not a politician." Yet she made her voice heard in many venues and exposed Americans to apartheid in numerous ways. She was, as one critic noted, "Africa's musical ambassador to the United States."[6] Makeba entered the United States just months before the first sit-ins in Greensboro and before the Sharpeville massacre in South Africa. In the aftermath of these events and during decolonization struggles in other African nations, American civil rights organizations across an otherwise diverse political spectrum developed a greater concern for the continent. This sense of connection between Africa and the United States increased among Americans across political and racial divides and was not restricted either to an interracial political left or to black nationalists.[7] Makeba's career suggests that these political interconnections developed not just in organizations, but also through popular culture.[8]

As critics and fans tracked Makeba's career and wrote about her rise from poverty in the apartheid state of South Africa to her celebrity status around the world, they tended to emphasize two themes, and that she was a black woman was relevant to both. First, a discourse in the United States tended to depict Makeba in terms of a so-called more primitive African space. A second theme, one that dated back to her remarkably successful career in South Africa, was that her success had everything to do with the more prominent men in her life. These ways of talking about Makeba drew on entrenched assumptions about blackness as akin to savagery and about femininity as intrinsically subordinate to masculinity.

Miriam Makeba never passively accepted the terms of conversations about her. Instead, she conformed to and pushed back against them. As a result, her success in the United States had multiple implications. Depictions of Makeba as authentically and almost inherently African, and the

ways in which as a South African black woman, she came to embody
Africa for Americans, black and white, reproduced long-standing perspectives of Africa as a primitive space where racial and gendered "others"
might live. Similarly, the emphasis on relationships that Makeba had with
prominent men did reinforce assumptions about her simultaneous racial
exoticism and gender subordination. But these descriptions of her were
never monolithic; even more, they were potentially productive. Like other
New York–based activists and entertainers who became her friends and
colleagues, Makeba mixed ambition and resistance. During her years in
the United States, representations of Makeba by others and by herself
enabled American consumers to engage with Africa generally, and anti-
apartheid politics specifically. When Makeba challenged apartheid and
challenged dominant assumptions about black female beauty, talent, and
sexuality—while she also pursued her commercial career—she affected
meanings of black power on two continents.

UNTIL SHORTLY BEFORE Makeba came to the United States, and certainly
through the early 1950s, most Americans were relatively uninterested in
and uninformed about Africa. One activist recalled a "Tarzan mentality"
among white as well as black Americans, one that Lorraine Hansberry
captured so effectively in *A Raisin in the Sun*. Faced with the prospect of
meeting her daughter's Nigerian boyfriend, the character "Mama," an
older, Christian, Southern-born working class black woman in Chicago,
notes, "I don't think I never met no African before." Her more sophisticated daughter urges her mother not to ask him "ignorant" questions, like
"do they wear clothes and all that."[9] This mentality started to recede as
resistance to European colonization and to apartheid in South Africa escalated. By the late 1950s, African independence efforts struck a chord in the
United States, even among Americans who were not especially politically
active. Despite Cold War concerns about the potential spread of communism in decolonizing countries, some Americans saw the fight against
fascism in World War II and the fight against communism in the Cold
War as connected battles against slavery and for freedom, and viewed African independence and anti-apartheid struggles in precisely that context.
Signs of this perspective were evident as early as 1952, when two prominent
African American newspapers compared the nonviolent Defiance Campaign that anti-apartheid activists waged in South Africa to the American
Revolution. It was this impulse to place resistance to fascism, American
racism, and apartheid on a continuum that animated filmmaker Lionel

Rogosin, and motivated him to make his anti-apartheid film *Come Back, Africa*.[10]

When it named 1960 the "Year of Africa"—the year that seventeen countries gained independence and over a dozen joined the United Nations—the U.N. captured the prevailing mood of Africa as a place of hope. Politicized entertainers based in New York related to this sensibility in both symbolic and substantive ways. Randy Weston gave a show for the United Nations Jazz Society, a group organized in March 1959 to bring together diplomats from around the world, jazz musicians, and critics to support new nations. Miles Davis and Dizzy Gillespie were among the many musicians who performed in honor of national independence in African countries or on behalf of American organizations—liberal, revolutionary, and the many in between—oriented toward countries in Africa gaining independence. Board members for the African-American Students Foundation (AASF), a group dedicated to bringing African students to the United States for their education, included Belafonte, Sidney Poitier, and Kenyan nationalist leader Tom Mboya. By the late '50s and early '60s, supporters of the American Committee on Africa (ACOA)—an organization formed in 1954 to bring events in the continent to the attention of more Americans and to aid in the development of newly independent countries—included Eleanor Roosevelt, Jackie Robinson, Arthur Schlesinger Jr., Sidney Poitier, Reinhold Niebuhr, and Martin Luther King Jr.; King served as the U.S. national vice chairman of the ACOA's "world-wide Day of Protest against apartheid" in 1960. As African American scholar St. Clair Drake put it in 1961, "pan-African identification" would "inject new meanings into the word 'Negro.'"[11]

The Sharpeville massacre marked a turning point in Americans' awareness of South African apartheid. Stories about the violence circulated in the media, generating international horror and condemnation. As the *New York Times* asked, "Do the South Africans think that the rest of the world will ignore such a massacre?" The African American newspaper the *Chicago Defender* forged cross-border racial connections more bluntly, as it declared that "the wanton slaughtering of men, women and children" had "shocked the conscience of the world into realizing the extent bestiality is resorted to in order to perpetuate a vicious anti-racial system." Jackie Robinson, the African American sports-icon-turned-newspaper-columnist, supported efforts to boycott South African goods and declared that "the fight against Jim Crow here is part of the same struggle in South Africa."[12]

The optimism suggested by the "Year of Africa" was short lived, and government policies in South Africa only hardened after Sharpeville. Nevertheless, protests and criticisms abounded from around the world. For the first time, the U.S. administration declared its "abhorrence" of the 12-year-old apartheid regime at the United Nations, though the administration did little officially to challenge policies in South Africa. The ACOA raised $15,000 for victims of repression in South Africa in a campaign that Harry Belafonte, Lorraine Hansberry, Roy Wilkins of the NAACP, and others cosponsored. Africa Freedom Day celebrations several weeks after the massacre included specific protests against apartheid and speeches by public figures ranging from NAACP legal star Thurgood Marshall to Malcolm X.[13] Activists who agreed on little else, along with Americans who were not members of organizations but considered themselves antiracist, came to support some degree of anti-apartheid activism and drew comparisons between race relations in the United States and South Africa. They did so even when events in Africa were far from their primary focus, and even as Cold War considerations and charges that some American organizations oriented toward Africa were harboring communists made opposing the anti-Communist white nationalist government in South Africa difficult.[14] Struggles against white supremacy took on an increasingly global cast across a political spectrum.

It was against this backdrop that Miriam Makeba moved to New York and entered the American entertainment industry. Her apartment became a hub for entertainers and diplomats from Africa, where Americans and non-Americans of color mingled when they found themselves in New York. Her celebrity bolstered a transnational perspective on black freedom and a developing consensus about Africa as a place of potential freedom and apartheid as a racial hierarchy worth challenging.

Lionel Rogosin had come to these conclusions several years earlier. The 38-year-old engineer-turned-filmmaker earned an Oscar nomination in the United States and best documentary awards from the British Film Academy and at the Venice Film Festival for his first film, *On the Bowery* (1956). The short drama made with documentary footage earned praised for its innovative style, its "overwhelming sense of veracity," and it compassionate portrayal of alcoholics who lived on "skid row"—the Lower East Side of New York. Rogosin arrived in South Africa in 1958, concerned about the fascist nature of the apartheid government and eager to direct his second movie.[15] Some 18 months later, the result was *Come Back, Africa,* filmed "secretly in order to portray the true conditions of life in

South Africa," as the onscreen text at the start declared. Rogosin initially saw Miriam Makeba on stage alongside thirty-five other performers in the *African Jazz and Variety* show, but it was Makeba alone whom he persuaded to join his cast. This required some effort because if the white authorities found out about *Come Back, Africa*, they would likely expel him from the country, but the black and white African cast "would be in real trouble," as Makeba later noted.[16]

When Makeba agreed to participate, she became part of an unusual film that blended a fictional story with elements of documentary. The protagonist, Zacharia, is a black South African who leaves his rural home for urban Johannesburg. Zacharia struggles to find work and build a life for his family in a multiracial area populated largely by blacks known as Sophiatown. He goes from job to job—he works in the mines, in a mechanic's garage, in a hotel, and as a "houseboy" in a private home—only to be fired for various infractions. Zacharia also faces violence from the powerful black gangster (or *tsotsi*), who terrorizes the neighborhood. Toward the end of the film, white Afrikaner officials arrest Zacharia because he does not have the correct form of identification, or "pass." While he is in jail, the tsotsi enters his one room home and assaults his wife. She resists and is murdered.[17]

Makeba mattered little to the plot of the *Come Back, Africa*. In one scene, she appeared as herself: as a local singer at an illegal drinking spot called a *shebeen*, where Zacharia and his friends gather. A mere four minutes after entering the shebeen and singing two songs, her part was done. Yet when Makeba left South Africa to join Rogosin at the Venice Film Festival, he greeted her by telling her that "everyone in Venice is clamoring for you"; she was the "Star of Venice," as the South African magazine *Drum* put it.[18] Her impact had to do with her ability to convey the film's central—and contradictory—message: that blacks in South Africa were suffering and degraded under white rule, *and* that blacks in South Africa were forging a vital and cosmopolitan community that was intellectually, emotionally, culturally, and politically rich. In communicating this theme, Makeba also intervened in a film otherwise dominated by men, and made black female sexuality relevant to the film's politics.

Come Back, Africa could not have developed its contradictory message about suffering and vitality without an unprecedented collaboration between South Africans and an American filmmaker. Rogosin, William "Bloke" Modisane, and Lewis Nkosi worked together on the story and the concept; there was no formal script, and the cast of amateur actors improvised a great deal.[19] Nkosi and Modisane, along with Can Themba, were well-known black South African public intellectuals and contributors to *Drum*, a magazine founded in 1951 that was at the center of Sophiatown life. *Drum* targeted the growing population of urban black readers in South Africa with fiction, political exposes about prison conditions and independence movements on the continent, and articles and advertisements featuring entertainers, American popular culture, gangs, and beauty products. Although it faced considerable constraints from ruling white authorities, the magazine bridged a chasm between protesting discrimination and celebrating a modern, cosmopolitan lifestyle. As Lewis Nkosi later explained, a "*Drum* man" was invested in "reporting the uncertainties of urban African life in the face of rigorous apartheid laws, as well as in reporting the wanton gaiety, lust and bravery of this life."[20]

Drum made these moves amidst growing activism in South Africa. After apartheid was established officially in 1948, the ruling white party passed legislation (along with other measures) to curtail the rights of the black majority. The Prohibition of Mixed Marriages Act (1949) outlawed marriage between whites and other races; the Immorality Amendment Act (1950) prohibited adultery and other extramarital sexual relations between whites and other races; the Bantu Education Act (1953) reshaped schools and syllabi to "retribalize" black Africans; and the Natives Resettlement Act (1954) allowed for the residential "relocation" of blacks. In opposition to these and other measures, the African National Congress increasingly became a mass movement with deeply committed supporters; this was most evident in 1952 when ANC activists organized the widespread "Defiance Campaign" of civil disobedience. This nonviolent campaign was designed to protest apartheid regulations and court arrest through passive resistance. Within months, white authorities arrested over 5,000 activists. As activism escalated, some blacks concluded that opposition to white rule was "possible" and that it "was a time of infinite hope and possibility."[21]

American popular culture played an important part in the sense of "hope and possibility" that percolated in Sophiatown, an area also known to some residents as "Little Harlem." Hollywood actors and African American musicians, including Lena Horne, Dorothy Dandridge, and Sidney Poitier, featured prominently in the "News from Hollywood" section of *Drum*. Beyond *Drum*, too, black South Africans drew on American popular culture. Singer Sathima Bea Benjamin received rave reviews for her performances of Duke Ellington's music. South African trumpeter Hugh

Masekela remembered how he and his friends "wore the gramophone out" listening to songs by Louis Armstrong, Ella Fitzgerald, Cab Calloway, and the Andrews Sisters, and teens saved their money to buy whatever albums were available from the United States, especially those of African American jazz musicians. Strongly influenced by American fashions and music, the Manhattan Brothers adapted hits from American groups like the Mills Brothers into Zulu and Xhosa; when the song "Lovely Lies" reached number 45 in March 1956, they became the first South African group to have a record on *Billboard*'s top 100 list. Makeba's "girl group," the Skylarks, loosely modeled after American groups like the Andrews Sisters, blended township music and tribal rhythms with American doo-wop and gospel music. And, when "several thousand" protesters supporting the upcoming Defiance Campaign marched in Johannesburg, they did so, according to the *New York Times*, "to the tune of Paul Robeson's songs played on a loud speaker."[22]

This *Drum* world, and the more widespread Sophiatown culture of which it was a crucial part, celebrated certain kinds of men and a certain kind of masculinity. Quite literally, far more black men than women participated in Sophiatown's intellectual and literary "renaissance," and this subculture helped to produce meanings of gender in Sophiatown. As Nkosi would later explain, in an essay evocatively titled "The Fabulous Decade: The Fifties," being a "*Drum* man" meant exhibiting a "unique" style, one that was "urbane, ironic, morally tough and detached. . . . A *Drum* man took sex and alcohol in his stride, or was supposed to, and stayed in the front line of danger so long as there was danger to be endured."[23] Few writers discussed violence against women, a common occurrence in black townships, as a serious social problem. Instead, in its journalism, fiction, advertisements, and entertainment-oriented stories, *Drum* tended to celebrate physically or economically powerful black men; heroes included boxers, wealthy entrepreneurs, brash entertainers with links to the United States, and aggressive tsotsis. The tsotsi was worthy of admiration, wrote Nkosi, because "even murder was a form of affirmation of one's presence and vitality." By contrast, *Drum* tended to subordinate women, including political activists and glamorous entertainers, to men.[24] An article about the Manhattan Brothers by Bloke Modisane celebrated the male band members as former "urchins" who now "had money in the bank" and credited them for having "discovered a great voice" in Makeba. "She was just a small-town girl," but they, according to Modisane, "saw possibilities in her."[25]

Strongly influenced by Italian neorealism, Lionel Rogosin was committed to developing his film from the perspective of black Africans and looked to the *Drum* community of male writer-intellectuals as his point of entry. As they had done with other visitors, Modisane, Nkosi, Can Themba, and others introduced the American to life in Sophiatown. But with Rogosin, more than with others, "there was a rapport," as Nkosi noted. The American lived in South Africa for over a year before he even started to film, listening to and recording conversations in Sophiatown, while also working to elude the attention of white authorities; when questioned, he told them he was making a travelogue.[26]

Under these circumstances, and with an international crew that used only two handheld cameras and a largely nonprofessional cast, *Come Back, Africa* developed a story that was largely about communities of black men. Makeba was a notable exception to Rogosin's use of amateurs; Themba, Modisane, and Nkosi also appeared in the film as themselves. There were women in the film, but they tended to appear in isolation from one another and in relation to men—as *the* wife, *the* bartender, *the* white boss, *the* prostitute of the more important, it seemed, groups of laboring black men.[27] With visual cues as well as dialogue, *Come Back, Africa* repeatedly rendered Zacharia one among many males. The plot suggested that white rule—the film never used the word *apartheid*—produced a combination of economic, political, and personal obstacles that black African men could not overcome.

Within this bleak story were glimpses of alternative narratives. The film's title was a slogan from the African National Congress (ANC) arsenal, and throughout black men resist apartheid in direct and indirect ways, offering coded references to an ANC perspective. Zacharia and his wife pass a graffiti-painted wall declaring "Hands off the Western Areas" as they walk through Sophiatown, in an allusion to the forced removals of blacks underway. While he is supposed to be working in a white family's home, Zacharia drinks alcohol and dances to jazz music playing on the radio; in another scene, in response to accusations from a white "boss," Zacharia's friend denies participating in a strike or being in the Communist Party. In the face of a degrading labor structure, cars, alcohol, and other consumer commodities offer black men pleasure; sex as well as family ties offer them joy and intimacy. Most of all, though, there is music. From the penny-whistling, drumming, and dancing of children on unpaved township roads to the commercialized popular jazz playing loudly in the background when Zacharia and his friend go for a ride in an

American car that they are supposed to fill with gas, and from the religious groups to the wedding parties that parade down streets, music abounds in *Come Back, Africa*. The film celebrated visually what one South African expatriate later described: "in the midst of all this terror, somehow township music was in its golden era, burgeoning as never before."[28]

The shebeen scene in which Miriam Makeba appeared was the moment when these political and cultural affirmations were most evident. Not coincidentally, it was also the most dramatic example of how the American and South Africans who conceptualized the film showcased the political perspectives of black South Africans. In this scene, Zacharia and his intellectual friends drink, smoke, and laugh. Because the tsotsi has just attacked Zacharia, the men discuss at length black-on-black violence in Sophiatown; they move on to argue over national politics and white liberals. In contrast to the whites who rule the country, "the liberals are trying to meet us halfway," asserts one "colored" member of the group. In response, the others laugh mockingly, and the Nkosi character offers a scathing critique. The white liberal "just doesn't want a grown-up African. He wants the African he can sort of patronize, pat on his head and tell him that 'with just a little bit of luck, someday you'll be a grown-up man, fully civilized.' He wants the African from the country, from his natural environment, unspoiled."

With this banter, the black men shatter the image of black men as deserving because of their supposed innocence. They confront—and reject—the liberal ethos evident in *Cry the Beloved Country*, the 1948 novel by white South African Alan Paton that was made into a film starring Canada Lee and Sidney Poitier in 1951, by suggesting that Zacharia, the rural migrant to Johannesburg, is no more or less deserving of rights than the violent gangster in urban Sophiatown.[29] White rule produces the tsotsi as aggressor as much as it produces Zacharia as victim. Crucially, this scene establishes a certain privileged common ground between two black men who at first seem to offer such different models of masculinity.

This is the context in which Makeba enters the film. Dressed in a tight, off-the-shoulder sheath dress that suggests professionalism, urban life, and independent black female sexuality, she comes into the male collective space of the shebeen. Like Lena Horne—as a pinup girl in World War II, as a patriotic performer for African America soldiers, and as the seductively single Georgia Brown in the 1943 film *Cabin in the Sky*—Makeba conveys a glamour that many popular films had denied black women. But in contrast to Horne, who in most 1940s films appeared before cameras alone and in a gown to sing one song that had nothing to do with the plot, Makeba becomes part of this formerly all-male community, and is more than just the object of their gaze. "Hey Miriam!" the men call with plea-sure and familiarity. "Sing us a song." Heeding the call to "sit next to me," she joins the men on the couch. There, swaying slowly to the music, she performs "Lakutshn, Ilanga," a song about a lonely man looking at the setting sun wondering what has happened to his lover. "I will come look-ing for you everywhere/in the hospital, in the jails, until I find you," sings Makeba (in Zulu) as she closes her eyes. "Sing us another!" call the men who have also been rocking their bodies to the mournful melody about missing loved ones. Smiling, Makeba rises and begins the lively "Intoyam." In this faster and more cheerful number about the joys of relaxing, the men provide a background chorus with their "ayahs" as Makeba sings, and moves to the beat.[30]

Makeba's presence was crucial to *Come Back Africa* because her body language, clothing, and professional performance strategies all helped to signal a cosmopolitan modern black identity—one that was transgressive

FIGURE 2.1 At a shebeen in the film *Come Back, Africa,* Can Themba and Bloke Modisane show their delight with Miriam Makeba as she sings "Intoyam." (Courtesy of Milestone Films and Rogosin Heritage)

precisely because it had simultaneous political and pleasurable dimensions and drew on multiple transnational sources. Her literal language was one source of such resistance. Most American films set in or about Africa had used English, whereas both Makeba and Zacharia sing or speak in Zulu. When Makeba sings in Zulu, to the delight of the English-speaking male intellectuals around her, she connects Zacharia and the poor miners who speak Zulu and discuss brutal labor conditions in the mining compounds at the outset of the film to the urban South African intellectuals who urge her in English to continue.[31] Makeba becomes part of the political declarations male characters make around but not completely apart from her. In a scene showcasing black social and political life that audiences agreed was filled with "humour, wisdom and warmth," her performance and sexualized appearance underscore and reinforce the declaration that Can Themba's character offers just moments earlier: "They [white liberals] can keep the vote," he says disparagingly. "We want the country—then *we'll* give *them* the vote."[32]

This political perspective could not have been as powerfully presented without Makeba's performance. In a period when underground music was "bursting the seams of apartheid," according to Nkosi, roles like Makeba's contributed to the sense of possibility and resistance that many black South Africans embraced.[33] Even though Zacharia was defeated over the course of the film, the overlapping possibilities of political resistance, cosmopolitan cultural creativity, and pleasure were not. Miriam Makeba's presence, though brief, was critical to the intertwined political and cultural affirmations that *Come Back, Africa* made.

Because of the nontraditional ways in which Lionel Rogosin made and then distributed his film, these affirmations had an impact on audiences around the world. Rogosin smuggled *Come Back, Africa* out of South Africa and took it to the twenty-first Venice Film Festival in September 1959; it won the prestigious Critics Award when he showed it out of competition. *Come Back, Africa* also opened to critical acclaim in Paris and London, and earned a prize at the Vancouver Film Festival. Shortly after its U.S. debut in April 1960, *Time* magazine selected it as one of the ten best pictures of the year.[34] With good reason, Rogosin felt that he had launched Makeba's career in the west. Even before she joined him in Venice, he had shown the film to television variety show host Steve Allen and Village Vanguard owner Max Gordon, both of whom wanted to book Makeba immediately.[35] Indeed, the film's debut at Venice created something of a sensation, and, in the process, the film and its female star stimulated a dialogue on both sides of the Atlantic about apartheid, race relations, and the documentary as a genre.

Many people who saw *Come Back, Africa* at film festivals or small art house movie theaters concluded that they were seeing an absolutely authentic depiction of black oppression. *Time* praised the film as the "horrifying study of life in the black depths of South African society." Influential *New York Times* film critic Bosley Crowther criticized the film for its "stilted" performances, but appreciated how it conveyed "the helplessness and frustration that the average African must feel in the face of the social dilemmas that exist in South Africa." "Make it a point to see *Come Back, Africa*," wrote Jesse Walker in a review for the *New York Amsterdam News* that emphasized blacks' agency as well as degradation, because this "drama of racial conflict . . . shows the true picture of South Africa."[36]

The film's aura of relevance and veracity increased because even as the cameras were rolling, white authorities had started to bulldoze Sophiatown and forcibly "relocate" blacks. *Come Back, Africa* documented Sophiatown on the cusp of its elimination.[37] In New York, this "timely and remarkable piece of cinema journalism" opened just weeks after the Sharpeville massacre. As the *Amsterdam News* critic explained, "inexperienced natives" had the "major roles" in the film, "but so do those we're reading about in today's headlines. And the impact is the same."[38] White South Africans responded to this negative publicity by criticizing the film's "sensationalism" and "distorted" perspective, and government officials accused Rogosin of having connections to communists. Nevertheless, even when a film critic for the *Rand Daily Mail* described *Come Back, Africa* as "one of the greatest hoaxes in cinema history," he also referred to it as a "documentary . . . about to gain worldwide fame."[39]

In valuing the film's "authenticity," many white viewers became aware of South African blacks as individuals, as political subjects with political aspirations, and as intellectuals with ideas and creativity. Anthony Carew, of the *London Daily Herald*, saw the film at Venice and wrote, "I have just seen a film that makes me ashamed of being white—ashamed of belonging to a race which can oppress and terrorise people of other colors." Andre Brink, a white South African writer who was living in Paris when *Come Back, Africa* opened there, recalled that until he saw this film, he had never conceived of a black as "anything but a servant or a labourer." As he explained, "The way blacks lived, the fact that they did all these things like eating and chatting and talking and singing, that was a closed book to me as a white." Seeing these activities on screen was "a revelation." Brink and others tended to focus on what one critic called the "most successful" shebeen scene and what *Time* referred to as an "exciting bull session among Negro intellectuals." Hollis Alpert, of the *Saturday Review*, praised the "cinematically crude scene" because the "talk is enlightening, and I should think somewhat frightening for any stray white Johannesburg politician who might happen to see this film." The episode that Rogosin himself regarded as "the climax" and filmed first was what made "the film worthwhile," said another. As one South African journalist put it, "That was not acting, in that that was what happened in shebeens every night."[40]

The implicit comparisons between African Americans and black South Africans that the film invited at times became explicit. When *Come Back, Africa* opened at the Los Feliz theater in Los Angeles, a reviewer asserted that "a verbal controversy" would "undoubtedly ensue" if a theater booked such an "inflammatory" film. According to this reviewer, only "communists" would "love the contrived story"; further, Rogosin had done an "extreme disservice to the Negro" with a film that was so filled with propaganda. The anticipated "verbal controversy" did in fact ensue when the owner of the city's leading art house cinema, Max Laemmle, countered the Cold War and racial logic spun together in this critique. Rogosin's film was worthy, according to Laemmle, not just because of its artistic credibility but because of its "subject matter as a social drama on one of the world's top topical hot spots," and, precisely because it fostered comparisons to American race relations: "As for the fact that this problem cannot help but provoke comparison with our American Negro situation that too is fine with me. If the compassion the onlooker might feel or the shame of it might transfer in some slight degree to his consciousness a similar feeling with regard to the American Negro, the showing of the film will be justified."[41]

The conversations which developed as a result of *Come Back, Africa's* release at international film festivals and art cinemas suggest how a film could draw attention to apartheid and introduce global ideas about race and anticolonialism to audiences who might not necessarily be involved in political organizing. The making of the film required Americans, Europeans, and South Africans to collaborate as cultural workers. The story itself depicted cosmopolitan and transnational black African cultures. And the reception of the film created opportunities for nonmainstream racial politics—and Miriam Makeba's voice—to circulate internationally.

TO SAY THAT a great deal changed in 26-year-old Miriam Makeba's life after the release of *Come Back, Africa* and her move to Manhattan would be an understatement. She was living in a society that was more racially integrated than that in apartheid South Africa; she was socializing with other celebrities across racial lines; she was performing on television and earning large sums of money. Although Makeba had been a professional singer for years, she now had an extraordinarily large fan base and support from experts who attended to everything from her backup band to her wardrobe to her transportation.[42]

Critics and fans who heaped exuberant praise on Makeba in her early years in the United States tended to focus on these and other changes.

FIGURE 2.2 Miriam Makeba poses for a portrait session in Chicago, circa 1960. (Michael Ochs Archives/Getty Images)

"There are few cases in show business where a performer's life has changed more suddenly, more dramatically, and with so much promise," noted the *New York Times* two months after her American debut. She may have been "too shy to realize it," according to a writer in *Time*, "but her return to Africa would leave a noticeable gap in the U.S. entertainment world, which she entered a mere six weeks ago."[43]

The critical discourse that swirled around Makeba in the aftermath of *Come Back, Africa* undoubtedly elevated her. Many agreed that she was "in a class by herself. It is very different kind of class, foreign to the usual kind of entertainment," and that she was a precious commodity akin to "A Pure Diamond from South African Mines," as the *Pittsburgh Courier* put it.[44] But this elevation had some unexpected and ironic results. Americans tended not to acknowledge Makeba's successful singing career in South Africa, the years of hard work she had invested to build that career under dangerous circumstances and in a male-dominated subculture, or the fact that American popular culture was important to blacks in South Africa. Instead, she emerged as a performer who stood "in contrast to the gimmicky approach of many American singers" and the "emotional, often artificial style of American negro singer." As the African roots of this "exotic" African performer—a "former housemaid from South Africa" with twelve "tribal names"—dominated Makeba's reception, the international routes of cultural exchange and the cosmopolitan nature of her life in Sophiatown often receded.[45] So too did her status as a sex symbol in South Africa. Few who focused on Makeba's "simplicity" would have guessed that the singer who "confessed" in her "almost unbelievable shy manner" that she had never received musical training, had enthralled young male fans in Johannesburg. Hugh Masekela, a fan, friend, and fellow musician in Sophiatown, remembered how in South Africa, "she wore sexy black high heels and a tight, hip-hugging strapless red dress that allowed us a bird's-eye view into her cleavage," but these perspectives were not prominent in the United States.[46] Some things did not change, however: Accounts of how Harry Belafonte had "discovered her and brought her to American audiences" and used his "powerful influence to get her TV exposure" echoed the Pygmalion-like discussions of her in South Africa in relation to the Manhattan Brothers and Lionel Rogosin. Representations of Makeba on two continents presumed that she always required discovering and was devoid of personal ambition herself, assumptions that could not have been further from the truth.[47]

While American critics praised Makeba's versatility and multilingual repertoire, they reserved their superlatives for her "native song stylings."

She "reaches her peak in African tunes," noted *Variety*'s critic, "since this is presumably where her heart is." In an early hit, "The Click Song," Makeba's distinctive Xhosa "click" sounds stood out as notably different from the sounds of American-born musicians. It seemed almost required for critics to observe that she used "a throat clicking only her people can do." Makeba was "the only entertainer now in New York," wrote Milton Bracker in the *New York Times*, who "can project the weird tongue-smackings of her native Xhosa language into night club songs." The "Click Song" secured Makeba's reputation as "a fascinating and exotic performer—she is Africa."[48]

Blacks in South Africa also described Makeba as rooted in Africa when they celebrated "our Miriam" and chronicled her overseas successes "in the big time." Three issues of *Drum* after Makeba's first American appearances on television and stage profiled "our Lady of Song" (or "our nightingale"), including extensive photo spreads of Makeba in South Africa and then in New York. The magazine *Zonk* published a letter from Makeba to her fans in South Africa. This coverage simultaneously conveyed a protective, even territorial, tone and a celebratory ethos, a combination that reinforced the ways "our Miriam" came to stand in for black South Africa in two countries. If "the world" was "just beginning to open up for our 27-year-old lady of song," then so too was the world of Sophiatown that she had just left, *Drum* seemed to suggest.[49]

"Our nightingale" was extremely careful about how she might, or might not, bring the world of Sophiatown to the attention of Americans. When she first arrived in the United States, Makeba avoided any direct discussions of apartheid. "South Africa will always be my home," she told one reporter, "though naturally I don't appreciate segregation. Everyone knows how I feel, but it isn't something I like to talk about." A well-known reputation for shyness offstage may have contributed to this reticence, but it was also a strategic decision. Makeba's entire family remained in South Africa, and they could face the consequences if she denounced the white nationalist government; this included her nine-year-daughter, who joined her mother in the United States in August 1960. Several of Makeba's relatives were killed at Sharpeville.[50] Shortly after her daughter's arrival in the United States, Makeba received word that her mother had died in South Africa. She tried to return for the funeral, only to learn that white South African authorities cancelled her passport. In her grief, Makeba realized that the "darling of the American newsmagazines" who had "started a fashion trend with her hair and clothes" was "nothing but a black native without rights" in New York's South African consulate.[51] A 30-year exile from her homeland had begun.

When they exiled Makeba, white South African authorities created a more effective symbol of apartheid's cruelty than she could have done herself. In addition to being the "First Lady of African Music," she was also a "Xosa [sic] tribeswoman who managed to elude South Africa's apartheid." This status as "unable to go home," as a headline in *Ebony* declared, broadcast the personal cost of apartheid to American consumers.[52] Makeba also became less reticent after white authorities cancelled her passport in 1961. She proactively performed anti-apartheid activism on an array of stages. As a result of these changed circumstances and the choices Makeba made, widespread depictions of the "doe-eyed Miriam Makeba," with her "exotic bag" of music, did more than simply reproduce a gendered primitivist discourse.[53] With a range of performance strategies, Makeba adapted this discourse.

Music and lyrics played an important part in how Makeba exposed Americans to the realities of apartheid and resisted the regime. She intentionally sang in English and in African languages but never sang Afrikaner songs—the language of ruling whites in South Africa. "When Afrikaaners sing in my language, then I will sing theirs," she declared, in a widely reproduced quote. Historically, English was a language of political resistance for many South African blacks precisely because the ruling all-white National Party had passed laws against blacks educating themselves. The Manhattan Brothers, Makeba's band in South Africa, was not allowed to record songs in English, a ban that made it harder for them to reach larger and international audiences. Some critics saw an "occasional slight commercialization" in Makeba's English-language songs, and one even saw a worrisome "hint of Lena Horne mannerisms" in her second American album, *The World of Miriam Makeba*; but most were impressed by the fact that Makeba could touch her fans with songs in both English and Xosa.[54]

Moreover, Makeba's songs in African languages were a means of affirming a resistant black South African identity that was independent of white authority. In the lively and fast-paced "Boot Dance," Makeba dressed in a (male) miner's costume and used dance and metaphors to evoke both the repressive apartheid regime and blacks' refusals to acquiesce to that regime. The song made manifest the bleak manual labor to which so many black men were subject under white rule even as it highlighted music as a means of resisting that degradation. Another, "Jikele Mayweni," was a slow and mournful song about an African warrior; with accompanying instruments and with the timbre of her voice, Makeba evoked the pain and loss of defeat in ways that resonated in post-Sharpeville years. "Wimoweh," a Zulu hunting song, quickly became one of Makeba's biggest hits in the United States. Most fans regarded the lyrics about warriors on a lion hunt in metaphorical terms: "One Day They'll Kill That Lion," noted a headline in the *Washington Post*. Even Americans who did not understand the Zulu ("If you don't wake up and go out hunting, / Time will pass you by, you'll always be behind. / So courage, warriors, there goes that lion. / Let's get after him") appreciated, as one reporter explained, that this song was "intended to give courage" to those who fought back, and that when Makeba sang "Wimoweh," she unleashed "feelings generated by 27 years of apartheid."[55]

Makeba resisted white rule and affirmed pride among black South Africans even in songs that were not seemingly about politics. When she introduced her famous "Click Song" on her first American album, for example, she claimed the very difference that others had imposed on her in ways that lightly drew attention to the shortcomings of her English-speaking audiences—albeit in an appealing and commercially strategic manner: The song "from my native village," she said to the audience in her inviting and lilting voice, "is called 'The Click Song' by the English because *they* cannot say . . . 'Qongqothwante.'"[56] By engaging her audiences, she did not simply assent to the assumption that the sounds that came out of her mouth were "weird." Instead, the "fascinating and exotic" woman destabilized assumptions about who and what was fascinating and exotic. In doing so, she raised questions about who was the "we" and who was the "they."

Offstage, Makeba's status as an exile and her ostensible difference as a black South African woman helped to create comparisons between American civil rights activism and anti-apartheid activism, contributing to an emerging liberal consensus that extremes of racial discrimination in or out of the United States were harmful. She and Belafonte often performed together and separately on behalf of the SCLC, SNCC, ACOA, Student Aid Association of South Africa, and other civil rights–oriented organizations.[57] Belafonte had a last-minute health emergency that kept them from performing at the SCLC annual convention in Nashville, Tennessee, in 1961, but the three-act concert they had planned highlighted connections between black struggles around the world: The first act was the "Sound of Two Continents," the second, "Tribute to the Freedom Riders," and the

third, "The Whole World Over." When they did perform at an SCLC benefit concert the following year, before an interracial crowd of over 5,000,
many agreed "that it was the event of the year," as Martin Luther King Jr.
put it in his letter of thanks, and the concert raised $15,000.[58] At these
events and others, Makeba supported organizations committed to im-
proving American race relations and those whose members focused on
Africa and especially apartheid in South Africa. Her very presence suggested the connections between these areas of struggle.[59]

Makeba also evoked associations between domestic black activism and
international protests against apartheid when she appeared in less overtly
political spaces, such as international film festivals, American television,
and college campuses. She was a "fave on the college circuit," where her
audiences tended to be younger, and a "first-rate draw" at smaller "supper-
clubs"—the chic nightclubs of mostly older white audiences where Lena
Horne's popularity had soared in the 1940s and '50s, and where Nina
Simone, Diahann Carroll, and Abbey Lincoln also made names for themselves.[60] In years when eighty-five percent of all American homes had a
television on some five hours a day, Makeba reached even larger audiences with her frequent appearances on variety shows like *The Steve Allen
Show* and *The Ed Sullivan Show*. She piqued the interest of live audiences
and those watching in their living rooms—most of whom were not club
goers or college students or activists—who might not otherwise encoun
ter her. As *Variety* noted after her television debut, "Her first public showcasing in the U.S. . . . was only a quickie shot that did little more than whet
the appetite for more of her native song stylings."[61] Makeba targeted and
reached many audiences, and her presence in this range of venues subtly
reinforced the ways that Americans across lines of race became more
aware of apartheid, and African Americans became more oriented toward
Africa in an era of decolonization. Consciously or not, a cross-section of
American audiences was paying attention to apartheid when they paid
attention to this woman who dressed and sang differently from American
performers, and who had so quickly become a phenomenon.

In 1962, after performing for the SCLC in Atlanta, Belafonte and
Makeba were denied entrance to one of the city's elegant restaurants. The
savvy Belafonte brought the media to the entrance of the restaurant and
declared, "What can we as Americans say to a guest like Miss Makeba?
She comes from a land of oppression, only to find a situation like this."
According to Makeba, she could not "get too excited or upset." As she later
explained: "I'm from South Africa, which makes Atlanta look like the

cradle of democracy."[62] Here and elsewhere, the exiled Makeba became a means through which liberal Americans who supported integration could compare South Africa to the United States. As a female victim of apartheid whom critics cast as shy, unsophisticated, and different, Makeba was an appropriate reminder for liberal Americans of all that they wanted their country not to be.

And yet, in the United States as in South Africa, Miriam Makeba was never just a symbol. She was more than a victim, more than an "African tribeswoman," and more than simply "Belafonte's protégé." Indeed, the challenges she posed, the locations for these challenges, and the ways in which she claimed her ostensible difference as a means of resistance increased in the mid-1960s. In 1962, Makeba returned to Africa for the first time since she had left in 1959. As the African American and white press noted, she could not enter South Africa, but did travel to Kenya to support Tom Mboya and the campaign for Kenyan independence. The following year, Makeba went to Addis Ababa, Ethiopia, for the founding of the Organization of African Unity (OAU), an organization committed to "African nationalism—and pan-Africanism" as "one of the determinant forces of the sixties," according to one observer. Years later, Makeba would write that she had "one thing in common with the emerging black nations of Africa: We both have voices, and we are discovering what we can do with them."[63] Even before she had offered that insight, she had earned the nicknames "Mama Africa" and the "Empress of African Song," and her close friends included delegates from the OAU, ambassadors to the United Nations from newly independent African countries, heads of state like Sekou Toure of Guinea, and ANC members and other activists who had left South Africa. Seven months after the founding of the OAU, Makeba and Belafonte both went to Kenya for its independence celebration as guests of prime minister Jomo Kenyatta; shortly after, Belafonte organized and funded a trip to Guinea for SNCC activists who "needed a hiatus"— one that could be had, he concluded, only in Africa.[64]

Makeba used her voice even more forcefully when she testified before the United Nations Committee on Apartheid in 1963. With Nelson Mandela in solitary confinement at a Pretoria prison and the political situation worsening (just days earlier, the raid at Rivonia led to the arrest of other ANC leaders; the subsequent trial would end with Mandela being sentenced to life in prison Robben Island), Makeba dressed in a tweed suit and sat alone at a long conference table. Her prepared remarks that ANC members wrote, according to her later accounts, touched on police brutality and mass arrests, and the economics of apartheid; four years after the African National Congress had issued a call for international economic sanctions against South Africa, she quietly and forcefully supported a boycott, especially of arms, to South Africa. "I have not the slightest doubt," she said, that the arms that major powers supplied to South Africa would "be used against the African women and children." Makeba also declared that the "great powers" must "act with firmness to stop those mad rulers from dragging the country" into further disaster.[65] When Makeba was "invited back" to the United Nations in March 1964, she re-emphasized the need for "quick and real action" in South Africa and concluded her statement by reading the lyrics to a song calling for an economic boycott of South Africa by anti-apartheid activist/entertainer Vanessa Redgrave.[66] Here Makeba defined herself as a political subject talking about global affairs, one who could draw on another singer's lyrics to illustrate the points she was making.

FIGURE 2.3 Miriam Makeba testified before the United Nations Committee on Apartheid in 1963, putting her family in South Africa and her career in the United States at risk.

(Photographs and Prints Division, Schomburg Center for Research in Black Culture, The New York Public Library, Astor, Lenox, and Tilden Foundations)

Makeba put her family in South Africa as well as her American career at risk. Her words at the United Nations, she knew, were an "act of treason" in the eyes of South African authorities, who sought to ban her records from stores and radio in retaliation. As one South African recalled, it was

> impossible to overstate how much of a role model Miriam Makeba became. The rarity of her records inside the country meant they were disseminated far and wide by underground means. If the cops found you with the music of Makeba, they would throw you in jail. Because the regime was aware of what she was doing outside, her music was seen as subversive—even if she was singing a love song.[67]

In the United States, Makeba continued to sing the songs considered subversive in South Africa and also continued to support the ACOA, the African-American Institute, and other groups oriented toward assisting Africans in the United States. She was fast becoming "the toast of New York's African community," in the words of one émigré.[68]

Belafonte and Makeba's Grammy-award-winning album *An Evening with Belafonte/Makeba: Songs from Africa* (1965), a collection of songs in Xhosa, Zulu, and other African languages, was a departure from their previously largely apolitical repertoire. Belafonte's considerable offstage activism had initially connected Makeba to civil rights struggles more than the music they performed, but on this album, several songs posed direct challenges to white authorities in South Africa: "Beware, Verwoerd," for example, warned the South African prime minister that the black man was "on the move"; "To Those We Love" told the story of Mandela and other leaders in prison. According to *New York Times* critic Robert Shelton, the album confirmed how "Mr. Belafonte's identification with African cultural and social movements has been growing during the years. Here he has a chance to indulge that musical interest with a singer steeped in several traditions."[69] Initially, Makeba may have largely separated herself from organized politics or confrontational stances and benefited significantly from Belafonte's celebrity and from his ties to the American civil rights movement. Nevertheless, when they collaborated on this album, Makeba, with her "striking blend of the highly sophisticated and the primitive," conferred a certain authenticity by association on to Belafonte.[70]

With and without Belafonte by her side, Miriam Makeba called attention to her status not just as South African, but as a South African woman. She did so in ways that further transformed common descriptions of her in the United States as an exotic "other." When her career first took off in South Africa, Makeba's sexuality was part of the public persona that she established.[71] In the United States, by contrast, American critics tended to emphasize how Makeba combined poise and "artistry," on the one hand, and a primitive exoticism, on the other. This combination of qualities converged in repeated references to Makeba's "simplicity" and related images of her as "shy," "soft-spoken and reticent," and "bashful."[72] Alternatively, and over time, critics and fans from around the world referred to Makeba in maternal terms, as "Mama Africa." In both instances, Makeba's ostensible difference as a black South African woman allowed her to emerge as a respectable performer in the United States; she sometimes appeared to be simple and refined and sometimes simple and exotic, but she was always distant from the images of sexuality and vice with which black women performers had been linked for many years.

Makeba also worked to alter assumptions made about her and to redefine black womanhood, sexuality, and beauty on her own terms. When she arrived in the United States, she refused to wear as much makeup as women performers generally did, and even more notably, after an initial disastrous experience, she would not straighten her hair. Before she opened at the Village Vanguard, "Mr. Belafonte's people" took Makeba to get her hair done, which, in 1959, meant straightened. "The long, elegant look like Diahann Carroll's" was the style, according to Makeba. Years later, she described this first experience at an American hair salon in this way: "I cannot look in the mirror. I'm too afraid. When I get back to the hotel I see what has been done to me. I cry and cry. This is not *me*. I put my head in the hot water and I wash it and wash it. I am not a glamor girl."[73]

Makeba was right—up to a point. Her trajectory in mainstream American popular culture did set her apart from the kind of glamour that Lena Horne, the "sepia sensation," defined and embodied in the 1930s and '40s. Makeba's dark skin, her unadorned designer clothing, her colorful jewelry that always, to audiences, hinted of Africa, and her quiet offstage demeanor which critics praised as "beguiling," rarely had the relentlessly eroticized dimensions common to depictions of Lena Horne as the desirable and unattainable black female "sex symbol."[74] Nevertheless, in South Africa and then the United States, the dark-skinned Makeba offered a different perspective on glamour, as well as respectability and sexuality, for black women. She first did so as part of the Sophiatown renaissance, when she became famous amidst a widespread valorization of lighter skinned black women. Nicknamed the "nut brown baby," she disapproved of the U.S.-made skin lighteners that were so popular in South Africa in the early 1950s, and refused to appear in advertisements for these products that sexualized and celebrated light-skinned black women.[75] Makeba continued to challenge meanings of female beauty in the United States when she appeared in a "chic gown" and what she called her "short and woolly" hair.[76]

Like African American women who made similar choices about their hair and clothes in this period, Makeba was rejecting standards of beauty defined by Americanness and whiteness.[77] Her self-representations had a particularly significant impact because of her fame, and because she was associated with a diasporic pan-Africanism, anti-apartheid activism, and American civil rights activism. Here was an incredibly talented and successful woman who performed on *The Ed Sullivan Show* and for SNCC, who seemed both exotic and elegant, and who embraced, on- and offstage, nonnormative models of female beauty and desirability. In 1966, Makeba—known as a sex symbol in South Africa, as a "simple" singer in the United States, and as "Mama Africa" around the world—explained her choices in ways that drew attention to the gender-specific and transnational dimensions of black pride and black power. Natural hair had spread among African American women, she said, because it "makes you have a good feeling. It's as though Negro women are finally admitting they're proud of their heritage. . . . A Negro woman should look natural, and that's what this new look is trying to say. . . . Those who press their hair and buy wigs are running away from themselves."[78] Makeba was putting into words the political ideas about black freedom and power for women that for six years she had performed and disseminated with her body. A woman who owned the *African Look*, one of the first stores in the country to sell African clothing exclusively, explained Makeba's impact this way: "The look is Miriam's. . . . She gave Americans the chance to see it on television, and that's where it all started."[79] This look may not in fact have started with Makeba; nonetheless, when Makeba chose to keep her hair "natural," she provided fodder for representations of her as the "Empress of Africa" and "Mama Africa" at the same time that she used mass culture to redefine black womanhood, female sexuality, and black power in a global context.

Many American fans reacted positively to Makeba's ability to bridge different worlds in her redefinitions of femininity and black womanhood. A critic for *Time* summed it up well: "The close-cropped woolly head and the sleek white Fifth Avenue gown come from different worlds, but the combination has a charm and grace of its own."[80] Makeba was known as beautiful and poised because of her "wooly hair" and not in spite of it. As she made this her look in the first half of the 1960s, she also bridged divides between politicized jazz subcultures in New York City and mass culture, between apartheid in South Africa and American race relations, and between pan-Africanism and black power in the United States. Her efforts were appealing to a range of fans across lines of race, region, nation, and even political affiliation.

Consequently, even though many Americans minimized Makeba's cosmopolitanism in the United States, they could not make assumptions about her based only on their preexisting assumptions about an imaginary Africa. Instead, Americans who paid attention to her engaged with anti-apartheid activism, decolonization, and representations of black women in ways that were markedly different from what had been common ten years earlier. Even though "black power" and "black is beautiful" were not yet common slogans, Makeba, along with other black women entertainers, was enacting a racial politics that emphasized black autonomy and took into account black women's experiences within and across national boundaries.

DESPITE ALL THAT she accomplished professionally and politically, Miriam Makeba's years in the United States did not end in triumph. For almost a decade, Makeba resisted essentialist representations of her in ways that were politically meaningful and professionally profitable. From 1959 until 1967, Makeba and Harry Belafonte—in their music and their celebrity status, separately and together—pushed against existing boundaries of race and music. They were creating multicultural and world music before those terms became popular and in ways that had broad mass appeal; theirs was a hybrid repertoire that, alongside their offstage activism, created connections among different groups and affirmed both the unique significance of Africa and a cultural pluralism. As liner notes to Makeba's best-selling 1967 album *Pata Pata* put it, her "multifaceted" music "knocks down walls, bridges, barriers, and transforms a dozen different languages into a universal tongue."[81] This "universal tongue" was contradictory because it relied on Americans' views of Makeba as specifically black and specifically African: "Don't let the chic gown worn by singer Miriam Makeba fool you!" *Variety* reminded readers. "When her voice sounds, it's the heart of Africa speaking to the world."[82] It was this contradiction—between singing a "universal tongue" and *being* the "heart of Africa"—that Makeba could not sustain.

In 1967, promotional material referred to Makeba as a "passionate Pan-Africanist, proud of her Continent and the people she has come to symbolize."[83] While that description might have been apt for years, what those terms meant was in flux. The American civil rights movement was never one monolithic organization or impulse, and multiple perspectives had always coexisted and competed. Makeba's career indicates how black power and liberal interracialism could connect; her mainstream appeal suggests that even in the late 1950s and early 1960s, Africa was relevant to black and white activists, across divides of liberal, radical, and nationalist politics, as a symbol of both anticolonialist freedom and black pride. Nevertheless, by the mid- to late 1960s, common ground with regard to meanings of Africa became harder to find.[84]

Events outside of the United States contributed to an eroding consensus on Africa's significance to Americans, and affected Americans' attitudes toward Makeba. For one, civil wars in newly independent African nations complicated what briefly had seemed to be "simple" anticolonialism in which black nationalists had struggled against white colonialists. The period when Americans caught up with Cold War concerns and wary of domestic red-baiting could get behind African independence efforts quickly passed in the face of wars in the Congo, Angola, and elsewhere. An escalating Vietnam War and antiwar activism in the United States also had an impact on relationships between domestic civil rights activism and anticolonialism in Africa and elsewhere in the world, especially after SNCC leaders and Martin Luther King Jr. officially came out against the war. Stokely Carmichael offered searing critiques and sharply brought the racial dimensions of American foreign policy into focus with an anticolonialist perspective. (The lyrics from the musical *Hair*—the draft was "white people sending black people to make war on yellow people in order to defend the land they stole from red people"—are often attributed to him.)[85] Finally, when Israel defeated Egypt, a founding member of the Organization of African Unity, during six days of battle in June 1967, civil rights alliances that were already stretched thin frayed further. Whereas many Christian and Jewish supporters, black and white, had regarded Israel in the first decades of its existence as having fought against

British colonialism for its own independence, after 1967, more people concluded that the country was itself a colonial power, and thus part of the problem that both the OAU and many American civil rights activists were challenging.[86]

With these developments, Miriam Makeba as a symbol of black Africa became a less palatable commodity across racial boundaries and across a political spectrum in the United States, and it became more difficult for her to use those symbolic connections productively. These dynamics became evident in the uneasy and changing relationship, or what she would call her "break up," with "Big Brother." According to Makeba's auto-biographical accounts, "African delegates" from the United Nations contacted her during her annual summer tour with Belafonte in June 1967. They were concerned that the Belafonte/Makeba concert program included Israeli folk tunes in Hebrew. Because "Egypt is an African nation," they asked her to "refrain" from singing those melodies. Makeba, who always claimed that she was just an entertainer and did not want to engage in political debates, regarded the numbers simply as "love songs." But she did tell Belafonte about this exchange. Again, according to Makeba, Belafonte agreed that this request was "ridiculous" because the songs in question were "not political"; he also felt that the request itself was inappropriate. It was their last tour together.[87] While the details of this conflict remain murky, what is clear is that being associated with Africa did not mean in 1967 what it had meant in 1960, dubbed the Year of Africa. Among some advocates of civil rights, there was a marked increase in attention to Africa and anti-apartheid activism in the late 1960s. SNCC activists, for instance, held a sit-in at the South African Embassy in Washington, D.C., and at the South African consulate in New York in 1966; Harry Belafonte and Sidney Poitier posted bail for the five arrested protesters. In 1967, H. Rapp Brown, the chairman of SNCC, called on African Americans to boycott General Motors cars: "We are fully aware," he declared, that "General Motors is a heavy investor in South Africa and the profits from exploited labor of our brothers in South Africa makes this company even richer."[88]

Yet, Miriam Makeba could not mesh and embody anticolonialist, anti-apartheid, and domestic civil rights agendas in mass culture in the ways that she had done just several years earlier. Her status as a female victim of apartheid and Belafonte's status as a black activist celebrity with mainstream success lacked the broad potency it once had; further, her personification of Africa and his relationships to domestic civil rights activism could not be as productively interwoven, regardless of their intentions or political beliefs, or the ways that Belafonte especially had long defied political labels and categories.[89] The irony was that Makeba, who for years had forged and performed her pan-African vision of black power in the United States, had less space to do so amidst proliferating calls for black power.

YEARS LATER, STOKELY Carmichael recalled that he had first met Makeba in 1961 when Harry Belafonte had invited him and other Freedom Riders to a concert in Forest Hills, New York. When the 19-year-old Carmichael heard that Makeba would be appearing with Belafonte, he hoped to meet her and thought carefully about what to wear: "After much thought and trying on for effect, I settled on a silky Harry Belafonte shirt. The kind with flared collars, a deep V neck, and billowing sleeves." To Carmichael's dismay, they met just briefly—so briefly, in fact, that Makeba quickly forgot all about it.[90] Their second meeting, at a music festival marking the Eighth Party Congress in Conakry, Guinea, in 1967, was more auspicious. Their romance began in Guinea and continued in the United States. At a party celebrating their wedding, the U.N. ambassador to Guinea hailed the marriage as "the beginning of stronger ties between black people on both sides of the Atlantic."[91]

As had been the case since she first came to the United States, Makeba remained emphatic about the fact that she was not an activist. Her relationship with Carmichael, she said at the time—and subsequently—had "nothing to do with politics"; further, she wrote in her first autobiography, "The man's activities do not interest me, only the man himself." In a second autobiography, Makeba noted that "Stokely is considered very radical and something of a menace when he talks about black power, but I don't see anything wrong with it. Why shouldn't power be black?" Given Makeba's history and the potential disingenuous feel that these and statements she made at the time have, it is unlikely that she completely cordoned off politics from this relationship.[92] Regardless of what she believed, her efforts to represent the romance as apolitical were not very effective at the time. The associations that had accrued to Carmichael and Makeba separately now had a cumulative impact through their connection to each other.

For Carmichael, this process had mostly positive results. He encountered criticism from some black activists that he had "sold out" or was "going bourgeois" after he and Makeba bought an expensive home in Washington, D.C. At Makeba's urging, he also became less inclined to wear overalls as a uniform, or a badge of authenticity for a black revolutionary.

More often than not, though, his marriage to a woman who was "the image of African womanhood, the gentle assegai [spear] that lets us know we are warriors," according to liner notes on Makeba's 1968 album, reflected well on his status as a pan-Africanist revolutionary.[93] The one "major difference" in how he made Africa matter to black power in the United States was Makeba herself: "Whenever possible, Miriam Makeba accompanied me on these speaking engagements. . . . And she certainly was a political asset at my speeches, big time. I'd introduce her from the stage. She'd stand, smile, bow, and the folks would go wild." In 1967, as the Afro became a symbol of militant black masculinity, Carmichael increasingly endorsed the style that black women like Makeba had started to wear some ten years earlier: "Don't ever," said Carmichael to a crowd in Harlem in which teenagers dominated, "don't ever, don't *ever* be ashamed of being black because . . . you are black, little girl with your nappy hair and your broad lips, and *you are beautiful.*" With Makeba by his side, the value of these words—and his own image as a black militant male—increased.[94]

The same could not be said for Carmichael's effects on Makeba's career. She felt the negative impact almost immediately after they wed, as shows were cancelled and opportunities dwindled.[95] Even when reporters did not dwell on their relationship, a marked decline in coverage suggests that Makeba had simply become less visible in the United States. Her appearance New York's Philharmonic Hall in 1969 was her first "in three years," as one reviewer observed.[96] In addition to losing recording and performing contracts, Makeba, like Carmichael, faced FBI surveillance and obstacles getting in and out of the country. "What hurt me," Makeba explained 15 years later, when she discussed the cancelled shows and what she considered to be a de facto blacklist, "was the silence of the Black press." She continued to perform around the world to much acclaim, but in the United States, as she described it, "Nobody even asked, 'Where is Makeba?' My records were not played."[97]

Miriam Makeba had found ways to use her associations with the masculine subculture of Sophiatown, with filmmaker Lionel Rogosin, and with activist-entertainer Harry Belafonte to her political and professional advantage. But she was unable to push back against representations of her as allied with Carmichael's politics—and perhaps she was unwilling to do so given her own commitments to black liberation. They both had relationships with Sekou Toure, the first president of Guinea, and both had opportunities that they could pursue in that country. In December 1968, they accepted Toure's invitation to Makeba and left the United States.

Makeba's career rebounded and continued for decades, and she remained important to anti-apartheid activism into the 1980s. But her years as the "voice of Africa" in and for the United States had ended.[98]

IN OCTOBER 1967, the magazine *Sepia* included a remarkably insightful profile of Miriam Makeba and her fans. "The fascination of her eloquent voice, the warmth of her quiet humility and the charm of her personality have combined to make Miriam Makeba the first South African songstress to attain international stardom," the short profile began, drawing on phrases and images that had become common refrains in popular coverage of Makeba. The unnamed reporter then took a more interesting turn. "She has been referred to as 'a high voltage star,' 'a typical example of the work camps, the bush villages and the city slums,' 'a highly disciplined performer with a chic, sophisticated style,' 'a totally untutored performer with the stark simplicity of a primitive style and a natural feeling for the jazz idiom,' 'a deliberate, very refined artist.' Makeba, it seems, is all things to all people."[99]

To some extent, for eight years, Makeba had been just that—"all things to all people"—and a repository for the meanings of Africa, anticolonialism, and apartheid that white and black Americans developed. Her popularity depended in part on her ability to reflect back the meanings of South Africa and blackness that many Americans put upon her. Yet Makeba did more than absorb preexisting political beliefs and assumptions. Through her music that seemed mostly apolitical and with her apparently nonconfrontational style, she used definitions of her as essentially African to defy that very essentialism: She linked race relations in South Africa and in the United States; she connected pan-African anticolonialism and American civil rights; and she articulated a position in which desirable black femininity and the racial pride associated with "black is beautiful" and black power coexisted.

Makeba's successes as a black woman who performed civil rights suggest the degree to which "civil rights" and "black power" ran parallel and shaped each other, especially in the context of popular culture, and the ways that foundations of black feminism developed in conjunction with black freedom struggles. But the obstacles she faced and the choices she made about how to position herself matter too. They serve as a reminder that the civil rights movement was not a consistent march toward progress, especially for black women wrestling with racial and gender discrimination. Makeba could not avoid the extent to which her name in the

United States was tied to the prominent men with whom she was associated. Nor could she control the meanings that circulated about her or the ways that other people represented her. As a result, many doors opened for Makeba, but others slammed shut.

One of the many people whom Miriam Makeba influenced from the time she arrived in the United States, and who in turn influenced her, was Nina Simone. The two women socialized and at times performed together; they remained close friends after Makeba left the United States and until Simone's death in 2003.[100] Years later, Makeba recalled that when she was frightened about being "a spokesperson for [her] people" at the United Nations in 1963, she reflected on her friend's strength: "Nina Simone speaking for her people . . . gave me courage."[101] Although the two women learned from and supported each other, Simone made quite different choices about how to perform civil rights as a black woman.

3

"More Than Just a Jazz Performer"

NINA SIMONE'S BORDER CROSSINGS

ON SEPTEMBER 15, 1963, Nina Simone learned that four young African American girls had been killed in the bombing of the Sixteenth Street Baptist Church in Birmingham, Alabama. Up to that point, Simone's repertoire was an eclectic blend of jazz, blues, gospel, and classical music. One critic had dubbed Nina Simone a "songstress for the elite," a phrase that echoed Lena Horne's many years on the cabaret circuit as well as Abbey Lincoln's pre-jazz career as a nightclub singer. Immediately after hearing about the events in Birmingham, however, Simone wrote the song "Mississippi Goddam." It came to her in a "rush of fury, hatred and determination" as she "suddenly realized what it was to be black in America in 1963." It was, she said, "my first civil rights song."[1]

"Mississippi Goddam" was a political anthem, one that expressed unqualified outrage at the violence inflicted on African Americans. The lyrics, filled with anger and despair, stood in stark contrast to the fast-paced and rollicking rhythm. Over the course of several verses, Simone vehemently rejected the notion that race relations should change gradually, that the South was unique in terms of discrimination, and that African Americans could or would patiently seek political rights. "Me and my people are just about due," she declared in her strikingly deep voice. Simone also challenged principles strongly associated with liberal civil rights activism: religion as a source of solace and protest for African Americans, and the viability of a beloved community of whites and blacks. Just one month after 250,000 black and white Americans gathered in front of the Lincoln Memorial and heard Martin Luther King Jr.'s "I Have a Dream" speech at the March on Washington for Jobs and Freedom, Simone sang, toward the end of "Mississippi Goddam":

> All I want is equality
> For my sister, my brother my people and me.
> Yes, you lied to me all these years
> You told me to wash and clean my ears
> And talk real fine, just like a lady
> And you'd stop calling me Sister Sadie.
> But this whole country is full of lies
> You're all gonna die and die like flies
> I don't trust you any more
> You keep on saying "Go Slow."[2]

Both Nina Simone and Lena Horne altered the content and style of their music to protest white Americans' acts of violence against African Americans, and both responded directly to the Birmingham church bombing and the murder of Medgar Evers. In the aftermath of these violent acts, Horne concluded that she could not "sing the same old songs"—standards like her trademark "Stormy Weather." But she also felt that she could not simply "get a guitar and start singing revolt songs." Her solution was "Silent Spring" and "Now." These were new tunes, or an old one with new lyrics in the case of "Now," which harnessed the typically festive Hebrew melody, "Hava Nagilla" to demands for civil rights, and that composers and lyricists Harold Arlen, Yip Harburg, Betty Comden, and Adolph Green wrote or arranged just for her. Horne was working to engage with black activism and politicized culture in a new way. In each of these songs, she grieved and also offered hope. She despaired that "the rains of hate rust the garden gate," but declared that "everyone should love his brother," and called on all Americans to "do what's right, constitutionally." Musically, the songs were not typical of the era's "freedom songs" like "We Shall Overcome," which Horne led in a march after Evers's murder. In terms of content and tone, though, they offered an affirmation. "It's thrilling. This is the beginning again," said Horne in an interview at the March on Washington with Walter Cronkite. Her decision to perform "Silent Spring" and "Now" shortly after her support for Evers and her televised participation in the March, reinforced her connection to what many regarded as the mainstream of the movement—interracial organizing and Southern-based efforts in the civil rights movement.[3]

"Mississippi Goddam" expressed grief, but also conveyed anger, and was just one of many songs that Simone wrote and performed in which she dramatically commented on, participated in, and thereby helped to

FIGURE 3.1 Lena Horne talks to a reporter at the March on Washington in 1963. (NBC/Getty Images)

recast black activism in the 1960s. In the decade that followed, she supported struggles for black freedom in the United States in a more outspoken manner than did many other African American entertainers, while
also building a career as a singer with international appeal. Simone
recorded nearly twenty albums and achieved critical and commercial success domestically and abroad; by the late 1960s, she had a global audience
for a songbook that ranged from recordings of Beatles songs to those that
considered segregation's effects on children, the assassination of Martin
Luther King Jr., romantic heartbreak, gender discrimination, and color
consciousness. There was a near-consensus internationally that Simone,
nicknamed the "High Priestess of Soul," was "one of the best jazz singers
of recent years" who had a magical ability to mesmerize her audiences.[4]
More than Lena Horne or Miriam Makeba, Nina Simone used music,
lyrics, and performance strategies on- and offstage to develop black power
perspectives that were free of misogyny and claimed black women's experiences as relevant. That she did so at all is significant; that she did so as

early as 1963—well before the apparent ascendance of black power or second-wave feminism in the late 1960s and '70s—is even more so.

Simone was surely not alone in her assessments of interracial liberal activism or in her gendered racial politics. The denunciations of the well-mannered politics of "going slow" in "Mississippi Goddam" made manifest the range of political perspectives that developed at many locations in this period.[5] Miriam Makeba claimed that she had nothing to do with politics at the same time that she used her body to affirm a kind of black power for women across national boundaries. She did so as part of male-dominated politicized subcultures in South Africa as well as in the United States. In the context of domestic civil rights organizations, SNCC leader John Lewis was a speaker at the March on Washington who referred to "black people" and not "Negroes" and incited controversy among planners when the initial draft of his speech included descriptions of pending civil rights legislation as "too little too late." Even before publication of his 1962 book *Negroes with Guns*, NAACP activist Robert Williams called for African Americans to arm and defend themselves. Attorney and civil rights activist Pauli Murray was a longtime advocate for legislation that would ensure equity based on race and gender. Simone was connected to many New York–based activist entertainers, men and women, with ties to the left and to radical racial politics. She learned about politics from playwright Lorraine Hansberry, and she chose to write explicitly political songs shortly after influential jazz critics censured vocalist Abbey Lincoln for doing just that.[6] Simone was not a voice out of nowhere, and she did not definitively cause a specific number of fans to change their behavior. But through her music and performances, the perspectives that she shared with others dispersed widely in the early 1960s. Reactions to Simone among critics and fans in the United States and abroad, her efforts to represent herself, and lyrics to "Mississippi Goddam" and other songs on her first overtly political album, all highlight the creative ways that Simone fused politics and performance as a black woman vocalist. Well before she recorded "Four Women" in 1966, a song that overtly addressed gender and racial discrimination in relation to each other and became one of her biggest hits, Nina Simone was bringing black women's voices into conversations about black freedom.

NINA SIMONE'S CAREER as a popular performer took off rapidly after the release of her 1958 hit song "I Loves You, Porgy," the album *Little Girl Blue*, and her move to New York. This "recent discovery," wrote a critic in

Down Beat, "rose to prominence virtually overnight"; as Simone later put it, "I was a sensation. . . . Suddenly I was the hot new thing."[7] At that point, press coverage of the "hot new thing" increased. Simone was the subject of discussion in publications that crossed racial, political, and cultural divides: She received reviews in the premier jazz journal of the day, *Down Beat*, and in the entertainment industry's bible, *Variety*; critics discussed her in African American newspapers and magazines like the *New York Amsterdam News* and *Ebony* as well as in the *New York Times* and *Time*. Even before her first performances in Europe in 1965, jazz magazines abroad had praised her extensively. In conversations about Simone from around the world, fans and critics agreed that her live performances offered an "excitement and spiraling intensity" that was truly rare, but they gave up on efforts to define the type of music she played. "She is, of course, not exactly a jazz performer—or possibly one should say that she is a lot more than just a jazz performer," wrote a reviewer for *Down Beat* after Simone performed at the Newport Jazz Festival for the first time in 1960.[8]

If critics could not define her music, they did agree that Simone's upbringing mattered to the kind of performer she had become. In a proliferating discourse, critics and fans repeatedly retold Simone's "origins" story. A profile in *Metronome* was typical: "Born Eunice Waymon in Tryon, North Carolina (population 1,985), the sixth of eight children, her father was a handyman, her mother a housekeeper who was an ordained Methodist minister. At four Eunice was able to play piano; at seven she was playing piano and organ. . . . The story itself is exciting, revealing, an American one."[9] The repetition of this "American" story about a poor African American girl from a small Southern town who received training in classical music and became a popular vocalist whose style defied musical categories was more than the recycling of promotional materials. In key aspects of her life and in numerous accounts of that life—those in which Simone represented herself and those in which others talked about her—she departed in several ways from then-dominant depictions of African American entertainers, and of African American women entertainers specifically.

Racial stereotypes of African Americans as "natural" entertainers had been a mainstay of a white-dominated entertainment industry for centuries, and for just as long, many black performers had worked to debunk those stereotypes. In the post–World War II years, many male jazz musicians issued these challenges in ways that marginalized women by linking artistry and masculinity.[10] Consequently, the biographical narrative that accompanied Simone's professional ascent was doubly subversive. Her "origins story," which emphasized her years of training and hard work as a classical pianist, countered a racial essentialism that transformed talent among African Americans into some inborn and racially determined inclination to entertain. As well, stories about Simone that emphasized her musical artistry and her scorn for mass culture simultaneously undermined assumptions that African American virtuosity was restricted to men.[11]

The Nina Simone who emerged in reviews and in conversations among fans straddled the worlds of high art and mass culture, of so-called authentic blackness and a universal genius. She was "at least a triple threat artist," according to the *Nashville Tennessean*, because she had studied classical piano at Juilliard and combined "musical range with her dramatic way . . . and composes, sometimes on the spot." A concert at Carnegie Hall showcased, in one critic's words, "artistic rarity": a woman who combined "flawless technical skill as a pianist" and "a superb sense of showmanship besides." It was no coincidence that when a British teenager formed a club devoted to Simone's career in 1965, he intentionally named it the "Nina Simone Appreciation Society" rather than the more common "fan club" that peers had formed for African American R&B musicians who had "cult followings" in England. "Because of the kind of music she was doing . . . because of her history in music . . . I felt it was just appropriate to call it an Appreciation Society and not a fan club. It just didn't sound right to me to say Nina Simone Fan Club."[12] With this biographical trajectory in place, Simone emerged as respectable in a certain kind of way. Unlike Lena Horne, she was not part of a Northern-based, middle-class family of reformers committed to racial uplift; still, because of her classical training, she escaped the association between popular African American women entertainers, vice, and a sexualized commercial culture geared toward pleasing white audiences. As she later described herself in this period when her career was taking off, "Unlike most artists, I didn't care that much about a career as a popular singer. I was different—I was going to be a classical musician."[13] Simone rejected racist assumptions about black performers at the same time that she rejected meanings of jazz that elevated black male creativity.

Place and class were the other two critical parts of Simone's origins story. Fans and critics frequently noted that Simone was a child prodigy who had grown up in the rural South and had played church music even before classical music. "Undoubtedly, her early training in the church and

FIGURE 3.2 Nina Simone bows for her audience at Carnegie Hall in 1965. (Photographs and Prints Division, Schomburg Center for Research in Black Culture, The New York Public Library, Astor, Lenox, and Tilden Foundations)

her years of singing in her father's choir, contributed strongly to the gospel patterns" in Simone's music, according to one portrait. "Regardless of sophisticated trappings," her "inner status as a true 'soul sister'" quickly became clear to black fans, according to another.[14] The many references to her artistry and musical virtuosity ran concurrent with an emphasis on region and class and confirmed Simone's "authenticity" as a black performer—a status that Lena Horne perceived herself as lacking in 1963. Just as Miriam Makeba's birthplace of South Africa coupled with her performance strategies allowed her to embody Africa for her American fans, Simone, with her rural Southern church background, became a credible representative of blackness. Paradoxically, this was the case for Simone whether or not she played the blues or other music associated with racial specificity or blackness, which frequently she did not.

While critics across lines of race depicted Simone in terms of both musical virtuosity and racial authenticity, few did so as vividly or evocatively as did Simone's friend, poet, and public intellectual Langston Hughes. In a description written in 1962 and reprinted in 1964 for promotional purposes, Hughes was expansive in his praise of Simone's technical skill: "She plays piano FLUIDLY well, SIMPLY well, COMPLICATEDLY well, THEATRICALLY well, DRAMATICALLY well, INDIVIDUALLY well, and MADLY well. Not just WELL." Yet, he noted reassuringly, "She is far-out, and at the same time common. . . . She has a flair, but no air." Her skill, he added, did not distance her from black people or blackness. "She is a club member, a colored girl, an Afro-American, a homey from Down Home." Nina Simone, he concluded, was as different as "beer is from champagne, crackers from crepes suzettes, . . . Houston from Paris—each real in their way, but Oh! How different—and how fake it is if it is not Houston you want but the 'city of light.'"[15] For Hughes, as for others, Simone simultaneously embodied an American-based racial authenticity and a cosmopolitan elegance, and she certainly could not be pigeonholed.

White Europeans similarly tended to regard Simone as quintessentially African American—emblematic of racial and national specificity—at the same time that they positioned her as a cosmopolitan artist whose skills transcended nation. Her concert performances of songs in French, her recordings of three French songs on her 1965 album *I Put a Spell on You*, her conversations in French with audiences, and her French-derived professional name strengthened associations between Simone and "the city of light." In fact, some initially assumed that she was a "French chanteuse." European fans also raved about Simone's ability to create a "blues atmosphere"; they associated her with African American women entertainers like Billie Holiday, Ethel Waters, Ella Fitzgerald, and Sarah Vaughan, and stressed Simone's unique ability to depict "the nightmare of segregation." According to one enthusiastic male British reviewer, Simone could "take a predominantly white and initially indifferent audience and by sheer artistry, strength of character and magical judgment, drive them into a mood of ecstatic acclamation."[16] Simone's background as a classically trained musician who bridged cultural hierarchies enabled her to bridge other seemingly contradictory positions. She did so in ways that were more readily accessible to her fans than did Miriam Makeba, whose cosmopolitanism American fans often suppressed, or Lena Horne, whose authenticity American fans, and Horne herself, often questioned.

Ultimately, though, Simone's biography weakened but could not dislodge gendered meanings of jazz. From the outset of her career, professional music critics and fans, advocates and detractors often noted that

Simone was "difficult to work with" and hostile to audiences, across lines of race, especially if they were not "sufficiently respectful." She recounted an incident at the celebrated Apollo, in Harlem: "I found out how rude the place could be when I started to introduce a song and people laughed at me." With that audience in mind, Simone declared that she would never play the Apollo again. Early in her career, critics associated this behavior with her origins and artistry. They explained Simone's high standards by referring to her professional and respectable training in classical music and to her overall disregard for mass consumer culture. She might yell at noisy audiences or even walk off a stage mid-show if fans were too "boisterous," but observers explained that the "stormy petrel of the piano" had a "deep-felt desire to be heard with the respect due an artist," and therefore emphasized the "social graces." According to one observer, Simone insisted that music should not be interrupted and that, whether she was in a club or a concert hall, "one must be neatly dressed and observe the proper decorum."[17]

As with her melding of classical and popular music, Simone's onstage hostility was not unique. Many jazz musicians in the postwar decades, especially those connected to bebop, defined themselves in opposition to mass culture and in opposition to their fans. When male musicians like Dizzy Gillespie, Thelonius Monk, or Charlie Parker distanced themselves from Louis Armstrong or at times cast him as an Uncle Tom–like entertainer, when they experimented musically far away from fans, and when they incorporated into their performances stances, clothing, and attitudes that conveyed hostility, alienation, or outright rudeness, the jazz press depicted them as unorthodox geniuses. As Ralph Ellison noted with regard to male musicians in the late 1950s, jazz audiences expected "the rudeness as part of the entertainment. . . . If it fails to appear, the audience is disappointed."[18]

If rudeness or hostility in male jazz musicians confirmed their genius, similar behavior came to confirm something else about Simone. "'Temperamental' is one word that is applied to her frequently; 'insulting' and arrogant' are also favorites," wrote a critic in 1963. Over time, critics and fans characterized her as notoriously "mean," "angry," and "unstable," or as beset by "inner fires" more than as a performer who cared little about crass commercial culture and for whom high standards and respectability were important.[19] Indeed, this refrain was almost as common as references to her classical training and placed Simone outside an exclusive club of innovative black male artists known for their virtuosity.

The themes that recurred in a celebrity discourse about Simone expose the rocky terrain of spoken and unspoken assumptions that she and other black women performers had to navigate. Simone's biography countered essentialist assumptions about race and talent by insisting on training and hard work. Her origins story emphasized a respectability that derived from her training as a classical musician and from her roots in the South. Simone's associations with respectability thus diverged from those of Horne—with her connection to a black elite and a commitment to racial uplift—as well as from the so-called sleazy blues woman.[20] Ultimately, even though Simone was cast as difficult or unstable in ways that isolated her from male musicians, she was rendered defiant in two important respects: Her music defied categorization, and, more than Horne or Makeba, she both captivated and was defiant toward her fans. These qualities were not incidental to Simone's racial politics, but were integral to her ongoing participation in black activism.[21] As a result, Simone was poised, after her initial successful albums, to expand the parameters of her activism.

IN THE EARLY 1960s, Simone was maintaining an extremely full schedule of recording and performing, but she was also accelerating her involvement in black freedom struggles. As with Makeba and other musicians associated with the New York–based jazz world, Simone supported national civil rights organizations like SNCC, CORE, the NAACP, and local organizations like the Harlem YMCA by offering her name as a "sponsor" and performing at benefit concerts.[22] At that point, she, like many other people in politicized subcultures of entertainers, was willing to take a stand, but did not think of herself as "involved." Simone explained this position further in her autobiography: "I was just spurring them [activists] on as best I could from where I sat—on stage, an artist, separate somehow." That feeling of detachment did not last, however. She later said that she soon became "driven by civil rights and the hope of black revolution," while others recalled Simone acquiescing to pressure from SNCC activists to increase her involvement.[23] Either way, in 1964, she headlined for SNCC several times in just a few months, including an event at Carnegie Hall that added to her reputation as a musician committed to the movement. The following year, Simone's husband/manager Andy Stroud volunteered her "services" to CORE, agreeing to a deal in which Simone would perform at CORE-sponsored fundraisers around the country at a minimal cost. These benefit concerts were very important to the treasuries of civil rights organizations. According to one estimate, CORE planned to raise close to $2,000 per Simone concert, considerably more than many other musicians and entertainers generated in benefit performances.[24]

Simone also traveled south to the site of many civil rights battles. The "ever-arresting Simone," as one journalist described her, was on the roster of stars scheduled to perform at an "unprecedented show" in Birmingham, Alabama, in the summer of 1963. There, the American Guild of Variety Artists, together with the SCLC, SNCC, CORE, NAACP, Urban League, and Negro American Labor Council, cosponsored a "Salute to Freedom '63" concert, designed in part to raise money for the upcoming March on Washington. The concert was originally planned for an integrated audience at Birmingham's city auditorium, but when organizers faced opposition from local whites, they moved it to a local all-black college. According to one estimate, the controversial concert, also featuring Ray Charles, Johnny Mathis, and Billy Taylor, raised $9,000 and attracted an audience of 15,000. Simone also performed in Atlanta and for marchers during the Selma-to-Montgomery march in 1965.[25]

This degree of visible political engagement on the part of African American popular musicians—those with commercial appeal among African American and white audiences—was relatively rare in the early to mid-1960s. In 1963, Lorraine Hansberry and her husband, Robert Nemiroff, wrote a letter to Lena Horne congratulating her for involving herself more directly in the movement and especially for traveling to the South to be with Medgar Evers: "Lorraine felt at once that you had said it perhaps better than anyone yet: 'the real drama has moved from Broadway to Mississippi.'"[26] Perhaps Hansberry and Nemiroff felt Horne deserved this acknowledgment because they knew that many popular entertainers were disinclined to go to Mississippi and other Southern states where daily battles for civil rights were ongoing. They risked alienating white fans as well as deejays who made choices about what music got airtime. Aspiring entertainers, versus celebrities like Horne, had even less security.[27] In part as a result of these attitudes, when SNCC organizers compiled lists of musicians and entertainers who were potential sponsors in these years, they often targeted a cultural avant-garde oriented around Greenwich Village, the political left, and jazz musicians as opposed to those with more popular mass appeal.[28] Simone was then recording with the (Dutch-based) Philips label, one that had an international reach and was associated with sophisticated, elite, and educated consumers of jazz across lines of race, and she was part of interracial communities in New York associated with "quality" culture.

Despite Simone's presumed respectable audience and her connections to a more elite jazz culture, it was not necessarily "safe" for her to make the political choices she did. As Makeba's 1968 marriage to Carmichael made clear, performers took significant risks when they supported (or when others concluded that they were supporting) certain kinds of African American activism. Two years before Simone wrote "Mississippi Goddam," when the seemingly apolitical Makeba was popular nationally and her own career was ascending, the jazz journal *Down Beat* published a scathing review of jazz singer Abbey Lincoln's 1961 album *Straight Ahead*, in which she warned against change happening too slowly, or "straight ahead, but awful slow" in the title track and sang about economic and social inequalities in the cacophonous "In the Red." The journal's influential critic Ira Gitler accused Lincoln of being a "professional negro" and discredited her artistically and politically. This criticism effectively, if temporarily, helped to silence Lincoln as a singer. While she continued to perform and write, Lincoln did not release another album under her own name until 1973.[29]

Organization activists were well aware that the participation of entertainers made for good public relations and helped in fundraising, but they knew that they could not assume the presence of performers who faced these and other risks. SNCC personnel courted stars to get them engaged with the movement, flattered them after the fact, and hoped that African American entertainers would attract even more popular white entertainers to their cause. "I would like to express our deep appreciation to you for your assistance," wrote one SNCC staff assistant to Simone after a benefit performance: "It is not often that we are incapable of expressing the beauty of a performance or the extent of our gratitude, but such was the case this time."[30]

While showing up was clearly a risky political choice for Simone, she did more than perform her standard "supper club" music at political events. The lyrics to the songs she wrote changed and became more explicitly political; her appearance changed as well. The album that marked this transition and the developing intersections between gender and music and between art and activism in Simone's career was *In Concert* (1964).[31] In certain respects, like many other albums by Simone, *In Concert* blended moods, styles, and genres. Over the course of seven songs, recorded at a live performance at Carnegie Hall, Simone moved from tender love songs to more classic blues to folk songs. Her expressive strategies, her skillful transitions between styles, and her very active engagement with the live audience all added to the album's power.[32] But coupled with these qualities, a different style of lyrics suggested that Simone was challenging political assumptions as well as conventional cultural categories. *In Concert* questioned patient nonviolence, Christianity, the interracial folk revival and the related celebration of freedom songs, and white-defined images of blacks. It also celebrated a woman-centered politicized black culture. Three songs indicate with particular clarity how relevant gender was to Simone's vision of black freedom and to her strategies of protest. Indeed, rejecting any singular definition of African American womanhood was part of the album's racial politics and remained central to Simone's participation in black activism beyond *In Concert*.[33]

In "Pirate Jenny," Simone transformed a song about class relations in London from Kurt Weill and Bertholt Brecht's *The Threepenny Opera* into a song about race, class, and gender relations in the American South. By maintaining ties to the original version and to the off-Broadway production adapted by Marc Blitzstein in 1956, Simone associated her own antiracism with Brecht's antifascism and evoked an alliance between African American musicians and a political left that dated back to the interwar years and continued to have an impact, politically and musically, in 1963.[34] Even as Simone gestured to the melding of opera and jazz and to a long history of civil rights–left activism, her version of a song about a poor and abused woman's fantasies of revenge was unique. After the ominous beating drum in the opening bars, the lyrics introduce a black woman scrubbing a floor:

> You people can watch while I'm scrubbing these floors
> And I'm scrubbing the floors while you're gawking.
> Maybe once you'll tip me and it makes you feel swell
> In this crummy southern town in this crummy old hotel.
> But you'll never guess to who you're talkin'.

In the verses that follow, the woman envisions violence and her own empowerment. She witnesses a "ship, the black freighter" come into the town "shooting guns from her bow" and leaving every building in the town but the hotel "flattened." The woman then determines the fate of the abusive town members, deciding whether or not they should be killed "now or later." In a powerful whisper, devoid of any musical accompaniment, Simone offers her protagonist's answer: "right now."

From the opening bars until the final drum, the rhythm, instrumentals, and Simone's rich and low voice, as well as the lyrics, communicated this woman's long-suppressed fury. Poor African American women and their labor were Simone's point of entry in "Pirate Jenny," the means through which she exposed the socioeconomic and gendered dimensions of racism and expressed a fantasy about vengeance that the white characters in the song can neither anticipate nor comprehend. In singing about this fictional woman in a Brecht-Weill song that had classical/jazz undertones and links to the Popular Front–era left, Simone rejected expectations of church-based freedom songs and protest music like "We Shall Overcome." "Perhaps it is a masterpiece; certainly it is a warning," suggested the liner notes.[35]

Like "Pirate Jenny," the song "Go Limp" featured a female protagonist, but this was a parody of folk songs at a time when politicized folk music was enjoying a celebrated revival.[36] During the live recorded performance, Simone repeatedly invited the audience to sing along during "hootenanny time," only to mock the participatory ethos of the genre. "And if I have a great concert, maybe I won't have to sing those folk songs again," she sang in one verse. More was at stake here than questions of musical style. "Go Limp" foregrounded Simone's ability to interweave—in a sometimes amusing and sometimes ironic manner—sexual and racial politics.

The song focuses on a young woman civil rights activist and begins with the woman defending to her mother her choice to join the marchers. In response to her mother's warnings, the daughter promises self-restraint: She will remain nonviolent, she assures her worried mother, and she will remain a virgin. In her performance, Simone uses humor to suggest that it will not be easy for the young woman to keep either promise. As she sings, in the voice of the young woman,

> Oh mother dear mother, no I'm not afraid
> For I'll go on that march
> And return a virgin maid
> With a brick in my handbag
> And a smile on my face,
> And barbed wire in my underwear to shed off disgrace.[37]

The high point of "Go Limp"—or the moment when the live audience is most involved—occurs when Simone teases the crowd with the fate of this young woman. Sings Simone,

> One day they were marching, a young man came by;
> With a beard on his chin and a gleam in his eye.
> And before she had time to remember her brick.

At this point, Simone stops singing. Over the course of the long indefinite pause that follows, the laughter and applause from the audience increase, crescendoing as the audience comes to its own conclusions about the implied rhyme with "brick." It is only after this long pause during which a laughing Simone encourages her audience to draw these conclusions that she repeats the verse and concludes:

> And before she had time to remember her brick
> They were holding a sit down on a neighboring hay rig.

With these performance strategies and lyrics, Simone rejected the image of herself as a respectable classically trained musician. She played with gender roles in ways that invited the audience in, making them complicit in this bawdy acceptance of premarital sex and the spoof of folk music. Yet she did not completely cast off her extratextual reputation either. Simone evoked a tradition of black female musicians who sang about sex, but she did so in a masterful performance of bawdiness.

In subsequent verses, the song explains what happens to the woman and why the brick and barbed wire are not more useful to her. She agrees to have sex, sings Simone, not in spite of her desire for respectable self-restraint. Rather, the sex takes place precisely because of the nonviolent civil rights training that the young woman has received. Activists have taught the young woman two important lessons: to "go perfectly limp" and to be "carried away" if anyone approaches her. Consequently, sings Simone slyly, again amidst considerable laughter from her audience, "when this young man suggested it was time she was kissed, she remembered her briefing and did not resist."

The song thus used sex to question the viability of nonviolence and to invoke the unanticipated consequences of "nonresistance" and of being "carried away." In the final verse, the young woman has a baby and the bearded young man vanishes. Despite this seemingly unfavorable outcome, Simone's young woman is upbeat, declaring in the final line that because of the choices she and the young man have made, the child will not have to march like his parents did. Progress, in this song's narrative, is possible as a result of the woman's commitments to nonresistance on the various battlegrounds of race and gender relations. In "Go Limp," Simone mocked, but did not completely reject, the value of passive nonresistance as a means to improve race relations, whereas in the more famous "Mississippi Goddam," Simone aggressively questioned nonviolence as a strategy. Like "Pirate Jenny," the song was musically, lyrically, and politically ferocious. Simone's public rage was intentionally incendiary and emphatically unladylike.

Gender was at the heart of Simone's racial politics in all three songs, each of which placed her far from the respectability of a classical musician. When Simone rejected the impulse to "talk like a lady" in "Mississippi Goddam," she effectively claimed that doing so would not halt discriminatory practices like calling black women "Sister Sadie." In a critique of both whites and blacks, she challenged the notion that behaving like a lady was a route toward improved race relations. Her lyrics unleashed a liberation from doing the right thing in the hopes of being recognized as deserving. Beyond the specific reference to "Sister Sadie," Simone's delivery and performance of rage in "Mississippi Goddam" was nothing short of a declaration of independence for "Sadies" everywhere, including in the civil rights movement.[38] Simone's focus on sexuality further allowed her to put women at the center of multiple struggles for civil rights. She inserted a playful sexual narrative into a song about marching in "Go Limp" and turned an ironic gaze on "self-restraint" and nonviolence, hallmarks of liberal civil rights activism.[39] In both songs, elements that potentially repressed black activism (nonviolence) and elements that potentially repressed female sexuality were linked in ways that challenged liberalism itself. Simone used the lyrics of her songs and her performance strategies to stage an assault on racism and expectations of female propriety, an assault that then circulated on vinyl records and on stages around the world.

The challenges to liberalism that Simone posed led many people to associate her with black power, and both fans and critics made sense of Simone's politics and her overall public persona in ways that often set her apart from her peers. In contrast to Makeba, Simone's appearances on television were few and far between. Especially in the second half of the 1960s, her considerable popularity and her notoriety always pushed up against each other. Fewer people noticed that Simone's perspective predated the end of the decade and differed significantly from that of many African American men with whom most white Americans equated this militancy.

Black power was an extraordinarily large tent, encompassing free breakfast programs and poetry, fashion and African American political candidates, anticolonial struggles in Algiers, Hanoi, and elsewhere around the world, school reform, health care, cultural centers and more.[40] Despite considerable diversity and a long history, many whites in the 1960s and '70s equated black power with Stokely Carmichael, his arm outstretched in a fist, or with leather-clad, sometimes gun-wielding members of the Black Panther Party, formed in Oakland, California, in 1966. Moreover, while African American women participated extensively in movements of black power and in expressions of black cultural nationalism—as leaders, grassroots activists, and writers, and in official organizations as well as countless grassroots enterprises—many organizations remained largely male-dominated.[41] Assertions of black male pride and a celebration of aggressive masculinity remained at the rhetorical and visual center of many expressions of black power, regardless of all that women activists were doing.[42]

Not surprisingly, then, few Americans, white or black, were likely to associate women with black power. In 1967, one critic suggested that part of what made a song like "Mississippi Goddam" so powerful was that the words sounded as if they should have been written by "some black power disciple of the caliber of Leroi Jones or Stokely Carmichael," while in fact, they came from a "woman who has become one of the show world's most popular and controversial entertainers."[43] The *New York Post* cemented the link between Simone and a black male racial militancy that the media publicized and that so many white Americans feared in the late '60s with its profile "Nina Simone: Soul on Voice." The headline alluded to Black Panther Eldridge Cleaver's *Soul on Ice* (1967), a prison memoir that shocked readers with its visions of black violence, and aligned Simone with that vision. From the time of its release, rumors circulated that "Mississippi Goddam," known for its "bold lyrics and profane title," was banned from radio stations in the South or from television. At least one observer suggested that it "was banned by radio stations because a woman dared put her feelings into song. . . . [T]he principal objection raised by most critics to the Mississippi song was apparently not so much its militant lyrics, but the fact that an entertainer, and a woman entertainer at that, had dared to put them to music."[44]

It is worth emphasizing that Simone had come up with these "militant lyrics" years before this critic's observation in 1969. Simone wrote "Mississippi Goddam" and "Go Limp" at a time when black male activists were

FIGURE 3.3 Nina Simone, known as the "High Priestess of Soul," in 1969. (Courtesy of the Jack Robinson Archive)

just beginning to articulate meanings of African American sexuality and civil rights under the rubric of black cultural nationalism. Simone regarded Stokely Carmichael and other black male leaders as friends and teachers. Yet she still, in her own music, exposed sexual aggression on the part of many male activists as potentially problematic. "Go Limp" frankly satirized the celebration of masculinity in black activism, in which allegedly authentic blackness and black power were made visible through male toughness and sexual potency. With its ambiguity and tongue-in-cheek nature, the song spoofed the sexual politics of civil rights activists.[45] It was unclear whether the woman "did not resist" male desire or was "carried away" by her own sexual desires; it was unclear as to the circumstances under which the brick should stay in her handbag (and against whom it should or should not be used); and, not the least, it was unclear who, or what, was going to "go limp." What was clear was that in her performance of this song and others, Simone claimed the power of sexuality from a woman's point of view, and this power was central to her vision of black political liberation.[46]

"Mississippi Goddam" and its genealogy suggest that Simone was among those who helped to create a version of black cultural nationalism as early as 1963 in ways that did not devalue women. According to Simone's account, the song "erupted out of me" right after she had heard about the church bombing. As she explained it years later, she had first used materials that her husband, an ex-police officer, had around the house, to try to build a gun. Then she realized: "I knew nothing about killing, and I did know about music. I sat down at my piano. An hour later I came out of my apartment with the sheet music for "Mississippi Goddam' in my hand."[47] The song thus anticipated the arguments that Amiri Baraka would make about the political purposes of culture when he moved from the Village to Harlem and organized the Black Arts Repertory Theater in 1965. With the formal development of the Black Arts Movement in the second half of the decade, Baraka and others explicitly tied together black culture and revolutionary politics; the one, advocates argued, could not exist without the other. This perspective had been developing for some years in New York–based subcultures and affected Lena Horne when she wrote her autobiography, Lena. But Baraka and others increasingly developed their ideas about revolutionary black culture by creating associations between militant poems, militant men, violence, and sex. "Poems that shoot guns," Baraka wrote in "Black Art," for example, were those "that come at you, love what you are, breathe like wrestlers, or shudder strangely after pissing."[48] Simone's creative contributions indicate that this type of masculinism, and even misogyny in some instances, was not inherent to expressions of black cultural nationalism and black power.[49]

AFRICA WAS ONE important resource that influenced how Simone envisioned black freedom. In December 1961, just days after her second marriage to former police officer Andy Stroud, Simone joined a group of thirty-three black artists, musicians, and intellectuals for her first trip to Africa, sponsored by the American Society for African Culture (AMSAC). The trip to Lagos, Nigeria, marked the opening of an AMSAC West African Cultural Center in Lagos and the beginning of an exchange program between African and African American performers. Langston Hughes, opera singer Martha Flowers, folk singer Odetta, dancers Al Minns and Leon James, jazz musicians Lionel Hampton and Randy Weston, and a range of educators and academics were among those with Simone.[50] What they shared—with each other and with other African and African American entertainers who traveled across borders in this period—was some commitment to an international vision of racial politics and culture. Simone later described her arrival:

> All around us were black faces, and I felt for the first time the spiritual relaxation any Afro-American feels on reaching Africa. I didn't feel like I'd come home when I arrived in Lagos, but I knew I'd arrived somewhere important and that Africa mattered to me, and would always matter. . . . [I]t wasn't Nigeria I arrived in—it was AFRICA.[51]

This perspective, romanticized as it was, repudiated the conception of Africa as backward or undeveloped—a perspective that Makeba and independence movements in numerous African countries had done much to diminish but not eliminate in the United States.

Upon her return to the United States, Simone emphasized the importance of Africa to African Americans. On- and offstage, she embraced physical markers of black power in ways that joined the struggle of African Americans to a vision of African freedom and made both visible through her female body. She dressed more frequently in what critics called African garb. She performed alongside Nigerian musician Michael Babatunde Olatunji and the African Dinizulu Band. She and Makeba became closer friends—as Simone later put it, "I loved her music the moment I heard it, but once I knew her I loved her more. . . . [S]he was so straightforward in what she said and thought, and at the same time so relaxed and so African." Makeba and Simone, "two incandescent women musicians," as a music critic for the *New York Times* described them, gave a benefit concert together at Carnegie Hall in 1961. In some promotional photos from 1961 onward, Simone appeared with her hair "natural"—in an Afro—which met with strong responses, pro and con, for years.[52] At New York's Philharmonic Hall in 1966, Simone "stirred up excitement in her audience," according to one critic, "by walking on stage in a stunning African motif hat and gown ensemble." While it was "difficult" to "select highlights" because "everything she did was great," the songs with "African back rhythms seemed to awaken much more feeling in both Nina and her audience."[53]

The ways in which Simone drew on Africa to perform black womanhood and to comment on racial politics were particularly significant outside of the United States. "Why am I so deeply moved by the different musics, the different folklores of Africa," she asked a French reporter rhetorically, when she was in Algiers for the Pan-African Cultural Festival in 1969. "Well, the 'gut bucket blues' . . . and the religious music of our people are evidently linked to the African tradition." As Simone elaborated, "that which we are more and more (but which we have never stopped being, in reality . . . despite appearances), is something very close to Africa."[54] In Algiers, and in England and France, statements like these, combined with her music and her celebrity, contributed to a different reception for African American women abroad than had been evident in earlier periods. In the 1920s and then the 1950s, Josephine Baker and Billie Holiday each had appeal and success in Europe. Neither, however, could contain assumptions among whites that black women performers had essential primitive qualities. By contrast, even though European fans and critics, white and black, may have regarded Simone as exotic, her well-known reputation for political activism coupled with the ways in which she aggressively claimed certain styles for herself made it difficult for her to be simply the object of a primitivist discourse. When critics described Simone as "looking almost tribal with her cone-shaped hairdo and an African-type habit" at the Antibes Jazz Festival in 1965, they also acknowledged both her power and the "vociferous" reception the crowd gave her.[55] Like Makeba in the United States, Simone in Europe took in and remixed potential essentialism.

Simone's proactive self-fashioning added to her stature in Europe as an activist-artist. With her appearance and her performances—especially of "Mississippi Goddam" and her version of the song Billie Holiday made famous, "Strange Fruit"—Simone highlighted American race relations for European audiences. "'Mississippi' is one of the most moving songs that I have been graced to hear," wrote one French reviewer; others appreciated how she "attacks 'Strange Fruit,'" or raised the hope for "a perfect world, one in which a white values a black." When she performed these and other civil rights songs in Antibes, she generated enthusiasm among both jazz lovers and the "larger public." She was, according to one fan, the "darling" of France.[56] A British teenager completed a school assignment on American race relations by playing Simone's version of "Strange Fruit" to his high school class because "she was my introduction to civil rights." While he had "read newspapers like everyone else," Simone's songs, he said, "totally opened my eyes to a reality that I didn't know."[57]

On and off stages in Europe, Simone was direct about her desire both to educate and entertain. As she put it to a French journalist toward the end of her first European tour, she considered herself an ambassador of sorts for her race: "Because of the lack of respect especially cruel in the last few years, each time I go to a new country, I feel obligated to include in my repertoire songs which proudly affirm my race."[58] In this context, as a female entertainer who produced and performed certain kinds of music—and who was an object of consumption herself—Simone helped to export American civil rights activism and black nationalism in particular. Her politics and her performances were deeply and self-consciously intertwined.

As a result of her experiences in and out of the United States, Simone also conceived of racism as an international problem. Many African American entertainers, including an "ever-increasing number of jazzmen making their homes in Europe," as *Down Beat* put it, achieved a degree of success among white audiences in other countries that eluded them domestically, and many compared non-American race relations favorably to those in the United States and positioned Europe as an oasis. Lena Horne and her husband were known as a "glamour couple" in Europe in the late 1940s and early '50s; they made Paris their home away from home because of the more intense racism they expected in the United States as an interracial couple and because of the professional opportunities only available to her abroad.[59] Simone's perspective stood apart. As she observed to European journalists: "[I] found prejudice in Britain, in Holland, and even Morocco. . . . Now I love being in London—it has its own personality and character and I love the way the people talk; but I don't really feel any more welcome in London than I do at home."[60] Simone was able to infuse her eclectic repertoire—including African-based melodies—with meanings that were not solely national or defined by race. Scholar Farah Jasmine Griffin has explained that when Billie Holiday sang "Strange Fruit" in Europe, audiences could indict violent abuses in the United States like lynching without having to consider histories of colonialism and race relations in their own countries.[61] By contrast, Simone was performing at a time of rising student and anticolonialist activism in Europe; that, combined with her own outspokenness and appearance, made it harder for audiences to distance themselves from the challenges she posed. At one concert in England, she declared that the performance was "for all the black people in the audience." Whites, including ardent fans, were shocked, and they were well aware that Simone was naming as black—and identifying with—her many fans who were of West Indian and African descent and not African Americans. Or, as she told one British reporter, "The Negro revolution is only one aspect of increasing violence and unrest in the world." In

1969, she questioned assumptions that the civil rights movement had improved the lives of African Americans, but she also suggested that her recording of the song "Revolution" was significant because it was about far more than "the racial problem."[62] As Makeba did in the United States, Simone in European countries used her body, her music, and her words to link Africa, African Americans, and people of color around the world.

SIMONE CONTRIBUTED TO civil rights as a black woman performer along-side and in relation to many other black women. Both Simone and Miriam Makeba affirmed a vision of black power that included women, even though their voices and relationships to commercial culture differed and the ways that they confronted discrimination differed even more. Similarly, Abbey Lincoln embraced jazz as a way to express her commitment to black free-dom struggles around the world and as a way to claim her dignity as a black woman much as Simone did in "Mississippi Goddam" and other songs. Black women writers like Alice Childress, Claudia Jones, and Lorraine Hansberry were among those whose fictional heroines from the 1950s anticipated a cross-class black feminism, and women in SNCC addressed the intersections of racism and sexism among activists in civil rights organizations. By 1968, members of the Third World Women's Alliance were just some of the women who criticized black men who "defined the role of black women in the movement. They stated that our role was a supportive one; others stated that we must become breeders and provide an army; still others stated that we had kotex power or pussy power."[63] Even before the Third World Women's Alliance issued this statement and before Frances Beale identified what she called the "double jeopardy" of racism and sexism that black women faced, Simone was among those who forged black power through the prism of gender, contributing to this proliferating discourse early in the decade and on stages around the world.[64]

Moreover, Simone identified "sisterhood" as a critical catalyst to her politicization around race. While she named many important influences, it was her friend Lorraine Hansberry—"the person who first took me out of myself," she wrote—who in 1961 helped her to think about power relations. As a result of Hansberry's influence, Simone later said, "I started to think about myself as a black person in a country run by white people and a woman in a world run by men."[65] Simone made similar points about Hansberry when she first introduced "To Be Young, Gifted, and Black" in 1968. Based on Hansberry's work, the song became an anthem of black pride and reached the top 10 on the R&B charts in 1969. In live performances, Simone repeatedly paid tribute to Hansberry, who died early in 1965. At a concert in Berkeley, for example, she called for the house lights to be put on, exhorted her audience to sing the chorus of the upcoming song with her, and then explained: "This song is dedicated to the memory of my dear, dear friend whom I miss very much, and if I don't control myself, I could talk about all night. Lorraine Hansberry, who wrote 'Raisin in the Sun' and died before her time." Here and elsewhere, Simone explicitly made relationships between women and gender solidarity central to the very idea of black pride. In her autobiography, she would note that in the early 1960s, she and her more politically informed friend had "never talked about men or clothes or other such inconsequential things when we got together. It was always Marx, Lenin, and revolution— real girls' talk."[66] Here as in her songs, Simone challenged those who might mistakenly assume that women first joined civil rights organizations only then to become cognizant of gender inequities.

FIGURE 3.4 Nina Simone performs at Lorraine Hansberry's funeral at the Presbyterian Church of the Master in Harlem on January 16, 1965.

(Photographs and Prints Division, Schomburg Center for Research in Black Culture, The New York Public Library, Astor, Lenox, and Tilden Foundations)

Nowhere was the intertwined relationship between black liberation and gender more evident than in "Four Women." Released on the album *Wild Is the Wind* in 1965, the slow-paced, four-and-a-half minute song offered minimal accompaniment beyond a bass background, as Simone brought black women throughout U.S. history from the margins to the center. Over four verses, Simone took on the voices of four black women, each burdened in her own way by gender and by skin color: the elderly "Aunt Sarah" with black skin and "woolly hair"; the young and "yellow" woman, "Saffronia," born as the result of a white man raping her mother; "Sweet Thing" a "tan" prostitute with "hair fine"; and the "brown" and "bitter" woman, "Peaches." The song came to a dramatic and emotional crescendo, as Simone sang about "Peaches," whose "skin is brown" and "manner tough," and who proclaims, "I'll kill the first mother I see 'cause my life has been too rough."[67]

To some extent, each of Simone's four women reproduced stereotypes of black women that white Americans had developed over the years—the hard-working "Mammy," the too-strong "matriarch," and the sexualized "Jezebel," for example. Yet with a voice that moved from soft and restrained to strong and fierce, and with a "spellbinding haunting tune," noted a critic from *Variety*, Simone infused each supposed type with realism, dignity, and pain.[68] Saffronia evoked the legacies of slavery and the reality of rape for slave women, while "Sweet Thing" was a reminder that black women migrants to the urban North often had limited economic options or resources beyond their own bodies. The elderly "Aunt Sarah," who was "strong enough to take the pain inflicted again and again," gestured to strong black women across generations, including the older civil rights activists in Simone's own era who risked everything—poorly paying jobs, homes, and their very lives—when they housed and cooked for civil rights activists. With regard to the song's final verse, Phyl Garland, a black woman and music critic writing in 1969, was just one among many who felt that the "loud-talking, no-shit-taking 'Peaches' of the final verse," came "closest to where so many black women of today stand, regardless of age." By bringing all four women together, Simone rejected the historical degradation of black women's bodies by whites, and the disparagement of dark skin and hierarchies of color that many women continued to experience in their own families and communities.[69]

These issues were a basic and very obvious part of daily life for black women, according to Simone. She later explained that "all the song did was to tell what entered the minds of most black women in America when they thought about themselves: their complexions, their hair. . . ." Her hope was that by offering this history she could also offer women the possibility of not being defined in these terms: "Black women didn't know what the hell they wanted because they were defined by things they didn't control, and until they had the confidence to defend themselves, they'd be stuck in the same mess forever."[70] "Four Women" was like consciousness-raising in song. But making this move in music was hardly commonplace; with its interweaving of skin color and class, sexuality and racial discrimination, "Four Women" was dramatically different from Aretha Franklin's demands for "Respect" in that rock classic from 1967, from Franklin (and Carole King's) more subdued "You Make Me Feel Like a Natural Woman," and from other music associated either with black freedom struggles or women's liberation, or, more occasionally, with both.[71]

Perhaps that is why "Four Women" quickly became one of Simone's most popular numbers, from her performance in 1965 at the Jazz Festival in Antibes, to the time she recorded it in 1965, until her death in 2003. It was the song that "brought the most reaction" at one concert in 1966, according to one critic, and it remained her "biggest hit" at a sold out concert in Detroit three years later. Critics praised the style of the song—it has "overtones of a contemporary classic"—but they also focused on the ways in which Simone inhabited the women's roles. According to a critic in *Down Beat*, "Four Women" got better over time because Simone was "more fully into the characters. . . . Nina *is* Aunt Sarah, Saffronia, Sweet Thing, Peaches and a lot of other people when she chooses to be. She is not only history, she contains it."[72] That she herself had abandoned "the straight-haired image of her supper club days to wear a natural hairstyle" confirmed her personal relationship to "Four Women," wrote another, reinforcing Simone's authenticity in the eyes of fans, and the degree to which so many people concluded that she was "a natural black woman in every sense."[73]

It would be anachronistic to impose second-wave feminism onto Nina Simone in 1963 and 1964, when she wrote and performed songs from *In Concert*, or after 1965, when she wrote and performed "Four Women" and "To Be Young, Gifted and Black." In the titillating "Go Limp," Simone played with an older tradition of African American female singers who sang about sex as much as she anticipated a tradition of second-wave feminists who wrote about sex in the late '60s and 1970s.[74] Simone distanced herself from feminism, explaining that even after she wrote "Four Women," she did not feel connected to "women's liberation" because "the questions that female radicals were asking had no relevance to me."[75] Nevertheless, gender and sexuality informed Simone's denunciation of racial discrimination and her articulation of a "black is beautiful" perspective. As with Makeba, elements of what we now call feminism were prefigured in this music and were integrally linked to Simone's black activism generally. Finally, it is important to recall the relevance of Simone's experiences in and attitudes toward places beyond the United States.[76] She was not a political leader, a traditional intellectual, or a diplomat. Instead, through her position as an African American female entertainer, she absorbed, developed, and disseminated a gendered vision of black freedom and culture in ways that were eminently consumable by her many fans around the world.

In all of these ways, Nina Simone was part of a larger cohort at the same time that she stood out. Her music defied categorization; she blurred the lines between jazz, classical, folk, blues, and soul music, and interviews and reviews that described her as a popular performer with classical training made it impossible to "fit" her into any one musical genre. With her explicitly political lyrics as early as 1963, Simone defied a liberal civil rights ethos. By making gender central to her racial politics, she defied links between racial progress, racial power, and masculine sexual power. Because she was a performer whose fans cut across lines of race, class, gender, and nation, these multiple and interconnected levels of defiance set Simone apart and reinforced both her celebrity and notoriety in the 1960s.

These same qualities have made it hard to incorporate Simone into collective memories, real or imagined, that Americans have of the 1960s or into more scholarly accounts of the period, whether the subject is music, women, racial politics, or the areas of considerable overlap between them. Simone's repertoire took shape on a different register from the "freedom songs" that so many Americans associate with the early to mid-'60s—the ubiquitous "We Shall Overcome," "This Little Light of Mine," and "Go Tell it on the Mountain"; her public persona could not have been more different from that of the Southern protesters who sang these and other melodies, often arm in arm and wearing clothing that was as appropriate for church as for marching.[77]

Such songs and singers have enduring power and appeal. According to editors of the anthology *We Shall Overcome: Songs of the Freedom Movement*, first published in 1963, freedom songs were "sung to bolster spirits, to gain new courage and to increase the sense of unity." Traditional "freedom songs" like "We Shall Overcome" and others resonate so strongly that it can be easy to overlook the effort and time it took to make them so canonical. SNCC organizers actively made the argument that this music mattered politically—as they produced songbooks and albums in 1963 and 1964 for fundraising, and when they organized tours that the Freedom Singers and others gave.[78] This canon-in-the-making tended to include songs that were easy for large numbers of people to sing, and with relatively few lyrics. Many were adapted from "church music"; "spiritual after spiritual began to appear with new words and changes," according to one activist. These and others songs were often "unrehearsed," or "improvisational." Many melodies came out of the Highlander Folk School where black and white activists had spent time, evoking associations with interracialism and with an ethos of folk music as pure and noncommercial.[79]

The process of canon formation that took place in the mid-1960s reinforced a myth that "authentic" civil rights music in the period before 1965 meant rural, grassroots, church-inspired freedom songs.[80] The iconic power of "freedom songs" has made it difficult to remember that a great variety of music mattered to and shaped black activism before 1965—including more urban-based, commercial, or complicated compositions with themes of sex or violence or expressions of rage like those that Nina Simone sang. Paradoxically, even though activists in the '60s regarded Simone as the "voice" or the "true singer" of the movement, subsequently, songs with sexual content, like "Go Limp," songs that considered the "whole country" implicated in racism, or songs like "Mississippi Goddam" and "Pirate Jenny" that did not necessarily embrace nonviolence, became something other than authentic freedom songs.[81] These are not the melodies worthy of recuperation and celebration in public schools eager to commemorate Martin Luther King Day every January; nor are they the likely "go-to" background music in documentaries about civil rights. For the most part, they are not part of how a dominant narrative in subsequent generations has remembered or commemorated this period. One result of this absence is that the politics of sex and gender have been segregated from the politics of race—far more so than they were at the time.

WHEN NINA SIMONE arrived on Long Island, New York, to rehearse for a concert scheduled at the Westbury Music Festival in April 1968, she saw people huddled around a television. That is how learned that Martin Luther King Jr. had been assassinated in Memphis. Simone's scheduled concert did take place on April 7, 1968, but included a new song: "Why? (The King of Love Is Dead)," a memorial to King that Simone's bass player

Gene Taylor wrote in the intervening days. The first performance of this song lasted 15 minutes, as Simone sang, spoke about, and performed the pain Americans were feeling. "We want to do a tune written for today, for this hour," she said in her introduction to the song, which included the question on the minds of so many Americans that week:

> Folks you better stop and think,
> Everybody knows we're on the brink
> What will happen now, that the King is dead?[82]

As Simone explained to a journalist from *Time* some time after the assassination, "When I'm on that stage . . . I don't think I'm just out there to entertain." The journalist then elaborated: "Nina is a Negro and proud of it: she is out there to share with the audience what Soul Singer Ray Charles calls her 'message things.'"[83]

Other black women performers came to different conclusions. They hoped to entertain and to avoid controversial "message things." In 1968, Abbey Lincoln and Diahann Carroll found roles in Hollywood films and on network television that they thought would allow them to do just that. Their efforts had mixed results.

4

"No One Asks Me What I Want"

ABBEY LINCOLN, DIAHANN CARROLL, AND THE PROMISE
OF INTEGRATION IN POPULAR CULTURE

WITHIN MONTHS OF the assassinations of Martin Luther King on April 4,
1968, and Robert Kennedy on June 5, 1968, a feature film and a television
show premiered, both with black women in starring roles. *For Love of Ivy*
opened in theaters across the country on July 17, and eight weeks later, the
television series *Julia* debuted on NBC. Featuring Abbey Lincoln, *For Love
of Ivy* told the story of Ivy Moore, maid to a wealthy white suburban family.
Ivy decides to leave her job, only to find herself in a romance with busi-
nessman/con man, played by superstar Sidney Poitier. The series *Julia*,
with Diahann Carroll as the title character, chronicled the life of a young
widow and mother who works as a nurse and cares for her son in a lovely
garden apartment in Los Angeles.[1]

By the late 1960s, when *For Love of Ivy* and *Julia* appeared, the topic of
race relations was receiving more airtime on television and in Hollywood
films than would have been imaginable ten years earlier when Lincoln and
Carroll were building their careers and when Lena Horne struggled to get
her own television special. One African American film critic suggested that
the situation in the film and television industries started to improve because
of concerted pressure from black actors and growing calls for black power.[2]
Regardless of the cause, the television shows *I Spy* (1965–1968), *The Mod
Squad* (1968–1973), and *Room 222* (1969–1974), and films like *In the Heat
of the Night* (1967) and *The Learning Tree* (1969) offered black actors more
substantive roles and touched on topics having to do with race relations.
Even the long-taboo subject of interracial marriage received mainstream
treatment in a film that Columbia Pictures marketed as a "light" comedy,
Guess Who's Coming to Dinner (1967). In addition to these fictional stories,
networks rushed numerous "race-themed" news-oriented specials into

production in the aftermath of King's assassination—so many that *Newsweek* referred to this development as having sparked "The Summer of the Negro."[3]

For Love of Ivy and *Julia* were noteworthy for several reasons. Strong female heroines played by prominent (and prominently politicized) women entertainers, black or white, remained unusual in popular culture. These productions also shared a commercial veneer, a focus on commodities and middle-class comforts across lines of race, and especially a positive perspective on integration and black-white social (though not romantic) relations. Both offered mainstream "integration narratives"—stories that were heavily marketed to consumers across lines of race about attractive blacks and whites who mostly got along and lived in middle-class settings. These qualities generated considerable attention and advance publicity. In the prerelease media blitz for *Ivy*, a critic for the *Film/TV Daily* offered the following prediction: "Take a solid, sophisticated situation comedy, interlaced with the racial overtones with which serious-minded people are so concerned today, and add one of the nation's top box office draws in Sidney Poitier, and you have Palomar Pictures International's '*For Love of Ivy*,' a can't miss picture at the box office." A headline in the *Los Angeles Times* declared that *Julia* was making a "bid for a historical niche."[4]

Despite the praise and considerable hype, many critics and fans concluded that both *Ivy* and *Julia* did, in fact, seem to "miss." Critics targeted many issues, from bad writing to bad politics. "A weak script is a weak script no matter what color you are," wrote one about *Ivy*. The most consistent refrain was that both *For Love of Ivy* and *Julia* were so geared toward middle-class comforts that they could not possibly be relevant to most African Americans.[5]

Certainly these productions did not engage with the issues that seemed to matter most in 1968, some three to four years after the passage of landmark civil rights legislation and months after the murders of King and Kennedy, a period when issues of class and poverty, and questions about black power increasingly dominated conversations about race relations. The year had started with the Tet offensive in Vietnam, major attacks by the North Vietnamese that reinforced opposition to the war in the United States. Black leaders and grassroots activists more readily protested American foreign policy as well as the disproportionate representation of working-class African Americans in the military. With regard to domestic race politics, conditions in urban areas were a major preoccupation. In February

1968, the government-sponsored Kerner Commission concluded that economic inequality, racism, unemployment, and police brutality had all contributed to the uprisings that were evident in cities around the country since violence in Watts, Los Angeles, in 1965, including in Newark and Detroit. Two months after the report's release, the national media offered extensive coverage of violence that gripped Washington, D.C., Chicago, Baltimore, and other cities following King's assassination.[6]

Affirmations of black power and black power activism that had circulated for years were becoming increasingly visible to more Americans. Nina Simone performed her hit "To Be Young, Gifted and Black" at concerts around the world; black nationalist Maulana Karenga's Organization US, which stressed the importance of African traditions among African Americans, had a significant impact nationally. In Newark, New Jersey, poet Amiri Baraka and grassroots activists drew on black power in community organizing and political campaigning after violence ruptured the city in 1967. SNCC activists and California-based leaders of the Black Panther Party forged a public (if brief) alliance. African American athletes at the 1968 Olympics in Mexico made international headlines when they gave a black power salute—heads bowed, one arm stretched upward, their gloved hands in a fist—with the U.S. national anthem playing in the background. The media scrutiny that these and many other events received generated further debates among Americans who neither agreed about nor necessarily approved of black power, but even the negative attention highlighted its proliferating political and cultural dimensions. Among activists, too, debates raged about the term itself, about the goals and strategies for ongoing organizing, and about the presence of whites in civil rights organizations, to name just a few. Indeed, a growing number of African Americans thought and spoke in terms of black power at the same time that people asked whether the civil rights movement was "finished" once major legislation passed, if it had not gone far enough in addressing intersections of racial discrimination and class inequities, or if it was changing into black power, with some regarding this as an evolution and others as a devolution. Meanwhile, throughout these years, state surveillance and repression of black-led organizations continued unchecked.[7]

In this atmosphere, placid commercial productions with integrated casts and suburban settings were easy to dismiss and to deride, and alongside the kudos *Ivy* and *Julia* each received, critics and ordinary viewers did plenty of both. *Julia* "would not recognize a ghetto if she stumbled into it," sniped a critic in *Time*, while the *New Yorker* mocked *For Love of Ivy* as "bourgeois to its bootheels."[8] Appraisals like these from black and white critics used class alongside race to discredit the film and the television show as trivial at best, if not inauthentic in more insidious ways. Yet integration narratives are worth another look precisely because they evoked hype and acclaim, on the one hand, and seemed easy to dismiss as less than serious and bad politics, on the other. *Ivy* and *Julia* are examples of how white and black Americans in the late 1960 used popular culture to evaluate black activism; they also suggest why the female leads proved to be a focal point for these evaluations.[9]

With starring roles in *Ivy* and *Julia*, Abbey Lincoln and Diahann Carroll became part of mainstream popular culture in ways that Nina Simone, Miriam Makeba, and even Lena Horne had not. As such, Lincoln and Carroll largely accommodated to genre and market imperatives.[10] Over the course of their careers, Horne, Makeba, and Simone juggled their ambition and commitments to black liberation. Their professional aspirations and their political investments were not necessarily mutually exclusive. *For Love of Ivy* and *Julia* illuminate the trajectories of two black women entertainers who negotiated a political and cultural terrain in a commodity culture that pointedly sought to de-emphasize political resistance. What, then, did these integration narratives offer Abbey Lincoln and Diahann Carroll, both politically and professionally, and on what options did they foreclose?

For Diahann Carroll, *Julia* was an opportunity for unprecedented exposure on a number 1 ranking series, one that was "slightly controversial," she later explained, but not enough to "interfere with the ratings."[11] Ever since Carol Diahann Johnson had changed her name to Diahann Carroll and left the home of her middle-class parents in the mid-1950s, she had been known as a "chic chanteuse" and as a star very much in the mold that Lena Horne had established in the 1940s.[12] Descriptions of her as a glamorous celebrity defined her for the next ten years, as she appeared in parts that included the high-class, well-dressed model in the Broadway show *No Strings* in 1962; the respectable, well-dressed school teacher who travels to Paris with her white friend in the film *Paris Blues* in 1961; and the glamorous, supremely well dressed Diahann Carroll in numerous singing engagements at venues like the elegant Persian Room at the Plaza Hotel, on Jack Paar's *The Tonight Show*, and at the Cocoanut Grove in Hollywood.[13] An aura of glamour clung to Carroll alongside her public support for civil rights. Like other entertainers in New York–based politicized subcultures, she lent her name, voice, home, and money to SNCC and other

civil rights organizations to support benefit concerts and fundraising dinners in the North. Carroll targeted the politics of popular culture specifically when she testified at congressional hearings about the limited
opportunities for black performers. In 1968, she joined an interracial
group of entertainers who participated in *King: A Filmed Record . . . Montgomery to Memphis*, a three-plus-hour documentary about Martin Luther
King that Sidney Lumet directed and released for a single showing at
movie theaters across the country in 1970. In all of these arenas and on
stages around the world, "the long fingernails and coiffed hair and designer clothes had become something of a personal trademark," Carroll
later recalled. The "alluring" Carroll was "sleek as a cheetah" and wore
designer "clothes like a thoroughbred clotheshorse," wrote critics.[14]

In 1968, the fictional Julia, heavily made up, attractive, respectable,
and well dressed, whose social circle included upwardly mobile whites
and blacks, extended Carroll's own middle-class upbringing as well as the
political and professional paths on which she had traveled. Producer Hal
Kanter decided to make *Julia* in 1967 after hearing NAACP executive Roy
Wilkins speak at an NAACP fundraiser in Hollywood about the "plight of
the black man," as Kanter later put it. Kanter left that luncheon determined to use television and humor in support of civil rights. His hope was
that *Julia* would be a series that allowed white audiences to "laugh *with*
and not *at* my characters," and that "sooner or later some of the verities
of African-American life would become apparent, some of the myths
exploded."[15] To some extent, the series sought to integrate middle-class
whites' living rooms by bringing fictional middle-class blacks into them.
Diahann Carroll was central to these goals. While television had not been
a major part of her career prior to *Julia*, the series allowed her to infuse the
small screen with her "new kind of glamour." The lines of continuity
between Carroll and the fictional Julia were apparent both to *Julia*'s supporters and detractors.[16]

By contrast, the production of *For Love of Ivy* was a marked departure
for its female star. Visually, the fictional Ivy looked and sounded dramatically different from Lincoln; as a narrative, the film had little to do with
Lincoln's jazz lyrics and pointed critiques of race relations in the United
States and colonial relations outside of the United States. With *Ivy*, Lincoln was performing black womanhood at what seemed to be a considerable distance from the wordless singing on *We Insist!*, vocals that
contemporary critics had compared to primal screams and that jazz critic
Nat Hentoff described as an "uncontrollable unleashing of rage and anger."[17]

FIGURE 4.1 Diahann Carroll as the lead in the series *Julia*, which premiered in September 1968.
(NBC Television/Getty Images)

Carroll would encounter a similar rupture between her off-screen persona and a film character in 1974 when she played the part of Claudine, a single mother on welfare. But in 1968, these disjunctures—Lincoln in the early '60s versus the late '60s, and the "real" Lincoln versus the fictional Ivy—help account for the contradictory reception the film had and the dialogues about black activism and culture that it set into motion. The integration narrative *For Love of Ivy*, even more than *Julia* and its apparent seamlessness between Carroll and her character, suggests how complicated and multilayered the notion of "resistance" could be for politicized black women performers.

FOR LOVE OF *Ivy* marked a turning point in a career that already had several, and quite different phases. Abbey Lincoln, like Lena Horne and Diahann Carroll, got started in show business as a glamorous nightclub singer. She was known for her suggestive clothing and for "sad, sexy lyrics

in a voice smoky with longing" that came from "her pouting lips," according to *Time*. Also like Horne, she appeared briefly on screen as a singer,
including in *The Girl Can't Help It* (1956).[18] But the similarities ended
there. In contrast to Horne and Carroll, Lincoln rejected these definitions
of glamour in the late 1950s when she claimed a name for herself as a jazz
vocalist, and as an outspoken critic of racial discrimination in the United
States and abroad. The "New Abbey Lincoln: A Voice of Protest" declared
a headline in the *Pittsburgh Courier*, an African American newspaper, in
1961.[19] For Lincoln, there was nothing respectable about being the type of
glamorous sex symbol that she had been at the start of her career.

Lincoln was direct about how jazz music and racial politics were related to each other and how being a black woman affected her commitments to both. As she explained why she had "deserted the champagne
circuit for jazz rooms" to *Jet* magazine in 1958, "I'm a black woman and I
have to sing about things I feel and know about, blues and jazz. At the
other places, something inside of me was not content. I didn't really fit in.
It was an act." Thereafter, as those charting Lincoln's "metamorphosis"
noted, she built a reputation as a jazz singer actively involved in black
independence movements.[20] Even more dramatically than Simone,
changes in Lincoln's musical repertoire and appearance went hand in
hand. Her "natural" hair, her avant-garde vocal styles, her marriage to and
musical collaborations with jazz drummer and composer Max Roach, her
support for organizations like CORE, the Cultural Association for Women
of African Heritage and others, her leadership in the protests at the U.N.
after the death of Patrice Lumumba—all of these, together with the content of her lyrics about domestic civil rights, apartheid in South Africa,
and economic inequities, reinforced her seriousness of purpose. Even the
way she stood, said jazz producer and critic Nat Hentoff, "had the smack
of authority" and the "pride of being black."[21]

The choices Lincoln made had significant costs. After *Down Beat*'s jazz
critic Ira Gitler harshly criticized the album *Straight Ahead* in 1961, both
for its politics and "banal" music, and dismissed Lincoln by characterizing
her as a "professional Negro," she did not record another album for over
ten years. Nonetheless, in live performances and interviews in the United
States and abroad, and in essays like "Who Will Revere the Black Woman?"
and "The Negro Woman in Literature," Lincoln continued to make herself
visible and retained her reputation as one of the "most vocal of socially
oriented jazz artists for much of the 1960s," as historian Eric Porter has
put it.[22] Just several months after Gitler's critical review of Lincoln and

Straight Ahead, Down Beat organized a panel discussion on "Racial Prejudice in Jazz" in which Lincoln participated. In the series published over
the course of two issues in 1962, she argued that Gitler had gotten it
wrong when he called her a "professional Negro." The term should refer
to performers who only tried to please white audiences—who "looked the
way Western people expect you to look" and wore "ridiculous dresses,"
explained Lincoln. As a performer with overlapping commitments to jazz,
dignified black womanhood, and racial equality, she simply did not meet
the criteria for being a "professional Negro," as she defined it. In making
this argument, Lincoln simultaneously affirmed her identity as a black
woman and as a politicized singer. When Gitler compared her to Billie
Holiday, she observed in the panel discussion, he implicitly suggested that
he preferred suffering black women performers to those who had agency
and developed political beliefs.[23]

Lincoln's transformation from a glamorous club singer to a politically
engaged performer persisted in her first major film role. In 1964, she
played the part of Josie in the low-budget and independently produced
black-and-white film *Nothing But a Man*. Josie, a subdued Southern
schoolteacher with straight hair, is deeply loyal to the men around her who
struggle with the emotional and economic effects of racism. She emerges
over the course of the film as the strong wife upon whom her working-
class husband can depend, and their love is a means through which they
resist the degrading effects of prejudice. *Nothing But a Man* was written by
two white filmmakers, Michael Roemer and Robert Young, and filmed in
1963 after their eight-week trip in the South that took place with the support of the NAACP. Like *Come Back, Africa*, it was the result of an unusual
collaboration and dialogue between white filmmakers, black actors and
writers, and young black activists; also like *Come Back, Africa* it premiered
at the Venice Film Festival. Roemer and Young, like Lionel Rogosin, were
steeped in traditions of avant-garde filmmaking and global antiracist politics.[24] *Nothing But a Man* had a limited commercial release in the United
States in 1964. Even so, Lincoln's performance got attention. As Josie,
Lincoln gave a "stirring" performance, according to *Ebony*, in a "timely
film masterpiece." Roemer admired the "untrained" actress who "was so
instinctive that she did things correctly with an almost uncanny skill."[25]

Reactions to Lincoln in her second feature film, *For Love of Ivy*, were
even more positive and far more widespread—even among those critics
who were not necessarily enthusiastic about the film as a whole. "In
Abbey," wrote a critic for the *Citizen News*, "a talented night club singer

turned picture performer, a star is born." Several suggested that her performance as Ivy was Oscar-worthy, and according to Renata Adler, in the *New York Times*, Lincoln "far outclasses anyone else in the film."[26] It appeared that the woman who had remade herself from Anna Marie Wooldridge to Gaby Lee to Abbey Lincoln, whom critics had "discovered" as the glamorous "girl in the Marilyn Monroe dress" and then rediscovered as a "voice of protest," had undergone yet another "metamorphosis" and process of discovery with this starring role in a Hollywood romance.

FOR LOVE OF *Ivy* was essentially a generic love story: between Ivy Moore and Jack Parks (Poitier), a successful businessman with legitimate and not-so-legitimate business interests. The soft-spoken Ivy sets the story into motion when she informs her white employers and their two hippie children that after nine years of employment, she has decided to leave their Long Island home; she wants to live in New York City and go to secretarial school. The entire family protests, but it is the sideburned Tim (Beau Bridges) and the mod Gena (Lauri Peters), prolonged adolescents and/or delayed adults, who concoct the plan to keep Ivy in their home. Tim blackmails the well-dressed, urbane Parks into asking Ivy on a date because he believes that with a man in her life who will date and flatter but emphatically not marry her, Ivy will remain in her job. Jack complies only because Tim knows that his trucking business is a front for an illegal gambling business housed in the back of a truck that drives along highways at night. And yet, to the surprise of every one (except the audience), Ivy and Jack fall in love. The twists and turns between them, and between them and the white family, make up the rest of the film, right up to the final few minutes when Jack gives up the gambling business and makes a commitment to Ivy. He carries her bag from the suburban enclave where the Austins live to his sedan, and he and Ivy drive off together to Manhattan, as the white family waves and looks on fondly.

Sidney Poitier spent three weeks in 1967 developing the ideas for *For Love of Ivy* into an extended story outline. When he shopped the film to the big studios, he received a lukewarm response. Only the little-known Palomar Pictures International, a subsidiary of the television network ABC, picked up this romantic tale. Executives there did so with considerable excitement, as they heralded the new subsidiary, and *Ivy* as its "first picture," as evidence for the rich cross-fertilization that was possible between television and Hollywood films. ABC president Leonard Goldenson was "proud to announce" that production on *Ivy* had started in October 1967 and that it was "but a start to what we confidently believe will be a very important factor in the ever-enlarging world of international entertainment." With an escalating crisis in Hollywood—five out of six films lost money by the end of the decade—executives tried to build bridges between television and film as a way to grow their audiences. One critic thought it "curious" that the big studios for which Poitier had made so much money "did not option to be associated with 'For Love of Ivy,'" but concluded that it was only "appropriate" that a new production outfit and new "distributor set up" be involved in this film that was "revolutionary" in "its very simplicity."[27] In contrast to the low-budget and independently produced *Nothing But a Man*, and the even lower-budget and furtively produced *Come Back, Africa*, everyone involved in the production and distribution of *For Love of Ivy* agreed that the film was designed to attract large audiences, entertain, and make money. The goals for *Julia* were similar. As Carroll noted, the show was "promoted and produced by two of the largest conglomerates in America—20th Century-Fox and NBC. . . . It was a new beginning."[28]

With the hope of expanding the "ever enlarging world of international entertainment" in mind, whites and blacks connected to *Ivy* were keen to downplay race. Poitier pointed out that he intended *Ivy* to be "lighthearted" and offer "loads of laughs." Despite his longtime connections to organized black activism, he had not tried to write a "turgid tale of social significance"; Poitier added that "race is only brought into the picture" designed as "entertainment" when Ivy encountered situations that "wouldn't be present if she were white." Palomar executive Ed Sherick went much further in stressing the "sheer entertainment value" of *Ivy*. As one reporter noted, "his answer was 'yes' when a reporter asked whether the story could be played just as easily by white actors." "No Racial Slant in 'Love of Ivy,'" declared a headline in *Film Daily*.[29] Producer Hal Kanter similarly sought to portray *Julia* as universal and in what he thought were race-neutral terms. He often repeated the story of how he had pitched the show to NBC without mentioning race, and the executives who "dropped the script in surprise" when they realized, midway through, that Julia was a black woman.[30]

Upon *Ivy*'s release, many critics and fans concurred with Poitier and Sherick about the unimportance of race to the film. Plenty of those who made this observation applauded this quality and praised *Ivy* as part of a racially unmarked mass culture. According to the white critic Stanley Kauffmann in *The New Republic*, the film followed in the familiar romantic comedy footsteps of Clark Gable and Claudette Colbert, "except—and the exception is the whole point—this time the lovers are black." In its extensive coverage, *Ebony* agreed that *Ivy* "marks a first . . . by casting black actors in romantic leads."[31] This refrain developed as part of a larger conversation about civil rights activism. Critics in 1968 who lauded *For Love of Ivy* because it was not politically oriented and did not address contemporary race relations directly were also affirming all that civil rights activism oriented around integration had achieved. In laying claim to the romance genre for black characters, *Ivy* offered "the ultimate in integration, rather like a Sidney Poitier *Pillow Talk*," said one. Or, in the words of Kauffmann, *Ivy* integrated "white America's heritage of 20th-century pop myths." *Ivy* was "quite obviously a breakthrough," noted film critic Charles Champlin in the *Los Angeles Times*. Its "significance" stemmed from its "rather deliberate insignificance: the fact that it seems to be a divertissement rather than a tract."[32]

These were the terms through which audiences who liked *For Love of Ivy* evaluated it: The film's "success" lay in its triviality, in the ability of fictional black characters to make race relations seem unimportant, and in the ability of these characters to claim the pleasures of romance and elegant accessories in lieu of protest. When a critic for *Newsweek* scorned the film for being "unrealistic," an angry reader wrote back that this was a ridiculous accusation because *For Love of Ivy* demonstrated "that we are not all superlovers chasing white women; that we do dig our black women; that we are not all good guys sweating the black revolution."[33] That the film was "just" entertainment and part of mass culture, and that its black characters were depoliticized components of that mass culture, became evidence for the success of the civil rights movement, according to this liberal logic that cut across a broad swath of public opinion. White critics employed this framework more frequently than did African American critics and fans, but it was not a racially specific response. One accomplishment of the civil rights movement, in other words, according to this strand in debates about *Ivy*, was to depoliticize leisure, mass culture, and the politics of racial representation. As *Ebony* declared, the "nonpolitical" nature of *Ivy* rendered it significant: "*Ivy* is more than just an amusing bit of fluff. . . . For it is the first film to feature blacks as ingénue and lover in a non-civil rights oriented script."[34] These and other reactions spoke to a longing, among some audiences, for African American film characters who could claim what seemed to be racially neutral pleasures. Television tapped into similar desires with *Julia*. Kanter described and praised the new series as one "that featured black characters as people first and black only incidentally," and as a means through which "a white audience could see blacks as people, not black people."[35]

Ivy's mass appeal and ostensible de-emphasis on race rested considerably on Lincoln and on the shoulders of its male lead. Sidney Poitier's astounding trilogy of successes in 1967—in *To Sir with Love*, *In the Heat of the Night*, and *Guess Who's Coming to Dinner*—eclipsed that of most stars white or black, and even overshadowed his own prior successes, including his Academy-award-winning performance in *Lilies of the Field* in 1963. As *To Sir with Love* and *In the Heat of the Night* broke box office records and anticipation for *Guess Who's Coming to Dinner* grew, *Variety* magazine even declared September 1967 to be "Sidney Poitier Month."[36]

Despite, or perhaps because of Poitier's celebrity and activism, he had plenty of critics and stirred up long-standing disagreements among African Americans about popular culture, racial politics, and authenticity. African American intellectual Harold Cruse was among those who led the charge in his book, *The Crisis of the Negro Intellectual*. In this wide ranging study of race and left-oriented politics that influenced a generation of younger black activists, artists, and intellectuals, Cruse argued that a destructive "one-star" system had "been manufactured around Sidney Poitier" and called on "Negro creative intellectuals" to "take action against the film-producing conspiracy." Several African American activists and intellectuals lambasted Poitier's roles as too "idealized" and as propping up an "Uncle Tom refurbished." According to a brutal critique in the *New York Times* by African American playwright Clifford Mason, Poitier was an "antiseptic, one-dimensional hero" and "a showcase nigger."[37]

In contrast to Lena Horne, who in the mid-1960s rejected earlier images of herself as a "good little symbol" and strove for what she regarded as greater authenticity and relevance with songs like "Now" and "Silent Spring," Poitier used the publicity around *Ivy* to counter the argument that he should be playing "all sorts of roles." As he told a reporter for *Variety* in the marketing blitz before the film's release, "I'm the only Negro actor who works with any degree of regularity. I represent 10,000,000 people in this country and millions more in Africa . . . and I'm not going to do anything they can't be proud of. Wait till there are six of us; then one of us can play villains all the time." Diahann Carroll shared this perspective. She responded to criticisms that *Julia* was not realistic by reframing the middle-class ethos of the series. The show's "middle-class aspect was a positive," she said. "There *is* a black middle class . . . and I had never seen it shown on TV before." Nonetheless, she also repeatedly asserted after the show's debut, "This is fairyland, you know." While Kanter had claimed that *Julia* would "show it like it is," Carroll embraced the show as entertainment. Carroll and Poitier's goals were neither authenticity nor topicality; they were not trying to represent the range of "real" African Americans in American society or make assertions about black cultural autonomy. Instead, as Poitier explained, he wanted to challenge preexisting cultural representations of black men in American popular culture. He wanted to "overcome," he explained, "all those frightened, bug-eyed maids and shuffling butlers."[38]

Jack Parks, the sophisticated, wealthy, well-dressed, and well-spoken hero of *Ivy*, never shuffled and was no butler. But as Palomar executives emphasized in their marketing for the film and as fans and critics were quick to point out, Poitier was doing something new relative to the rest of his career. In the first starring role that he helped to craft and define, his character is essentially a con man and hustler, though one who ultimately mends his ways. As the romantic lead, Poitier's Jack Parks not only "gets the girl"—an ending that the romance genre essentially required—but he and "the girl" also get into bed together. "Saint Sidney finally smooches," wrote Joseph Morgenstern in *Newsweek*, sardonically. Many people admired this sex scene because it offered a glimpse into the private lives of black characters and freed them from storylines tethered to politics and noble causes. As a critic for *Playboy* explained, "Never on the screen have black lovers been treated this way—abed in elegant surroundings, just digging each other far from the clamor of racial strife and the war on poverty." For critics and fans, Poitier's presence provided further evidence that the absence of confrontational racial politics in *Ivy* was politically significant and evidence of progress. The film's depiction of sexuality and romance proved that claiming the right to pleasure could be an unnamed political strategy. "Jack and Ivy are just characters in the story," as London's *Punch* magazine put it after the film opened to favorable reviews in that city, "which is exactly as it should be."[39]

Shortly before *For Love of Ivy*'s release, producer Jay Weston predicted that it would be "one of the best things abroad for America's image. There are no Uncle Toms in it. There are three-dimensional characters." Weston was articulating a well-established Cold War logic, one that presumed that it was good foreign policy to make race relations in the United States look better.[40] The film was a reasonable success—it broke records during its opening weekend in four American cities; when it played in London,

reviews of the "delightful comedy" about a "charming, natural relationship between a man and woman who just happen to be colored" were
enthusiastic; and it won several award nominations, including an Oscar
nomination to Quincy Jones for his score, and a Golden Globe nomination to Lincoln for best supporting actress.[41] However, even in his efforts
to sell *Ivy*, Poitier encountered domestic limits to his own status as an international celebrity and was openly bitter that three big studios "for
whom I had worked and made money—some of them are making money
in various parts of the world this minute on my pictures" turned him
down.[42] The camera further contained the story—*Ivy* was shot almost exclusively in interior domestic spaces, with an urban landscape hovering
tantalizingly near, but mostly very far away from its main characters.[43]
From a strictly financial perspective, five years after *Ivy*'s release, according to one report, the film had made a profit of $390,000, but the acclaim
could not compare to that that of another ABC-Palomar production, *They
Shoot Horses, Don't They*, which was nominated for nine Oscars and won
one.[44] Lincoln remained far better known for her jazz vocals, in and outside of the United States, and Poitier's other films garnered far greater
recognition and profits than did *Ivy*. *Ivy* simply did not become part of an
"ever enlarging world of international entertainment," in the ways that
Makeba's "Pata Pata" or Simone's "Mississippi Goddam" did.

Not everyone agreed that there was "no racial slant" in *Ivy*. Many people
who watched the film concluded that its alleged de-emphasis on race was
neither consistent nor worth saluting in any case, and questions and criticisms abounded about the film's racial politics. Why, some wondered, had
Poitier not demanded an African American director? Why the "coyness"
about race relations in the storyline? Why was "Negro culture . . . nowhere
in evidence"? *Newsweek* criticized the film for offering "black decorations
in a white world" at a moment when "a whole black world waits, less and
less patiently."[45] That many white critics in mainstream publications on
both sides of the Atlantic objected to the absence of a specifically black
culture and black power perspective in the film indicates the broad impact
that the black arts movement and the broader emphasis on black power of
which it was a part had in these years.

As viewers also observed, occasional glimpses of African Americans'
political perspectives beyond integration and upward mobility did seep
into *Ivy*. Jack Parks makes money only off of wealthy whites in his illegal
gambling business, and he employs only African Americans with families
to support; "we don't take from blood," he explains to Ivy when she learns

about this side of his life and sees that his employees are part of a community that he has established. While there is no evidence of movements or organizing on the part of the black characters, there are subtle suggestions about how much the white characters don't know. Gena asks Jack what he thinks about black power, for example; his initial response, offered slowly and in Poitier's famously recognizable cadence—"I think about it . . . a lot," precedes his assertion "I don't talk about it." This exchange conveys some sense of an underlying threat, one that the film's white characters do not detect but which some audiences did. In a letter to the *New York Times*, a white viewer explained that that the newest Poitier vehicle "was trying to tell us—very subtly—that the Black community is angry, very aggravated and fed up. . . . [T]he American Negro is stepping up to claim what is his— not what the white community thinks he *ought* to want." For these and other more critical consumers, *Ivy* was anything but what Stanley Kauffmann described as a "brief respite" that signified that "Negroes have now reached a position to exercise the franchises of genuinely mass fantasy." Rather, the "fantasy" was evidence for an unfinished political agenda, and the "sadly dishonest" film confirmed all that black activism still needed to accomplish. "I am certain," wrote a critic in *Film Quarterly*, "that I speak for the majority of my fellow black Americans in suggesting that Poitier cease deluding himself that cinematic debris such as this is beneficial to the black cause."[46] Audience members who saw subtle gestures toward African American culture and community building in *Ivy*, and those who critiqued the absence of such qualities, were dismayed with the film's apparent emphasis on integration, romance, and social mobility.

Whether or not *Ivy* was "beneficial to the black cause," Poitier did hope that it would benefit one very small group in particular. A theme that recurred in the pre-film publicity was that Poitier had developed his story because his four daughters wanted to see African Americans in Hollywood romances. "Very rarely can they see Negro women on screen. They go to movies all the time but they rarely see themselves reflected there," noted the celebrity dad, motivated by the gaps in his daughters' lives as black female consumers of popular culture.[47] No one at the time remarked that when Poitier named black girls as his imagined audience at the same time that he insisted that the story was not about race or politics, he isolated women from questions about race. One person, however, did put black women into the center of the film's contradictory representations of race, black culture, and black activism: Abbey Lincoln. Lincoln offered multiple perspectives on *For Love of Ivy* and her role as a domestic. There were instances when she participated in the widespread conversation emphasizing *Ivy*'s appeal and success as depoliticized entertainment, especially when she talked about how *Ivy* offered "universal identification" for both blacks and whites.[48] But there were many ways in which Lincoln claimed the racial, class, and gender particularity that so many others who endorsed the film's mass appeal denied.

IN THE PLETHORA of media coverage about *Ivy*, Lincoln spoke highly of the film and the process of working on it and explained both with reference to what she regarded as progress in the United States. In a lengthy profile in the *Los Angeles Times*, she responded to a question about prejudice by comparing the United States favorably to other countries in Europe and Africa: "This country is big enough for everybody," she said, "because everybody is here. People of European extraction can live together here while in Europe they're looking at each other suspiciously. In Africa, the people are having civil wars. I don't believe the Creator made us unintelligent. I think we'll all get together eventually." When jazz critic Nat Hentoff, in a profile for the *New York Times*, asked Lincoln if she and husband Max Roach were "still involved in black organizations working to change the country," Lincoln answered: "We stay involved . . . on a level at which an artist can best contribute. We have to stay in tune with what's going on, stay close to black people, and try to project what they feel." But, she added, "I'm feeling very positive about things these days. It's another time now. I think everything is going to right itself. I don't mean we can just relax, but I don't think people have to be hit on the head any more. . . . I feel now I can relax as a woman and let the guys take care of things." Lincoln concluded that "personally" she did not "feel panicky or frustrated about anything."[49] In this interview, Lincoln's optimism about race relations and patriarchy were intertwined.

This perspective was vastly different from that of other black woman entertainers in 1968—a time that "felt like the shutters were coming down on anyone who dared to suggest there was something seriously wrong with the state of our country," according to Nina Simone, and when Miriam Makeba was experiencing the negative impact of her marriage to Stokely Carmichael.[50] For many years Lincoln had worked to maintain her political commitments without alienating the audiences on whom she depended, and sometimes these efforts had meant containing a radical political perspective; the more cheerful tone and a de-emphasis on political strife evident in her comments to the mainstream press about *Ivy* were not, in fact, unprecedented. In 1962, for example, shortly after the controversy erupted over the politics on her album *Straight Ahead*, Lincoln insisted in the *New York Amsterdam News* that while she had "sung some protest songs," she had been "misrepresented as being a nationalist." Many people, she explained, mistakenly assumed that she was "some kind of a freedom fighter" or that she used "the stage as a political platform." But she vehemently refuted their claims: "Nothing is further from the truth." Sounding a bit like Miriam Makeba, she defined her music not as political, but as being about "dignity."[51]

While Abbey Lincoln may have strategically positioned herself in the marketplace and chosen her words with care for years, she also had good reason to feel optimistic in 1968. Much was made about the fact that Lincoln had earned the starring role in *Ivy* after a four-month search during which 300 women had auditioned. Even with this level of competition, "it wasn't even a test," according to director Daniel Mann. "She was five light years ahead of all the rest." Poitier had initially looked for "a very glamorous girl in the part to make the love story more commercial," Mann continued, and changed his mind after Lincoln's audition. Lincoln, said the director, "is beyond 'glamour.' She's a woman of great physical appeal, but she doesn't organize herself around her sex. She organizes herself around her directness, and *that* makes her sexy."[52] Or, in the words of another critic, also a white man, what was most impressive about Lincoln was her "assurance—a gyroscope-like awareness of self from which she speaks mildly, carefully and firmly."[53] These were quite startling descriptions of a black women performer, especially one who was known some years earlier for her "sexy lyrics," her "pouting lips," and her image as a black Marilyn Monroe.

For Love of Ivy was the biggest commercial endeavor of Lincoln's career, and with it came numerous predictions that she was on her way up. She was fast becoming "the female Sidney Poitier!," as one of the producers put it; a reporter observed that at one press conference, Poitier introduced Lincoln as the star who was "going to eclipse 'all of us.'" Years later, she referred to this as a period when her "life reached a peak." After *Ivy*, Palomar producers hoped to make a film based on Billie Holiday's life, *Lady Sings the Blues*, and according to Lincoln, they were discussing the leading role with her.[54] Here was a moment of potential promise for Lincoln on many fronts—politically, professionally, and in the intermingling of these arenas. Seven years after being censured as a "professional Negro," doors were opening for her. She had gained entry to a celebrity culture for a

FIGURE 4.2 Sidney Poitier and Abbey Lincoln with the script of *For Love of Ivy* in September 1967. Lincoln secured the part for which 300 women auditioned and was "beyond 'glamour,'" according to director Daniel Mann.
(John Pedin/*New York Daily News* Archive/Getty Images)

performance of black womanhood that would reach audiences across lines of race, region, and class, in ways that jazz performances at small clubs and benefit concerts rarely did, and no one, it seemed, was telling her to be a good little symbol, to be on her best behavior, or not to be "too" outspoken, as had been the case the case when Lena Horne signed a contract in Hollywood some 25 years earlier. These positive reactions to Lincoln and to the ways she spoke up in the marketing of *Ivy* were not a given. Diahann Carroll faced numerous constraints in her conversations about *Julia*. Journalists expected her to speak about "the overall state of black people in this country" at the same time that director Hal Kanter repeatedly stressed that she should not see herself as "spokeswoman for her entire race. She's Julia Baker, not Joan of Dark."[55] Carroll, whose history was less controversial than Lincoln's, had to negotiate with competing expectations about *Julia*. She often encountered opposition when she talked about the series and her character in ways that Lincoln, in her statements about *Ivy*, did not.

Perhaps because Lincoln did not seem to be policed in her conversations about *Ivy*, she did not always stay "on message" or adhere to a single party line. She commended the film and expressed optimism for what it said about American race relations and the civil rights movement, but she also used her performance of Ivy to articulate the concerns of working-class black women and as a platform for a black nationalist perspective that critiqued racially specific standards of beauty. *Ivy* was not, then, simply evidence for the triumph of liberal interracialism and the politics of pleasure, according to Lincoln. On screen as Ivy and off screen when she talked about herself in relation to the fictional character, Lincoln developed multiple perspectives on the film and her role in it.

As the fictional Ivy, Lincoln generated a model of black femininity that was unusual in American popular culture and noticeably different from the film's depiction of white women. She portrayed Ivy Moore as subdued but fiercely independent, as restrained yet passionate. In her quiet way, the character demands that people—the white "family" and Jack Parks—listen to her. "No one asks me what I want," she says to both the Austins and Jack near the end of the film, as they all battle over her fate. Early on, when Ivy first tells her white employer Doris Austin (Nan Martin) that she plans to leave her job so that she can move to Manhattan, earn a high school diploma, and attend secretarial school, Doris is so panic-stricken that she cannot even listen to Ivy—if, indeed, she ever could, in any meaningful way. She asks whether Ivy is pregnant and offers her more money; she insists that since she had "found" Ivy in Florida, they had been like family, and asks Ivy to call her "Mother"; she then offers to pay for an extended vacation: "We'll send you anyplace you want to go—Africa?" There was nothing subtle about the intertwined expressions of race and class privilege on the part of a white woman who clearly considers herself antiracist.[56]

The film repeatedly ties Doris Austin's racial privilege to expressions of women's liberation that many black women associated with whiteness. Her liberation—she works in the family business instead of running the household and perceives domestic work as oppressive—rests on Ivy, and that dynamic keeps the white woman from acknowledging Ivy's desire for nondomestic opportunities. Toward the end of the film, Doris renounces both shopping and her job, declaring that she "used to run this house" and "can run it again." Given her evident incompetence in the kitchen, however, there is little reason for Ivy or her own family to believe her. "Very few of these women [in the white women's liberation movement] suffer the extreme economic exploitation that most Black women are subjected to day by day," Frances Beale would write in 1969 in her classic essay "Double Jeopardy: To Be Black and Female." The "joke" about Doris Austin that audiences were expected to get in *For Love of Ivy* was essentially a Hollywood version of the pointed political critique that black women were developing about the racial and class chasm that separated many black and white women, and that black women were politicizing. "The Black woman was needed and valued by the white female as a domestic," wrote Pat Robinson and a black women's group from Mt. Vernon and New Rochelle in 1968. "The Black female diluted much of this actual oppression of the white female by the white male."[57] Significantly, when audiences were invited in on this joke—in scenes that transformed the white characters into buffoon-like figures of comic relief once reserved for black actors in white-dominated films—they were also invited to distance themselves from these expressions of white privilege.

Ivy's version of femininity is as different from that of the young white woman as it is from the older white woman. Like her mother, Gena Austin willfully ignores the ways in which her behavior reproduces racial hierarchies. At an elaborate matchmaking dinner for Jack and Ivy (that Ivy cooks), she boasts about her own civil rights credentials and urges Ivy to sit with them, only to vaguely insist that Ivy do all of the dishes at the end of the night ("Oh, there aren't that many, Ivy"). The film exposes both Tim and Gena as vapid and as merely clinging to countercultural props—long hair and beads for Tim, and birth control pills and miniskirts for Gena. When the two first hatch their plot to fix Ivy up with a man and are trying to think of who they might know who might be right for her, Gena explains, "I'm afraid my friends won't qualify." The film evokes taboos against interracial sex, only to have it seem that Gena and Tim don't care about such matters. Tim tells his sister that "none of them [her friends] are good enough" for Ivy. His infatuation with Ivy becomes a running joke, one that gestures toward the possibility of an interracial romance that "everyone" knows could never really happen or possibly be serious, and more implicitly gestures to the history of sexual abuse to which black women domestic workers had been subject for centuries.[58]

Ivy stands apart from both Gena and Doris Austin. She is financially independent, hard-working, sexually active, and, as she asserts to Jack on their first date, uninterested in marriage. She does not go on a lot of second dates, but "These are the dues you pay for being free," she says matter-of-factly. While the young white woman embraces her right to have many boyfriends and provides Ivy with birth control, Ivy does not just want to "score" and does not have "more action" than she "can use," as Tim describes his sister. The much commented on sex scene between Ivy and Jack Parks actually consists of two sexual encounters. The first is the more typical romantic fare: At the end of a date, Ivy and Jack are in his Manhattan apartment, a sophisticated urban space decorated with African art and other hints of a cosmopolitan black identity. Earlier, the black children of his employees had wandered in and out, reminding audiences that Jack Parks lives in this space as part of an urban black community that contrasts with the Austin's isolated white suburban luxury. The anxiety and sexual tension build—"I ought to take you home," says Parks—until their first kiss and the sex that follows. The second and more significant episode of intimacy comes later. Ivy, clad in a robe, sits at the window looking at the urban landscape while Jack is in bed; as they talk, she says insistently, "I like you." When she comes back to his bed, she is initially on top of him. For years, from her earliest days as a jazz singer and in essays she wrote and interviews she gave, Lincoln had emphasized the importance to black life of strong black men and heterosexual relations. In many respects, so does the fictional Ivy, but explicitly on her own terms.

In addition to how she performed Ivy, Abbey Lincoln talked about the film in ways that highlighted black female strength and dignity. She agreed with Poitier that countering Hollywood's representations of African Americans on screen was an important goal and observed that for many years too many black women in Hollywood had been relegated to subordinate roles as maids. At the same time, for Lincoln, ordinary African American women's lives were as important as what fictional women in movies were doing. At a widely covered press conference in New York prior to the film's release called "in her honor" to introduce her as Poitier's costar, Lincoln elaborated on Poitier's claim that Ivy was a domestic, but was not "that kind of maid." She explained that the part would resonate with many Negro women in the country who had experienced domestic work because Ivy was a multidimensional character whose professional and personal desires the film acknowledged.[59] Just as Nina Simone's "Four Women" drew on historical stereotypes from the perspective of black women, the character of Ivy injected some degree of realism into what had so often been a white-inspired construct.

Lincoln made this idea concrete when she drew connections between herself and Ivy. "Very many Negro women (including herself)," according to reporters, "have worked as domestics at one time or another."[60] By

FIGURE 4.3 Lincoln as Ivy and Poitier as Jack in *For Love of Ivy*. (ACADEMY OF Motion Picture Arts and Sciences)

comparing the character's domestic work to her own experience, Lincoln inserted class directly into the conversation about *Ivy*, noting that economic insecurities limited the choices available to working black women. Lincoln also used her own experiences to subvert myths that many middle-class white Americans, including the white characters in the film, maintained. She remarked that she had worked as a domestic to help her family, "not by choice." She had learned to do the work and to do it well, but had always "resented" it and "didn't want to do domestic work." Lincoln made clear that the labor that she and millions of other women did never defined them and was just a small piece of far fuller lives in which women retained their power and dignity: "When I was working as a domestic, maybe I was playing a domestic then," said Lincoln.[61] Far more than anyone else involved in making and marketing the film, Lincoln insisted on seeing the character of Ivy in terms of race, gender, and class, not just as a woman longing for heterosexual romance.

On and off screen, then, Lincoln reengaged with Lena Horne's attempts in the 1940s to position black women as modern entertainers.[62] In the 1940s, Horne's efforts had largely revolved around her refusal to play the part of a domestic, coupled with her glamour and sexual appeal, and her own family's ties to a middle-class-oriented ethos of racial uplift. This was, as noted, quite a difficult balancing act. "Neither fancy character nor Topsy," a journalist in St. Louis wrote about Horne in 1949, "she sometimes finds it hard to walk the wobbly line between these two conceptions."[63] By contrast, in 1968, Abbey Lincoln embraced the opportunity to play the part of a black domestic, but she put the character's quest for independence and autonomy—economic and sexual—at the center of the story about a modern black woman; moreover, she connected her own family story to those efforts. Her claims on behalf of black women were not the "typical" assertions of black power that other black entertainers, often men, made. The fictional Ivy, with her stylish sweater sets and straight-haired wig, had none of the outrageousness that many people associated with James Brown's "I'm Black and I'm Proud," or the assertiveness of Linc, the Afro-coiffed undercover cop in the trio that made up *The Mod Squad*. Instead, the radical dimensions of black feminism's liberal roots—its focus on workplace equity, labor issues, and reproductive control—were on display here in mass culture via Lincoln.[64] Lincoln, like Makeba, revised glamour as Horne had claimed and defined it for modern black women entertainers in the 1940s and as Carroll extended it in the 1960s in another way too: Her skin color set her apart. With this range of approaches, Lincoln used mainstream mass culture to alter meanings of beauty and power for black women.

Ivy was not the first fictional "maid" that black women made their own with a series of on- and off-screen strategies. In taking on this role, Lincoln was participating in a long tradition—one that in different ways Hattie McDaniel, Louise Beavers, Alice Childress, and Beah Richards developed in films and in print.[65] But Lincoln joined aspects of civil rights and second-wave feminism, and claimed her fictional role as a site for black female dignity, respectability, and sexual desirability in a mainstream Hollywood production in a unique way. The film mocked a strand of women's liberation associated with married, middle-class white women and their efforts to free themselves from domestic responsibility; it also mocked a strand of women's liberation associated with younger white women and their efforts to free themselves to sexual expression. Through Lincoln, *Ivy* gestured toward a black feminist perspective that took into account the aspirations of working-class black women. It did so, moreover, based on prior associations between Lincoln and black power.

LINCOLN'S POLITICIZED PERFORMANCE of Ivy is worth yet another look, because it had more than one set of meanings. Ultimately, to celebrate the film as one in which Lincoln articulated elements of black feminism through her on-screen performance as Ivy and countered critiques of the film as lacking racial specificity through her off-screen commentary—to consider *Ivy* primarily in terms of resistance—is difficult for several reasons. First, Abbey Lincoln consistently rejected the term feminist.[66] Second, her outspoken critiques of racism and her attention to questions of class always depended on her support for black men and a certain kind of patriarchal, heterosexual gender relations. "Lincoln advocated a black nationalist politics," explains scholar Farah Jasmine Griffin, "where black women would finally have access to femininity, protection and domesticity."[67] This perspective was evident when Lincoln explained her transition from sexy nightclub singer to serious jazz vocalist by referencing her husband, Max Roach, as "the master" in their "master-apprentice relationship" and credited him for shifts in her music, politics, and appearance; it was a worldview that persisted in the dialogues around *For Love of Ivy*.[68]

Finally, Lincoln and others established a contrast between herself and Ivy in ways that limited the fictional character's resistance to the status quo. Much was made of the fact that Lincoln, known since the late 1950s for her "natural" hairstyle, played the role wearing a straight-haired wig. Numerous critics, mostly, but not all self-identified antiracist whites, drew attention to the disconnect between Lincoln's politics and looks and those of her fictional counterpart. A lengthy profile in the *Los Angeles Times* juxtaposed a photo of Lincoln as herself with a large Afro to one of Lincoln as Ivy, with straight hair and pearls. The caption between the two emphasized the contrast: "The two hair-dos of Abbey Lincoln; As she appears off-screen, left, and in movie '*For Love of Ivy*,' right. Miss Lincoln is proud that she is the first of black glamour queens to adopt the bushy style." In the text of the article, Lincoln explained that the "Afro" was a "natural style for a woman of African heritage"; in another interview, she noted that black women "didn't start imitating white hair-styles until about 50 years ago."[69] *Ebony* covered *Ivy* with an extensive photo spread and article, including three photos of Lincoln and Poitier from the film on the cover and another dozen inside. The lengthy piece set up a contrast between Abbey Lincoln and Ivy Moore with images and words. Two pages of photos of her as the straight-haired Ivy preceded a page with a photograph of Lincoln, her hair in an Afro and clad in African-inspired dress and jewelry. The unattributed copy noted the following:

Off screen she presents a sharp contrast to the maid she plays. With her crown of bouffant au-naturel hair, dangling earrings matched with flowing African dresses, Abbey brings with her an aura of soft femininity and black pride. Her eyes light up, smiling, when would-be critics point to the discrepancy between her role as a maid (hair straightened), and her real life militancy and beauty.[70]

Some fans did prefer to see Lincoln with her natural hair. "One disgruntled black youth complained to a friend, 'I wish she wasn't wearing that wig. She looks more like a soul sister in her natural,'" according to *Ebony*. Lincoln cited professional reasons for wearing a wig, and affirmed the value of her role. "As an actress, I must be truthful to the character I am portraying and the Ivy's in this country don't wear their hair natural."[71] Amidst repeated references to Lincoln's pride in her Afro, critics also observed that she was equally proud to wear a wig in a performance that allowed her to reach out to black women who made different choices in their own lives.

The reception of *Ivy* and the dialogue about black women that it sparked might suggest the degree to which Lincoln countered assumptions that the film was only a liberal success story or a depoliticized romance about upwardly mobile African Americans. Her reputation prior to *Ivy* could have an impact on the production and consumption of the film. In this reading, Lincoln's Afro alongside Ivy's wig might speak to political resistance and a black woman's unique perspective on "black is beautiful."[72] Lincoln could acknowledge the reality that many black women continued to straighten their hair, and that older black women in particular tended to regard "natural" hair with suspicion, while also elevating the alternative: her own hair, with its connotations of political commitments and racial pride. In fact, the part of Ivy seemed to validate Lincoln's personal metamorphoses. She had once dressed in ways that other people defined as "glamorous." But when "reviews and people said [she] was lovely to look at and things like that," she had stopped performing because, as Lincoln explained after *Ivy*'s release, she "didn't get a feeling of accomplishment." By contrast, once she started to wear her hair natural and practiced her "craft," she could be "in a film like 'Ivy' and go in at the top."[73]

And yet Lincoln's potential resistance in this film was limited, as were her prior connections to black power. Palomar Pictures marketed *For Love of Ivy* by emphasizing Lincoln's hair, body, and femininity, all of which

FIGURES 4.4 and 4.5 The *Los Angeles Times* juxtaposed these two photos, with the following caption between them: "The two hair-dos of Abbey Lincoln; As she appears off-screen, left, and in movie '*For Love of Ivy*,' right. Miss Lincoln is proud that she is the first of black glamour queens to adopt the bushy style."

(Courtesy of the *Los Angeles Times*)

stood in for, and ultimately supplanted, her politics. In 1965, years before Poitier had started to work on *Ivy*, a journalist for *Jazz* who interviewed Lincoln "the day after the first attempted march from Selma to Montgomery," asked whether race relations could be "resolved nonviolently." Lincoln responded by emphasizing how important it was for black Americans to think of themselves as "African American" and not "Negroes." She mourned the links to Africa that were lost when "we were forced to give up our languages, names, and identity" and compared the U.S. government's acceptance of violence against black citizens to parents who spoil and do not discipline their children when they mistreat others. "From all that I can see, violence is *not* being avoided. Violence is the order of the day in this country," she concluded.[74] Three years later, the mainstream marketing and the reception of the *For Love of Ivy* commodified black power radicalism by quoting Lincoln in ways that blunted these political critiques and further reinforced masculine authority. The article titled "Lincoln's Brand of Domestic Tranquility" recorded Lincoln as saying, "I really wear the style for beauty reasons. I try as every woman to be as attractive as possible."[75] Again and again, profiles of Lincoln explained her hair and dress, so different from those of Ivy's, in traditional gender terms and as a cosmetic choice. The discourse about *For Love of Ivy* made black power primarily an aesthetic experience, isolated from any discussion of structural changes or power dynamics.[76] Many people referred to Lincoln's "militance," but the primary evidence for this militance had become her hair and earrings.

IN THE EARLY 1960s, Lena Horne had distanced herself from her own political past and started to identify with a younger generation of New York–based black activists, partially in response to how the civil rights movement was redefining the politics of popular culture. Because one goal of the black arts movement was to develop an "art that would reach the people, that would take them higher, ready them for war and victory," a range of African Americans took popular culture very seriously; many people connected to criss-crossing circles which linked black power, the black arts movement, and black cultural nationalism made African American culture and performing arts a locus in their quest for self-determination.[77] By the late '60s—and *Ivy* is just one example—many white critics, producers, and consumers of popular culture felt the impact of these critiques and felt the impact of ongoing black activism. They were now invested in determining who and what constituted "authentic" blackness and a distinctive black culture, and had decided that Lincoln met these standards in ways that Diahann Carroll in *Julia* did not, largely because of her appearance. "Black is beautiful" was a popular slogan and a galvanizing idea.[78] For many young black women and men, the phrase consolidated demands for greater participation in the political process and made style part of larger struggles: to establish ties to Africa, to consider the racial dimensions of American foreign policy, and to affirm identity, citizenship rights, and cultural creativity in positive ways. But the slogan was a resource for whites, too, who could support the style as an "authentic" representation of blackness without necessarily engaging the demands that accompanied political movements.

These contradictions seeped into *For Love of Ivy* and Lincoln's role. Her reputation as a jazz singer with longtime commitments to black freedom struggles around the world and her associations with black power did create fissures in the production and reception of Poitier's story. Her presence at times brought contemporary politics back into what seemed to some like a largely apolitical narrative, and there were ways in which Lincoln's extratextual reputation allowed her, and fans of the film, to resist the film's "lightness" and apparent color-blind logic. Largely due to Abbey Lincoln, even a film like *For Love of Ivy*—commercial to its core, intended to be uncontroversial in all ways, and, as many critics noted, poorly written—generated questions about black women's labor and class, about black female sexuality and independence, and about what black activism had and had not accomplished. Ivy-as-Lincoln was a domestic who was sexy and chic; she got the man on screen and got an Afro off screen. In her on-screen and real-life performances of black womanhood, Lincoln at times deployed a kind of class-based gender politics, one easy to overlook precisely because it was so rooted in consumer culture. She brought to the fore issues that black women were wrestling with in and out of social movements in the late '60s.

At the same time, this resistance was limited. In the discourse around *Ivy*, Lincoln emphasized working-class black women's needs while she celebrated the film as universal and the United States as a country where race relations had improved and was continuing to improve; she claimed black women's sexual agency while she promoted black male authority; and she affirmed gendered expressions of black power while she subordinated that affirmation to matters of personal style. Lincoln's prior connections to black power and the claims she made on behalf of working-class black women were contained by the commodity culture of which the film was a part. Ultimately, Abbey Lincoln helped constitute what was resistant and reactionary in this mass culture integration narrative.

Much had changed between 1961, when jazz critic Ira Gitler tarred Lincoln as a "professional Negro," and the release of *For Love of Ivy* in 1968. Gitler had critiqued Lincoln's performance of Negro identity on the album *Straight Ahead* and charged her with elevating black politics over aesthetic considerations. Lincoln then used the panel discussion "Racial Prejudice in Jazz" to challenge Gitler's terms. She argued that a politicized performer like herself was not a "professional Negro"; rather, it was the less-than-authentic black performers who cared only about pleasing white audiences who deserved the label. In 1968, the terms of the conversation over Lincoln's career had changed. White and black critics and fans were deeply invested in Lincoln's performance of black identity and politics; although the term Negro had fallen out of favor in the intervening seven years, it seemed appropriate and desirable for Lincoln as a black woman to be a professional embodiment of black power; it was a way to market the film and a way for white audiences to align themselves with antiracism. As with Lena Horne, the question of who and what constituted authentic blackness, and who and what was a "professional Negro," haunted Lincoln throughout her career, from her early years as a glamorous nightclub singer, into her years as a politicized jazz vocalist, and through her movie performances. Ironically, this integration narrative released in 1968 positioned her as an authentic representation of black power—in opposition to Ivy—and that authenticity legitimized Lincoln as an actress and became a way to sell the film.

The inconsistencies in Lincoln's relationship to *For Love of Ivy* should not be completely surprising. A binary model—was Lincoln as Ivy a character of resistance or accommodation? Was she anticipating elements of what would later be called feminism or not?—simply does not work, given the ways that Lincoln performed black womanhood over the course of her career. As a black woman artist, Lincoln was both ambitious and politically aware. She moved between worlds of avant-garde jazz and Hollywood celebrity in years when ideas about black activism and strategies of protest were changing and fraught, evident, in part, in the ways that fans and critics alternatively castigated and celebrated her as a politicized black woman entertainer. It makes sense that she did not hew consistently to one position about black activism or gender relations. To note the complex minefield Lincoln and other black women negotiated in mainstream mass consumer culture and to consider *For Love of Ivy* as one moment in Lincoln's intertwined professional and political trajectories is to grapple with black women entertainers' talents, dreams, and political commitments.

Years later, Diahann Carroll recalled that it had been hard for her to go from nightclubs to television and then, after *Julia* went off the air, back again to the nightclub circuit. She compared the twists and turns in her own professional life to that of Cicely Tyson, a performer who "moved in a straight line her entire career—just say her name, and you think of black ladies who are purpose oriented."[79] Tyson's "straight line" ascended in the 1970s, some years after *Ivy* and *Julia*. As Tyson became more famous, Carroll rerouted her own career to find a more "purpose-oriented" role. These "purpose-oriented" black female characters and the popular productions from the 1970s in which Tyson and Carroll starred, even more than late '60s integration narratives, became a means to remember, as well as to judge, black activism.

5

"So Beautiful in Those Rags"

CICELY TYSON, POPULAR CULTURE, AND
AFRICAN AMERICAN HISTORY IN THE 1970S

ON JANUARY 23, 1977, and for seven consecutive days thereafter, Africa—
and African American history—made it to U.S. television in ways that
seemed unprecedented. The first episode in the miniseries *Roots* was set
in a small tribal village in Gambia, West Africa, in 1750. An unseen nar-
rator announced that the series was about "the triumph of an American
family." The actual story began with an excruciating natural childbirth
sequence. Screaming and sweating, a woman labors intensively, clutching
a tree trunk. A midwife and other women assist her while a man who is
obviously her husband paces outside the tent. Finally, the woman gives
birth to a son, later named Kunta Kinte. In terms of minutes on screen,
the mother's role in this episode was small. Yet, when the credits rolled,
she received top billing. She was not just Binta: She was "Cicely Tyson AS
Binta."[1] Clearly, when *Roots* aired on ABC in 1977, television audiences
knew Tyson well.

   Roots, based on the book by Alex Haley about his ancestors, began with
Kunta Kinte (LeVar Burton) and his idyllic family and tribal life in West
Africa. The story continued with Kunta Kinte's capture in 1767 by slave
traders and his life in what would become the United States. Through the
heroic Kunta Kinte and his descendants, television audiences witnessed
the horrors of the middle passage, the brutality of slavery, and slaves' resistance to that brutality. By the final episode set after the Civil War, they saw
free blacks and "good" whites elude the Ku Klux Klan and acquire their own
land in Tennessee. The series culminated with Haley coming on screen to
bring the story up to the present. With its chronological and geographical
expanse, its huge cast, and its setting in the past, *Roots* had a grandeur that
set it apart from the gritty and amateur realism of *Come Back, Africa*, from

the glitzy sheen and middle-class ethos in integration narratives like *For Love of Ivy* and *Julia,* and from other films and television shows about African American life that were made and also set in the 1970s.[2]

Roots producers David Wolper and Stan Margulies wanted to attract as large an audience as they possibly could. But in contrast to Hal Kanter or Daniel Mann, the white men involved in making *Julia* and *For Love of Ivy,* their goal was more than light entertainment. When *Time* critic Richard Schickel called *Roots* "middle brow," the producers embraced that designation as one that allowed them to reach, and educate, large numbers. Some 135 million Americans ("120 million of them whites," according to Wolper) watched at least one episode of *Roots,* and the 12-hour series became the highest-rated television show in history up to that point. The producers took a number of steps, particularly with regard to casting, to increase the appeal of this series that they hoped would educate white Americans about slavery.[3]

Cicely Tyson was just the type of African American celebrity that Wolper and Margulies felt they needed—a known star "with whom whites felt comfortable." She had been active in television, stage, and screen dramas since the late 1950s, including roles in the off-Broadway show *The Blacks* (1961), the television show *East Side, West Side* (1963), and the film *The Heart Is a Lonely Hunter* (1968), but Tyson's big breakthrough came in 1972, when she played Rebecca, a Depression-era poor black mother, in the film *Sounder.* Two years later, she took on the title role in *The Autobiography of Miss Jane Pittman.* In this made-for-television movie, Jane's life unfolded from her years as a slave girl to her decision, as a woman of 110, to drink from a "whites-only" water fountain. Both *Sounder* and *Jane Pittman* were enormously successful productions in the United States and around the world. Tyson was nominated for an Oscar for *Sounder* and won multiple Emmys for *The Autobiography of Miss Jane Pittman.* Critics praised "the first great black heroine on the big screen" for her "sublime achievement" and for performances "so special they go beyond all the awards." Wolper and Margulies recruited Tyson for the part of Binta because she was able to infuse this opening episode set in a foreign land with the authority that she had acquired since her role in the film *Sounder* five years earlier. She helped to domesticate and Americanize this exotic opening episode of *Roots,* making it a national story about "an American family," as both the novel and the series declared.[4]

Because *Roots* was such a landmark, it has been relatively easy to consider its representation of history in isolation.[5] In fact, *Roots* extended an interest in genealogy and family history that was widespread in the 1970s and not consistently aligned with a specific political agenda. This preoccupation could be seen in films like *Fiddler on the Roof* (1971), *The Godfather* (1972), and *Mean Streets* (1973); books like Philip Roth's *Portnoy's Complaint* (1969) and Maxine Hong Kingston's *The Woman Warrior* (1976); the rise in organizations and clubs for those of Polish, Irish, Mexican, Italian, and Serbian descent; the development of ethnic studies departments on college campuses; and a restoration project at Ellis Island—a location that was once a mark of shame.[6] Still, despite the popularity of roots-like stories, most white Americans did not see much in popular culture about African American history, especially from the perspective of black people. The stunning successes of *Roots* and the other historically oriented productions in which Tyson starred suggest that they told stories that Americans wanted and were able to hear in the 1970s.

Sounder, The Autobiography of Miss Jane Pittman, and *Roots* may have been set in the Depression and in the era of slavery, but by gesturing back in time they spoke, if indirectly, to issues that were on the minds of American consumers in the 1970s, specifically with regard to race relations. These included how African Americans should continue to resist ongoing segregation and prejudice, years after passage of civil rights legislation, and the deaths, jailing, or exile of visible leaders; why family life mattered to black activism, and what kinds of African American families were—or were not—healthy; and what constituted "authentic" and politically meaningful African American culture. The film and television specials through which Tyson vaulted to the upper echelons of the entertainment industry offered "solutions" to these contemporary concerns, in part by providing what seemed to be memories about the past. The paradox was that even as African American activism persisted and developed in many political and cultural venues in the 1970s, films and television shows about earlier eras manufactured nostalgia and helped to suggest that Americans were now in a post–civil rights era.[7] The characters that Cicely Tyson chose so carefully, her performances, and their reception shed light on what role black women played in popular culture that took up black history, and how they helped create the sense that the civil rights movement was finished.

LIKE MANY CELEBRITIES, Cicely Tyson's background mattered enormously to her fans. Well before her appearance in *Roots*, her own "roots" story circulated widely. Three features recurred consistently in stories about Tyson's past: first, that although she had grown up in Harlem, her childhood was not typical of poor black urban youth; second, that she was a model before she just happened to become an actress; and third, that she was always determined to choose the content, style, and location of her performances, mostly by locating herself solidly in the world of quality drama and avoiding the music industry.

If this last quality set her apart from many of her peers, Tyson did have something important in common with Abbey Lincoln, Diahann Carroll, and Lena Horne. Like them, Tyson got her start before cameras and audiences by being glamorous. For the working-class daughter of West Indian immigrants, modeling was a stepping stone, a source of social mobility that offered a way out of what felt like a dead-end office job. In 1958, after becoming a top model, Tyson met a black actress who suggested that she read for a part in an upcoming film. The movie was never made, but Tyson was "enthralled" and began her training at "top New York acting schools." More than one critic compared Tyson's stumble into show business, which "started as a fluke," to that of Lana Turner— discovered, according to Hollywood lore, at a drugstore soda fountain. Numerous accounts by critics and fans, white and black, reported that Tyson had never even considered acting or show business before that moment because she was "too nervous" and "too shy" to act; even more, her mother "kept her out of movie houses. . . . Life revolved around the church instead."[8]

This roots story was quite different from Lena Horne's, with its emphasis on her illustrious and racial uplift–oriented family; Nina Simone's, with its emphasis on the many years she had spent studying classical piano since childhood; and Miriam Makeba's, with its assumptions about her exoticism and "natural" talent. Instead, a refrain about Tyson's religious working-class mother, her consequent isolation from American popular culture, and her brief modeling career created a reassuring set of associations. Repeated references to how Tyson's mother "had church oozing out of her every pore" and "felt exposure to movies and plays was sinful," placed the star's childhood at odds with the majority of urban youth, black or white. Or, as Tyson would recall, "All our friends went to the movies every single Saturday, but we weren't allowed." Tyson's mother may have kept her daughter from movies and boys and popular music, journalist Phyl Garland observed to readers of *Good Housekeeping*, but she had instilled in her daughter the self-discipline that Tyson would later draw on as an actor. As one headline declared, "Her Mother Made Her a Star." Tyson concurred, noting that her family had always been "on relief" and "hemmed in by crime and prostitution"; given this atmosphere, she "was grateful" to her mother for her many rules.[9]

This discourse about Tyson's childhood as virtuous and disciplined took shape in the same years that critiques of African American families in the urban North as enmeshed in corruption, crime, and sexual pathology abounded. In 1965, assistant secretary of labor Daniel Patrick Moynihan offered his "Report on Black Families" to President Johnson, in advance of the president's speech at Howard University in which he declared that "it is not enough just to open the gates of opportunity." The "Moynihan Report" identified overly weak black men and overly strong, or matriarchal, black women as evidence for a "tangle of pathology" in black families, especially among those who lived in Northern cities. The controversy that followed the release of the report placed questions about black activism in the urban North center stage. Some whites who considered themselves supporters of civil rights agreed with Moynihan and concluded that family dynamics had more to do with ongoing racial inequities than economic or structural issues. This perspective reinforced calls among some politicians and others to cut back on Aid to Families with Dependent Children (welfare) and other government programs. Whereas many black activists blasted the report and its defenders for pointing to family problems as the cause of ongoing discrimination rather than the result of institutional racism and long-term inequities in housing, employment, and education. For them, the report proved that ongoing black activism and additional federal policies were necessities.[10] The War on Poverty was oriented, in part, around giving poor people more agency. By the 1970s, however, Richard Nixon was president, and his "Southern strategy" and policies of "benign neglect" brought growing numbers of white Southerners and Northerners who wanted to halt desegregation into the Republican Party. More white Americans agreed that antipoverty programs had created even greater dependency in allegedly dysfunctional black families and that these programs supported corrupt and inefficient bureaucracies.[11]

The myth of the undeserving and promiscuous black urban woman who would not stop reproducing or scamming the government to get her welfare check and who did not really care for her children persisted among politicians, in the media, and in popular culture in the 1970s. The counterpart to that figure was the deadbeat dad, the mythical African American man who was not interested in fatherhood or other responsibilities associated with successful masculinity. In 1970, the song "Welfare Cadillac" by Guy Drake was on the charts for six weeks. Two years later, Nixon asked

Johnny Cash to perform the song at the White House to bolster his own antiwelfare credentials. As governor of California and then presidential candidate in 1976, Ronald Reagan declared war on welfare, and made the "welfare queen" part of the national conversation.[12]

Repeated references to Tyson's childhood suggested that she and her family were different from these familiar images of urban African Americans—that the Northern-born-and-bred Tyson had more in common with a rural, southern, ostensibly more "simple" and authentic African American past, imagined as this premigration past was. The discussions of Tyson's youth to which she contributed set an authentic black culture, a work ethic, and a religious mother in opposition to urban-based vices and dysfunctional families.

Tyson's early career as a model was a second feature that came up repeatedly in discussions of her background and reminded her fans in the '70s that the actress who was becoming famous for seeking out distinctly unglamorous parts was making a choice. *Sounder*'s Rebecca had braided cornrows wrapped in a rag and worked hard, sweating, in the fields. The stooped and wrinkled Jane Pittman had discolored eyes and a gold front tooth. In both instances, Tyson opted for realism and historical accuracy over glamour, and critics lauded these choices. When she claimed her protagonists represented all black women, she offered "at long last," according to one reporter, "some sense of the profound beauty of millions of black women of a certain kind whose tale has almost never been told." (This was a theme that Toni Morrison also explored in her first novel, *The Bluest Eye*, in 1970.) One profile quoted Tyson as declaring, "I'm proud of Rebecca. I think she's what life is all about."[13] Several years earlier, Nina Simone, Miriam Makeba, and Abbey Lincoln had each performed in her own way to remake the meanings of glamour with which Lena Horne and Diahann Carroll were associated; Tyson's poor, Southern, and rural fictional characters, by contrast, seemed to reject glamour completely, and profoundly challenged the equation between whiteness and beauty.

Still, these challenges had their limits. The same profile that drew attention to Rebecca as standing in for the beauty of all ordinary black women observed that the "stylish former model seemed a long way from barefoot, housedress-clad Rebecca Morgan." Similarly, in an effusive review of *The Autobiography of Miss Jane Pittman*, *New Yorker* critic Pauline Kael wrote that as Jane Pittman, Tyson "never bathes us in the ravishing smile of her modeling years. . . . Tyson won't allow her beauty to carry her; she plays Jane with supreme integrity."[14] In the fan culture chronicling

Tyson's journey from "slum to stardom," she was able to claim her un-glamorous performances of black womanhood as authentic expressions of "black is beautiful" and as expressions of black feminist thought that challenged racially specific definitions of beauty. At the same time, readers received reassurance that these were just performances on Tyson's part, because in fact she was a stylish former model whose beauty was unique and transcended race.[15]

A final ingredient in the fan discourse about Tyson's past was her seri-ousness of purpose. That Tyson stumbled into acting and then committed herself to the "long, steady, arduous trek" of learning her "craft" suggested that she was motivated more by her commitment to quality representa-tions of blackness than by money.[16] People who read the entertainment sections, women's or teen magazines, and the African American press in the 1970s were likely to learn about Tyson's struggles. Ten years earlier, she had received awards for her dramatic stage performances and gar-nered among the first serious (and nonmusical) parts for black women on television, but she had endured a great deal. Tyson was always determined to act in dramas in which she would not be "typecast" as a prostitute and could "play different types of women," with "pride, dignity, and strength." Interviewers observed that she was neither materialistic nor enmeshed in consumer culture and profiles emphasized her modest, even ascetic life-style and the financial hardships she endured because of her "concern for black women's image."[17] These stories politicized the choices Tyson made about her professional visibility.

Perhaps even more notably, the biographical narrative about Tyson in the '70s also politicized her absence from stage, television, and films. After 1964, Tyson had fewer significant roles, and from 1968 until 1972— between the films *Heart Is a Lonely Hunter* and *Sounder*—just a handful of television appearances. She "seemed to drop out of sight" after 1965, was "broke before *Sounder*," and did not even own a car when she lived with her agent in Los Angeles, according to profiles in *Redbook, Ms. Magazine,* and *Essence: A Magazine for Today's Black Woman.* But, the media sug-gested, she was not just a passive supplicant to the Hollywood industry. As coverage in the 1970s of Tyson's career from the '60s noted, she had waited "four long years" because she had become "increasingly discrimi-nating." In contrast to so many other entertainers, the "soul which is so much hers, she did not sell en route; and that took guts when she had nothing else with which to barter."[18] In fact, Tyson's romantic relationship with Miles Davis played at least some part in her relative absence from the stage and screen in the mid- to late 1960s.[19] The point is not to determine what kept Tyson out of the public eye during turbulent and vital years of African American activism.[20] What stands out is how once she did achieve superstar status in the 1970s, black and white fans and critics tended to explain even her professional invisibility in terms of her authenticity and her commitments to African American culture. Consequently, what might have been narrated as a fallow professional period instead became part of a seamless story about political convictions and politically significant performances of black womanhood.

As Tyson became a celebrity in the early 1970s and with these pieces of her background in place, many retold the story of how she had decided, some ten years earlier, to wear her hair "natural." Tyson had first cut her hair in 1959 when she portrayed an African woman who resists her husband's efforts to modernize himself in an episode of the television drama *Camera Three*, "Between Yesterday and Today," during which she consulted with Miriam Makeba. She maintained her short Afro in her role as secretary to a white social worker on *East Side, West Side*. Tyson was thus part of a larger group of black women entertainers who stopped straightening their hair in this period. But in the 1970s—after Abbey Lincoln's "natural" hair became one way to sell *For Love of Ivy*; after Angela Davis's Afro became the definitive symbol of both radical politics and fashion, or "revolutionary glamour," as she has put it; and after James Brown's hit song "I'm Black and I'm Proud" became a mainstream hit—Tyson's hair and her reputation as the "first" offered her '70s self certain credentials.[21]

Hair became another piece of evidence that Tyson had always been willing to make unpopular choices because of her investment in black culture and black liberation. By taking the "then daring step of having her hair cut into television's first Afro-natural," according to *People* magazine, she had "set off a national furor—and trend—among blacks," wrote *Ebony*. In interviews in the 1970s, Tyson asserted that performing dignified black women with natural hair had been her way of doing political work: "I had to make a choice and I decided that I could not afford the luxury of just being an actress. I had some very definite statements to make. It was my way of picketing." As a profile in *Ms.* observed, Tyson had always been "discreet" about her politics, but "during those early years," her "style was interpreted as revolutionary."[22] Mostly, though, discussions in the 1970s of Tyson's hair ten years earlier affirmed progress. Tyson was able to look back and say, "We have come a long way from that day in 1959 when I first cut my hair. The fact that we have gone from imitating white people's hair to the close crop to the big bush to the braids was an immense progress."[23]

These narratives about Cicely Tyson's past connected her to black activism stretching back into the late 1950s and stretching forward into the 1970s, and legitimated her status as an entertainer who could perform black womanhood authentically. She could denote respectable church-based activism and boycotts, and declarations that "black is beautiful" and various aspects of black power, including the welfare rights movement. Tyson's roots stories and the assumptions they evoked—about her vice-free childhood, her beauty, and her hair as evidence of the progress that African Americans had made through the civil rights movement—contributed to the impact that *Sounder*, *Miss Jane Pittman*, and *Roots* would have. Stories about Tyson set the stage for the subtle ways in which audiences viewed her characters from the past in relation to their own lives and contemporary concerns.

SET IN RURAL Louisiana in 1933, *Sounder* offered a straightforward narrative about a black family's efforts to cope with poverty and hunger. At the outset, the father, Nathan Morgan (Paul Winfield) goes hunting at night with his eldest son David Lee (Kevin Hooks) and the family dog, Sounder. When they fail to catch anything, Nathan slips out of the house again. He steals a ham from a white landowner to feed his wife and three children. They eat well, but the next day the white sheriff arrests Nathan; he is quickly tried, convicted of trespass and robbery, and sentenced to a year of hard labor. The film then shifts its attention to the family, especially the eldest son. David Lee works the fields with his mother, Rebecca. He helps her care for his younger siblings and even makes the long journey on foot to another county in search of the prison camp where Nathan may be. While he is looking for his father, David Lee comes upon a one-room school for black children. The African American teacher (Janet MacLachlan) welcomes him and later invites the education-hungry David Lee to live with her so that he may go to the school on a regular basis. David Lee is initially reluctant to leave home, especially after his father and the dog return, both limping. But his father encourages him to take advantage of this opportunity. The film ends as Nathan drives his son in mule and buggy away from their rural shack and toward the future.

Celebrated for its realism and quality, *Sounder* was directed by Martin Ritt, a white filmmaker known for his independence, and for his long-term investment in left politics, antiracism, and resistance to red-baiting. His earlier films *Edge of the City* (1957) and *Paris Blues* (starring Diahann Carroll

in 1961) both featured interracial friendships and emphasized the importance of committing to a cause. Ritt worked on *Sounder* in collaboration
with the toy company Mattel, producer Robert Radnitz, and screenwriter
Lonne Elder, an African American writer-actor who was part of a black
avant-garde left and the Black Arts Movement. Elder's 1969 play, "Ceremonies in Dark Old Men," developed in the Negro Ensemble Company, a
black-controlled company, and then moved to an extended off-Broadway
run. "Ceremonies" was "as meaningful a theatrical event as Lorraine Hansberry's 'Raisin in the Sun,'" according to theater critic Mel Gussow. *Sounder*
thus marked a successful fusion between independent filmmaking, Hollywood, and the black arts movement; and between the old Left and black
activism in the '70s.[24] The team that worked on *Sounder* believed in the
democratic potential of mass culture. As would be the case with *Roots* a few
years later, everyone in this production team was committed to blending
quality culture with relevant questions about race in ways that had wide
commercial appeal. The reception of *Sounder* suggested that this formula,
coupled with an aggressive marketing campaign, could be effective.[25]

Audiences and critics across lines of race, region, and political affiliation saluted *Sounder* in extravagant and emotional terms. "A Beautiful
Black Movie" was the headline in the *New York Amsterdam News*. "Like
most classics, simply beyond imitation," said another reviewer. "Soviet
leaders weep at 'Sounder' screening," noted *Variety*. In February 1973,
Sounder made Hollywood history when it was nominated for four Academy
Awards (for best actor, actress, screenplay, and film). "Wild horses couldn't
drag me away," wrote one African American journalist in anticipation of
the televised Oscars ceremony.[26]

Two other movies set in the past, Francis Ford Coppola's *The Godfather*
and Bob Fosse's *Cabaret* won the lion's share of Academy Awards, but the
acclaim that *Sounder* received went beyond film critics or awards ceremonies. Accolades came from Coretta Scott King, Harvard University
president Derek Bok, who spoke to faculty and students on what was designated Cicely Tyson Day, and even members of Congress. In March 1973,
Senator Claiborne Pell (RI) endorsed *Sounder* in Congress, as a film that
went "beyond mere entertainment to produce a work of art" that "appeals
to all of us human beings." Michigan congressman Charles Diggs introduced a "personal resolution" to "highly recommend *Sounder* to all [his]
Colleagues in the Congress and to audiences through the world."[27] *Sounder*
was thus celebrated as a story with universal appeal and as an effective
means through which to teach African American history. Schools and

religious groups booked blocks of seats for student trips to see the film; the studio assembled and distributed sample "letters to educators" and offered a *Sounder* study guide designed to provide "many ways for a teacher to lead students in provocative discussions" after seeing the film.[28]

In the chorus of praise, one theme stood out. Critics, fans, educators, and organization leaders lauded *Sounder*'s loving black family: *Sounder*, wrote the reviewer in the *Wall Street Journal*, offers a "rare" and "much needed picture of loving and responsible black family life." "At last," wrote *Time*, "a compassionate and loving film" about black families. Roy Innis, director of the civil rights organization CORE, offered similar sentiments: "I have long awaited black films which black families could view without feeling insecure or ashamed."[29] At the emotional center of *Sounder* were Nathan and Rebecca Morgan, black parents who love each other and their children in ways that seemed remarkable to audiences in 1972. As Pauline Kael noted in the *New Yorker*, "the ironic miracle of *Sounder*," was "that whites could respond to its black family far more intensely than they could conceivably now respond to a white family."[30]

FIGURE 5.1 "At last," wrote *Time*, about *Sounder*, "a compassionate and loving film" about black families.

(Academy of Motion Picture Arts and Sciences)

The loving black family in *Sounder* appealed to diverse audiences in part because it was a source of reassurance at the same time that it was a source of resistance. Progress beckons to parents and children not because anyone challenges the status quo overtly or violently, or because laws or policies change, or because anyone joins an organization whose members agitate for anything. The situation for the Morgans improves and David Lee gains access to a good education simply because as a family, they work hard, love each other, and are able to get along with both whites and blacks. With its pastoral settings, its hard-working and loving black men who wear overalls and hard-working black women whose hair is braided or wrapped, and its soundtrack consisting of acoustic guitar and harmonica by folk-blues musician Taj Mahal, *Sounder's* vision of family life seemed to negate the calls for black power and the urgency of black activism that was prevalent in 1972. It seemed to celebrate all that Nina Simone had rejected so vehemently in 1963 with "Mississippi Goddam." Together, Nathan and Rebecca as loving parents suggested that "survival with injustice can be heroic," one observer noted. This was a comforting message to some audiences in an era of inflation and rising rates of unemployment as well as a backlash against the civil rights movement among groups of white Americans.[31]

Alongside this moderate message, *Sounder's* family did offer occasional glimpses of anger and overt resistance to white supremacy. Critics and fans agreed that family life in *Sounder* revolved around Cicely Tyson as Rebecca—"so beautiful in those rags," as Toni Morrison described her in *Ms.* in 1972.[32] At several junctures, Rebecca confronts the inequities in her life directly. She challenges a white sheriff who will not let her see her imprisoned husband, declaring, "You got yourself a low-life job, Mr. Sheriff." Later, she even takes on a traditional source of African American authority: the black church. When the Morgan's suit-clad, African American minister tells her that he will not help the family locate Nathan, the usually deferential Rebecca says that "it's a damn shame" he feels that way. To his response that she should not be bitter because "we brought nothing into this life, we carry nothing out," she merely says, "Is that a blessing, Reverend?" In these scenes, Rebecca rejects those who passively accept the status quo and is impatient with older African American authorities—sentiments that many younger black activists felt in the '60s and into the '70s when they formed their own organizations without clergy at the helm.

For the most part, Rebecca, far more than Nathan, endures heroically and in relative silence as she supports her husband and props up her eldest son. An incomplete list of adjectives and descriptions that critics used to praise Rebecca suggest what qualities in black women garnered approval in 1972: she was the "stoic wife" with a "quiet strength" who "suffers in quiet," and "THE strong black woman" and "rip-cord-tough mother who binds the family tightly together with sheer will."[33] According to yet another extensive discussion of Tyson-as-Rebecca: "Rebecca functions basically as a follower and a sustainer. . . . The role is historically accurate because the black family, no less than the white, is patriarchal." Moreover, by recovering this overlooked history, "Tyson may have provoked another revolution."[34]

FIGURE 5.2 Cicely Tyson as Rebecca Morgan in *Sounder*, "so beautiful in those rags," according to *Ms*.

(Academy of Motion Picture Arts and Sciences)

This praise for *Sounder's* patriarchal black family provoking "another revolution" appeared in a profile of Tyson in *Ms.*, the magazine perhaps most closely associated with second-wave feminism and its critiques of patriarchy. Tyson repeatedly offered similar sentiments in many other interviews. Before the film opened to rave reviews in London, she told a reporter that *Sounder* was "the first black positive film which shows us as human beings and says something about the unity of the black family." It was "significant" because there was "never, ever, a positive image of a full home life with both mother and father figures and with warmth, beauty, love and understanding," she said in *The New York Times*. In fact, "if it weren't for that kind of family," Tyson noted in an interview in *Seventeen*, "we would not be where we are today as a race of people."[35] In these and other conversations about the film, a consensus developed that Rebecca mattered because she was a wife and mother who supported her family, especially the husband/father. Her strength did not make her a dangerous matriarch. Together, the fictional Rebecca and Nathan Morgan did more to challenge Moynihan's "tangle of pathology" than many social scientists and activists could.

Like Rebecca, Nathan Morgan is a tremendously appealing character. Even more than Rebecca, his appeal lies in his contradictory qualities: He is a smiling, hard-working, and warm man, but he is occasionally aggressive and angry. Nathan can move between these positions of accommodation and resistance only because his position as father and husband is so secure. For example, immediately before Nathan steals the ham, he hunts with his son and dog, and then returns home to his loving wife, who wraps him in a hug. By juxtaposing the off-screen theft with his loving family life, *Sounder* does not question Nathan's morality or his masculinity, since both are tightly bound to his position as head of this family. At a time when images of black men as violent criminals or lazy deadbeats were invoked by politicians and sociologists, and appeared regularly in popular culture, Nathan stood out. The film implicitly endorsed his technically illegal act of resistance against a white landowner. "I did what I had to do," he says to Rebecca, to survive not just a bad harvest, but also a system of white supremacy that kept black sharecroppers in poverty.

Similarly, the crucial scene in which Southern white men arrest Nathan comes just after his victory as a pitcher in a baseball game with other black men as his wife, children, and neighbors cheer him on. Many of them walk home together, joking and laughing, and with one friend playing the harmonica and singing, only to find the sheriff's truck waiting. As with the theft, Nathan's encounter with a white-controlled power structure comes immediately after audiences are reassured of his authority as loving father and husband. Initially, Nathan neither challenges the white men's claims verbally nor resists arrest physically. In contrast to other disaffected 1970s film heroes who lived in cities and who loved to take on established authorities, including the African American actor Melvin Van Peebles in *Sweet Sweetback's Baadasssss Song* and the white Clint Eastwood in the original *Dirty Harry* (both in 1971), Nathan does not resist a white-controlled power structure.

Nathan's relationship to authority evoked mixed responses. Some critics and fans applauded his initial acquiescence as further evidence of the film's realism and of the character's dignity. One British journalist loved that the film did not "impose on its hungry black sharecroppers the aggressive militancy of another generation of Negroes." Pauline Kael said that *Sounder* evoked "the memory of the black people in the recent civil-rights demonstrations who put on their Sunday clothes to be beaten up in."[36] But the source for one critic's nostalgia could be the source of another's ire, and the relatively few voices that disapproved of *Sounder* objected to the "dated" and "deliberately apolitical social drama" in which "all aggression is sublimated into an ideology of self-help." *Sounder* placed audiences "back in Sidney Poitier land," according to one review, while another reported that one "black actor told me angrily that he would never lay a part in which a black man was shown as submissive."[37]

As other critics also noted, Nathan does not only submit to white authority. When the white sheriff lifts his gun to shoot the dog that is chasing their truck, a chained Nathan knocks the gun with his leg. The bullet hits Sounder, but Nathan saves the beloved family dog from a lethal injury. With this kick, the film departed conspicuously from the white-authored novel on which the film was based, and altered the tenor of the film significantly. Such an action in the 1930s would have resulted in violence to Nathan. Audiences in 1972 may imagine but do not see such white-on-black violence on screen, which provides even more evidence of his heroism. This was a moment when more confrontational strategies of black activism made their way into this mainstream Hollywood film in ways that kept the noble Nathan from being "too" noble and outside of "Sidney Poitier land," according to most fans of *Sounder*.[38]

Thus, the loving family reinforced the film's emphasis on survival and a politics oriented around accommodation and at several junctures, also did the opposite: *Sounder* relied on family to negate the apparent emphasis on endurance as resistance.[39] Especially through its depiction of a loving black father and mother, *Sounder* fleetingly forged a hybrid black politics in which acquiescence coexisted with more confrontational strategies of resistance.

Placed in the context of the early 1970s and an even longer history of performing black women, Rebecca as loving wife and mother did stand out as "revolutionary," as *Ms.* put it. The character marked a dramatic departure in historically entrenched images of black women on screen: She was not one of many desexualized "mammies" to white children as Hattie McDaniel had been in *Gone with the Wind*, and she was not a "sex symbol," respectable or otherwise, as Lena Horne's Georgia Brown had been in *Cabin in the Sky*. Rebecca also provided an alternative to the chic middle-class respectability associated with just a few, usually light-skinned, black women stars like Diahann Carroll in her role as Julia. Even more than Abbey Lincoln as Ivy, Tyson as Rebecca, with her worn clothes, sweaty face, and wrapped head, valued black women's labor and under-mined racially specific standards of beauty and sexuality, as well as as-sumptions about black mothers as undeserving. As one white woman wrote to Tyson, "I never knew that kind of love went on between a black man and woman. I thought you were sexual animals." Perhaps this letter-writer was thinking of the reunion between Nathan and Rebecca when he returns from prison, an intensely loving and romantic scene that affirms loyalty, family, and passionate desire in both Nathan and Rebecca.[40] A pho-tograph from this scene—a rear view shot of Nathan surrounded by his wife and children with their arms around each other—became the visual marker for *Sounder* most commonly used in advertisements and other marketing material in and out of the United States.[41]

As a result of all that she stood for, the fictional Rebecca and Tyson as a representative of her became figurative allies to activist women around the country. In 1967, local groups of poor women who had been meeting in cities, towns, and rural areas for years to discuss their rights as welfare recipients formed the National Welfare Rights Organization. At its peak in the late 1960s, the welfare rights movement may have included up to 100,000 people, including black and white women. Notable successes of welfare activists supported by the NWRO included winning higher monthly benefits and, in Nevada in 1971, reversing decisions to terminate benefits. Although many demands remained unmet and the NWRO col-lapsed in 1975, numerous groups challenged negative depictions of wel-fare recipients and used innovative strategies to expose the connections between economic justice, black liberation, and women's rights. These

issues were at the heart of *Sounder*'s family and Rebecca Morgan's struggles in the 1930s, and shaped Tyson's conversations about the film.[42] In
interviews, Tyson emphasized that while her own mother had received
welfare, she had "instilled in her children a sense of self-sufficiency," and
that receiving aid had not made her family suspect. Further, Tyson was so
determined to get the part of Rebecca because she wanted to counter a
widespread cultural and political discourse about black families in general
and black mothers in particular. As she explained:

> I felt Rebecca in every sinew of my body. I knew her. She was every
> Black woman throughout history, every Black woman that society
> forces into the role of protector when it either takes away, or
> threatens to take away her husband. She was the glue that held the
> family together, the glue and the guts. Here was the love that made
> him, the head of the house, stand just a little bit taller. And this was
> what I had to be.[43]

The Black Woman, the 1970 landmark anthology edited by Toni Cade,
included poetry, manifestos, and essays about bodies, beauty, and birth
control, about welfare rights and theater; about black men's attitudes
toward women; and about events in Mississippi and Algiers. It did not
offer a consensus, but consolidated the range of concerns black women
had been voicing since the 1950s at the same time that it set the stage for
a flourishing of what more black women were calling black feminism and
what Alice Walker would identify as a "womanist" perspective some years
later.[44] *Sounder*'s reception placed Tyson at the center of this outpouring. If
Rebecca was the "every Black woman" that Tyson "had to be," then, as a
result of portraying Rebecca, Tyson became that "every black woman" to
her fans. She remained so well after *Sounder* left the theaters.

IT WOULD BE two years before audiences got another glimpse of Cicely
Tyson acting on screen. On January 31, 1974, *The Autobiography of Miss
Jane Pittman*, a made-for-television film, aired on CBS. Its major sponsor,
Xerox, felt the story was so important that it interrupted the lengthy special only once during the entire two hours for a commercial break. Critics
agreed. "Don't let anything or anyone prevent you from being near a television set when 9 p.m., Thursday rolls around," declared one reviewer the
day before the special aired. By the next morning, the program had already
become, according to one ad, "what Americans are talking about."[45]

In the months that followed, *The Autobiography of Miss Jane Pittman* won numerous awards, including a record-breaking nine Emmys. Several years before the VCR became a common household item that freed consumers to watch what they liked on television whenever and as often as they wanted, CBS took the unusual step of airing the special a second time. Pauline Kael gave *The Autobiography of Miss Jane Pittman* what was perhaps the ultimate seal of cultural approval when she declared, in her *New Yorker* film column, that it was "quite possibly the finest movie ever made for television."[46] Even before Tyson won the Emmy for best actress, she attended a champagne reception to honor her and *The Autobiography of Miss Jane Pittman* at the Kennedy Center in Washington, D.C., where politicians from both sides of the aisle discussed the Watergate scandal and shared the spotlight with entertainers like Jack Valenti, president of the Motion Picture Association of America, and John Schneider, president of CBS.[47] This second role for which Tyson received such exuberant recognition reinforced her reputation as an international celebrity who had the authority to represent a certain type of black women from the past in a certain type of way. Because of the qualities in the women she portrayed, she remained deeply associated with entertainment that had mass appeal, and with progressive antiracist politics.

The Autobiography of Miss Jane Pittman used the fictional "Miss Jane" to narrate African American history from slavery to civil rights. It was direct about its relationship to contemporary racial politics in ways that *Sounder* was not. Over the course of the two hours, the 110-year-old Jane describes her life to a young white male reporter from New York who is interested in writing a "feature story" about the oddity of a woman who was once a slave. "A what?" asks the elderly Jane when she hears the word "feature," confusing newspapers, radio, and Ed Sullivan's television show before starting to talk to the young man. In the first of a series of flashbacks, audiences learn, as does the reporter, about Jane's childhood as a slave on a plantation. In the immediate aftermath of the Civil War, former slaves debate whether or not to head north. The active and aggressive "Big Laura," played by folk singer Odetta, leads a group of former slaves who choose mobility, but they face danger and brutal violence from a gang of white men. "Big Laura" fights back against the men and is killed; her son is left to Jane. The two are unable to make it to their destination in Ohio, and they remain in the South.

Flashbacks to key moments in Jane's life continued, and through this device, the series brought to light daily life for ordinary African Americans living in the rural South from the 1870s into the twentieth century. The focus remained on those who were not "the one," Jane's phrase for unique black men who were potential leaders. Director John Korty was attentive to the ways that economic and racial hierarchies in the South combined to keep many African Americans "in their place"—literally—by tying them to manual labor on land that they did not own. *The Autobiography of Miss Jane Pittman* also repeatedly exposed as myth the "we're all a family" ethos; one white landowner utters these words to suggest interracial domestic intimacy immediately before he threatens black sharecroppers with eviction. The show culminated in what the film designated as Jane's "present," 1962, as the wrinkled and hunched woman slowly walks to a "whites only" water fountain in her hometown of Bayonne, Louisiana. She does so before white authorities wielding nightsticks and guns, and as members of the black community look on. The now-awestruck reporter, who had left the region to cover John Glenn's space landing, returns as a witness; he has realized that Jane Pittman is, as he tells his editor, far more than "just another human interest story." *New York Times* critic John O'Connor was one among many who applauded this "splendid" and "ingeniously constructed format for a history of black people in the United States, specifically in the South."[48]

In part because it was so unusual for an illiterate African American woman to sit at the center of a story without a charismatic leader as protagonist, it was Tyson herself who critics singled out for the most kudos. "It is possible that other actresses could have given adequate performances, but Miss Tyson was sheer perfection," wrote a typically enthusiastic reviewer in the *Chicago Defender*.[49] The focus on Tyson was also the result of the film's use of a single heroine across a century to suggest what mattered to black history. And what mattered in this production was the insistent theme of violence by whites against blacks. Over the decades, Jane endures discrimination, even racist brutality, with honor and forbearance; that she and her loved ones do not necessarily succeed in making big changes does not make her less heroic. As one white critic observed, "Miss Jane watches history from the sidelines. . . . Her main accomplishment is that she has survived, but that survival somehow embodies the activity of her people."[50]

When critics described Jane as embodying "the activity of her people" by surviving, they consolidated a certain narrative about black "activity"— and activism—that included a seemingly unimportant woman like Jane, but that also excluded a great deal. Narrow geographical boundaries were one means through which the film confined the story politically. As was the case with the intensely personal and domestic *Sounder*, issues and events having to do with black history beyond the rural South were rarely mentioned. Moreover, because Jane was so emphatically ordinary, organizations—Southern or national—in which groups of African Americans worked together toward change prior to 1962 were rarely part of the storyline. The three (male) characters whose strategies of resistance are different from Jane's, those who might be "the one" as she puts it, are eliminated. This trilogy of loss begins during the Reconstruction era, when Jane's adopted son, Ned, must flee the South and Klan violence after he organizes a Negro rights committee. Even before the audience sees him head north, the elderly Jane tells the reporter that "Reconstruction never really worked," a declaration that frames this segment.

The theme of loss and endurance continues when, twenty years later, Ned returns to the South. Now married, college-educated, and a veteran of the Spanish-American War, he bravely starts a school for black children. But he continues to take these stands alone and with the mantle of martyr upon him. In a speech Ned gives to the small black community, he rejects the word "nigger," but also rejects any connections to Africa, to pan-African movements like Marcus Garvey's Universal Negro Improvement Association, or to any other organization for that matter. Instead, he casts black African tribes as responsible for slavery and makes patriotic claims for African American citizenship: "I want my children to be black and proud of it. This land, America, belongs to us all." Ned concludes this speech with a whisper to Jane, "I'm gonna die, Mamma." And indeed he does—at the hands of a Cajun hit man. Ned refuses the order to "crawl" after being shot once, but he otherwise does not resist what feels like the inevitable. He insists that a black ally who is with him when the shooter confronts them leave the scene, even though this friend insists that together they could "take him."

Similar dynamics of violence and loss structure Jane's other relationships. As a young woman, Jane marries Joe Pittman, a fiercely independent and attractive black cowboy; he sells his shotgun and horse to free them both from sharecropping, and they move to an interracial ranch in Texas. Here there are the moments of joy and evidence of Jane's sexuality. However, when Joe tries to tame a white stallion—over Jane's objections— he is killed, and Jane returns to sharecropping in the rural South.[51] Finally, Jane loses Jimmy, another surrogate son, whom Jane calls "the one" from the time of his birth. It is Jimmy, early in the film, who asks Jane to protest publicly against segregation. He wants her "to inspire the others," but she refuses. Only after he too is killed, in prison, does Jane makes the long and solitary walk to the water fountain.

Through its aging female heroine, *The Autobiography of Miss Jane Pittman* narrated African American history and the development of the civil rights movement as rooted in "ordinary" African Americans, and in nonviolent, largely individual, and passive struggles for integration with whites in the South. The charismatic characters, mostly men, who insist on their political rights are killed by racist whites (or white horses). Their deaths are easy to anticipate, but no less painful because of their predictability; the recurring violence refocuses the attention on to the suffering but enduring Jane. Even before her climactic walk to the water fountain, the barren Jane raises two young boys into strong and courageous men. As critics noted, through this act of raising other African Americans as well as in that final scene, *The Autobiography of Miss Jane Pittman* figured Tyson-as-Jane as mother of the race.[52]

By eliminating certain characters, *The Autobiography of Miss Jane Pittman* suppressed the internationalist perspective that had informed decades of black activism as well as calls for global black power that continued in the 1970s. Over 8,000 people attended the National Black Political Convention in Gary, Indiana, in March 1972, for example, where participants included Black Panthers, Nation of Islam members, Democratic Party activists, and a range of public figures from Amiri Baraka to Coretta Scott King. Resolutions against apartheid in South Africa and for Palestinian independence passed alongside discussions of urban renewal, education, and welfare rights. It was a disparate agenda and group, united only in support of the idea that it was "Nation Time!" for black Americans and confirming the *Washington Post*'s headline: "Black Power Comes of Age."[53] A few months later, African Liberation Day (ALD) brought together Black Power grassroots activists and prominent leaders in cities throughout the Americas. Demonstrators generally supported a pan-African sensibility and progressive governments in Africa, and sometimes had more specific agendas. In Washington, D.C., participants at a "massive demonstration" (estimates ranged from 10,000 to 30,000) protested apartheid and U.S.–South Africa relations. While African Americans in the 1970s did not have one single global vision or agree on a particular goal or strategy, these and other developments—including an increased interest in Africa among members of the Congressional Black Caucus, a "sports boycott," and the targeting of American corporations that invested in South Africa, and the growth of black studies programs at universities around the country—were among the expressions of a vital pan-African diasporic sensibility.[54] The rural and consistently Southern *Autobiography of Miss Jane Pittman* excluded this black diasporic experience and African American urban cultures and politics, rendering Jane Pittman's story the representative narrative for all African American people.

In the many conversations that this television special set in motion, female heroism had as much to do with Tyson the actress as with Jane the character. It was not always clear whether the fictional Jane Pittman or the actress Cicely Tyson stood in for "the" race. For weeks, critics discussed extensively the transformations in Tyson's body and what she endured and accomplished physically to play this part. The *Baltimore Afro-American* was just one among many publications to feature a five-photo "evolution" sequence showing Tyson at different points in the film alongside photos of the makeup experts at work. Reviewers and fans repeatedly noted that Tyson's "make-up took six hours to prepare." The "shoulder twitches, the shaking hands, the loss of voice . . . Tyson had them all," wrote poet Nikki Giovanni.[55] In a two-hour show that covered 100 years, Tyson's body itself became a visible sign for African American suffering and endurance.

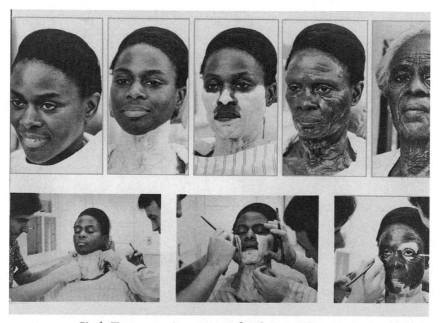

FIGURE 5.3 Cicely Tyson at various stages of makeup application during the filming of *The Autobiography of Miss Jane Pittman*. Many critics emphasized all that Tyson endured to become Jane Pittman.

(Hulton Archives/Getty Images)

As a result, Tyson emerged as heroic and politically relevant because she could play the part of Jane, at the same time that Jane emerged as heroic and politically relevant because Tyson played her. But in neither arena did an African American woman engage in organized activism in any consistent way. This dynamic was also in play when numerous civil rights organizations gave Tyson awards for performing the roles of Jane and Rebecca; in these instances too, the political significance of Tyson and her fictional counterparts stood in for each other, and it was the performance of black womanhood in and of itself that emerged as significant.[56]

The Autobiography of Miss Jane Pittman was not without its critics. One bemoaned the "cosy [sic] assurance" white audiences received in the final scene. "If Jane can drink at the fountain, then America is safe. . . . *It's all over now.*" According to another skeptic, the final minutes created the impression that the "real" political story had only started in 1962. But these perspectives did not have much traction. When the article "Did 'Jane Pittman' Really Show Us Black History?" raised these and other limitations, the *New York Times* got angry reprisals, including a full-page response from poet Nikki Giovanni, with the headline "'Jane Pittman' Fulfilled My Deepest Expectations."[57] Critical perspectives simply could not counter the appeal that the film had or the deep investment so many people made in a production that merged high-quality culture, commercial appeal—more than 50 million viewers watched it during its first showing, according to CBS—and progressive politics. *The Autobiography* elevated the status of television, and television elevated the appeal of *The Autobiography*. Here was a version of black history that was "too good for television," as representative Charles Diggs put it.[58]

SOUNDER AND *THE* Autobiography of Miss Jane Pittman celebrated ordinary African Americans and their capacity for endurance and love. In both, white directors associated with independent filmmaking were determined to tell a meaningful story about black characters and some degree of interracial cooperation in ways that had commercial appeal. In both, black heroines supported the men in their lives, engaged in arduous manual labor while claiming their respectability, and were not sexualized objects of white male desire or caretakers of white children. Critics' admiration for Jane echoed the acclaim that Rebecca had received two years earlier. Finally, many critics and fans across lines of race agreed that the film and television show represented African American people and black culture in authentic and politically meaningful ways. This was an important political goal among advocates of black power from the late 1950s onward. In the 1970s, it was evident in poetry and literature and local black political and cultural organizations, but it also had an impact on popular music and the mainstream media.[59]

If many African Americans and whites welcomed the productions in which Tyson starred, other versions of blackness on screen did not meet these high standards. Reactions to other performances of blackness in popular culture in this period highlight the stakes in battles over how African Americans and African American history would appear in popular culture, and also suggest the role that gender played in these debates.

In 1967, William Styron's novel about the slave rebellion that Nat Turner led in 1831 garnered commendation and condemnation. *The Confessions of Nat Turner* won the Pulitzer Prize and earned the approval of respected scholars, including the preeminent African American historian John Hope Franklin and C. Vann Woodward, a noted white historian of the South who declared that the book was "the most profound fictional treatment of slavery in our literature."[60] The novel also inspired fierce criticism, including an anthology by prominent African American intellectuals and activists. "No event in recent years has touched and stirred the black intellectual community more than this book," wrote writer and historian John Henrik Clarke in his introduction to *William Styron's Nat Turner: Ten Black Writers Respond*.[61] Contributors argued that Styron's account was inauthentic and historically inaccurate. He had gotten the facts, slaves' speech patterns, family dynamics, goals, and religion all wrong, and, as a result, had transformed slave resistance into pathology. As Charles Hamilton, author with Stokely Carmichael of *Black Power* (1967), wrote, Nat Turner's rebellion remained important to black Americans "because its lesson is that there will be leaders who *will* rise up—against all odds—to strike blows for freedom." Above all, the "ten black writers," all black men, charged Styron with distorting Turner's masculinity and with transforming the "virile, commanding, courageous figure" into a psychologically damaged, "impotent, cowardly, irresolute creature" who was "pining for white women." Ossie Davis would observe in his review of this anthology that the collection expressed "more than anger" and "more than blackness." Responses to Styron, he said, constituted "scholarship, justice, high confrontation" and even "warning."[62]

When producer David Wolper bought the rights to make Styron's novel into a film in 1967, the controversy escalated. Wolper hired Norman Jewison to direct and James Earl Jones to star in the lead role. Louise

Meriwether, a black woman novelist and journalist then working for Universal Studios, spearheaded a campaign in Hollywood to oppose the film. She and actor Ossie Davis formed the Black Anti-Defamation Association (BADA), which, under Meriwether's leadership, received support from a broad spectrum of Los Angeles civil rights organizations—the NAACP, Urban League, and Black Panther Party—as well as leaders like Amiri Baraka, Stokely Carmichael, and H. Rap Brown; Meriwether also wrote to Martin Luther King about the group's efforts shortly after meeting with him in Los Angeles in March 1968. The ad hoc group involved both African American consumers and well-known performers and writers in the protest. Meriwether advertised in African American newspapers nationally, solicited letters of support from readers, organized students who passed out brochures about the campaign against the film, and collected supporting signatures on college campuses. BADA also took out advertisement on the back page of the *Hollywood Reporter* addressed "To All Black Actors." This full-page ad included a statement from Ossie Davis, with the names of forty supporting organizations, calling for a black boycott of the "dangerous" film. "For a black actor," Davis wrote, "to lend his craft, his body, and his soul to such a flagrant libel against one of our greatest heroes, would be to have one of us become an agent for the enemy. . . . It is quite possible I would despise such a man who would do such a thing."[63]

Since *Birth of a Nation* in 1915 and *Gone with the Wind* in 1939, African Americans had protested representations of African Americans and African American history on film. Although *Cabin in the Sky*, one of the few films in which Lena Horne starred and was not just "pasted to a pillar," had a Broadway pedigree, a story that featured black actors as heroes and villains, and a cast with a record of success and crossover appeal among blacks and whites, many African American leaders and some white critics nevertheless felt that the film's apparently nostalgic depictions of rural African Americans were insulting if not dangerous; *Cabin* reinforced "misconceptions of the Negro," wrote Ramona Lewis in the *New York Amsterdam News*, as simple "folk" with "heads tied up with crap shooting inclinations and prayer meeting propensities." Representatives from the NAACP concluded that the film "follows the same old pattern" and that "in its present form the picture is a disservice to racial relations"— although they did not officially condemn it or seek to boycott theaters that showed it, as some critics had hoped.[64] Regardless of these perspectives, fans of Lena Horne, Ethel Waters, Eddie "Rochester" Anderson, Duke

Ellington, and other stars loved *Cabin in the Sky*; crowds of African Americans stood on long lines around the block to buy tickets at the Capitol Theater in New York.[65]

Twenty-five years later, there was no such split, as protests against a possible movie about Nat Turner included ordinary fans, organizations, and celebrity/activists. Moreover, these protests had a significant impact. In a series of meetings between Meriwether's and Wolper's groups, the Hollywood insiders agreed to BADA's main demands. The extraordinary contract that both sides signed in 1969 included guarantees that "the picture will project a positive image of Nat Turner as a black revolutionary" and that it would not "be based solely upon 'The Confessions of Nat Turner' by William Styron, but upon a variety of source materials." The title of the proposed film would not even be *The Confessions of Nat Turner*. Meriwether and other opponents of the proposed film, in turn, agreed to stop "picketing, demonstrations and boycotts."[66]

There is no way of knowing what the film's final name might have been because it was never made. Louise Meriwether and William Styron were among those who felt that the pressures BADA had exerted and the politics that surrounded the proposed film contributed to this decision, while other evidence suggests that Twentieth Century-Fox cancelled production for economic reasons.[67] Either way, this episode suggests the degree to which debates about how popular culture narrated black history were also debates about black power, resistance, and activism. Meriwether, Davis, and so many others objected to the proposed film because of what it suggested about black activism and resistance in the past and the present; to besmirch and degrade the former was akin to besmirching and degrading the latter. Numerous talented black actors in Hollywood were willing to threaten to boycott because so many people assumed that African American culture was central to ongoing political activism. Much had changed since the 1940s, when Walter White, executive director of the NAACP, saw Lena Horne as an ally because she would not portray maids on screen, and when some African American actors in Hollywood resented her presence and the roles that she did receive. The controversy over Nat Turner also illuminated the significance of gender to debates about black culture. Styron's rendering of Turner's masculinity was perhaps the strongest piece of evidence that his version of African American history was inauthentic and dangerous. As Meriwether explained in a letter to Wolper, Styron "divests Turner of all his strength, fortitude and manhood. . . . He castrates Nat mentally, physically, and sexually."[68]

Celebrated by some, vilified by others, and contested by all, Nat Turner's failed sojourn in Hollywood throws into sharper relief the stories about African American history that Hollywood did tell. Some, like *Sounder* and *The Autobiography of Jane Pittman*, emerged as uncontroversial and worthy of praise. The fact that both had white directors did not discredit these productions or preclude them from getting rave reviews as authentic black culture. Martin Ritt and John Korty worked to avoid the battles that David Wolper encountered with Nat Turner and that Wolper largely circumvented seven years later when he bought rights to Alex Haley's book *Roots*.

Sounder and *The Autobiography of Miss Jane Pittman* also could not have been more different from films made in the 1970s about black life in the urban North. The genre that became known as "blaxploitation" when it was copied over the course of the decade started in 1971 with Gordon Parks's film *Shaft*—about a "black private dick" who was both a "bad mother" and a good detective, according to the film's Oscar award–winning theme song by Isaac Hayes. The same year that the mustached private eye in a leather jacket who battles the white mob and the black mob without breaking sweat made *Shaft* a surprise hit, Melvin van Peebles developed a far more violent urban black male hero in *Sweet Sweetback's Baadasssss Song*, a film about a young black hustler besting the Los Angeles police. These and many other low-budget, action-oriented blaxploitation films were enormously popular and controversial in the same years that Cicely Tyson became something of a household name.[69]

Shaft, Sweet Sweetback's Baadasssss Song, and others in this genre usually featured hyper-heterosexual and violent African American urban antiheroes who outsmart white authorities and dominate women. Only a few, notably *Coffy* (1973) and *Foxy Brown* (1974), both with Pam Grier as a sexy heroine, featured women battling, and sometimes castrating, villains. Some fans argued that a film like *Shaft* was simply entertaining—good "date night" fare, according to Vincent Canby in the *New York Times*.[70] More often, advocates and opponents invested the genre with either positive or negative political significance. One radical black newspaper said that *Sweetback* was about "decolonization." According to Black Panther Party leader Huey Newton, the character Sweetback was a revolutionary and the film affirmed "the need for unity"; the Black Panther Party, he said, would require that its members watch the film. Many fans appreciated seeing working-class, urban black characters who did not seek to assimilate into white society or acquire middle-class values on screen.[71] Even those who did not like the content agreed that these films had some political and economic value because they opened doors for African Americans in Hollywood.[72]

Sounder and *The Autobiography of Miss Jane Pittman* entered this fray by countering the cinematic focus on Northern black urban life and blaxploitation's emphasis on violence as resistance. Many African Americans and almost all whites commended *Sounder* as a crucial alternative to what one critic referred to as the "slick, bloodletting tribal fantasies of the new commercial black cinema." Pauline Kael explicitly rejected the argument that blaxploitation films were authentic expressions of urban black culture or on-screen extensions of black power when she asserted that it was *Sounder* that marked "the birth of black consciousness on the screen," whereas "*Shaft* and its ilk" did so "merely in blackface." It was not just white critics who regarded the pastoral vision of *Sounder* as authentic: *Sounder* is "black, black black, and beautiful, beautiful, beautiful," wrote Loften Mitchell, a prominent African American playwright, in a large multipage spread about the film in the *New York Amsterdam News*.[73]

Tyson herself became something of a spokesperson for critiques of blaxploitation films. Elaborating on "The Emancipation Orgasm: Sweetback in Wonderland," an essay in *Ebony* in which editor Lerone Bennett would argue that *Sweetback's Baadasssss Song* was "neither revolutionary nor black because it presents the spectator with sterile daydreams and a superhero who is ahistorical, selfishly individualist with no revolutionary program," Tyson repeatedly repudiated blaxploitation films.[74] The challenge that *Sounder* posed, she said, was far more extensive, historically accurate, and politically effective than any in *Shaft* and other films that followed Gordon Parks' lead. "The story of *Sounder* is part of our history," said Tyson in one of many interviews that moved into a discussion of blaxploitation and black culture. "Our whole black heritage is one of struggle, pride and dignity."[75] Tyson specifically objected to women's roles in these films: "Take your clothes off, girl, and it's a fast $10,000. Shake your butt, baby, it's five grand more. Black sexploitation. That's where it's at, but not for me. . . . I may be broke, but I'm not broken." She contrasted representations of African American women in blaxploitation films—as a "kind of Barbie Doll sexpot . . . in trash like '*Shaft*' and '*Sweetback*'"—to those in *Sounder*: "The black woman has never been shown on the screen this way before. She has always been a prostitute, a drug user, or someone who slept around. She has never been given any dignity at all. This is the first time it's happened." She had stopped even going to blaxploitation films, Tyson often said, and she would never, ever act in one: "I have pride in myself as a black woman," she said. "I couldn't portray an empty-headed, turned-on, spaced-out swing chick."[76]

Blaxploitation films were not the only examples of movies about black urban life in this period, and Tyson-dominated films set in the past were not the only on-screen challenges to them. In 1974, *Claudine*, starring Diahann Carroll, introduced a 36-year-old single mother of six who lived in Harlem as its protagonist.[77] With its urban landscape, contemporary soundtrack, sexually active men and women, and leather jacket-clad characters, *Claudine* seemed to share a great deal with blaxploitation films. Yet, as many critics noted at the time, in direct and indirect ways *Claudine* offered an alternative. The challenges in this film were not the same as those in *Sounder* and *Miss Jane Pittman*, and Carroll's public statements were very different from the critiques that Cicely Tyson launched in her many off-screen conversations about race, popular culture, and blaxploitation. The two female stars performed black womanhood in drastically different ways. Not surprisingly, perhaps, the impact these performances had varied as well.

In 1971, Ossie Davis announced the establishment of Third World Cinema "to produce in New York City films and documentaries utilizing talents and providing jobs for Blacks, Puerto Ricans and other minority groups and for their distribution to motion picture houses and television." With funding from African American celebrities and from state and local agencies, Third World Cinema combined a long history of independent black filmmaking companies with the War on Poverty and its attention to economic development projects. The goal of the company was to film stories that were "dealing with the real problems about real people in the black community," Davis explained.[78]

Claudine revolved around the themes of family and romance, and the obstacles facing a single black mother of six as she tried to balance the one with the other. Critics repeatedly noted how the film took on the welfare system and exposed it as an unfair bureaucracy in which white administrators policed hard-working African American women and made privacy virtually impossible.[79] Claudine must conceal her wage work and her relationship with garbage man Rupert Marshall (James Earl Jones), lest she jeopardize the below-subsistence welfare checks and lose her benefits. In one powerful scene, the family works together to hide from the welfare administrator the toaster, iron, and any other "extras" that Claudine's clandestine job as a domestic affords; in another, the white welfare administrator, Miss Kabak, finds Rupert in a closet. These scenes were among those that demonstrated the "harm the system does," said one reviewer.[80] *Claudine* is surely not a "happily ever after" movie: By the end, Claudine's 15-year-old daughter is pregnant and her son is running away from the police after a protest for "jobs not welfare" goes awry. Nevertheless, through it all, and despite the fact that Claudine curses often and even beats her daughter, she loves her children. Most audiences agreed that she is a powerful, nurturing, and positive force in their lives. In the final minutes, she and Rupert marry and the family is together—albeit arrested and in the back of a police paddy wagon. It was through this vision of family and domesticity as resistance that *Claudine* affirmed African American activism, far more than in its depiction of the eldest son's alliances with an urban militant black organization.[81]

The contrasts to blaxploitation films were apparent to reviewers who praised *Claudine*. "Unlike the worst black action pictures, it shows the ugliness of Harlem with out itself becoming ugly," wrote a critic from *Rolling Stone*. "The super-jive, super-spade, cocaine desperado image of the ghetto that has been flashing across the screen in superabundance of late is given its rightful place in the Harlem of 'Claudine,'" according to the *Chicago Defender*, "off in the shadows." With its tenderness and emphasis on a loving family, noted an effusive review in *Variety*, *Claudine*, "like 'Sounder,'" was a film "for all ages and audiences."[82] For some, *Claudine* even had qualities that *Sounder* lacked: "Unlike 'Sounder,'" *Claudine* "doesn't need the remote past or distant locations to find a positive side to black life." A critic in the *Chicago Defender* applauded a film that could "uplift" those who had "been ignored on film until now, the ADC mother."[83] In this African American family, there was love and commitment, and there were struggling but strong women and men. In all of these ways, *Claudine*, like *Sounder*, foregrounded hard-working black mothers and affirmed families as a source of resistance—upending assumptions in the Moynihan Report and those who said welfare recipients were undeserving, as well as blaxploitation films with their emphasis on violence and hyper-masculine sexual aggression.

While Diahann Carroll was nominated for an Oscar, critics were divided in their responses to her performance. In part, this was a genre issue. *Claudine* was "promoted as, of all things, a comedy," wrote a reviewer in *Time* with disbelief.[84] Some viewers objected to a black mother who used "four letter words." "I thank heavens for the star, Cicely Tyson," wrote an African American woman to the *Chicago Defender*, "whom I hope will never stoop to play such a role as 'Claudine.'"[85] Critics were most divided in their responses to Carroll because the role was such a departure. While a handful observed that a "deglamorized Diahann Carroll is surprisingly effective as

a 36-year-old city wise and world weary mother who battles welfare department bureaucracy," many more could not relinquish associations between
Carroll and glamour and concluded that she could not represent working-
class black women effectively. "Even without makeup, she still looks and
acts like Julia," said one. A "gap" between the star and the film's "ghetto
environment," noted Molly Haskell in the *Village Voice*, was "made more
glaring by those inevitable attempts at sociological authenticity." And *Time*
attacked Carroll for a "slumming expedition by a woman best known for
playing the upwardly mobile Julia on TV."[86]

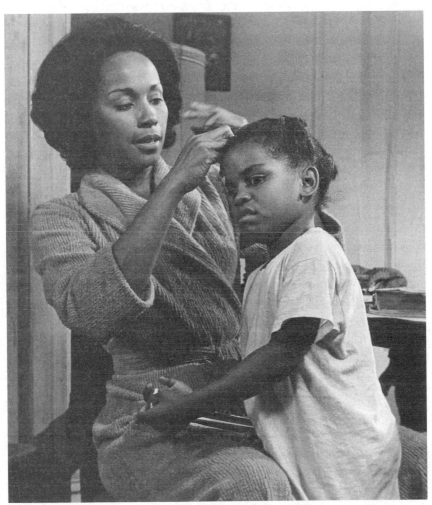

FIGURE 5.4 Diahann Carroll as the single mother of six in the film *Claudine* (1974).
(Hulton Archives/Getty Images)

Tyson's performances of Rebecca Morgan and Jane Pittman, combined with a biographical discourse about Tyson's own background, allowed her to speak for all black women and as all black women. By contrast, Diahann Carroll, who "led a sheltered life," could not "presume to speak for all black women"—or for any black women, for that matter. Ultimately, Carroll was unable to navigate the chasm between her off-screen persona and the character of *Claudine* productively, diminishing *Claudine*'s impact as a film. Third World Cinema did train hundreds of African Americans who would work in Hollywood industries, but made just one more movie. Carroll's Oscar nomination was a milestone, but offers were few and far between thereafter, and she felt that her career was "floundering."[87] Neither she nor the film acquired the authority that Cicely Tyson garnered from *Sounder* and *The Autobiography of Miss Jane Pittman*.

AMIDST THE POLARIZED arguments over blaxploitation films and black culture, *Sounder* screenwriter Lonne Elder stood out when he observed that the gap between blaxploitation films and productions like *Sounder* or *The Autobiography of Miss Jane Pittman* was narrower than it seemed. Both, he explained, suggested that African American audiences wanted to see themselves represented in a variety of ways on screen after "sixty years" of being "starved for any kind of image at all."[88] Their interests could not be distilled into one definitive story or one definition of black culture. What Elder did not note was the subject on which these and other stories agreed: gender relations. The monogamous Nathan Morgan, the cowboy Joe Pittman, the swinging single Shaft (or the abusive Sweetback), and the charming but not always dependable Rupert in *Claudine* seemed to offer quite different models of African American manhood, but they all asserted their masculinity and heterosexuality in ways that Styron's imagined Nat Turner—deemed inauthentic by so many African Americans— did not. Ultimately, the emphasis on courageous and dominant heterosexual men and on fatherhood in *Sounder* and *Claudine* reproduced an assumption that was as evident in the Moynihan Report as it was among many male advocates of black power, and relied on a premise implicit in critiques of welfare and in blaxploitation films: that what African American communities really needed was stronger black men.

Why, then, did *Ms.* describe Tyson's performance in *Sounder* as "revolutionary" for her character's support for a patriarchal family? That this claim appeared in a feminist periodical suggests that a burgeoning body of black feminist writings challenging the Moynihan Report, literature by black women like Toni Morrison, Alice Walker, and others, and black women activists who asserted their rights as mothers and citizens and rejected the sexualization of black women were having an impact on a women's liberation movement often associated with white women. Tyson's repertoire inserted African American women into historical narratives about African American strength and endurance. Her roles affirmed the resistant positions black women were making in these years.

And yet Tyson's fictional black women offered a qualified affirmation of resistance and strength. Even though both white and black women and men praised her characters as strong, their strength was evident only through the support they offered their families (or in the case of Jane Pittman, the race as a whole). Positive reactions to Tyson suggested that strong black women mattered to African American history but not to feminism. The reception of Tyson again resegregated black activism and gender activism and placed them on parallel but unrelated tracks despite the fact that Tyson's characters, like those in Simone's song "Four Women," made clear how intertwined these were. Further, Tyson's women may have been central to narratives of black history taking shape in popular culture, but only certain types of women and femininity had access to this increasingly authoritative memory bank. In contrast to Carroll as Claudine and Lincoln as Ivy, Tyson's strong black women tended to live in the past and in the rural South. Her most famous black women stood out because they endured. They suffered nobly but quietly. They did not join organizations. They might have some sexual desire but, in contrast to Claudine and Ivy, not a lot of sexual agency. Of perhaps greatest importance, they mattered largely in relation to more heroic and more active men or extended kin networks. As a black mother, Rebecca "was every black woman throughout history," said Tyson.[89] These were the terms through which many black and white Americans in the 1970s regarded Cicely Tyson as politically relevant and as subverting myths about black women.

In the 1970s, Tyson's performances of black womanhood were saturated with political significance because of her characters' qualities and their location in time. This dynamic set her apart from Lena Horne and from the cohort of performing black women around whom she had first come of age professionally. Horne's role as the sultry Georgia in *Cabin in the Sky* mattered to black audiences in the 1940s because they loved to see Horne "mosey on" down to see—and tempt—Little Joe (Eddie Anderson), but also because they knew about her off-screen activism on behalf of the

NAACP and her participation in the interwar black Left. The African American press applauded Horne's refusal to play maids on screen and viewed that in relation to Horne's alliance with Walter White and the NAACP. Over 20 years later, Abbey Lincoln's demure characters and "straight" hair in *Nothing But a Man* and *For Love of Ivy* (wigs in both instances), stood in direct contrast to her off-screen appearance and her off-screen denunciations of American domestic race relations and her anticolonial politics. As was the case with Lena Horne, these contrasts were well known, even when the subversive potential of her off-screen activism was not fully realized in the late 1960s. Diahann Carroll's off-screen aura of glamour was so strong that it could not displace the commitments to civil rights organizations that she made or the content of her performance in *Claudine*, a film that in many respects, deeply engaged critiques of liberalism and communicated black power and black feminist politics. What set Tyson apart as a celebrity was the degree to which she came to stand in for her characters living in the past, sharing with them the qualities of dignity, racial authenticity, and a certain type of female strength.

These, then, were the roots of *Roots*. When Tyson appeared as Binta, the quintessential African American woman was birthing the quintessential heroic African man. She established the origins for this story about "an American family." By doing so, she also helped to bring this eighteenth-century tribal village into the present. In an analysis of *Roots* in relation to racial politics in the 1970s, film studies scholar Linda Williams argues that Alex Haley was "simultaneously incorporating and criticizing the civil rights tradition that had used moral supremacy and martyrdom as the means to integration," and "incorporating and criticizing a 'Black Power' tradition that eschewed martyrdom for more virile expressions of separatist black pride." Williams suggests that it was precisely the potentially contradictory aspects of *Roots* that made it so appealing to mass audiences in the 1970s.[90]

Roots was able to accomplish all that it did not only because of its story and unique production history, but also because of preexisting patterns in popular culture. The opening minutes of this blockbuster series set the stage for a series of narrative themes that developed over the following seven nights, and that Cicely Tyson had already helped make familiar in ways that Diahann Carroll, for all that *Claudine* accomplished, could not. Four key features that critics and scholars have located in *Roots* had already played a part in the discourse about Tyson and popular culture that took up African American history.

First, these productions shared a setting largely in the rural South, the site for loving black families, authentic black culture, and nonviolent strategies of resistance, all of which stood apart from urban-based activism and global analyses of race relations and anticolonialism. Second, these productions celebrated African American characters who resist oppression in mostly—but not exclusively—nonviolent ways. Like Nathan Morgan and the murdered Ned, Joe, and Jimmy, the male heroes in *Roots* from Kunta Kinte to Chicken George to Haley himself are emphatically not "Uncle Toms," but the challenges they pose to white authority are offset by their roles in families. Third, all of these stories offered hopeful endings. Progress had been achieved, or the struggle was over. As critics noted at the time, in *The Autobiography of Miss Jane Pittman*, the trembling Miss Pittman walks to the water fountain with her cane—alone—and drinks in triumph. She rides away from the water fountain on a chair in the back of a pickup truck as other African Americans assemble behind the vehicle, and as the white reporter watches from a distance. In *Sounder*, the young David Lee receives reassurance from the teacher—the voice of wisdom: "You did all you could. . . . You did your job." As Nathan drives him away from the shack and toward the future in the final scene, David Lee tells his father, "I'm going to miss this raggedy old place, but I sure ain't going to worry about it." By the end of *Sounder*, all of the characters have done all they can. Audiences in 1972, in turn, were reassured that they, too, had done all they could. The story of suffering and endurance, and of anger and resistance, was over. Finally, all of these dynamics were set into motion by the fourth shared element—love in African American families.

Cicely Tyson's efforts to remake black womanhood in the 1970s helped tie these themes together in *Roots*. Consequently, when the series aired in 1977, many white Americans presumed the civil rights movement to be not a contemporary struggle, but a historical success story. To quote an editorial in the *Washington Post*, "The greatest contribution of the *Roots* phenomenon probably lies . . . in what it confirms about where we are, and how far we have come."[91]

Epilogue

THE "NEW STAR" (Makeba). The "greatest singer" (Simone). The "hottest new thing" and a surprising "arrival" (Lincoln). The "entertainer of the year" (Carroll). The "rising star" (Tyson).[1] To read the reviews that Miriam Makeba, Nina Simone, Abbey Lincoln, Diahann Carroll, and Cicely Tyson received, one would never guess that they were peers and sometimes friends whose careers ascended contemporaneously, 25 years after Lena Horne started dancing at the Cotton Club. The lavish praise tended to presume that each woman existed in isolation, as an exception. This reception at the time as well as the subsequent trajectories of their careers has made it easy to think of each as the lone anomaly whom critics discovered and wisely elevated in singular ways as the star.

These narratives were not just the result of an entertainment industry that produced celebrity culture by emphasizing novelty more than networks. The reality was that the styles and performance strategies that these women employed varied. Makeba sang folk songs in her native Xhosa and incorporated songs in English and other languages into her repertoire. She never felt comfortable with the designation "jazz singer" even though she made a name for herself with American audiences at the Village Vanguard and moved in circles associated with both jazz and folk. Diahann Carroll felt even more uncomfortable with jazz; her style was "Broadway perfectionist," she said, and she felt "intimidated by the great jazz and blues artists." Cicely Tyson avoided music altogether, in part because she wanted to get away from the assumption that black performers were destined by nature to sing and dance. Abbey Lincoln was influential in the flourishing New York jazz scene of the late 1950s and early '60s; even though she did other kinds of work writing essays and appearing in films over the course of the '60s, she was—and has remained—primarily associated with a jazz canon. Fans and critics never could decide how to classify Nina Simone and the porousness of jazz, blues, classical, rock, and other styles in her music.[2]

Moreover, in considering the distinctions among these women performers, there is no question that Abbey Lincoln as Ivy and Diahann Carroll as Julia were not producing a resistant culture of protest in the ways that Nina Simone did with "Mississippi Goddam," or in the ways that Miriam Makeba did more subtly in "The Click Song." Even taking into account differences in genre and the degree to which musicians and lyricists might sometimes have greater creative control and autonomy than did film actors, *For Love of Ivy* and *Julia* simply did not celebrate urban black cultures and racial cosmopolitanism or challenge racism and whites' definitions of blackness in the (very different) ways that were evident in *Come Back, Africa* or the album *In Concert*. The political dimensions of the women's cultural work varied as much as the political positions they embraced offstage. In front of cameras and microphones and away from them, black women performers weighed multiple and sometimes competing variables that included ambition, political investments, and their sense of professional opportunities. No one label—radical, liberal, or some space in between or beyond either of these designations—fit them all; in fact, no one label fit any one of them given how varied each woman's performances were and how many meanings any one song, film, or television show could have.

In concluding, then, it is worth reconsidering that period when communities of entertainer-activists came together in the late 1950s. While their careers and political perspectives varied in those years, these six black women performers were affected by one another and their overlapping friends, acquaintances, and mentors. James Baldwin, Lorraine Hansberry, Leroi Jones, Odetta, Ossie Davis, and Harry Belafonte were among those who interacted with and had an impact on them all. Sometimes, this meant sharing the same stage or song: Belafonte collaborated with Lena Horne and with Miriam Makeba; Sidney Poitier costarred with Lincoln and with Carroll. Lena Horne, Nina Simone, and Diahann Carroll all performed Oscar Brown's song "Brown Baby," and Miriam Makeba and Nina Simone performed together at Carnegie Hall in 1961. Several years later, Simone and Lincoln collaborated on "Blues for Mama," a song that rejected the assumption that abused black women somehow brought that abuse on themselves.[3]

This was not a "sisterhood" devoid of conflict or competition. It was, however, an informally connected universe in which women had relationships with each other and with sometimes more prominent men. Scholar Sherrie Tucker has suggested that women jazz musicians can be

conceptualized as a "border community, not as a community with a unified core, but as a community on the edge, that has, as its closest thing to
common experience, scattered patterns of unbelonging, partial belonging,
loose connections, and guerilla tactics."[4] To extend this metaphor to a
range of women performers in New York–based circles of activist entertainers in the 1950s, there was no one "unified core" among them; still,
"loose connections" joined them. They shared ambition and commitments to cultural creativity and political activism; they encountered
common obstacles as black women.

All five younger women bumped up against Lena Horne, literally or
figuratively, and her larger-than-life reputation. In the 1930s and '40s,
Horne had produced a new kind of black female celebrity. At nightclubs in
New York, critics described the "tantalizing singer" as a "siren" and a
"sepia sensation" who was as "voluptuous as crushed grapes," and as a
singer in a "simple white gown" who performed with "quality" and "complete poise."[5] Just as Horne's family marked her as different from many
other African American women entertainers who got their start in vaude-
ville and minstrel shows, and just as she moved between her work on
behalf of the NAACP and a black Left, her performances of black womanhood differed when she secured her status as a glamorous star who
deserved the right to be looked at as an unavailable object of sexual desire
and who deserved respect as well.

Over a decade later, Makeba, Simone, Lincoln, Carroll, and Tyson each
inherited and negotiated with Horne's strategies for performing black
womanhood. Diahann Carroll invited numerous and direct comparisons
to Horne, and critics repeatedly highlighted the similarities between the
two "tawny" singers who received as much attention for their bodies, skin,
and wardrobes as for their singing and other roles. A critic for *Time*
observed that Lena Horne was "the sophisticated lady with a past, Diahann is the ingénue of the trade—sweet but sexy, and eager to learn"; in the
New York Post, a reviewer seeking to praise Carroll in her own right
acknowledged that "Diahann Carroll has been called the second Lena
Horne—but historians of our musical culture are more likely to memori-
alize her as the first Diahann Carroll."[6] In the 1960s, Carroll worked to
update and maintain Horne's insistence that that a black woman could
simultaneously be respectable, sexual, and glamorous, even when Horne
herself began to repudiate those representational strategies. Carroll's
efforts had mixed results, evident when associations with glamour limited
the impact of her subtle and subversive performance as Claudine.

Like Carroll, Miriam Makeba, Nina Simone, Abbey Lincoln, and Cicely Tyson grappled with Horne's image, but they did more to redefine celebrity culture for black women. Cicely Tyson, for instance, seemed to draw on Horne when she would accept only parts that she felt offered respectable and dignified representations of black womanhood. At the time that she joined the cast of *East Side, West Side* in 1963, African Americans, especially women, were largely absent from television; when they did appear, it was usually on news reports about civil rights battles in the South or on variety shows as musicians, dancers, and comics.[7] Tyson's character, Jane, neither cleaned nor sang. But as secretary and general assistant to the social worker Neil Brock (George C. Scott), she was not marginal or "pasted to a pillar," as Horne had been in so many Hollywood films. In *East Side, West Side* and even more so as Rebecca in *Sounder* and as the lead in *The Autobiography of Miss Jane Pittman*, Tyson portrayed women whom other characters and fans embraced as beautiful and dignified, minus Horne's gowns, jewels, and political alliances.

Hair was one of the crucial props that four of the younger women drew on to develop their representational strategies. Lincoln, Tyson, and Carroll all emerged as public figures as models or in the context of high fashion and an allure that Lena Horne had done so much to make viable for black women. Lincoln and Tyson both explicitly rejected the definitions of glamour and sexuality that emanated from this world as their careers ascended. For them, as for Makeba and Simone as vocalists, hair was a potent means of doing so. When Abbey Lincoln left the world of nightclubs and declared that "I demand that I be respected as a dignified Negro woman," she started to wear her hair natural; in 1958, her album *It's Magic* featured a cover photograph of her with hair short and cropped.[8] Starting in 1959 on *Camera Three*, a Sunday morning television variety show that emphasized the arts, and as the fictional Jane on the CBS drama *East Side, West Side* in 1963, Tyson also wore her hair in a short, cropped Afro. Makeba, from her opening night at the Village Vanguard in 1959 and during all of her years of celebrity in the United States, refused to straighten her hair—opting instead for what she called her "short and woolly" style.[9] Nina Simone wore her hair in dramatically different styles from one performance to the next, including straight-haired wigs, but as early as 1961 these styles included a natural Afro style. Like Lincoln, a change in her physical presentation was one part of the change in her musical repertoire and became visual evidence of Simone's willingness to sing as a black woman about racial politics in ways that took on white Americans and interracial activism and affirmed her femininity.

All of these women, then, were involved in a process of politicized self-fashioning in which race and femininity played intersecting parts. Makeba, Simone, Lincoln, and Tyson insisted that how they looked mattered to their racial politics and insisted, despite prevailing racialized aesthetics that equated beauty with light skin and straight hair, that how they looked made them desirable and desiring black women. They were part of a larger group of artists and musicians, writers and singers who freed themselves artistically and individually in relation to more collective struggles for black freedom.[10] The singer Odetta, the modern dancer Ruth Beckford, jazz trombonist and composer Melba Liston, Lorraine Hansberry, and the fictional Beneatha—heroine of Hansberry's *Raisin in the Sun*—were just some of the other women who wore their hair "natural" in New York in the late 1950s or early '60s or otherwise challenged normative meanings of black womanhood and sexuality, and whose choices affected ordinary black women around the country.

Yet, as with their prowess on stage and in recording studios, critics at the time and subsequently tended to speak about each woman—and her hairstyle—in isolation. Many agreed that, as a *New York Times* headline about Miriam Makeba put it in 1966, "Her Hairdo Started the 'Afro' Trend." There was also a consensus that Abbey Lincoln was the pioneer and that "she wore an Afro . . . when that coiffure was almost an obscene curiosity in the world of Black women with their jars of grease and straightening combs." Tyson's choices evoked similar declarations that her "short, African cut" had "set the 'au natural' trend," and that she was "the mother of the Afro hairstyle."[11]

When critics praised any one artist (and her hair) as unique, they elided the important similarities among black women entertainers and their strategies for performing black womanhood. Considering them together changes the question from "Who was the first woman artist to wear her hair natural?" to "What does it mean that groups of women entertainers made that same choice in this same period?" Reproducing the assumptions that critics made from the late 1950s onward may suggest that each woman was exceptional, early, or "ahead of the times." Taken together, they appear far less isolated than critics at the time indicated. Here was an emergent collectivity: an ambitious cohort of women living and working amidst larger male-dominated communities of performers and activists, women who built careers, supported black liberation struggles, and sought to control their own self-representations.[12] As they drew on changing meanings of blackness and racial pride, and as some of them also used meanings of Africa in their own styles and dress, they offered evidence for female activism at work.

The tendency to talk about each woman in isolation that made it hard to see how these networks of activism took shape in the late '50s has also obscured the impact black women of different generations had on one another. One evening in February 1960, Lena Horne and husband Lennie Hayton were at the Luau, a "swank" restaurant in Hollywood, when a white male patron nearby started to talk about Horne as "just another black nigger." A short verbal exchange escalated, and an enraged Horne threw an ashtray and then a lamp at the man.[13] Horne later described this incident as important because she received so much support from African Americans around the country; their responses, she said, "made me feel that they wanted to identify with me, as I wanted to identify with them."[14]

The timing of Horne's "unscheduled performance," as she put it, was likely not random. Horne's starring role in the Broadway hit *Jamaica* had recently come to a close. With music and lyrics by Harold Arlen and E. Y. Harburg, the team for *Cabin in the Sky*, the show seemed to gesture back to the 1940s and to Horne's years in Hollywood. But with a plot about a Caribbean woman who longs to move to Manhattan, with what scholar Shane Vogel calls a subtle "diasporic political consciousness," and with its young interracial cast of actors and dancers, *Jamaica* was anchored firmly in the present: an increasingly multiethnic New York, the late '50s craze for calypso music, and more opportunities for politicized African Americans in theater.[15] It was during her stint in *Jamaica* that Horne encountered a younger generation of activists, entertainers, and the many artists and performers who defined themselves as both. According to Horne's version of herself in *Lena*, *Jamaica* was as important to her political development as it was to her career.[16]

The timing of this incident is significant for another reason as well. Just three weeks earlier, four black students staged a scheduled performance at a Woolworth's counter in Greensboro, North Carolina. Like Horne, the four wanted service at a restaurant; like Horne, the result was rage and violence—only in Greensboro, the rage came from white people who opposed the young African Americans. By the evening of this altercation in Hollywood, sit-ins as a form of protest had spread around the country and would soon lead to the formation of the Student Nonviolent

Coordinating Committee (SNCC), the youth-based civil rights group that was a nerve center for black activism over the next decade.

According to Horne, before she had thrown anything, she had first held a lamp to her face and yelled, "Here I am you bastard, I'm the nigger you can't see."[17] A woman who had been in front of audiences since she was 16 years old demanded to be seen—or more accurately, perhaps, to be looked at and seen anew. This demand further linked Horne to the protesting young students at Greensboro and to younger politicized performers in New York. Both groups staged their protests before cameras or audiences and demanded that the world see them anew. Both groups were using types of performance strategies to transform what it meant to be a black person in the United States.[18] Lines of influence circled from Horne to younger performers, and back again to Horne, and help to explain why in 1965 she redefined her own political and creative life in the context of the black activism developing around her.

In 1966, in a special issue of *Ebony* on "The Negro Woman," Lena Horne coauthored what she called an "epilogue" to *Lena*, an article titled "The Three-Horned Dilemma Facing Negro Women." The "horns" of the dilemma that virtually all "privileged Negro women" faced, she wrote, were their "rapport with Negro males, the lowly poor, and white liberal women." Horne explored the myth of matriarchy and tensions between black men and women, the widening divide and exacerbated class tensions among black women, and the growing difficulties white and black women had connecting to each other. She concluded that "solidarity" among black women was most important and called upon other "professional women performers" to intensify their work "with our sisters."[19] This essay took up themes that younger women had been performing onstage and in song for years. The sexual and racial dynamics in Simone's "Go Limp"; the chasm between white and black women that Lincoln exposed in *For Love of Ivy*; the loving and struggling and sexually active mothers that Diahann Carroll and Cicely Tyson captured in *Claudine* and *Sounder*; the political power of performance and culture that Miriam Makeba communicated in every appearance—were all in this essay. In print and in film, on records and onstage, black women engaged in black activism and grappled with the intersections of race and sex in their lives in ways that influenced one another.

These circles of influence between women across generations expanded and have had an ongoing impact. Yet, in part because of the memories of civil rights that prevail today, they often remain hidden and are all too easy to erase. In 2002, for example, Halle Berry became the first black woman to win an Oscar for best actress in a leading role. Sobbing at the podium, she held the small statue and said, "This moment is so much bigger than me. This moment is for Dorothy Dandridge, Lena Horne, Diahann Carroll." Berry seemed to be naming a history of black women performers and the longer tradition of which she was a part. But she then declared that the award was "for every nameless, faceless, woman of color that now has a chance because this door tonight has been opened." Moreover, curiously absent from her initial list was Hattie McDaniel, the one other black woman who had received an Oscar, in 1939, for her supporting role in *Gone with the Wind*. Berry was identifying herself as another first, another woman like no one else, and another performing black woman who was a pioneer. By contrast, when Denzel Washington accepted his award for best actor at that same awards ceremony, he raised his statue to Sidney Poitier, to whom he had presented a lifetime achievement award earlier in the evening, and declared, "I'll always be chasing you, Sidney. I'll always be following in your footsteps. There's nothing I would rather do sir. Nothing I would rather do. God bless you."[20] As Washington and Poitier each raised his golden statue to meet that of the other in midair, Washington affirmed a brotherhood, or almost a paternal line from father to son; he located himself on that celebrated historical trajectory of black male performers. This is not an indictment of Halle Berry; rather, the incident suggests how easy it continues to be to overlook a history of black women performers who are connected to one another through their cultural and political work, even when that history seems to be evident or the topic of the conversation.

Consequently, the narratives that isolated the women in this cohort from one another and rendered them exceptional performers earlier in their careers continued to affect responses to them decades later. Each one earned recognition and kudos later in life or sometimes posthumously. Even so, the political dimensions of their cultural work, the interventions that they made into two pivotal social movements, and their connections to one another are harder to detect. Theirs are stories of struggle and success, of new developments and regression, and of the multiple ways that race and gender shaped the choices they could, and sometimes could not, make.

MIRIAM MAKEBA MAY have left the United States in 1968, but she remained a popular and beloved performer around the world, as well as an enduring symbol of African liberation and anti-apartheid struggles, until her death in November 2008. She lived and worked in Guinea for 15 years, well after she and Carmichael separated in 1973, before moving to Brussels in 1985. In 1974, she invited Nina Simone to join her in Liberia for an Independence Day celebration. Simone visited with Makeba and then made Liberia her primary home for several years, returning to Guinea to be with her old friend periodically. Makeba also hosted Abbey Lincoln's trip to Africa in the early 1970s. All the while, Makeba traveled, recorded, and entertained audiences in Africa, Europe, and Asia. An incomplete account of her more famous performances includes her role in the three-night concert that preceded the fight between Muhammad Ali and George Forman in 1974 in Zaire, hyped as the "Rumble in the Jungle"; shows around the world with Paul Simon as part of the Graceland Tour in the late 1980s; and, after her dramatic return to South Africa in 1990 at the invitation of Nelson Mandela, concerts and the album *Eyes on Tomorrow*, made in collaboration with Dizzy Gillespie and Nina Simone.[21]

Even as she struggled with family tragedies, health issues, and financial stress, Makeba continued to combine political activism and cultural work. Over the years, she served as a United Nations goodwill ambassador, earned Grammy nominations, gave sold-out shows, played roles in films about apartheid, supported South African exiles and activists who struggled against apartheid rule, and supported facilities for children in South Africa with AIDS after the demise of apartheid—all the while continuing to declare "I'm not a political singer." As had been the case during her years in the United States, such assertions both de-emphasized her activism and enabled it; similarly, her international status as "Mama Africa" elevated her as an icon of the continent and "mother" of liberation movements even as it rendered that defiant and sometimes revolutionary political work into something nurturing, natural, and safe.[22]

Makeba continued to perform until the very end of her life. Partly this was due to economic considerations and the poor management that she, like many other black entertainers, received in the entertainment industry. "We knew nothing about royalties," she explained in her second autobiography, written after she returned to South Africa. "There were no pensions for artists. That's why I was still touring and singing at 70."[23] During a global "farewell tour" that started in 2005, during which she performed the eclectic repertoire that by then had become known as world music, Makeba continued to control where, for whom, and for what reasons she would perform. She died in 2008 after a concert in Italy, held in support of a journalist who had written about organized crime and whose life had repeatedly been threatened.

That level of control eluded Nina Simone, who suffered a series of setbacks in the 1970s. Her marriage to Andy Stroud (also her manager through the '60s) ended, and she had numerous financial difficulties and legal conflicts with the IRS. With the repression of black radicalism by the U.S. government, she grew increasingly pessimistic, if not despairing. In the face of considerable personal, legal, and political difficulties, she performed and recorded infrequently, and her popularity diminished. Simone led a peripatetic if not nomadic life, living in Barbados, Liberia, France, and Switzerland over the course of the 1970s and '80s, while continuing to compose and record. Her friendship with Makeba was an ongoing source of solace. "If I ever needed a friend it was then, and I'd almost forgotten that I had such things until Miriam Makeba called," Simone wrote, recalling Makeba's call urging her to join her in Liberia. In the 1980s and '90s, Simone had several big hits ("My Baby Just Cares for Me," used as background music in Chanel perfume ads, and songs for the film *Point of No Return*, for example). She received numerous honors around the world and occasionally returned to the United States for tours—to much adoration from old and new fans, but also with mixed reviews. Ongoing conflicts with managers and audiences, and ongoing accounts that emphasized her instability, reinforced Simone's reputation as difficult.[74]

When Simone died in April 2003, obituaries around the world affirmed her relationships to civil rights activism (according to *Jet*, her voice had "helped define the Civil Rights Movement"), and several referred to her internationalism. At the funeral service in France, Miriam Makeba offered the "condolences of the whole South Africa" and celebrated the friend she called "sister" as "not only a great artist, but also a freedom fighter." According to some accounts, Simone's cremated body was to be scattered across several African countries. Many reports, however, depicted Simone as a relic of a bygone era or as a difficult entertainer with a "terrifying reputation" who had supplied background music for the civil rights movement rather than as an activist or thinker in her own right. Even in acknowledging her contributions, then, many posthumous narratives about Simone implicitly reinforced a dichotomy between culture and politics, or spoke in terms of pathology reminiscent of the Billie Holiday biopic *Lady Sings the Blues*. Simone has become increasingly iconic only since her death.[25]

Like Simone, Abbey Lincoln experienced personal and professional setbacks in the '70s that included divorce, declining professional opportunities, and depression. The quality film roles that she hoped would follow *For Love of Ivy* never materialized, and for some time, she largely withdrew from public life and focused on artwork and teaching. During a trip to Africa in 1974, Lincoln joined her friend Miriam Makeba and received the African names of Aminata from the president of Guinea and Moseka from the minister of information in Zaire—quite literally renaming herself again, as Aminata Moseka. Thereafter, she started to write her own music and lyrics. *People in Me*, her first album since *Straight Ahead* in 1961, was recorded in Japan and in the United States in 1979. It marked her return to writing, performing, and arranging, a "remarkable comeback," according to the *Washington Post*, "as a singer, songwriter and spiritual elder" that accelerated in the 1990s after release of *The World Is Falling Down* (1990).[26] The ten albums that followed with Verve—the last, *Abbey Sings Abbey* (2007), released while she was recovering from open heart surgery—included introspective songs that looked back on her life and looked ahead to the future, collaborations with younger musicians, and tributes to Billie Holiday. Lincoln's acclaim in the 1990s came from critics, old fans, and new followers; her role in Spike Lee's *Mo' Better Blues* (1990) also introduced her to another generation of consumers. As a critic in the *Wall Street Journal* observed, she "manages to exude both an elder's wisdom and a child's wonder."[27]

Lincoln's death in 2010 brought almost reverential affirmations of her "unshakable integrity" and her "one of a kind" importance as "a singular figure" and "guiding conscience" in jazz.[28] Obituaries emphasized her "militant" politics in the past, including her rejection of the "glamorous ingénue" role and her choice to wear an Afro. She had been "in the forefront of it all," according to a tribute in *Ebony*; she had gone from "a slinky chanteuse to an oracle of hard-won wisdom," according to the *Washington Post*. Accounts of her life from South Africa recalled her global vision of black liberation that dated back to the album *We Insist*, and especially the song "Tears for Johannesburg." But many agreed that Lincoln had reached her peak musically in the last ten years of her life, when her repertoire "retreated from the polemic."[29] The ways in which she had performed black womanhood over the course of her life became evidence for a certain kind of progress that allowed Lincoln into a pantheon of great performers. It was as if true artistic greatness ultimately required a severing of music and politics.

Diahann Carroll's popularity did not peak until years after *Julia* and *Claudine*, even though she had been a familiar celebrity since the late '50s and had won both a Tony award and Oscar nomination. The turning point came in 1984, when Carroll was cast as Dominique Deveraux on *Dynasty*, a television series that pioneered the new genre of prime-time soap opera. As Deveraux, Carroll had a lavish wardrobe of furs and diamonds, romances with black and white men, infamous "catfights" with the character of Alexis Carrington (Joan Collins), and even a history as a nightclub singer. The role was a great match and a rare professional opportunity for an African American performer in her 40s whose career had been in slump just a few years earlier.

As Dominique, Carroll, like Horne, continued to be associated with politically significant "firsts"—in this instance by embracing and being so closely identified with a fictional woman who was the "first black bitch" on television, as she put it. *Dynasty*-related hype emphasized that Carroll saw the part as a way to fill a "void." Television had "done incest, homosexuality, murder," she said in *People Magazine*, but had not yet allowed black women to be "wealthy and ruthless." Carroll was striking "a blow against one of TV's last WASP bastions: the prime-time soap"; moreover, as "the only black actress with a continuing role on a current evening serial," she was also "breaking boundaries" and extending her "pioneering" work as a black female performer. *Dynasty*, with its emphasis on excessive wealth and older women in competition with one another—for whom sisterhood was anything but powerful—was one of the highest-rated television shows during the Reagan presidency amidst what would soon be called a backlash against second-wave feminism.[30] Only in this particular context did Carroll's decades-long associations with glamour and opulence become both unproblematic and evidence of her political work. Ironically, then, it was this role that reinserted Carroll into a longer narrative about civil rights activism and ensured her status as a pioneer in that narrative. In August 2011, Diahann Carroll received an NAACP Lifetime Achievement Award, "presented to an individual whose theatrical contributions have been revolutionary, and whose efforts have 'made a historic difference' in the entertainment industry."[31]

Cicely Tyson remained active on- and offstage after *Roots* and other productions made in the 1970s and set in the past. In the late 1970s and '80s, many of the parts that Tyson chose continued to be historically oriented; Coretta Scott King, Harriet Tubman, and the mother of Olympic athlete Wilma Rudolph were some of the black women from other eras whom she portrayed in television specials. Tyson also sought out roles in productions set in the present that engaged contemporary racial politics in progressive ways. As a homeless "bag lady" (*Samaritan: The Mitch Snyder Story*, 1986), the mother of teenage heroin addict (*A Hero Ain't Nothin' but a Sandwich*, 1978), and a working-class wife and mother who must wrestle with tensions between her family's life in urban Detroit and her roots in the rural South (*Just an Old Sweet Song*, 1976), Tyson continued to negate assumptions about black families as damaged and reject representations of black women as sexualized and promiscuous or as mammy-like caretakers.

Since the 1990s, Tyson's work has cut across genres and topics more so than at any other point in her career. She has appeared in films ranging from the heart-warming—*Fried Green Tomatoes* (1991) and *Because of Winn-Dixie* (2005)—to the comedic—Tyler Perry's *Diary of a Mad Black Woman* (2005) and *Madea's Family Reunion* (2006), both particularly popular among Perry's target audience of African Americans. More recently, consumers have been able to see "the incomparable Cicely Tyson" in Willow Smith's music video for "21st Century Girl," where she appears to bring the sexualized tween singing about female power to life in the desert, and as the elderly maid, Constantine, in *The Help* (2011), a film that became a flashpoint over who defines acceptable or politically productive representations of black women. In 2013, the 88-year-old Tyson won the Tony Award for best leading actress for her role as Carrie Watts in *The Trip to Bountiful*.[32]

Despite this relative diversity, the tendency to conflate Tyson's significance and dignity with the significant and dignified women from the past whom she has portrayed persists. Her "body of work," noted *Jet* after the Tony awards ceremony in 2013, "speaks to her commitment to choosing purpose-driven projects." The authority she acquired in the 1970s thus remains relevant to the ways her performances do political work. In April 2009, for example, Tyson participated in a ceremony at the U.S. Capitol. First lady Michelle Obama unveiled a bust of nineteenth-century abolitionist and feminist Sojourner Truth—the first memorial to an African American woman in the U.S. Capitol. Elected officials and lawmakers from both sides of the aisle, schoolchildren, activists, and organizers attended, marking the culmination of ten years of work on the part of the National Congress of Black Women. Tyson's task was to reenact Truth's most enduring speech, her address to the 1851 women's convention in Akron, Ohio, where she asked the now famous and rhetorical question,

"Aren't I a woman?" The dramatic reenactment drew laughs and a huge round of applause when Tyson-as-Truth declared, "Then that little man in black there, he says women can't have as much rights as men, 'cause Christ wasn't a woman! Where did your Christ come from? Where did your Christ come from? From God and a woman! Man had nothing to do with Him!" She recovered the history of Truth as an abolitionist and suffragist who had exposed gender and racial oppression—and liberation—as historically and inextricably linked. C-SPAN identified each of the many speakers at this ceremony by name ("HILLARY CLINTON," for example), with a smaller description of his or her role below that name ("Secretary of State"). In filming Tyson, however, C-SPAN displayed "SOJOURNER TRUTH" in large, capital letters below Tyson, and "portrayed by Cicely Tyson," in smaller white letters beneath that.[33]

Tyson's performance of Truth was compelling and dramatic. But just as she became Truth in front of her audience in Emancipation Hall and for television viewers, so too her place in the Capitol performing Truth had everything to do with how she had performed black women from the past. Her characters gave her a credibility that Lena Horne never acquired as a glamorous star from 1930s into the 1960s. Critiques of Tyler Perry's movies as modern versions of the blaxploitation films that Tyson lambasted in the '70s seem not to affect Tyson. Her presence, including in *The Help*, lent a certain integrity to contested representations of blackness in popular culture today. If Tyson's performances of black women in *Sounder*, *The Autobiography of Miss Jane Pittman*, and *Roots* helped to signal an imagined post–civil rights moment in the 1970s, they now signal an imagined postracial moment in the new century.

What of Lena Horne, the woman who in many respects created the template for the modern and glamorous politicized female black celebrity that other women played with and bent sometimes beyond recognition, only to break that mold after she joined James Baldwin, Harry Belafonte, and Lorraine Hansberry at the meeting with Robert Kennedy in 1963? Horne remained active in different venues for years to come. In 1969, she finally had her first U.S. television special, a musical review in which she redefined herself as modern and contemporary; she wore her hair in a style that was similar to an Afro; and her repertoire included music by Blood, Sweat and Tears, and "Turning Point," a powerful song about children grappling with prejudice that Nina Simone recorded in 1967.[34]

In 1981, after years of personal turmoil, her last film (*The Wiz*, in 1978), and an announcement of her official retirement in 1980, Horne starred in a remarkably successful one-woman Broadway show. *Lena Horne: The Lady and Her Music* was a musical retrospective based on Horne's life and career. It ran for 14 months to packed crowds that cut across lines of race and received rave reviews, earning Horne a special Tony Award and two Grammy awards. The show offered an account, mostly through song and with some connecting narrative from Horne, of her musical prowess and the discrimination that she had faced—in the past—as a symbol in the entertainment industry. To convey this trajectory musically, Horne sang "Stormy Weather" twice: first, early on in the show, in the restrained manner that echoed her performance in the 1943 film of that name, and the second time toward the end, in a far more exuberant and expressive style. Steven Holden captured what many others felt when he wrote in *Rolling Stone* that Horne "hits peaks of ferocity, tenderness, playfulness and sheer delight that would have seemed unthinkable in her glamour-girl days. . . . [H]er performance here is a sustained cry of affir- mation . . . because that affirmation acknowledges the bitterness, cyni- cism and toughness of the world."[35]

The before-and-after dynamic that had characterized Horne's 1965 autobiography and fan culture about her was still evident in the 1980s. However, the decisive turning point had shifted. Accounts of her life during the one-woman show tended to contrast Horne of the 1960s— when she had been an "outspoken proponent of black rights"—to the ap- parently less angry Horne who had now "mellowed." The new and improved Horne was "in better form than she's ever been" and was achieving even greater and unprecedented critical and commercial suc- cess. In the 1940s, Horne had been "cold as an iceberg" and a "good girl"; in the 1960s, the quality of her performances and American race relations together had both improved; but it was not until the '80s that "Time Cooled Her Anger," as a headline in the *New York Times* suggested. As with Abbey Lincoln, reactions to Horne and her self-representations in the '80s and '90s affirmed progress; that she declared herself "free to be me" as a black woman seemed to confirm a post–civil rights discourse and her own aspirations toward authenticity.[36]

Obituaries for Horne in 2010 emphasized her role as a trailblazer and celebrated her many "firsts." In his tribute, Barack Obama observed that Horne had "worked tirelessly to further the cause of justice and equality." Posthumous accounts also tended to break away from the "before-and- after" model that critics and Horne herself had used to make sense of de- fining moments, instead foregrounding the longer trajectory and changing circumstances on which her support for civil rights had expressed itself. But in these accounts, Horne, the "passionate champion" for racial justice, emerged as the pioneer and the exception; moreover, recent coverage tended to focus on her racial politics or her sex appeal, but rarely considered the ways that race, gender, and sexuality converged in the political choices and commitments she made.[37] Horne is "sentimentalized and, now, eulogized," according to critic Stanley Crouch, when in fact, the "show business world in which women chose to make their livings by being looked at and listened to was not always kind to Lena Horne."[38] "Not always kind" may be putting it mildly, but Horne also did an enormous amount to change what it meant for black women to be looked at and listened to, and she herself changed as the result of how other politicized black women got the world to listen to and look at them.

More than eight decades after Lena Horne entered show business, and over 50 years after Miriam Makeba, Nina Simone, Abbey Lincoln, Diahann Carroll, and Cicely Tyson started performing regularly in New York City, they are once again familiar names, and their music, films, and television work are widely available. Even as a new generation of consumers watches, listens to, and celebrates them, and remixes or reissues their work, the connections between gender and the racial liberation for which they all fought often remain suppressed.[39] These are women who remain the backdrop to conversations about what some might consider to be real racial politics, and they remain stubbornly outside mainstream narratives about civil rights history and women's liberation. Yet, if the outcry over white director Cynthia Mort's choice to cast Zoe Saldana as Nina Simone in the film *Nina* suggests anything, it is that the intersections of racial and sexual politics that Simone sang about with poignancy in "Four Women" and humor in "Go Limp" are with us still.[40] The question of who owns black women's stories and who gets to tell these stories was central to all six of these women and the political contributions they made. Their collaborations and enduring friendships, their shared and diverse commitments, and their varied struggles and successes as politicized black women performers offer a new window into civil rights/black power history and its gendered dimensions, as well as the role race placed in the history of second-wave feminism. In the 1980s, a group of black women declared, "All the women are white, all the blacks are men, but some of us are brave."[41] Decades earlier, black women performers were being more than brave: In direct and indirect ways, they were crossing (and refusing) the divides between black liberation and women's rights.

From *Cabin in the Sky* in 1943 to *Roots* in 1977, Lena Horne, Miriam Makeba, Nina Simone, Abbey Lincoln, Diahann Carroll, and Cicely Tyson created music and fictional characters that electrified audiences and continue to resonate. Often, their activism and their artistry reinforced each other and became one and the same. These six women offer a glimpse into the centrality of popular culture to black activism, and to the ways in which black activism and feminism developed across borders and in conversation with each other. In 1967, Nina Simone recorded "I Wish I Knew How It Would Feel to Be Free," in which she sang about breaking chains, speaking freely, flying, loving, and giving—her examples of "how it feels to be free." She may not ever have felt that sense of freedom in her own life, but in singing and performing, she affirmed a vision of liberation that was felt around the world.[42]

In the age of Facebook, YouTube, and Twitter, it is easy to document the ways in which politics is shaped, if not supplanted, by technologies of entertainment and popular culture that circulate in just seconds across national boundaries. It is also easy to forget that innovative meshings of progressive political movements and cultural commodities seemed possible in the 1960s, and that many people concluded that doing so would invigorate and transform both arenas. The stardom of Lena Horne, Miriam Makeba, Nina Simone, Abbey Lincoln, Diahann Carroll, and Cicely Tyson—their music, films and television work, their activism and their lack of activism, their resistance and their accommodation, their reception and self-representation, and the intersection of all of these in their highly visible public personas as celebrities—helps us to rewrite narratives of black activism and feminism, and render these social movements in all of their messy complexity and richness.

Acknowledgments

THIS PROJECT WAS born over a decade ago during a conversation with Melani McAlister. What might we assign, we wondered, if we were teaching about the civil rights movement, popular culture, and women, and wanted our students to think about how these issues related to each other? Since that initial phone call, there have been more conversations with more people than I can possibly remember. I have benefited from rich and exciting scholarship on these and related topics, and from the input I've received from so many colleagues, friends, and relatives (and apologies to whomever I inadvertently omit). For conversations and questions, and for comments on chapter and article drafts and on lectures and conference papers, my enormous thanks to: Paul Anderson, Joyce Antler, Daphne Brooks, Mari Jo Buhle, James Campbell, Susan Carruthers, Kornel Chang, Lizabeth Cohen, Nancy Cott, Kimberly DaCosta Holton, Carolyn Dean, Alice Echols, Barbara Foley, Jane Gerhard, Saverio Giovachinni, Jim Goodman, Matthew Guterl, Nancy Hewitt, Ann Holder, Daniel Horowitz, Jacqueline Jones, Mark Krasovic, Andrea Levine, Eric Lott, Jane Mangan, Melani McAlister, Lisa McGirr, Joanne Meyerowitz, Ingrid Monson, Kimberly Phillips, Uta Poiger, Suzanne Raitt, Beryl Satter, Jessica Shubow, Judith Smith, Rob Snyder, Lynn Thomas, Judith Tick, Salamishah Tillet, Sherrie Tucker, Allen Tullos, Laurel Thatcher Ulrich, Penny Von Eschen, Gayle Wald, Jessica Weiss, and anonymous readers for the *Journal of American History*, *Feminist Studies*, the anthology *Race, Nation and Empire*, and Oxford University Press. Thanks to Michele Rubin, for representing me, and to the incomparable Susan Ferber for her patience and wisdom, and to the entire team at Oxford University Press. For research support, thanks to Natalie Borisovetz, Barbara Burg, Anders Griffen, Tad Hershorn, Kristine Krueger, Diana Lachatanere, Thomas Lisanti, Antony Toussaint, the Women's Studies Research Center at Brandeis University, the Charles Warren Center for Studies in American History, Harvard University, the Schlesinger Library, Radcliffe Institute, Summer Seminar in Gender History, and the Women's and Gender Studies Research Grant, Rutgers University, Newark, as well as research assistants Maggie Gardner, Janine Mandel, Sara Mixter, Shana Russell, and Jennifer Thompson, and translators Eren Murat and Samantha Hackney. Thanks to my colleagues at Rutgers University, Newark, in the history department, in the program in American Studies, and throughout campus for your belief in rigorous scholarship and rigorous teaching in a welcoming atmosphere, and to Christina Strasburger for making everything work, and a special thanks to Dean Jan Lewis for her support. For asking great questions, keeping me on my toes, and for helping me to keep up with popular culture today beyond *West Wing* or *Mad Men* (or trying to), thanks to my students at Harvard University and at Rutgers University, Newark. Thanks to Mari Jo Buhle, again, for the training she provided. I feel grateful to have been able to discuss my research with the late Jack Thomas, Roy Rosenzweig, and Lawrence Levine, and value the feedback that each one offered. For more conversations, more readings (and rereadings), more help with research and more general propping up than any one person might expect to get in a lifetime, my deepest gratitude to Melani McAlister and Uta Poiger—and especially Jane Gerhard, who has been there every day and in every way. To the extended family of Nixons and Feldsteins, and especially to Asa Nixon, Sara Feldstein-Nixon, Max Feldstein-Nixon, Elizabeth Feldstein-Nixon (Elizabeth, welcome to acknowledgments!), to Rachel Garber and to Oakley—thanks for making my life so full and crazy and happy. When I think of all of you, I know how blessed I am that it's taken me so long to finish this book.

Brookline, Massachusetts

2013

Notes

INTRODUCTION

1. Lena Horne with Richard Schickel, *Lena* (Garden City, NY: Limelight, 1986; orig. pub. 1965), pp. 206–224; for the original essay on which *Lena* was based, see Lena Horne, "I Just Want to Be Myself," *Show*, September 1963, pp. 62–65; republished in the *New York Post*, September 29, 1963, in Schomburg Center on Black Culture Clipping File, Volume I, 1925–1974, "Lena Horne" (hereafter, "Horne," SCBCCF, v. I); for published excerpts from *Lena*, see, for example, Lena Horne, "My Life with Lennie," *Ebony*, November 1965, pp. 174–186.

2. In addition to *Lena*, accounts of this meeting include Taylor Branch, *Parting the Waters: America in the King Years, 1954–1963* (New York: Simon and Schuster, 1988), pp. 809–813; Harry Belafonte with Michael Shnayerson, *My Song: A Memoir* (New York: Alfred A. Knopf, 2011), pp. 266–269; Rebeccah Welch, "Spokesman of the Oppressed? Lorraine Hansberry at Work: The Challenge of Radical Politics in the Postwar Era," in Manning Marable, ed., *The New Black History: Revisiting the Second Reconstruction* (New York: Palgrave, 2011), pp. 69–89; *New York Amsterdam News*, June 8, 1963, p. 11; Layhmond Robinson, "Robert Kennedy Consults Negroes Here About North; James Baldwin, Lorraine Hansberry and Lena Horne Are Among Those Who Warn Him of 'Explosive Situation,'" *New York Times*, May 25, 1963, p. 1. Several of Baldwin's associates also attended. For *The Fire Next Time* and "sounded a warning," see Sheldon Binn, "Books of the Times," *New York Times*, January 31, 1963, p. 6; see also "Best Seller List," *New York Times*, March 2, 1963, p. 7n. For the Birmingham campaigns, see Branch, *Parting the Waters*, pp. 703–815.

3. Horne with Schickel, *Lena*, pp. 209–210; Belafonte with Shnayerson, *My Song*, p. 268. For Freedom Rides, see Raymond Arsenault, *Freedom Riders: 1961 and the Struggle for Racial Justice* (New York: Oxford University Press, 2007).

4. While there are (and historically, were) important differences between civil rights, black power, black liberation, black freedom struggles, and more, my emphasis is on the sometimes overlapping and concurrent strategies that a broad spectrum of those involved with black activism drew on and developed, and not on a distinction between a good or "heroic" phase of interracial activism versus its "evil twin"—black power, as Peniel Joseph has described this perceived dichotomy. See Joseph, "Waiting till the Midnight Hour: Reconceptualizing the Heroic Period of the Civil Rights Movement, 1954–1965," *Souls* 2 (Spring 2000): 6-17; Joseph, "The Black Power Movement: A State of the Field," *Journal of American History* 96 (December 2009): 751–776, quote p. 752. Scholarship on these issues is extensive. For a focus on the South, see John Dittmer, *Local People: The Struggle of Civil Rights in Mississippi* (Urbana: University of Illinois Press, 1995), and for the North, see Beryl Satter, *Family Properties: Race, Real Estate and the Exploitation of Black Urban America* (New York: Metropolitan Books, 2009), and Thomas Sugrue, *Sweet Land of Liberty: The Forgotten Struggle for Civil Rights in the North* (New York: Random House, 2009); for an expansive and invaluable history of black power, see Peniel Joseph, *Waiting 'Til the Midnight Hour: A Narrative History of Black Power* (New York: Holt Paperbacks, 2007); for the Southern roots and transnational dimensions of black power, see Timothy Tyson, *Radio Free Dixie: Robert F. Williams and the Roots of Black Power* (Chapel Hill: University of North Carolina Press, 2001); for a landmark study of relationships between events within and beyond the United States, see Brenda Gayle Plummer, *Rising Wind: Black Americans and U.S. Foreign Affairs, 1935–1960* (Chapel Hill: University of North Carolina Press, 1996). For the "long civil rights movement" as a fruitful paradigm, see Jacquelyn Dowd Hall, "The Long Civil Rights Movement and the Political Uses of History," *Journal of American History* 91 (March 2005): 1233–1263; see also Robert Korstad and Nelson Lichtenstein, "Opportunities Found and Lost: Labor, Radicals, and the Early Civil Rights Movement," *Journal of American History* 75 (December 1988): 786–811; Nikhil Pal Singh, *Black Is a Country: Race and the Unfinished Struggle for Democracy* (Cambridge, MA: Harvard University Press, 2005); Peniel Joseph, ed., *The Black Power Movement: Rethinking the Civil Rights–Black Power Era* (New York: Routledge, 2006). For questions about this framework, see Sundiate Keita Cha-Jua and Clarence Lang, "The 'Long Movement' as Vampire: Temporal and Spatial Fallacies in Recent Black Freedom Studies," *Journal of African American History* 92 (2007): 265–288; Eric Arnesen, "Reconsidering the 'Long Civil Rights Movement,'" *Historically Speaking* 10 (April 2009): 31–34. See also John Dittmer and Danielle McGuire, eds., *Freedom Rights: New Perspectives on the Civil Rights Movement* (Lexington: University Press of Kentucky, 2011).

5. For Gregory's role, see Branch, *Parting the Waters*, p. 809; Lorraine Hansberry, "A Challenge to Artists," *Freedomways* 3 (Winter 1963): 31–35.

6. Brian Ward, *Just My Soul Responding: Rhythm and Blues, Black Consciousness, and Race Relations* (Berkeley: University of California Press, 1998), pp. 316–322; Judith

Smith, "Becoming Belafonte: Black Artist, Public Radical" (Austin: University of Texas Press, forthcoming); Belafonte with Shnayerson, *My Song;* Dick Gregory, *Nigger: An Autobiography* (New York: Pocket Books, 1990); Ossie Davis and Ruby Dee, *With Ossie and Ruby: In This Life Together* (New York: HarperCollins, 2000; orig. pub. 1998); Bernice Johnson Reagon, "The Song Culture of the Civil Rights Movement," liner notes, *Voices of the Civil Rights Movement: Black American Freedom Songs, 1960–1966* (Smithsonian Folkways Recordings, 1997).

7. For Cooke, see Ward, *Just My Soul Responding,* pp. 292–293; for Reeves, see Suzanne Smith, *Dancing in the Street: Motown and the Cultural Politics of Detroit* (Cambridge, MA: Harvard University Press, 1999), pp. 1–4; Richard Iton, *In Search of the Black Fantastic: Politics and Popular Culture in the Post-Civil Rights Era* (New York: Oxford University Press, 2008), pp. 23–25; Mark Kurlansky, *Ready for a Brand New Beat* (New York: Riverhead Books, 2013); for "party song," see Martha Reeves with Mark Bego, *Dancing in the Street: Confessions of a Motown Diva* (New York: Hyperion Press, 1994), p. 147; also quoted in Smith, *Dancing in the Street,* p. 2.

8. Craig Werner, *Higher Ground: Stevie Wonder, Aretha Franklin, Curtis Mayfield and the Rise and Fall of American Soul* (New York: Crown, 2004).

9. For how women entertainers "improvised" gender and womanhood, see Sherrie Tucker, "Bordering on Community: Improvising Women Improvising Women-in-Jazz," in Daniel Fischlin and Ajay Heble, eds., *The Other Side of Nowhere: Jazz, Improvisation, and Communities in Dialogue* (Middletown, CT: Wesleyan University Press, 2004); pp. 244–267. The literature on black women, race and performance is extensive. In addition to work cited in each chapter, useful theoretical and historical analyses include Jayna Brown, *Babylon Girls: Black Women Performers and the Shaping of the Modern* (Durham, NC: Duke University Press, 2008); Donald Bogle, *Brown Sugar* (New York: Crown, 1980); Stephanie Baptiste, *Darkening Mirrors: Imperial Representation in Depression-Era African American Performance* (Durham, NC: Duke University Press, 2012); Nicole Fleetwood, *Troubling Vision: Performance, Visuality, and Blackness* (Chicago: University of Chicago Press, 2011); Melissa Harris-Perry, *Sister-Citizen: Shame, Stereotypes and Black Women in America* (New Haven, CT: Yale University Press, 2011); Fred Moten, *In the Break: The Aesthetics of the Black Radical Tradition* (Minneapolis: University of Minnesota Press, 2003), pp. 85–169. For black women musicians negotiating race and gender, see Eileen M. Hayes and Linda F. Williams, eds., *Black Women and Music: More Than the Blues* (Urbana: University of Illinois Press, 2007).

10. In considering black women entertainers as activists, intellectuals, and political subjects, and not exclusively as performers or the object of an audience's gaze, I draw on Hazel Carby's essential *Reconstructing Womanhood: The Emergence of the Afro-American Woman Novelist* (New York: Oxford University Press, 1990). See also James C. Hall, "The African American Musician as Intellectual," in

Jerry G. Watts, ed., *Harold Cruse's The Crisis of the Negro Intellectual Reconsidered* (New York: Routledge, 2004), pp. 109–119. Although work on the women who are my focus has increased (in part since the deaths of Nina Simone, Miriam Makeba, Lena Horne, and Abbey Lincoln), they remain ancillary to most civil rights histories oriented toward traditional political organizing and movements, including important work oriented toward women as movement leaders or local grassroots activists. Josephine Baker and Billie Holiday remain the black women entertainers about whom a great deal has been written. See, for example, Jeanne Scheper, "'Of la Baker, I Am a Disciple': The Diva Politics of Reception," *Camera Obscura* 65 (2007): 72–101; Mathew Guterl, "Josephine Baker's 'Rainbow Tribe': Radical Motherhood in the South of France," *Journal of Women's History* 21 (2009): 38–58; Farah Jasmine Griffin, *If You Can't Be Free, Be a Mystery: In Search of Billie Holiday* (New York: Ballantine, 2001).

11. For the development of black feminist theory, see, for example, Patricia Hill Collins, *Black Feminist Thought: Knowledge, Consciousness, and the Politics of Empowerment* (New York: Routledge, 1990); Gloria T. Hull et al., eds., *All the Women Are White, All the Blacks Are Men, but Some of Us Are Brave: Black Women's Studies* (New York: Feminist Press, 1982); Joy James, *Shadowboxing: Representations of Black Feminist Politics* (New York: St. Martin's Press, 1999). For black feminist organizing (and the term's meanings among African American women), see especially Kimberly Springer, *Living for the Revolution: Black Feminist Organizations, 1968–1980* (Durham, NC: Duke University Press, 2005).

12. For a classic and still influential analysis of second-wave feminism developing out of and after a commitment to civil rights, see Sara Evans, *Personal Politics: The Roots of Women's Liberation in the Civil Rights Movement and the New Left* (New York: Vintage, 1979). For analyses of the intertwined relationships between black activism and black feminism, see, for example, Angela Davis, *Blues Legacies and Black Feminism: Gertrude "Ma" Rainey, Bessie Smith, and Billie Holiday* (New York: Vintage, 1998); Lisa Gail Collins, "The Art of Transformation: Parallels in the Black Arts and Feminist Art Movements," in Lisa Gail Collins and Margo Natalie Crawford, eds., *New Thoughts on the Black Arts Movement* (New Brunswick, NJ: Rutgers University, 2006), pp. 273–296; Dayo Gore, *Radicalism at the Crossroads: African American Women Activists and the Cold War* (New York: New York University Press, 2011); Christina Greene, "What's Sex Got to Do with It?: Gender and the New Black Freedom Movement Scholarship," *Feminist Studies* (March 2006): 163–183; Cheryl Higashida, *Black Internationalist Feminism: Women Writers of the Black Left, 1945–1995* (Urbana: University of Illinois Press, 2011); and Anne Valk, *Radical Sisters: Second-Wave Feminism and Black Liberation in Washington, D.C.* (Urbana: University of Illinois Press, 2010). For the multiple histories, origins, and implications of second-wave feminism, see, for example, Dorothy Sue Cobble, *The Other Women's Movement: Workplace Justice and Social Rights in Twentieth-Century America* (Princeton, NJ: Princeton

University Press, 2005); Jane Gerhard, *The Dinner Party: Judy Chicago and the Power of Popular Feminism, 1970–2007* (Athens: University of Georgia Press, 2013); Benita Roth, *Separate Roads to Feminism: Black, Chicana, and White Feminist Movements in America's Second Wave* (New York: Cambridge University Press, 2003).

13. Work on gender, culture, and the transnational dimensions of civil rights that has shaped my thinking includes Paul Gilroy, *The Black Atlantic: Modernity and Double Consciousness* (Cambridge, MA: Harvard University Press, 1993); Kevin Gaines, "From Center to Margin: Internationalism and the Origins of Black Feminism," in Russ Castronovo and Dana Nelson, eds., *Materializing Democracy: Toward a Revitalized Cultural Politics* (Durham, NC: Duke University Press, 2002), pp. 294–313; Penny Von Eschen, *Satchmo Blows Up the World* (Cambridge, MA: Harvard University Press, 2004).

14. Stuart Hall, "Notes on Deconstructing 'the Popular," (1981), in Raiford Guins and Omayra Zaragoze Cruz, eds., *Popular Culture: A Reader* (London: Sage, 2005), pp. 64–71; Stuart Hall, "What Is This 'Black' in Black Popular Culture?," in Gina Dent, ed., *Black Popular Culture* (New York: New Press, 1992), pp. 21–33; Richard Dyer, *Stars* (London: British Film Institute, 1998); Richard Dyer, *Heavenly Bodies: Film Stars and Society* (New York: Routledge, 2004).

15. Cicely Tyson's Tony-award-winning performance in *The Trip To Bountiful* in 2013 stood out because it marked her return to the Broadway stage for the first time in 30 years, and also because the actress long associated with dramatic roles also sang (the hymn "Blessed Assurance").

16. Robin D. G. Kelley, "Dig They Freedom: Meditations on History and the Black Avant-Garde," *Lenox Avenue: A Journal of Interarts Inquiry* 3 (1997): 13–27; Robin D. G. Kelley, *Africa Speaks, American Answers: Modern Jazz in Revolutionary Times* (Cambridge, MA: Harvard University Press, 2012); for attention to the "shared experiences of racism, sexism, decolonization, and exile" among women musicians, including Simone, Makeba, and Lincoln, see Jacqueline Castledine, "Gender, Jazz and Justice in Cold War Freedom Movements," in McGuire and Dittmer, eds., *Freedom Rights*, pp. 223–246.

17. Renee Romano and Leigh Raiford, eds., *The Civil Rights Movement in American Memory* (Athens: University of Georgia Press, 2006).

18. Horne with Schickel, *Lena*. For other versions of these events, see, for example, Mel Watkins, "Lena Horne Films Are Headline Act in a Festival," *New York Times*, November 28, 1980, p. C6. *Lena* was not the first time that the famously private Horne offered autobiographical accounts or was the subject of biographies. See, for example, Lena Horne, "My Search for Happiness," *True Confessions*, April 1949, n.p., "Horne," SCBCCF, v. I; for an earlier, and quite different autobiography, see Lena Horne, as told to Helen Arstein and Carlton Moss, *In Person: Lena Horne* (New York: Greenberg, 1955). Other biographies of Horne include James Haskins with Kathleen Benson, *Lena: A Personal and*

Professional Biography of Lena Horne (Chelsea, MI: Scarborough House, 1991, orig. pub. 1984); Gail Lumet Buckley, *The Hornes: An American Family* (New York: Applause Books, 1986); James Gavin, *Stormy Weather: The Life of Lena Horne* (New York: Atria Books, 2009).

19. Horne with Schickel, *Lena*, p. 210, pp. 216–17. For Horne's new songs, see Harold Arlen and Ira Gershwin (music), and Yip Harburg (lyrics), "Silent Spring," performed by Lena Horne, *Back in My Baby's Arms* (20th Century-Fox Records 1963); Adolph Green and Betty Comden, "Now," performed by Lena Horne, *Here's Lena Now* (20th Century-Fox, 1964).

20. For "good" and "spent," see Horne with Schickel, *Lena*, p. 203; for "was ice," see Ponchitta Pierce, "Lena at 51," *Ebony*, July 1968, pp. 124–135, quote p. 134; see also, Michiko Kakutani, "Lena Horne: Aloofness Hid the Pain Until Time Cooled Her Anger," *New York Times*, May 3, 1981, p. A1. For "I was," see Pierce, "Lena at 51," p. 133; for "I was," see Horne with Schickel, *Lena*, p. 218; for "cold hard," "absolutely joyful," and "determined," see Bob Thomas, "Lena Horne's Long Wait: First Dramatic Film Role," *New York Post*, July 1, 1968, n.p., in "Horne," SCBCCF, v. I. For similar themes, see also Joan Barthel, "Lena Horne: 'Now I Feel Good About Being Me,'" *New York Times*, July 25, 1968, p. 81; Marcia Gillespie, "Lena Horne Finds Her Music, Her Daughter, and Her Self," *Ms.*, August 1981, n.p., in Schomburg Center on Black Culture Clipping File, Volume II, 1975–1988, "Lena Horne" (hereafter, "Horne," SCBCCF, v. II); Josephine Premice interviewed and quoted in Susan Lacy, director/executive producer, *An American Masters Special: Lena Horne, in Her Own Voice* (New York: PBS, 1999), the Paley Center for Media, New York. For how Horne started to talk and write more about issues affecting black women in this period, see, for example, Lena Horne, "The Three-Horned 'Dilemma' Facing Negro Women," *Ebony*, August 1966, pp. 118–122, 124. For Horne's tendency toward "revisionism," see Gavin, *Stormy Weather*, pp. 428–429; for "disowning" her past and her history of relationships with whites, see pp. 347–351; for Horne's relationship to biography and autobiography, see also Shane Vogel, *The Scene of Harlem Cabaret: Race, Sexuality, Performance* (Chicago: University of Chicago Press, 2009), pp. 167–193; Shane Vogel, "Lena Horne's Impersonas," *Camera Obscura* 23 (2008): 1–22; Kwakiutl Dreher, *Dancing on the White Page: Black Women Entertainers Writing Autobiography* (Albany: State University of New York Press, 2008), pp. 29–60.

21. For "pretty Negro actress" and "hardworking gal," see Earl Wilson, "It Happened Last Night: A 'Dynamite Interview'—Lena Horne on Prejudice," *New York Post*, June 30, 1947, n.p., in "Horne," SCBCCF, v. I; for Horne's sense of her upbringing and her repertoire in contrast to "decadent jazz" and the blues, see Horne with Schickel, *Lena*, pp. 55, 91; for "have broadened the roles," see Eleanor Roosevelt to "To Whom It May Concern," February 17, 1942, NAACP Papers, Part 18, reel 15, #00417, Widener Library, Harvard University. For how the NAACP used visual representations of Horne as part of its larger political

goals, see Megan E. Williams, "The *Crisis* Cover Girl: Lena Horne, The NAACP and Representations of African American Femininity, 1941–1945," *American Periodicals: A Journal of History, Criticism, and Bibliography* 16, no. 2 (2006): 200–218; for Walter White's campaigns in Hollywood, see Thomas Cripps, *Slow Fade to Black: The Negro in American Film, 1900–1942* (New York: Oxford University Press, 1977). For respectability, race, and reform, see especially Evelyn Brooks-Higginbotham, *Righteous Discontent: The Women's Movement in the Black Baptist Church, 1880–1920* (Cambridge, MA: Harvard University Press, 1993); for Horne representing herself as an heir to this legacy, also known as "the politics of respectability," see Horne, "I Just Want to Be Myself," p. 4. For race and Hollywood in the 1940s, see Daniel Widener, *Black Arts West: Culture and Struggle in Postwar Los Angeles* (Durham, NC: Duke University Press, 2010), pp. 21–52.

22. For "too" outspoken, see Horne, "I Just Want to be Myself," p. 6; for White rebuking Horne, see Buckley, *The Hornes*, pp. 159, 172 (according to Buckley, Horne recalled that he "was writing letters saying 'remember your position' (in other words, don't disgrace us)," and on at least one occasion, he said that she'd worn an inappropriate dress to an MGM photo shoot); for "tired and overworked," see "Meet the Real Lena Horne," *Ebony*, November 1947, pp. 9–14, quote (and her support for Robeson) on p. 9. For Horne's range of activism in this period, see, for example, "Thousand Artists, Writers Back Davis," *Daily Worker*, September 25, 1945, p. 12; "Open Drive for Negro Vets' Terminal Pay," *Daily Worker*, July 2, 1947, p. 4; "Civil Rights Parley Saturday," *Daily Worker*, October 6, 1947, p. 5; "Protest Deportations," advertisement in the *Daily Worker*, March 3, 1948, p. 7; "Mobilize Against the Un-American Activities Committee," *Daily Worker*, October 6, 1947, p. 8; "Lena Brings Colored, White Newspaperman Together in Dee Cee," *Los Angeles Sentinel*, November 14, 1944, p. 23, in Margaret Herrick Library, Academy of Motion Pictures and Sciences, Special Collections, "Lena Horne" (hereafter, "Horne," Herrick Library); for *Ebony*'s coverage of Horne's support for Wallace, see "Meet the Real Lena Horne." See also Charlene B. Regester, "Hazel Scott and Lena Horne: African American Divas, Feminists, and Political Activists," *Popular Culture Review* 7 (1996): 81–95.

23. Horne with Schickel, *Lena*, pp. 103–107; for "biggest news," see William Thomas Smith, "Hollywood Report," *Phylon* (1st Qtr., 1945), pp. 13–16. For a slightly different account of these negotiations and the role Horne's father played, see Gavin, *Stormy Weather*, pp. 104–106; see also James Haskins with Kathleen Benson, *Lena: A Personal and Professional Biography of Lena Horne* (New York: Stein and Day, 1984), pp. 60–61.

24. For Horne's account of these events in *Lena*, see Horne with Schickel, *Lena*, pp. 132–135; for "crowded in," see "Lena Horne Meets Army Jim Crow," January 10, 1945, untitled source, n.p., in "Horne," SCBCCF, v. I; for paying her own way when she performed for black soldiers, see "Lena Horne Big Hit with Men in

Service," *Pittsburgh Courier*, March 20, 1943, n.p., in "Horne," Herrick Library; see also Kakutani, "Lena Horne"; Edmund Scott, "Lena Horne and the South," *PM*, March 29, 1945, n.p., in "Horne," SCBCCF, v. I; Alfred Smith, "Lena Horne Quits USO in Row Over Army Jim Crow: Star Charges Snub by Army Commander," *Chicago Defender*, January 6, 1945, pp. 1, 4. Details about the USO tours vary slightly from one source to another. For a later account that refers to Italian and not German prisoners of war, see Lena Horne, "A Measure of What Has Gone Before," *The Crisis*, August/September, 1983, p. 38.

25. See, for example, Frank Nugent, ". . . She's Nobody's Mammy," *Liberty*, April 7, 1945, pp. 30–31, 52–53, in "Horne," Herrick Library.

26. For "first black pin up" and "sex symbol," see Horne with Schickel, *Lena*, p. 132, p. 100; for "radiantly beautiful," see Brooks Atkinson, "The Play: Lew Leslie Gets His 'Blackbirds of 1939' on to the Stage of the Hudson Theatre," *New York Times*, February 13, 1939, p. 12; it is worth noting that Atkinson's full description of Horne was a "radiantly beautiful sepia girl"—a characterization that, in 1939, set the stage for later (and ongoing) tributes to Horne as "one of the world's most beautiful women." For Horne as a pinup girl, see also, "Backstage," *Ebony*, May 1946, p. 4; Letter from Alta Corinne Payne, *Ebony*, March 1947, p. 4; for the significance of black pinups, see Williams, "Meet the Real Lena Horne"; Maria Elena Buszek, *Pin-Up Grrrls: Feminism, Sexuality, Popular Culture* (Durham, NC: Duke University Press, 2006), p. 248; and Charissa Threat, "Searching for Colored Pin-Up Girls: Race, Gender and Sexuality During World War II," paper presented at the Berkshire Conference on Women's History, Amherst, MA, June 2011. For black women and beauty, see especially Maxine Leeds Craig, *Ain't I a Beauty Queen: Black Women, Beauty, and the Politics of Race* (New York: Oxford, 2002); Susannah Walker, *Style and Status: Selling Beauty to African American Women, 1920–1975* (Louisville: University Press of Kentucky, 2007). For an alternative reading of Horne's aloofness as "an acute response to the interracial intimacy produced by performance across the color line," see Vogel, *The Scene of Harlem Cabaret*, quote p. 35, and pp. 167–193; see also Richard Dyer, *Heavenly Bodies: Film Stars and Society* (New York: Routledge, 2003; orig. pub. 1986), pp. 15, 64–136.

27. Nugent, "She's Nobody's Mammy," p. 30, in "Horne," SCBCCF, v. I; for this scene, see Bud Friedkin, director, *That's Entertainment, III* (MGM, 1994); for her aloofness as Georgia Brown, see Vogel, "Lena Horne's Impersonas."

28. Elsa Maxwell, "Glamour vs. Prejudice," *Negro Digest*, January 1944, reprinted in Maureen Honey, ed., *Bitter Fruit: African American Women in World War II* (Columbia: University of Missouri Press, 1999), p. 334; Maxwell was discussing both Horne and dancer Katherine Dunham. For the category of "glamour" with regard to other black women, see "Introduction" in Honey, *Bitter Fruit*, pp. 28–29; Karen Chilton, *Hazel Scott: The Pioneering Journey of a Jazz Pianist, from Café Society to Hollywood to HUAC* (Ann Arbor: University of Michigan

Press, 2010); Kristin McGee, *Some Liked It Hot: Jazz Women in Film and Television, 1928–1959* (Middletown, CT: Wesleyan University Press, 2009); Shane Vogel, "Performing *Stormy Weather*: Ethel Waters, Lena Horne, and Katherine Dunham," *South Central Review* 25 (Spring 2008): 93–113.

29. Horne with Schickel, *Lena*, p. 211.

30. Horne with Schickel, *Lena*, pp. 222; 199–200; Davis and Dee, *With Ossie and Ruby*, p. 271; for *Jamaica*, see Shane Vogel, "*Jamaica* on Broadway: The Popular Caribbean and Mock Transnational Performance," *Theater Journal* 62 (2010): 1–22.

31. See also Kakutani, "Lena Horne"; Barthel, "Lena Horne: 'Now I Feel Good About Being Me,'" p. 81.

32. Daphne Brooks, *Bodies in Dissent: Spectacular Performances of Race and Freedom, 1850–1910* (Durham, NC: Duke University Press, 2006), p. 8; see also Kevin Gaines, "Artistic Othering in Black Diaspora Musics: Preliminary Thoughts on Time, Culture, and Politics," in Robert G. O'Meally et al., eds., *Uptown Conversation: the New Jazz Studies* (New York: Columbia University Press, 2004), pp. 204–223.

33. For Walker, see Brooks, *Bodies in Dissent*, pp. 326–342; Nugent, "She's Nobody's Mammy." For black women and modern womanhood, see Davarian Baldwin, *Chicago's New Negroes: Modernity, the Great Migration, and Black Urban Life* (Chapel Hill: University of North Carolina Press, 2007), pp. 53–120; Erin Chapman, *Prove It on Me: New Negroes, Sex and Politics in the 1920s* (New York: Oxford University Press, 2012).

34. For women blues singers, see Davis, *Blues Legacies and Black Feminism*; Hazel Carby, "'It Jus Be's Dat Way Sometime': The Sexual Politics of Women's Blues," (1986), in Vicki Ruiz and Ellen Dubois, eds., *Unequal Sisters: A Multicultural Reader in U.S. Women's History* (New York: Routledge, 1994; orig. pub. 1990), pp. 330–342; Chapman, *Prove It on Me*. For women musicians and the jazz canon of the 1920s, see Jeffrey Taylor, "With Lovie and Lil: Rediscovering Two Chicago Pianists of the 1920s," in Nichole Rustin and Sherrie Tucker, eds., *Big Ears: Listening for Gender in Jazz Studies* (Durham, NC: Duke University Press, 2008), pp. 48–63. For Baker, see Charlene Regester, "The Construction of an Image and the Deconstruction of a Star—Josephine Baker Racialized, Sexuality, and Politicized in the African American Press, the Mainstream Press, and FBI Files," *Popular Music and Society* 24 (Spring 2000); 31–84; Anne Cheng, *Second Skin: Josephine Baker and the Modern Surface* (New York: Oxford University Press, 2011). For black women's attempts to use images of black female sexuality, see bell hooks's analysis of Tina Turner, "Selling Hot Pussy: Representations of Black Female Sexuality in the Cultural Marketplace," in hooks, *Black Looks: Race and Representation* (Boston: South End Press, 1999), pp. 61–78.

35. For criticisms from Walter White and others, and for controversies over *Gone with the Wind* more generally, see Jill Watts, *Hattie McDaniel: Black Ambition, White Hollywood* (New York: HarperCollins, 2005); for different versions of

this story, see Watts, *Hattie McDaniel*, p. 139; Donald Bogle, *Toms, Coons Mulattoes, Mammies, and Bucks: An Interpretive History of Blacks in American Films* (New York: Continuum, 2001; orig. pub. 1973), p. 82. For recent controversies about black women entertainers that draw on this story, see Anthony Kaufman, "How Racist Is 'The Help'?," *IndieWIRE*, http://blogs.indiewire.com/anthony/archives/how_racist_is_the_help/ (August 22, 2011).

36. Linda Dahl, *Morning Glory: A Biography of Mary Lou Williams* (Berkeley: University of California Press, 2001); Tammy Kernodle, *Soul on Soul: The Life and Music of Mary Lou Williams* (Boston: Northeastern University Press, 2004); Nichole Rustin, "'Mary Lou Williams Plays Like a Man': Gender, Genius and Difference in Black Music Discourse," *South Atlantic Quarterly* 104 (Summer 2005): 445–462; Karen Chilton, *Hazel Scott: The Pioneering Journey of a Jazz Pianist from the Café Society to Hollywood to HUAC* (Ann Arbor: University of Michigan Press, 2008); Gayle Wald, *Shout, Sister, Shout! The Untold Story of Rock-and-Roll Trailblazer Sister Rosetta Tharpe* (Boston: Beacon Press, 2007); Raymond Arsenault, *The Sound of Freedom: Marian Anderson, the Lincoln Memorial, and the Concert That Awakened America* (New York: Bloomsbury Press, 2009); Janell Hobson, "Everybody's Protest Song: Music as Social Protest in the Performances of Marian Anderson and Billie Holiday," *Signs* 33 (2008): 443–448. For popular culture as a mediated space, see Baldwin, *Chicago's New Negroes*, pp. 236–239.

37. See especially, Lizabeth Cohen, *A Consumer's Republic: The Politics of Mass Consumption in Postwar America* (New York: Knopf, 2003), pp. 166–192.

38. For black activism, the media and citizenship, see Sasha Torres, *Black, White, and in Color: Television and Black Civil Rights* (Princeton, NJ: Princeton University Press, 2003); Allison Graham, *Framing the South: Hollywood, Television and Race During the Civil Rights Struggle* (Baltimore: Johns Hopkins University Press, 2003); Clayborne Carson, David J. Garrow, Bill Kovach, and Carol Polsgrove, eds., *Reporting Civil Rights, Part One: American Journalism 1941–1963* (New York: Library of America, 2003). For black expressive culture, identity, and activism, see also Waldo Martin, *No Coward Soldiers: Black Cultural Politics in Postwar America* (Cambridge, MA: Harvard University Press, 2005), pp. 25–37; Robin D. G. Kelley, *Freedom Dreams, The Black Radical Imagination* (Boston: Beacon Press, 2003); Kobena Mercer, "1968: Periodizing Politics and Identity," in Lawrence Grossberg and Cary Nelson, eds., *Cultural Studies* (New York: Routledge, 1992), pp. 424–449; and Jane Rhodes, *Framing the Black Panthers: The Spectacular Rise of a Black Power Icon* (New York: New Press, 2007).

39. Watts, *Hattie McDaniel*, pp. 158–179; Widener, *Black Arts West*.

40. See, for example, Amiri Baraka, *Blues People: Negro Music in White America* (New York: William and Morrow, 1963).

41. James Baldwin, "Sweet Lorraine," in Lorraine Hansberry (adapted by Robert Nemiroff), *To Be Young, Gifted, and Black: An Informal Autobiography* (New York: Signet, 1970; orig. pub. 1969), p. xiii.

CHAPTER I

1. Lena Horne with Richard Schickel, *Lena* (Garden City, NY: Limelight, 1986; orig. pub. 1965), p. 200.

2. Maya Angelou, *The Heart of a Woman* (New York: Random House, 1981), p. 115; Hugh Masekela with Michael Cheers, *Still Grazing: The Musical Journey of Hugh Masekela* (New York: Crown, 2004), p. 137.

3. For activism in New York, see especially Martha Biondi, *To Stand and Fight: The Struggle for Civil Rights in Postwar New York City* (Cambridge, MA: Harvard University Press, 2006); for the Nation of Islam, see especially Peniel Joseph, *Waiting 'Til the Midnight Hour: A Narrative History of Black Power in America* (New York: Henry Holt, 2006), pp. 9–34; for other organizing, see Adina Black, "Exposing the 'Whole Segregation Myth': The Harlem Nine and New York City's School Desegregation Battles," in Jeanne Theoharis and Komozi Woodard, eds., *Freedom North: Black Freedom Struggles Outside the South, 1940–1980* (New York: Palgrave Macmillan, 2003), pp. 65–92; Rebeccah Welch, "Black Art and Activism in Postwar New York, 1950–1965" (Ph.D. diss., New York University, 2002). In addition to work cited in other chapters, important scholarship exploring the impact of the Cold War on the black left includes Kate Baldwin, *Beyond the Color Line and the Iron Curtain: Reading Encounters Between Black and Red, 1922–1963* (Durham, NC: Duke University Press, 2002); Antoinette Burton, "Cold War Cosmopolitanism: The Education of Santha Rama Rau in the Age of Bandung, 1945–1954," *Radical History Review* (Spring 2006): 149–172; and Dayo Gore, *Radicalism at the Crossroads: African American Women Activists in the Cold War* (New York: New York University Press, 2011). For a contemporary critique of Cold War liberal antiracism, see "Cold War Casualty," in "Letters," *The Nation*, July 2, 1949, p. 173: "Suppose Stalin recants and returns to God . . . and the cold war simply comes to its end—what then? No more need to oppose colonialism and lynching and civil rights? . . . The liberal movement would be caught with its ideological pants down."

4. See Penny Von Eschen, "The Cold War Seduction of Harold Cruse," in Jerry Watts, ed., *Harold Cruse's The Crisis of the Negro Intellectual Reconsidered* (New York: Routledge, 2004), pp. 169–182; for "to link," see Larry Neal, quoted in Joseph, *Waiting 'Til the Midnight Hour*, p. 256.

5. For this growing sense of cultural and political possibility, see especially Robin D. G. Kelley, *Africa Speaks, America Answers: Modern Jazz in Revolutionary Times* (Cambridge, MA: Harvard University Press, 2012); Joseph, *Waiting 'Til the Midnight Hour*; for the significance of the Bandung Conference, see Ryan Irwin, *Gordian Knot: Apartheid and the Unmaking of the Liberal World Order* (New York: Oxford University Press, 2012), pp. 4–6; Fanon Che Wilkins, "Beyond Bandung: The Critical Nationalism of Lorraine Hansberry, 1950–1965," *Radical*

History Review 95 (Spring 2006): 191–210; Cynthia Young, *Soul Power: Culture, Radicalism, and the Making of a U.S. Third World Left* (Durham, NC: Duke University Press, 2006), p. 2; for radical and nationalist black politics in this period, see Van Gosse, "More Than Just a Politician: Notes on the Life and Times of Harold Cruse," in Watts, ed., *Harold Cruse's The Crisis of the Negro Intellectual Reconsidered*, pp. 17–40. Of course, there were many other events—the brutal murder of Emmett Till in September 1955, for example—that generated more outrage than optimism.

6. For the black left and anticolonialism, see especially Penny Von Eschen, *Race Against Empire: Black Americans and Anticolonialism, 1937–1957* (Ithaca, NY: Cornell University Press, 1997); for the impact independence movements in Ghana had, see Kevin Gaines, *American Africans in Ghana: Black Expatriates and the Civil Rights Era* (Chapel Hill: University of North Carolina Press, 2006).

7. Lorraine Hansberry, *Les Blancs: The Collected Last Plays: The Drinking Gourd/ What Use Are Flowers*, ed. Robert Nemiroff (New York: Vintage, 1994; orig. pub. 1973); Max Roach, *We Insist! Freedom Now Suite* (Candid Records, 1960); Melba Liston and Randy Weston, *Uhuru Afrika* (Roulette Records, 1960); see also Kelley, *Africa Speaks, America Answers*.

8. Angelou, *The Heart of a Woman*, pp. 104–120, 135; Miriam Makeba with James Hall, *Makeba: My Story* (New York: New American Library, 1987), p. 91; Plummer, *Rising Wind*, p. 282. For black internationalism on a longer chronological trajectory, see Robin D. G. Kelley, "'But a Local Phase of a World Problem': Black History's Global Vision, 1883–1950," *Journal of American History* 86 (December 1999): 1045–1077.

9. For Harlem and for "blacks on the street," see Conrad Lynn, *There Is a Fountain: The Autobiography of Conrad Lynn* (Brooklyn, NY: Lawrence Hill Books, 1993; orig. pub. 1979), p. 169; for the 1961 protest, see Joseph, *Waiting 'Til the Midnight Hour*, pp. 38–44; Angelou, *Heart of a Woman*, pp. 143–170; for Lincoln and other women preparing, see pp. 147, 153.

10. For "like a long-lost brother" and "how glad," see Masekela with Cheers, *Still Grazing*, pp. 137, 150; for "how does," see Makeba with Hall, *Makeba*, p. 92.

11. For "saloon for sophisticates," see Makeba with Hall, *Makeba*, p. 80. For Brooklyn as another nerve center, especially for culturally and politically innovative black musicians, see Kelley, *Africa Speaks, America Answers*, pp. 41–57.

12. Ossie Davis, quoted in Welch, "Black Art and Activism," p. 41; for a similar perspective, see also Masekela with Cheers, *Still Grazing*, p. 127. For the significance of Harlem, see Joseph, *Waiting 'Til the Midnight Hour*, pp. 40–41; James Smethurst, *The Black Arts Movement: Literary Nationalism in the 1960s and 1970s* (Chapel Hill: University of North Carolina Press, 2005), p. 11; Eric Porter, *What Is This Thing Called Jazz? African American Musicians as Artists, Critics, and Activists* (Berkeley: University of California Press, 2002), pp. 58–59.

13. Angelou, *The Heart of a Woman*, pp. 147, 153.

14. For "two damn crowded," see Lorraine Hansberry, *To Be Young, Gifted and Black: Lorraine Hansberry in Her Own Words* (New York: Random House, 1995; orig. pub. 1970), p. 77; for "artistic," see Nina Simone with Stephen Cleary, *I Put a Spell on You: The Autobiography of Nina Simone* (New York: Da Capo Press, 1993; orig. pub. 1991), pp. 65–70, quote p. 67.

15. Joseph, *Waiting 'Til the Midnight Hour*, p. 42; Makeba with Hall, *Makeba*, pp. 90–94, 106; Diahann Carroll with Ross Firestone, *Diahann! An Autobiography* (New York: Ivy Books, 1986), pp. 77–83; for discrimination and violence in the Village, see Amiri Baraka, *Autobiography of Leroi Jones/Amiri Baraka* (Brooklyn, NY: Lawrence Hill, 1995; orig. pub. 1984), p. 133; see also pp. 168–172; Judith Smith, *Visions of Belonging: Family Stories, Popular Culture, and Postwar Democracy, 1940–1960* (New York: Columbia University Press, 2006); pp. 304–306; for "harassed," see Miriam Makeba in conversation with Nomsa Mwamuka, *The Miriam Makeba Story* (Johannesburg, South Africa: STE, 2004), pp. 68, 70. For Hansberry's race and sexuality in the context of village subcultures, see Lisbeth Lipari, "The Rhetoric of Intersectionality: Lorraine Hansberry's 1957 Letters to the *Ladder*," in Charles Morris III, ed., *Queering Public Address: Sexualities in American Historical Discourse* (Columbia: University of South Carolina Press, 2007), pp. 220–248; for Hansberry's race, sexuality, and anticolonial politics in relation, see Cheryl Higashida, "To Be(come) Young, Gay, and Black: Lorraine Hansberry's Existentialist Routes to Anticolonialism," *American Quarterly* 60 (December 2008): 899–924.

16. Simone with Cleary, *I Put a Spell on You*, p. 67.

17. For a conference in 1959 organized by the Harlem Writers Guild and AMSAC on "The American Negro Writer and His Roots," see AMSAC, ed., *The American Negro Writer and His Roots: Selected Papers from the First Conference of Negro Writers, March 1959* (New York: AMSAC, 1960). For AMSAC and the CIA, see Gaines, *American Africans in Ghana*, pp. 48–49, 219; Kelley, *Africa Speaks, America Answers*, pp. 64–66; Lawrence P. Jackson, *The Indignant Generation: A Narrative History of African American Writers and Critics, 1943–1960* (Princeton, NJ: Princeton University Press, 2010), pp. 462–463.

18. Ossie Davis and Ruby Dee, *With Ossie and Ruby: In This Life Together* (New York: HarperCollins, 2000; orig. pub. 1998), p. 202; see also Smethurst, *Black Literary Nationalism*, p. 133; Gaines, *American Africans in Ghana*, p. 154.

19. Makeba with Hall, *Makeba*, pp. 91–92; Simone with Cleary, *I Put a Spell on You*, pp. 60–63; Alan Ebert, "Inside Cecily" [sic], *Essence*, February 1973, p. 41. For black entertainers and financial stress, see also Welch, "Black Art and Activism," pp. 39–90.

20. For *Porgy and Bess*, see Aram Goudsouzian, *Sidney Poitier: Man, Actor, Icon* (Chapel Hill: University of North Carolina Press, 2003), p. 151; Michael Eldridge, "Remains of the Day-O: A Conversation with Harry Belafonte," *Transition* 92

(2002): 110–137; for Davis, Roach and the ARF, see Ingrid Monson, *Freedom Sounds: Civil Rights Call Out to Jazz and Africa* (New York: Oxford University Press, 2007), p. 189.

21. Arnold Shaw, *Belafonte: An Unauthorized Biography* (New York: Pyramid Books, 1960), pp. 40–42; Eldridge, "Remains of the Day-O," pp. 114, 117–118; Davis and Dee, *With Ossie and Ruby*, pp. 129–138; Sidney Poitier, *This Life* (New York: Knopf, 1980), pp. 68–79; Baraka, *The Autobiography of Leroi Jones/Amiri Baraka*, pp. 95–123; Van Gosse, "More Than Just a Politician," p. 20. For black veterans as the "shock troops of the modern civil rights movement," see John Dittmer, *Local People: The Struggle for Civil Rights in Mississippi* (Urbana: University of Illinois Press, 1994), p. 9.

22. Simone with Cleary, *I Put a Spell on You*, pp. 86–87.

23. For "a kind of," see Lorenzo Thomas, "Alea's Children: The Avant-Garde on the Lower East Side, 1960–1970," *African American Review* 27 (Winter 1993): 573–78, quote pp. 575–576; John Cassavetes, director, *Shadows* (Lion International Films, 1959); for "established the beginning," see Albert Johnson, "The Negro in American Films: Some Recent Works," *Film Quarterly* 18 (Summer 1965): 14–30, quote p. 20. For discussions of interracialism in these communities, see Welch, "Black Art and Activism," pp. 19–25; Smith, *Visions of Belonging*, p. 303; Smethurst, *The Black Arts Movement*.

24. Horne with Schickel, *Lena*, pp. 155–169; "Meet the Real Lena Horne," *Ebony*, November 1947, pp. 9–14; Lena Horne, "My Life with Lennie," *Ebony*, November 1965, pp. 174–186; Belafonte with Shnayerson, *My Song*; Simone with Cleary, *I Put a Spell on You*, p. 57; Carroll with Firestone, *Diahann!*, pp. 70–77; Jones, *The Autobiography of Leroi Jones/Amiri Baraka*, pp. 129, 168. See also Renee Romano, *Race Mixing: Black-White Marriage in Postwar America* (Cambridge, MA: Harvard University Press, 2003).

25. For "three distinct," see Smethurst, *The Black Arts Movement*, p. 135; for "jazz scene," see Simone with Cleary, *I Put a Spell on You*, p. 68.

26. Simone with Cleary, *I Put a Spell on You*, p. 67.

27. The literature on jazz in this period is extensive. For musicians' relationships to civil rights organizing and to benefit concerts, see especially Monson, *Freedom Sounds*; for women, gender, and jazz, see especially Sherrie Tucker and Nichole Rustin, eds., *Big Ears: Listening for Gender in Jazz Studies* (Durham, NC: Duke University Press, 2008). While Diahann Carroll was a vocalist who recorded several albums in this period, because roles on stage and in films were crucial to her professional persona from the start of her career, I consider her in that context.

28. Here and throughout the following chapters, biographical information is based on consistent accounts in memoirs and biographies, and sources from the period. For "knew I was going to be," see Oral History with Abbey Lincoln/Animata Moseka, by Cobi Narita and James Briggs Murray (September 1996), Louis

Armstrong Jazz Oral History Projects, Schomburg Center for Research in Black Culture, New York, SC-visual, VRA-178; for "sultry dish," see "New Acts: Abbey Lincoln," *Variety*, August 21, 1957, p. 55; for "sepia Marilyn Monroe," see "Abbey Lincoln Opens Tuesday," *New York Amsterdam News*, December 7, 1957, p. 13; for signed photographs of her as "Ann Marie," see Abbey Lincoln Collection (MC 101), Institute of Jazz Studies, Rutgers University Libraries, Box 33, "Abbey Lincoln Photographs, 1940–60s." Lincoln's autobiographical writings are part of this collection but are currently restricted.

29. For Lincoln at the Village Vanguard, see John Wilson, "Pop Music, Abbey Lincoln Returns," *New York Times*, August 24, 1979, p. C12; for "arrival," see Dom Cerulli, "The Arrival of Abbey," *Down Beat*, June 12, 1958, p. 19; for the "girl in," see "The Girl in the Marilyn Monroe Dress," *Ebony*, June 1957, pp. 27–31 (and cover); for her changing styles, see Barbara Gardner, "Metamorphosis," *Down Beat*, September 14, 1961, pp. 18–20. For an invaluable discussion of Lincoln's changed appearance and moves toward innovative jazz music and political commitments as intertwined, see Farah Jasmine Griffin, *If You Can't Be Free, Be a Mystery: In Search of Billie Holiday* (New York: Free Press, 2001), pp. 161–191; see also Porter, *What Is This Thing Called Jazz?*, pp. 149–192.

30. Abbey Lincoln, *Abbey Is Blue* (Riverside, 1959); Lincoln quoted in Nat Hentoff, "Liner Notes," *Straight Ahead* (New York: Candid Records, 1961); also quoted in Porter, *What Is This Thing Called Jazz?*, p. 154.

31. Simone with Cleary, *I Put a Spell on You*, p. 42; Nadine Cohodas, *Princess Noire: The Tumultuous Reign of Nina Simone* (New York: Pantheon, 2010), pp. 5–60. Jazz giants Thelonius Monk and Miles Davis also studied at Juilliard.

32. "I Loves You Porgy" reached the top 20 on Billboard in the summer of 1959, after Simone had moved to Manhattan. See Joel Whitburn, *Top R&B Singles, 1942–1995* (Menomonee Falls, WI: Hal Leonard, 1996), p. 402; David Nathan, liner notes, *The Very Best of Nina Simone, 1967–1972* (RCA, 1998); Nina Simone, *Little Girl Blue* (Bethlehem, 1957). "I Loves You Porgy" was one of several songs associated with Billie Holiday that Simone recorded. For Holiday's complex legacy, see Griffin, *If You Can't Be Free, Be a Mystery*.

33. For "the greatest compliments," see Sidney Lazard, *Chicago Sun-Times*, quoted in Phyl Garland, *The Sound of Soul* (Chicago: H. Regnery, 1969), p. 175; for "singularly arresting," see "Nina Loves Porgy," *Ebony*, December 1959, p. 169; for "cocktail and supper club," see Garland, *The Sound of Soul*, p. 171.

34. For "interpreted," see "New Singer in Town," *Look*, February 2, 1960, p. 60D; for her arrival in the United States and initial performances, see Makeba with Hall, *Makeba*, pp. 84–86; "African Girl Tops: A Name's, A Name's A Name," *Pittsburgh Courier*, February 6, 1960, p. 24.

35. Makeba had to leave school to earn money, which she did first as a nanny, and then by doing laundry for white families. In 1950, Makeba married and had a daughter, but the marriage was brief; she left her first husband because

he physically abused her. See Makeba with Hall, *Makeba*; William Modisane, "Manhattan Brothers Mellow," *Drum*, January 1956, pp. 37–39; Casey Motsisi, "Miriam in New York, Part I," *Drum*, April 1960, pp. 26–31; Muff Anderson, *Music in the Mix: The Story of South African Popular Music* (Johannesburg, South Africa: Ravan Press, 1981), pp. 35–37.

36. For Makeba's years of performing in Africa, see Makeba with Hall, *Makeba*; for Venice, see "Miriam: Star of Venice," *Drum*, October 1959, p. 65; for the film, see Lionel Rogosin, director, *Come Back, Africa* (currently distributed by Milestone Films, Harrington Park, NJ; orig. release 1959); for Makeba and the film's reception in Venice, see Lionel Rogosin, *Come Back, Africa: A Man Possessed* (Johannesburg, South Africa: STE, 2004), pp. 124–125. Rogosin and others helped Makeba leave South Africa, although the specifics regarding who did what vary from one account to another. According to Rogosin's diaries, he worked with Myrtle Berman, a white South African liberal (and a housewife in the film), who paid $500 to Pretoria officials for Makeba's exit permit; Makeba was able to leave the country almost a year after he had; see Rogosin, *Come Back, Africa*, p. 124. According to other accounts, to get a passport from the South African government officials who did not know that the film existed, Makeba claimed that she had been invited to Venice to be honored for her role in *King Kong*. See Masekela with Cheers, *Still Grazing*, p. 100. The precise nature of the professional relationships Makeba had with Rogosin and Belafonte also remains unclear. Rogosin's manuscripts suggest that she was under contract with him, and that Belafonte encouraged her to "break her contract" so that he could promote her; Rogosin's son explains that Lionel Rogosin was acting as Makeba's "agent" and felt "betrayed" by both Belafonte and Makeba. See Rogosin, *Come Back, Africa*, p. 126; Michael Rogosin, interview with author, June 24, 2005; for this perspective, see also Lorraine Gordon interview in Mika Kaurismaki, director, *Mama Africa* (Trigon-Film 2011). Belafonte suggests that Makeba was not being well served professionally; see Belafonte with Shnayerson, *My Song*, pp. 203–205. Makeba's first autobiography offers a mostly positive account of her move from a relatively dependent relationship on Rogosin to a similarly dependent relationship with Belafonte but does not discuss agents or official representation. See Makeba with Hall, *Makeba*.

37. Monson, *Freedom Sounds*, p. 170; see Leroi Jones, *Blues People* (New York: William Morrow, 1963) for an influential articulation of blues as *the* authentic black culture; for debates from this period about jazz and race, see Ira Gitler, Abbey Lincoln, et al., "Racial Prejudice in Jazz, Part I," *Down Beat*, March 20, 1962, pp. 20–26; "Racial Prejudice in Jazz, Part II," *Down Beat*, March 29, 1962, pp. 22–25. For a rich intellectual and cultural history of African American jazz musicians, see Porter, *What Is This Thing Called Jazz?* For experimental music in New York in this period, see Benjamin Piekut, *Experimentalism Otherwise: The New York Avant-Garde and Its Limits* (Berkeley: University of California Press, 2011).

38. Dizzy Gillespie with Al Fraser, *To Be or Not to Bop* (New York: Da Capo, 1970), pp. 287–291; also quoted in Porter, *What Is This Thing Called Jazz?*, pp. 58–59. For bebop, see also Guthrie Ramsey Jr., *Race Music: Black Cultures from Bebop to Hip Hop* (Berkeley: University of California Press, 2003), pp. 96–130; Eric Lott, "Double V, Double-Time: Bebop's Politics of Style," in Robert G. O'Meally, ed., *The Jazz Cadence of American Culture* (New York: Columbia University Press, 1998), pp. 457–468.

39. Charles Mingus, "Fable of Faubus," *Mingus Ah Um* (Columbia, 1959); Mingus, "Original Faubus Fables," *Charles Mingus Presents Charles Mingus* (Candid, 1960); Mingus, "Work Song," *Mingus at the Bohemia* (Debut, 1955); Mingus, "Haitian Fight Song," *The Clown* (Atlantic, 1957); Porter, *What Is This Thing Called Jazz?*, p. 128. For these musical subcultures in relation to domestic civil rights and anticolonial politics, see especially Monson, *Freedom Sounds*; Kelley, *Africa Speaks, America Answers*.

40. Charles Mingus, "Prayer for Passive Resistance," *Mingus at Antibes* (Rhino, 1960); Roach, *We Insist!*; see also Monson, *Freedom Sounds*, pp. 171–185; Porter, *What Is This Thing Called Jazz?*, pp. 167–169; 129; Salim Washington, "'All the Things You Could Be By Now': *Charles Mingus Presents Charles Mingus* and the Limits of Avant-Garde Jazz," in Robert O'Meally, et al. eds., *Uptown Conversation: The New Jazz Studies* (New York: Columbia University Press, 2004), pp. 27–49. It is worth noting that Lincoln later said that it was Roach's idea for her to scream and that it "wasn't an approach to music that I would have chosen"; see Monson, *Freedom Sounds*, p. 178.

41. For "had to take politics seriously," see Simone with Cleary, *I Put a Spell on You*, p. 86; Randy Weston *Uhuru Afrika* (Capitol, 1960); Sonny Rollins, *The Freedom Suite* (Riverside, 1958); Michael Babtunde Olatunji, *Drums of Passion* (Columbia, 1959); see also Kelley, *Africa Speak, America Answers*.

42. Suzanne Smith, *Dancing in the Street: Motown and the Cultural Politics of Detroit* (Cambridge, MA: Harvard University Press, 2001); Joslyn Layne, "Smokey Robinson and the Miracles," http://www.billboard.com/artist/smokey-robinson-the-miracles/bio/170243#/artist/smokey-robinson-the-miracles/bio/170243, (accessed July 3, 2011); Harry Belafonte, *Harry Belafonte—Calypso* (RCA-Victor, 1956); Eldridge, "Remains of the Day-O," p. 137; Matthew Frye Jacobson, "Take This Hammer: Odetta, Coffeehouse Publics, and the Tributaries of the Left, 1953–1962," paper presented at the American Studies Association Conference, Washington, DC, November 2009.

43. For the political energy of various musical genres and spaces in this period, see also John Gennari, "Hipsters, Bluebloods, Rebels, and Hooligans: The Cultural Politics of the Newport Jazz Festival, 1954–1960," in O'Meally, ed., *Uptown Conversation*, pp. 126–150; Scott Saul, *Freedom Is, Freedom Ain't: Jazz and the Making of the Sixties* (Cambridge, MA: Harvard University Press, 2003).

44. See especially Ingrid Monson, "The Problem with White Hipness: Race, Gender, and Cultural Conceptions in Jazz Historical Discourse," *Journal of the American*

Musicological Society 48 (Autumn 1995): 396–422; for the gendered dimensions to notions of jazz "genius," see Nichole T. Rustin, "'Mary Lou Williams Plays Like a Man!': Gender, Difference and Genius in Black Music Discourse," *South Atlantic Quarterly* 104 (Summer 2005): 445–462.

45. Porter, *What Is this Thing Called Jazz?*, pp. 191–239.

46. Horne supported Robeson and wrote columns and gave interviews defending those convicted by HUAC into the 1950s at the same time that she did what she could to get her name off of Red Channels and expand her options professionally. For example, she met with Theodore Kirkpatrick, the ex-FBI agent who published *Counterattack* and *Red Channels* in an effort to clear her name; according to some accounts, she also did distance herself from Robeson. See Lena Horne, "From Me to You," *People's Voice*, September 16, 1947, n.p., Schomburg Center on Black Culture Clipping File, Volume I, 1925–1974, "Lena Horne" (hereafter, "Horne," SCBCCF, v. I); John Roddy, "Lena Horne's Manager Says 'Counterattack' Clears Her," *Daily Compass*, October 10, 1951 n.p., "Horne," SCBCCF, v. I; "Lena Horne's Manager Says She'll Refuse to 'Name Names'" *Daily Compass*, October 11, 1951. For a slightly different account of these events, see Ed Sullivan, "Little Old New York: Behind the Scenes," *Daily News*, October 10, 1951; James Gavin, *Stormy Weather: The Life of Lena Horne* (New York: Atria Books, 2009), pp. 234–237.

47. For this "cross-fertilization" process as it dated back to the 1930s and 1940s, see especially Michael Denning, *The Cultural Front: The Laboring of American Culture in the Twentieth Century* (New York: Verso, 1996), pp. 283–322; Smith, "Becoming Harry Belafonte," p. 27. For the shifts between genres among writers, see Welch, "Black Art and Activism," pp. 207–210.

48. Carroll with Firestone, *Diahann!*, pp. 8–9, 30–45, 46.

49. Carroll with Firestone, *Diahann!*, p. 47; "The Entertainer of the Year," *Cue: The Complete Entertainment Guide for New York and Suburbs*, December 30, 1961, n.p., in "Diahann Carroll," Schomburg Center on Black Culture Clipping File, Volume I, 1925–1974 (hereafter "Carroll," SCBCCF, v. I).

50. For "what more," see Dolores Calvin, "Diahann Carroll, Ella, Dizzy, Duke Make Week's News," *Chicago Defender*, October 22–28, 1960, p. 19; for Cairo and other countries, see Henderson Cleaves, "Diahann Uses the Method," *New York World Telegram*, February 22, 1961, n.p., in "Carroll," SCBCCF, v. I; for "an entertainer of international import," see Don Nelsen, "A Shooting Star with Melody," *New York Daily News*, undated, n.p., in "Carroll," SCBCCF, v. I.

51. Yvonne, "The Importance of Cicely Tyson," *Ms.*, August 1974, p. 77; published accounts of Tyson's birth year vary, but 1933 is the date that recurs most consistently.

52. For "from the typing pool," see Robert Windeler, "Cicely Tyson: From the Typing Pool to an Emmy," *People*, June 3, 1974, pp. 36–40; for her commitment, see "Cicely Was Once Too Shy to Act," *New York Amsterdam News*, September

23, 1972, p. D-2; Jerry Tallmer, " Unmasked Talent, " *New York Post*, August 15, 1966, n.p., in Schomburg Center on Black Culture Clipping File, Volume I, 1925–1974, "Cicely Tyson," (hereafter "Tyson," SCBCCF, v. I).

53. Tyson's first starring role on stage was in *Dark of the Moon* (1957), a play written by Howard Richardson and William Berney, and directed by Vinnette Carroll, a black woman actress, director, and producer, with choreography by 26-year-old Alvin Ailey. Early films included *The Last Angry Man* (1959), and *Odds Against Tomorrow* (1959); on television, she appeared in *Brown Girl, Brown Stones* (1960), several soap operas, and, a few years later, on *I Spy* (1966). For "first-class," see David Susskind, quoted in Richard F. Shepard, "News of TV and Radio," *New York Times*, June 30, 1963, p. 75.

54. For black theater, see Smethurst, *The Black Arts Movement*, pp. 108–109, pp. 114–132; Errol Hill, ed., *The Theater of Black Americans: A Collection of Critical Essays* (New York: Applause, 1987; orig. pub. 1980). For *Raisin*, see Lorraine Hansberry, *A Raisin in the Sun and The Sign in Sidney Brustein's Window*, introduction by Robert Nemiroff (New York: Vintage, 1995; orig. pub. 1958). For its reception, see Smith, *Visions of Belonging*, pp. 318–322. For black left-wing theater as it developed in the 1940s, see Davis and Dee, *With Ossie and Ruby* (New York: William and Morrow, 1998); Smith, "Becoming Harry Belafonte," pp. 10–17.

55. For opportunities African Americans had on television after *Raisin*, see Davis and Dee, *With Ossie and Ruby*, pp. 289–90, quote p. 290. For the opportunities African Americans had in theater, see "Fresh Faces On and Off Broadway," *New York Times*, May 6, 1962, p. 257; "Five Productions Off Broadway Take Up the Story of the Negro," *New York Times*, March 15, 1964, p. XI.

56. Jean Genet, *The Blacks: A Clown Show*, trans. Bernard Frechtman (New York: Grove Press, 1958); for "was delicious," see Angelou, *The Heart of a Woman*, p. 179; for "fairly free," see James Earl Jones with Penelope Niven, *Voices and Silences* (New York: Limelight Books, 2004; orig. pub. 2002), p. 119, see also 115–120; for "on that small New York stage," see Angelou, *The Heart of a Woman*, p. 179. For Abbey Lincoln and Max Roach's involvement with the production, see Angelou, *The Heart of a Woman*, pp. 180–185; for the play's significance, see John Warrick, "*The Blacks* and Its Impact on African American Theatre in the United States," in Clare Finburgh, ed., *The Politics of Jean Genet's Later Theatre: Spaces of Revolution* (London: Palgrave Macmillan, 2006), pp. 131–143; for Hansberry and *The Blacks*, see Higashida, "To Be(come) Young, Gay and Black," pp. 902–905.

57. For "fixture," see Sam Zolotow, "Tonight's Performance to Mark 1,000th Showing of 'The Blacks,'" *New York Times*, September 25, 1963, p. 37; for 1,400 performances, see Robert Simonson, "Sightlines: Jean Genet's *The Blacks: A Clown Show*," *Village Voice*, February 13, 2003, n.p., http://www.villagevoice.com/2003–02–18/theater/theater/ (March 15, 2009); for how black actors who circulated in and out of the production wrestled with its content, see Angelou, *Heart of a Woman*.

58. Angelou, *Heart of a Woman*, p. 219.

59. Carroll with Firestone, *Diahann!*, p. 85.

60. Smith, *Visions of Belonging*, p. 323.

61. Martin Ritt, director, *Paris Blues* (United Artists, 1961).

62. Michael Roemer, director, *Nothing but a Man* (Cinema V, 1964); Judith Smith, "Close Up: Civil Rights, Labor, and Sexual Politics on Screen in *Nothing but a Man* (1964)," *Black Camera* 3 (Spring 2012): 164–193.

63. Kristin Thompson and David Bordwell, *Film History: An Introduction* (New York: McGraw Hill, 1994), pp. 410–411, 518. The San Francisco and London film festivals started in 1957, and the Moscow film festival began in 1959.

64. Thompson and Bordwell, *Film History*, p. 384.

65. A. H. Weiler, "By Way of Report," *New York Times*, February 28, 1960, p. 7; for "small but steadily growing," see "A Camera in Johannesburg," *Time*, April 25, 1960, n.p., Margaret Herrick Library, Academy of Motion Pictures and Sciences, Special Collections, "Lionel Rogosin clipping file" (hereafter, "Rogosin," Herrick Library).

66. Monson, *Freedom Sounds*, p. 170; for race, music, and television, see Matthew Delmont, *The Nicest Kids in Town: American Bandstand, Rock 'n' Roll, and the Struggle for Civil Rights in 1950s Philadelphia* (Los Angeles: University of California Press, 2012).

67. For Belafonte and television, including his historic appearance as guest host of Johnny Carson's *The Tonight Show* in 1968, see Genia Fogelson, *Harry Belafonte: Singer and Actor* (Los Angeles: Melrose Square, 1980), pp. 78–79, 141; Donald Bogle, *Prime Time Blues: African Americans on Network Television* (New York: Farrar, Straus, and Giroux, 2001), p. 76; "Harry Belafonte," Southern Christian Leadership Conference Papers, 1962, Part 3, Reel 3, #00239, Widener Library, Harvard University; Henry Louis Gates, "Belafonte's Balancing Act" (1996), in Gates, *Thirteen Ways of Looking at a Black Man* (New York: Random House, 1997). It is worth noting that the sponsor cancelled additional episodes of his show in 1959. See Smith, "Becoming Harry Belafonte."

68. Their individual and joint appearances on *The Ed Sullivan Show* include, for example, TV.com, *The Ed Sullivan Show*, April 22, 1962, http://wwwtv.com/the-ed-sullivan-show/april-22–1962-harry-belafonte-miriam-makeba-thelma-lee/episode/126759/summary.html, (accessed July 10, 2000); *The Ed Sullivan Show*, January 31, 1965, http://www.ovguide.com/tv_episode/the-ed-sullivan-show-season-18   episode-18-lesley-gore-burt-lancaster-mickey-rooney-miriam-makeba-27372, (accessed July 5, 2011); *The Ed Sullivan Show*, December 31, 1967, http://new.music.yahoo.com/miriam/makeba/albmus/pata-pata-performed-live-on-the-ed-sullivan-show—218930465, (accessed July 5, 2011).

69. For Carroll, see, for example, *The Steve Allen Show*, May 17, 1959, http://www.ovguide.com/tv_episode/the-ed-sullivan-show-season-18-episode-18-lesley-gore-burt-lancaster-mickey-rooney-miriam-makeba-27372, (accessed July 5, 2011);

for Lincoln, see, for example, *The Steve Allen Show*, August 18, 1957, http://www
.tv.com/the-steve-allen-show/andy-williams-lous-costello-liberace-abbey-lincoln-
jean-fenn/episode/664173/summary.html, (accessed July 7, 2011). Simone appeared
on television less frequently, especially after her music became more explicitly political. Notable exceptions include an appearance on *The Steve Allen Show*, September 10, 1964, and on the premier episode of *The Great American Dream Machine*.
See Cohodas, *Princess Noire*, pp. 155–58; Jack Sameth, director, *The Great American
Dream Machine*, January 6, 1971, The Paley Center for Media, New York, New York.

70. Belafonte's success and desire for creative control even enabled him to play television rivals off of each other. According to one account, during a fierce ratings
war between two leading variety shows in 1958, Belafonte accepted an offer to
appear on Steve Allen's show and not Ed Sullivan's because the former allowed
him more creative control, including a longer segment that he was able to produce himself. See Fogelson, *Harry Belafonte*, p. 141.

71. *The Steve Allen Show*, March 16, 1958, The Paley Center for Media, New York,
New York; for Horne's efforts to get a show of her own, see Horne with Schickel,
Lena, p. 193. For Horne's relationship to television in relation to that of other
women performers, see Kristin A. McGee, *Some Liked It Hot: Jazz Women in
Film and Television, 1928–1959* (Middletown, CT: Wesleyan University Press,
2009), pp. 201–244.

72. For a "wall of frustration," see Hy Gardiner, *New York Herald Tribune*, quoted in
Bogle, *Prime Time Blues*, p. 57; for Robeson, see Smith, *Visions of Belonging*, pp.
289–293; "Protests Block Robeson as Guest on Mrs. Roosevelt's TV Program,"
New York Times, March 14, 1950, p. 1; for Nat "King" Cole, see Bogle, *Prime Time
Blues*, pp. 75–77; for the NAACP committee, see Welch, "Black Art and Activism," p. 211; for "limited" and "star treatment," see Eliot Tiegel, "TV Showcasing
Black Artists," *Billboard*, August 24, 1968, p. 66. For an alternative reading of
television in the 1950s as a "sympathetic, even breakthrough medium" for African Americans, see Thomas Doherty, *Cold War, Cool Medium: Television: Mc-
Carthyism, and American Culture* (New York: Columbia University Press, 2003),
pp. 70–80, quote p. 71.

73. Letter from David Susskind and Daniel Melnick to Roy Wilkins, December 18,
1963, in Papers of the NAACP, Part 24-C, Reel 34, #00540, Widener Library,
Harvard University; Arnold Perl, "Who Do You Kill?," *East Side/West Side* [*sic*],
completed script, September 20, 1963, pp. 1–72, in Papers of the NAACP Part
24-C, Reel 34.

74. For "for the first time," see *Variety*, November 6, 1963; also quoted in Bogle,
Prime Time Blues, p. 110. For "achieving total integration," see Shepard, "News
of TV and Radio," p. 75; for "the vigorous campaign," and "produced," see "More
Negroes Winning Roles in TV," *New York Times*, November 12, 1963, p. 31.

75. Susskind in *Newsday* (1964), quoted in Bogle, *Prime Time Blues*, p. 112; see
also Aniko Bodroghkozy, *Equal Time: Television and the Civil Rights Movement*

(Champaign: University of Illinois Press, 2012), pp. 155–180; Stephen Bowie, "East Side/West Side," *Classic TV History Blog: One Writer's Research in the History of American Television*, http://www.classichistory.com/EpisodeGuides/east_side_west_side_.html (2007; orig. 1997; accessed July 10, 2011).

76. Carroll with Firestone, *Diahann!*, p. 42.

77. For Carroll and SNCC, see "SNCC Backers," *New York Amsterdam News*, July 6, 1963, p. 5; "Sponsors of Carnegie Hall, February 1st [1963] Benefit for SNCC," undated, Student Nonviolent Coordinating Committee Papers, microfilm reel 45: B1–13, #1094, Widener Library, Harvard University; letter from James Forman to Miss Diahann Carroll, February 13, 1963, SNCC Papers, reel 5-A-TV-69.

78. Makeba with Hall, *Makeba*, p. 93. For Makeba's importance to the film, see also "Lionel Rogosin, the Documentary Filmmaker Who Made *Come Back, Africa*, Starring Miriam Makeba, Dies Dec. 8 in Los Angeles," *Hollywood Reporter*, December 13, 2000, n.p., in "Rogosin," Herrick Library.

CHAPTER 2

1. For "feel" and "thunder," see Miriam Makeba with James Hall, *Miriam Makeba: My Story* (New York: New American Library, 1987), pp. 86–87; for Horne, see "Chocolate Cream Chanteuse," *Time*, January 4, 1943, n.p., in Schomburg Center on Black Culture Clipping File, Volume I, 1925–1974, "Lena Horne" (hereafter, "Horne," SCBCCF, v. I); see also Earl Wilson, "It Happened Last Night: A 'Dynamite Interview'—Lena Horne on Prejudice," *New York Post*, June 30, 1947, n.p., "Horne," SCBCCF, v. I. For an analysis of Horne's onstage aloofness and restraint, see Shane Vogel, *The Scene of Harlem Cabaret: Race, Sexuality, Performance* (Chicago: University of Chicago Press, 2009), pp. 171–176.

2. For "African tribeswoman," see Lee Zhito, "Makeba Too Hip for Ciro's," *Billboard*, October 31, 1960, p. 52; for "import," see "Miriam Makeba," *Variety*, December 9, 1959, p. 65; for "she is easily," see *Newsweek*, January 25, 1960, p. 84.

3. For "first matinee idol" see *Look* (1957), quoted in Henry Louis Gates, "Belafonte's Balancing Act" (1996), in Gates, *Thirteen Ways of Looking at a Black Man* (New York: Random House, 1997), p. 158; for "Miss Makeba," see Makeba with Hall, *Makeba*, p. 81; for their meeting in London and subsequent events, see also Harry Belafonte with Michael Shnayerson, *Harry Belafonte: My Song* (New York: Knopf, 2011), pp. 201–205; for Belafonte as "Big Brother," see Makeba with Hall, *Makeba*, p. 83; for "as the first South African Negro," see Arthur Gelb, "Miriam Makeba and Leon Bibb Open Shows," *New York Times*, May 5, 1961, p. 24; for "Belafonte's Protégé," see "Belafonte's Protégé," *Ebony*, February 1960, p. 109. For the role that director Lionel Rogosin played in Makeba's move to the United States, see Lionel Rogosin, *Come Back, Africa: A Man Possessed* (Johannesburg, South Africa: STE, 2004), pp. 120–125.

4. For these and other milestones, see Makeba with Hall, *Makeba*; Mika Kauris-maki, director, *Mama Africa* (Trigon-Film, 2011); for "personal appreciation," see "Meet Miriam Makeba" (Irvington, NJ: Gii Kravette, 1967), unpaged pro-motional pamphlet.

5. "Stokely Takes a Bride," *Ebony*, July 1968, pp. 137–139; "Miriam Makeba En-gaged to Stokely Carmichael," *New York Times*, March 16, 1968, p. 34; "Make-ba-Carmichael Romance 'Sizzled' for Six Months, Pals Say," *Jet*, March 28, 1968, pp. 44–45. For Carmichael's work in Mississippi, see Henry Hampton and Steven Fayer, *Voices of Freedom: An Oral History of the Civil Rights Move-ment from the 1950s Through the 1980s* (New York: Bantam, 1990), pp. 267–297; Peniel Joseph, "Revolution in Babylon: Stokely Carmichael and America in the 1960s," in Manning Marable and Elizabeth Hinton, eds., *The New Black History: Revisiting the Second Reconstruction* (New York: Palgrave Macmillan, 2011), pp. 169–193; for "stirred up a storm," see Edwin Newman, "Meet the Press," August 21, 1966, National Broadcasting Company; transcript in John H. Bracey Jr., and Sharon Harley, eds., *Papers of the NAACP*, Part 28: Special Subject Files, 1966–1970, Series A: Africa-Poor People's Campaign, Part 28-A, Reel 5, #00552, Widener Library, Harvard University; for Carmichael, black power and the Black Panther Party, see Peniel Joseph, *Waiting 'Til the Midnight Hour: A Narrative History of Black Power in America* (New York: Henry Holt, 2006), pp. 181–240; for uses and meanings of black power among activists and for subsequent scholars, see Peniel Joseph, "The Black Power Movement: A State of the Field," *Journal of American History* 96 (December 2009): 751–776; for "the young man," see Gordon Parks, "Whip of Black Power—Stokely Carmichael: Young Man Behind an Angry Message," *Esquire*, May 19, 1967, n.p., Schomburg Center on Black Culture Clipping File, Volume I, 1925–1974, "Stokely Carmichael" (hereafter "Carmichael," SCBCCF, v. I); for surveillance and the variables that shaped their decision to leave, see Makeba with Hall, *Makeba*, pp. 161–166; Stokely Carmichael with Ekwueme Michael Thelwell, *Ready for Revolution: The Life and Struggles of Stokely Carmichael (Kwame Ture)* (New York: Scribner's, 2003), pp. 652–666, 672–676; Miriam Makeba in con-versation with Nomsa Mwamuka, *The Miriam Makeba Story* (Johannesburg, South Africa: STE, 2004), pp. 115–119.

6. For Makeba's reference to herself as "no diplomat," see Kathleen Teltsch, "Miriam Makeba, at U.N., Scores South African Race 'Nightmare,'" *New York Times*, July 17, 1963, p. 7; for "Africa's musical ambassador," see Robert Shel-ton, "2,800 Hear Concert by Miriam Makeba," *New York Times*, April 22, 1963, p. 23.

7. Thomas Borstelmann, *Apartheid's Reluctant Uncle: The United States and South Africa in the Early Cold War* (New York: Oxford University Press, 1993); Thom-as Borstelmann, *The Cold War and the Color Line: American Race Relations in the Global Arena* (Cambridge, MA: Harvard University Press, 2001); Van Gosse,

"More Than Just a Politician: Notes on the Life and Times of Harold Cruse," in Jerry Watts, ed., *Harold Cruse's The Crisis of the Negro Intellectual Reconsidered* (New York: Routledge, 2004), pp. 17–40; James Meriwether, *Proudly We Can Be Africans: Black Americans and Africa, 1935–1961* (Chapel Hill: University of North Carolina Press, 2002); Francis Njubi Nesbitt, *Race for Sanctions: African Americans Against Apartheid, 1946–1994* (Bloomington: Indiana University Press, 2004).

8. Scholarship on these cultural and political interconnections is extensive, and useful discussions include Iain Anderson, *This Is Our Music: Free Jazz, The Sixties, and American Culture* (Philadelphia: University of Pennsylvania Press, 2007); James Campbell, "The Americanization of South Africa," in James Campbell and Robert Lee, eds., *Race, Nation and Empire* (Chapel Hill: University of North Carolina, 2008), pp. 206-249; Veit Erlmann, *Music, Modernity, and the Global Imagination: South Africa and the West* (New York: Oxford University Press, 1999); Robin D. G. Kelley, *Africa Speaks, America Answers: Modern Jazz in Revolutionary Times* (Cambridge, MA: Harvard University Press, 2012); Ntongela Masilela, "New Negroism and New Africanism: The Influence of U.S. Modernity on the Construction of South African Modernity," *Black Renaissance* 2 (1999): 46–59; Ingrid Monson, ed., *The African Diaspora: A Musical Perspective* (New York: Garland, 2000); Rob Nixon, *Homelands, Harlem, and Hollywood: South African Culture and the World Beyond* (New York: Routledge, 1994). For a rich analysis of Makeba and the "discourse of voice," see April Sizemore-Barber, "The Voice of (Which?) Africa: Miriam Makeba in America," *Safundi: The Journal of South African and American Studies* 13 (July 2012): 251–276. For Makeba in relation to other South African and African American women jazz singers, see especially Jacqueline Castledine, "Gender, Jazz and Justice in Cold War Freedom Movements," in Danielle McGuire and John Dittmer, eds., *Freedom Rights: New Perspectives on the Civil Rights Movement* (Lexington: University Press of Kentucky, 2011), pp. 223–246.

9. For a lack of interest and "Tarzan mentality," see George M. Houser, "Meeting Africa's Challenge: The Story of the American Committee on Africa," *Issue: A Journal of Opinion* 6, no. 2/3 (Summer 1976): 16–26, quote p. 16; see also Meriwether, *Proudly We Can Be Africans*, pp. 90–100; for "I don't think," see Lorraine Hansberry, *A Raisin in the Sun* (1959), in Hansberry, *A Raisin in the Sun; The Sign in Sidney Brustein's Window* (New York: Vintage Books, 1995, also pub. 1987), p. 57.

10. For a cross-section of African Americans who related to Africa, see Joseph, *Waiting 'Til the Midnight Hour*, pp. 18–23; Nikhil Pal Singh, *Black Is a Country: Race and the Unfinished Struggle of Democracy* (Cambridge, MA: Harvard University Press, 2005), pp. 187–189; for this perspective in the African American press, see Meriwether, *Proudly We Can Be Africans*, p. 114; for Rogosin's perspective, see Rogosin, *Come Back, Africa*; see also interview with

Michael Rogosin, Harry Belafonte, and Robert Downey Sr., by Leonard Lopate, *The Leonard Lopate Show*, January 27, 2012, http://www.wnyc.org/shows/lopate/2012/jan/27/.

11. For the "Year of Africa," see Houser, "Meeting Africa's Challenge"; for Randy Weston, see Kelley, *Africa Speaks, America Answers*, pp. 56–62; for Miles Davis and Dizzy Gillespie, see Ingrid Monson, *Freedom Sounds: Civil Rights Call Out to Jazz and Africa* (New York: Oxford University Press, 2010), pp. 188–189; for relationships to Africa and for the AASF, see James Meriwether, "'Worth a Lot of Negro Votes': Black Voters, Africa, and the 1960 Presidential Campaign," *Journal of American History* 95 (December 2008): 737–763; for the ACOA, see Richard Knight, ed., *African Activist Archive Project: Preserving the History of the Solidarity Movement*, http://www.peaceworkmagazine.org/african-activist-archive-project-preserving-history-solidarity-movement; George Houser, *No One Can Stop the Rain: Glimpses of Africa's Liberation Struggle* (New York: Pilgrim, 1989); for support of the ACOA among prominent liberals, see sponsors listed in Theodore W. Kheel to Mrs. Hutson, March 20, 1959, Schomburg Center on Black Culture Clipping File, Volume I, 1925–1974, "American Committee on Africa" (hereafter "ACOA," SCBCCF, v. I); see also the flyer "The American Committee on Africa Announces the celebration of Africa Freedom Day," April 13, 1960, "ACOA," SCBCCF, v. I; for King, see Martin Luther King Jr. to "Dear Friend," November 12, 1959, "ACOA," SCBCCF, v. I. For Americans for South African Resistance, a short-lived organization that preceded the ACOA, see Meriwether, *Proudly We Can Be Africans*, pp. 110–112, 170–172. For the Council on African Affairs, a more left-oriented organization with an internationalist perspective and with a longer history, see especially Penny Von Eschen, *Race Against Empire: Black Americans and Anticolonialism, 1937–1957* (Ithaca, NY: Cornell University Press, 1997); for "pan-African identification," see St. Clair Drake, "The Relations of the American and the African Negro in the Context of Pan-Africanism," American Society of African Culture, Summary Report, 4th Annual Conference (June 21–21, 1961): 9–12; also quoted in Singh, *Black is A Country*, p. 187.

12. For "do the South Africans," see "The Tragedy at Sharpeville," *New York Times*, March 22, 1960, p. 36; for the "wanton slaughtering," see "Massacre in South Africa," *Chicago Defender*, March 24, 1960, p. A12; for Jackie Robinson, see Meriwether, "Worth a Lot of Negro Votes," p. 751. For reactions to Sharpeville, see Nesbitt, *Race for Sanctions*, pp. 36–38; Nixon, *Homelands, Harlem, and Hollywood*, p. 38; for *Drum's* coverage within South Africa, see especially Humphrey Tyler, *Life in the Time of Sharpeville: And Wayward Seeds of the New South Africa* (Cape Town, South Africa: Kwela Books, 1995).

13. For the United States and the U.N., see Kenneth Mokoena, ed., *South Africa and the U.S.: The Declassified History* (New York: New Press, 1993), pp. xx–xxi; for the ACOA's activism, see Nesbitt, *Race for Sanctions*, pp. 37–38, 45–46. For

antiapartheid activism, decolonization in Africa, and U.S. foreign relations, see especially Ryan Irwin, *Gordian Knot: Apartheid and the Unmaking of the Liberal World Order* (New York: Oxford University Press, 2012).

14. Meriwether, *Proudly We Can Be Called Africans*, pp. 90–123; see also Pamela Brooks, *Boycotts, Buses and Passes: Black Women's Resistance in the U.S. South and South Africa* (Amherst: University of Massachusetts Press, 2008); Irwin, *Gordian Knot*. For the "Americanness" of African Americans' identifications with Africa, see Borstelmann, *The Cold War and the Color Line*, p. 169. For the ways in which white Americans who *supported* segregation compared the United States to South Africa, see, for example, "Mississippi Senate Lauds South Africa," *Chicago Defender*, April 23, 1960, p. 1.

15. Lionel Rogosin, director, *On the Bowery* (currently distributed by Milestone Films, Harrington Park, NJ; orig. release 1955); for "overwhelming," see Arthur Knight quoted in Jon Thurber, "Lionel Rogosin; Made Films with Political Edge," *Los Angeles Times*, December 12, 2000, n.p., in Margaret Herrick Library, Center for Motion Picture Study, Academy of Motion Picture Arts and Sciences, Beverly Hills, CA, Lionel Rogosin Clipping File (hereafter, Herrick Library, "Rogosin"); for this film and Rogosin's crucial role in the development of the New American Cinema, see "Lionel Rogosin: *Come Back, Africa*," Venezia 61 Orizzonti Eventi speciali (2004), p. 178; Thurber, "Lionel Rogosin; Made Films with Political Edge"; Jonas Mekas, "The Film-Maker's Cooperative: A Brief History," www.film-makerscoop.com/history/htm.

16. Lionel Rogosin, director, *Come Back, Africa* (currently distributed by Milestone Films, Harrington Park, NJ; orig. release 1959). For Rogosin's perspective on apartheid and fascism, see Peter Davis, *In Darkest Hollywood: Exploring the Jungles of Cinema's South Africa* (Athens: Ohio University Press, 1996), p. 47; for the making of the film, see especially Lewis Nkosi, "*Come Back, Africa*: On Making a Film," *Fighting Talk*, 1960, pp. 12–13; Lionel Rogosin, "Interpreting Reality (Notes on the Esthetics and Practices of Improvisational Acting)," *Film Culture* (1960): 20–28; Elinor Rogosin, *Chasing Love: A Mother's Journey* (iUniverse, 2011); Earl Lloyd Ross, director, *An American in Sophiatown* (2007); for "would be in real trouble," see Makeba with Hall, *Makeba*, p. 66.

17. Zachariah Mgabi played the part of Zacharia; while the character's name appears as Zachariah in some sources, I follow Rogosin's lead and refer to him as Zacharia. See Rogosin, *Come Back, Africa*.

18. Rogosin, *Come Back, Africa*, pp. 124–125; for "everyone is," see Makeba with Hall, *Makeba*, p. 77; for "star of Venice," see "Miriam: Star of Venice," *Drum*, October 1959, p. 65.

19. Peter Davis, "Lionel Rogosin, 22 January 1924–8 December, 2000," in Rogosin, *Come Back, Africa*, pp. 8–10; Nkosi, "*Come Back, Africa*: On Making a Film."

20. For *Drum*, see Ezekile Mphahlele, "History and Change in Black Literature: Landmarks of Literary History in South Africa," quoted in Michael Chapman,

"More Than Telling a Story: *Drum* and Its Significance in Black South African Writing," in Michael Chapman, ed., *The Drum Decade: Stories from the 1950s* (Pietermaritzburg, South Africa: University of Natal Press, 1994), pp. 183–232; J. Schadenberg, *The Finest Photos from the Old Drum* (Johannesburg, South Africa: Bailey's Photo Archives, 1987); for "*Drum* man," see Lewis Nkosi, "The Fabulous Decade: The Fifties," *Home and Exile and Other Selections* (London: Longman, 1983; orig. pub. 1965), pp. 3–24, quote p. 9.

21. For a concise political history, see Meriwether, *Proudly We Can Be Africans*, pp. 90–123; for "possible" and "was a time," see Nkosi, "The Fabulous Decade," pp. 6, 16.

22. For "little Harlem," see Kelley, *Africa Speaks, America Answers*, p. 127; for *Drum*, see Lindsay Clowes, "Masculinity, Matrimony and Generation: Reconfiguring Patriarchy in *Drum* 1951–1983," *Journal of Southern African Studies* 34 (2008): 179–192; for Benjamin, see Carol A. Muller, "Musical Echoes: Composing a Past in/for South African Jazz," in Grant Olwage, ed., *Composing Apartheid: Music For and Against Apartheid* (Johannesburg, South Africa: Wits University Press, 2008), p. 139; Kelley, *Africa Speaks, America Answers*, pp. 120–161; Carol Muller, "Sounding a New African Diaspora: A South African Story (1958–1978)," *Safundi* 13 (July–October 2012): 277–294; for "wore," see Hugh Masekela and Michael Cheers, *Still Grazing: The Musical Journey of Hugh Masekela* (New York: Crown, 2004), p. 22; for the Manhattan Brothers, Skylarks, and other groups, see Makeba with Hall, *Mukebu*, pp. 46–57, Muller, "Musical Echoes"; Craig Harris, "All Music Guide," *The Manhattan Brothers, Biography*, http://mp3/the-manhattan-brothers/390569/biography.html (accessed May 4, 2005); Makeba in conversation with Mwamuka, *The Miriam Makeba Story*, pp. 39–42; Rob Allingham, liner notes, *Miriam Makeba and the Skylarks, Pt I* (Teal Records, 1991; orig. recorded between 1956 and 1959, Gallotine). For Robeson and "to the tune of," see "Defiance of Malan over 'Unjust' Laws Set in South Africa," *New York Times*, April 7, 1952. That protesters played Robeson may suggest political affinities as well musical preferences. For the political dimensions of music in South Africa, see also David Coplan, *In Township Tonight: South Africa's Black City Music and Theater* (New York: Longman, 1985), pp. 143–182; Veit Erlmann, "Black Political Song in South Africa—Some Research Perspectives," *Popular Music Perspectives* 2 (1985): 187–209.

23. For "a *Drum* man," see Nkosi, "The Fabulous Decade," p. 9; for women, gender, and Sophiatown, see Dorothy Driver, "*Drum* Magazine (1951–9) and the Spatial Configurations of Gender," in Kate Darian-Smith et al., ed., *Text, Theory, Space: Land, Literature and History in South Africa and Australia* (New York: Routledge, 1996), pp. 231–242; Nixon, *Homelands, Harlem and Hollywood*, pp. 17–23; Sandra Gunning, et al., eds., "Introduction: Gender, Sexuality, and African Diasporas," *Gender and History* 15 (November 2003): 397–408; Lindsay Clowes, "Are You Going to be MISS (or MR) Africa? Contesting Masculinity in

Drum Magazine 1951–1953," *Gender and History* 13, no. 1 (2001): 1–20; Shula Marks, ed., *Not Either an Experimental Doll: The Separate Worlds of Three South African Women* (Bloomington: Indiana University Press, 1988).

24. Nkosi, "The Fabulous Decade," p. 12; Lara Allen, "Introduction: South African Women of Song, Their Lives and Times," in Z. B. Molefe, *A Common Hunger to Sing: A Tribute to South Africa's Black Women of Song, 1950 to 1990* (Cape Town, South Africa: Kwela Books, 1997), n.p.; see also Mac Fenwick, "'Tough Guy, Eh?' The Gangster-Figure in *Drum,*" *Journal of South African Studies* 22 (December 1996): 617–632; Clive Glaser, "Swines, Hazels and the Dirty Dozen: Masculinity, Territoriality and the Youth Gangs of Soweto, 1960–1976," *Journal of Southern African Studies* 24 (December 1998): 719–736.

25. William Modisane, "Manhattan Brothers Mellow," *Drum,* January 1956, pp. 37–39; Makeba with Hall, *Makeba,* pp. 50–51, 53–62. For violence that Makeba specifically faced, in a story celebrating how singer Nathan Mdledle, "at the risk of his own life, stood between the gunman and his Nutbrown baby," see Casey Motsisi, "On the Way Up, Lady of Song, Part II," *Drum,* May 1960, p. 42.

26. For "there was a rapport," see Nkosi quoted in Peter Davis, "Introduction," in Rogosin, *Come Back, Africa,* p. 10; for Rogosin in South Africa, see Nkosi, "*Come Back, Africa,*" p. 13; Rogosin, *Come Back, Africa.* For efforts to elude the authorities, see "Compulsion," *New Yorker,* June 18, 1960, p. 31.

27. The film does show black women suffering; Vinah, Zacharia's wife is the ultimate victim when she is killed at the hands of the tsotsi, Marumu. But black women generally do not participate in the film's political discourse.

28. Masekela with Cheers, *Still Grazing,* p. 69; see also Lara Allen, "Circuits of Recognition and Desire in the Evolution of Black South African Popular Music: The Career of the Penny Whistle," *South African Journal of Musicology* 25 (2005): 31–51.

29. Alan Paton, *Cry the Beloved Country* (New York: Scribner's 1948); Zoltan Korda, director, *Cry the Beloved Country* (British Lion Film Corporation, 1951). For urban/rural tensions in the film, see Isabel Balseiro, "*Come Back, Africa*: Black Claims on 'White' Cities," in Isabel Balseiro and Ntongela Masilela, eds., *To Change Reels: Film and Film Culture in South Africa* (Detroit: Wayne State University Press, 2003), pp. 88–111.

30. "Lakutshn, Ilanga," includes the lyrics (translated), "I will come looking for you everywhere/in the hospital, in the jails, until I find you," an allusion to the frequent arrests and disappearances in black African communities under the apartheid regime. "Intoyam" (or "Into Yam" in some versions) is translated as "My Man," with lyrics about a woman who loves her man in spite of his fondness for alcohol. See Jonas Gwangwa and E. John Miller, eds., *Miriam Makeba, The World of African Song* (Chicago: Quadrangle Books: 1971), pp. 50–52. For "the ability of cryptic lyrics to accommodate multiple interpretations" as "particularly useful in a repressive political climate," see Lara Allen, "Commerce,

Politics and Musical Hybridity: Vocalising Urban Black South African Identity During the 1950s," *Ethnomusicology* 47 (2003): 228–249, quote p. 235. The woman who serves the alcohol in the shebeen remains marginal, though she too claps for Makeba on the sidelines.

31. Masilela, "*Come Back, Africa* and South African Film History," p. 65; Davis, *In Darkest Hollywood*, p. 51.

32. Paul Rotha, "Eyes on the World," *Films and Filming* 6 (1960): 21.

33. Nkosi, "The Fabulous Decade," p. 17.

34. For Venice and after, see Rogosin, *Come Back, Africa*, p. 135; for Vancouver, see Lewis Nkosi, "*Come Back, Africa*: On Making a Film," pp. 12–13; John Cocchi, "Lionel Rogosin Planning to Reissue His Production '*Come Back, Africa*'" *B. O.*, May 29, 1978, n.p., in Herrick Library, "Rogosin"; for ten best, see "Cinema: A Camera in Johannesburg," *Time*, January 2, 1961, p. 92. For the film as a sensation, see Robert F. Hawkins, "Annual Film Festival in Retrospect," *New York Times*, September 13, 1959, p. X9; Program, Production Notes, and Credits, "The Bleecker Street Cinema Gala Opening Party" (April 1960), Beril Becker Associates, in Schomburg Center on Black Culture Clipping File, Volume I, "Moving Pictures—*Come Back, Africa*" (hereafter "*Come Back, Africa*," SCBCCF, v. I).

35. Makeba with Hall, *Makeba*, p. 77.

36. For "horrifying study," see "Cinema: A Camera in Johannesburg"; for "stilted" and "helplessness," see Bosley Crowther, "Screen: Social Dilemma Documented," *New York Times*, April 5, 1960, p. 45; for "make it a point," see Jesse H. Walker, "Theatricals," *New York Amsterdam News*, April 12, 1960, p. 17; for a similar perspective, see Michèle Firk, "Come Back Africa: Que Viva Africa," *Positif*, May 1960, pp. 58–61.

37. Nixon, *Homelands, Harlem and Hollywood*, p. 12; Masilela, "*Come Back, Africa* and South African Film History," p. 64.

38. For "timely and remarkable," see "A Camera in Johannesburg"; for "inexperienced natives," see Walker, "Theatricals," p. 17.

39. Julian Neal, "South Africa Through a Distorted Lens," *Rand Daly Mail*, August 12, 1959, n.p., quoted in Davis, *In Darkest Hollywood*, p. 57; for a critique of the characters as distorted stereotypes, see Fred Carson, "Les homes oubliés de Dieu," *Cahiers du Cinéma* 18 (March 1960): 51–53. *Come Back, Africa* was not officially shown in South Africa until 1988.

40. Anthony Carew, *London Daily Herald*, September 4, 1959, quoted in Davis, *In Darkest Hollywood*, p. 56; Andre Brink interview (1990), quoted in Davis, *In Darkest Hollywood*, p. 56; for "the most successful," see "Current Non-Fiction and Short Films," *Monthly Film Bulletin* 27 (June 1960): 87; for "one exciting bull session" and "cinematically crude," see *Time* and the *Saturday Review* reviews compiled in "*Come Back, Africa*," *Film Facts*, May 20, 1960, pp. 9–13; for "flows easily," see Davis, "Rogosin and Documentary," p. 28; for "the climax,"

see Rogosin, *Come Back, Africa*, p. 84; for "makes the film worthwhile," see Rotha, "Eyes on the World," p. 21; for "that was not acting," see Arthur Maimane, quoted in Davis, *In Darkest Hollywood*, p. 53.

41. Nadine M. Edwards, "At Los Feliz: African Negro Is Depicted in Film," *Hollywood Citizen-News*, August 29, 1963, n.p., "Rogosin," Herrick Library; letter from Max Laemmle to "Miss Flynn," *Hollywood Citizen-News*, September 7, 1963, n.p., "Rogosin," Herrick Library. For Los Feliz as the "premier arthouse theater" in Los Angeles, see Burt Folkart, "Max Laemmle Dies at 82; Showcased Foreign Films," *Los Angeles Times*, January 24, 1989, n.p., http://articles. latimes.com/1989-01-24/local/me-907_1_french-film-festival. For the film inviting these comparisons, see Saul Gross, "Movie, *Come Back, Africa*," *The Worker*, April 4, 1960, n.p., "*Come Back, Africa*," SCBCCF, v. I.

42. Makeba with Hall, *Makeba*, pp. 77, 83–96; Masekela with Cheers, *Still Grazing*, p. 113; Nixon, *Homelands, Harlem and Hollywood*, pp. 43–76. The government in South Africa regulated television until 1976, considering it a source of potentially dangerous information.

43. For "there are few cases," see Milton Bracker, "Xhosa Songstress," *New York Times*, February 28, 1960, p. 32; for "too shy," see "Nightclubs: Good to My Ear," *Time*, February 1, 1960, p. 52.

44. For "in a class," see "Cocoanut Grove, L.A.," *Variety*, April 19, 1968, p. 65; for a "pure diamond," see "Makeba . . . A Pure Diamond from South African Mines," *Pittsburgh Courier*, June 9, 1962, p. 21.

45. For "in contrast," see "New Singer in Town," p. 60f; for "emotional, often artificial style," see "Good to My Ear," p. 53; for "exotic" and "former housemaid," see Bracker, "Xhosa Songstress," p. 32; for twelve "tribal names," see "Good to My Ear," p. 52. See also Sizemore, "The Voice of (Which) Africa."

46. For "simplicity," see "New Singer in Town," p. 60f; for "confessed" and "almost unbelievable," see "With a Touch of Zulu," *Newsweek*, January 25, 1960, p. 84; for "she wore," see Masekela with Cheers, *Still Grazing*, p. 65. Masekela and Makeba were married in 1964 and divorced in 1966. For representations of Makeba's sexuality and her alleged exoticism, see Castledine, "Gender, Jazz and Justice in Cold War Freedom Movements," pp. 232–234.

47. For "discovered her," see Robert Shelton, "ABC's of Xhosa, Yoruba and Zulu," *New York Times*, November 14, 1965, p. X19; for "powerful influence," see "Belafonte's Protégé," p. 109. For exceptions—coverage that named ambition and the influence that American popular culture had in South Africa—see, for example, "New Singer in Town," *Look*, February 2, 1960, p. 60f.

48. For praise of her versatility, see Shelton, "ABC's of Xhosa, Yoruba and Zulu"; for "native song stylings," see "New Acts," *Variety*, December 9, 1959, p. 65; for "reaches her peak," see "Blue Angel, N.Y.," *Variety*, April 20, 1960, p. 147; for "The Click Song," see Miriam Makeba, *Miriam Makeba* (RCA, 1960); for "a throat clicking," see "Ash Grove, L.A.," *Variety*, January 31, 1962, p. 59;

for "the only entertainer," see Bracker, "Xhosa Songstress," p. 32; for "a fascinating and exotic performer," see Alan Barnes, liner notes, Miriam Makeba,
The World Of Miriam Makeba (RCA, 1963).

49. For "our Miriam," see "Miriam: Star of Venice," *Drum*, October 1959, p. 65; for
"big time," see "Our Miriam Makeba in the Big Time: Writes to *Zonk* from New
York," *Zonk*, February 1960, p. 18; for "our lady of song," and "our nightingale,"
see Modisane, "Manhattan Brothers Mellow," p. 38; "Miriam: Star of Venice,"
p. 65; Casey Motsisi, "Miriam Makeba in New York, Part I," *Drum*, April 1960,
pp. 26–31, quote p. 28; for "the world" and "just beginning," see "Miriam: Star
of Venice," p. 65; Motsisi, "Miriam Makeba in New York, Part I," p. 28.

50. Gelb, "Miriam Makeba and Leon Bibb Open Shows," p. 24; Teltsch, "Miriam
Makeba, at U.N., Scores South African Race 'Nightmare,'" p. 7; Makeba with
Hall, *Makeba*, p. 97; Belafonte, *My Song*, p. 204.

51. Makeba with Hall, *Makeba*, p. 98.

52. For "First Lady," see Shelton, "ABC's of Xhosa, Yoruba and Zulu"; for "Xosa
tribeswoman," see O. B. B., "Miriam Makeba," *High Fidelity*, December 1960,
p. 93; for "unable to go home," see "Miriam Makeba: Unable to Go Home,
Vocalist Takes Substitute Trip to Kenya," *Ebony*, April 1963, pp. 74–80.

53. "With a Touch of Zulu," *Newsweek*, January 25, 1960, p. 84.

54. For "when Afrikaaners sing," see "Good to My Ear," p. 52 (also reprinted in
liner notes to her first album); for the Manhattan Brothers, see Makeba with
Hall, *Makeba*, p. 48; for "occasional" and "hint," see "The World of Miriam
Makeba," *High Fidelity*, January 1964, p. 102.

55. Miriam Makeba, "Kilimanjaro (Hunting Song and Boot Dance)" and "Jikele
Mayweni (The Retreat Song)," *Miriam Makeba: The Many Voices of Miriam
Makeba* (Kapp Records, 1962); Solomon Linda, "Wimoweh (The Lion Sleeps
Tonight)," also recorded as "Mbube" by Miriam Makeba, *Miriam Makeba* (RCA,
1960); William McPherson, "One Day They'll Kill That South African Lion,"
Washington Post Times Herald, June 25, 1961, p. F5. For the song's capacity to in-
cite riots, see "Crescendo, L.A.," *Variety*, November 28, 1962, p. 53; for reactions
to the "Boot Dance," see Shelton, "2,800 Hear Concert by Miriam Makeba."

56. Makeba, "The Click Song," *Miriam Makeba*.

57. For the SCLC, see for example, the concert program, "'Belafonte': Featuring
Miriam Makeba, Chad Mitchell Trio, George Kirby," September 27, 1961, Nashville, Tennessee, sponsored by the Southern Christian Leadership Conference,
in the Southern Christian Leadership Conference (hereafter SCLC) Papers,
Part 2, Reel 3, #00194, Widener Library, Harvard University; "Belafonte," a
program for an SCLC-sponsored concert in Atlanta, Georgia, on June 25, 1962,
in SCLC Papers, Part 2, Reel 14#, 00568-572. For SNCC, see for example, letter from James Forman to Harry Belafonte, December 4, 1963, in Student
Nonviolent Coordinating Committee (hereafter SNCC) Papers, Subgroup A,
Series 4, Reel 5, #48, Widener Library, Harvard University; for the American

Committee on Africa, see, for example, "Africa Freedom Day," Program at Carnegie Hall, April 15, 1959; "Africa Defense and Aid Fund" advertisement, December 13, 1965; "Africa Freedom Day," Program, April 17, 1961; "Program for Human Rights Day Rally and Benefit for South African Victims of Apartheid," December 10, 1965, all in "ACOA" SCBCCF, v. I.

58. "'Belafonte': Featuring Miriam Makeba, Chad Mitchell Trio, George Kirby"; for the interracial crowd of 5,000 and for $15,000 for the SCLC, see "News Release from Southern Christian Leadership Conference," June 13, 1962, SCLC Papers, Part 3, Reel 3, #00256; for "the event of the year," see letter from Martin Luther King Jr. and Wyatt Tee Walker to Mrs. Geneva Haugabrooks, June 25, 1962, in SCLC Papers, Part 2, Reel 14, #00550.

59. "Aid for South Africans," *New York Times*, March 11, 1964, p. 33. For Makeba's role in a "giant 12 hour civil rights rally" in New York, see *New York Amsterdam News*, August 24, 1963, p. 14.

60. "Mister Kelly's, Chi," *Variety*, March 27, 1968, p. 96.

61. For television, see Sasha Torres, *Black White and in Color: Television and Black Civil Rights* (Princeton, NJ: Princeton University Press, 2003), p. 20; for "her first," see "New Acts," *Variety*, December 9, 1959, p. 65.

62. Makeba with Hall, *Makeba*, p. 101; Taylor Branch, *Parting the Waters: America in the King Years, 1954–1963* (New York: Simon and Schuster, 1989), p. 593. For slightly different accounts of this incident, see SCLC Papers, Part 2, Reel 14, #00592; Belafonte, *My Song*, pp. 251–252.

63. For Kenya, see "Miriam Makeba: Unable to Go Home, Vocalist Takes Substitute Trip to Kenya," pp. 74–80; for Ethiopia, see "New York Beat," *Jet*, June 20, 1963, p. 64; Makeba with Hall, *Makeba*, pp. 110, 116–118; Nesbitt, *Race for Sanctions*, p. 51; for "African nationalism" and "one of," see "After Addis Ababa" (unsourced publication), May 27, 1963, in "Organization of African Unity," SCBCCF, v. I; for American reactions to the founding of the OAU, see Jay Walz, "African Showplace: Addis Ababa Meeting Hall Is Symbol of Haile Selassie's Goal for Continent," *New York Times*, May 18, 1963, p. 10; Mokoena, *South Africa and the U.S.: The Declassified History*, pp. 54–55; for "one thing," see Makeba with Hall, *Makeba*, pp. 127–128.

64. Sally Hammond, "U.S. Singer Is in Tune with Africa," *New York Post*, January 26, 1964, p. 45; for "needed a hiatus," see Henry Hampton and Steve Fayer, *Voices of Freedom*, p. 204; see also Taylor Branch, *Pillar of Fire: America in the King Years, 1963–65* (New York: Simon and Schuster, 1998), pp. 480–483.

65. United Nations General Assembly, "Special Committee on the Policies of Apartheid of the Government of the Republic of South Africa: Summary Record of the First Part* of the Eighteenth Meeting," New York, New York, July 16, 1963, pp. 5–6; for her later account that ANC representatives Duma Nokwe and Robert Resha prepared her remarks, see Makeba in conversation with Mwamuka, *The Miriam Makeba Story*, p. 86; for sanctions, see Nesbitt, *Race for Sanctions*, p. 36.

66. For "invited back," see "U.N. Hears Anti-Apartheid Song," *New York Times*, March 10, 1964, p. 5; for "quick and real action," see "Special Committee on the Policies of Apartheid of the Government of the Republic of South Africa, Summary Record of the Twenty-Sixth Meeting," March 9, 1964, New York, New York, pp. 7–8; "The Proceedings in the U.N.," *New York Times*, March 10, 1964, p. 2; see also Makeba with Hall, *Makeba*, pp. 111–113. For reactions to U.N. measures in South Africa, see Clyde Sanger, "Toward Unity in Africa," *Foreign Affairs*, January 1964, pp. 260–281.

67. For "an act of treason," see Makeba with Hall, *Makeba*, p. 112; for Makeba's records being banned and "impossible to overstate," see Mandla Langa quoted in Paul Walters, University Public Orator at the Rhodes University Special Graduation Ceremony and award of the Degree of Doctor of Music, *Honoris Causa*, to Zensi Miriam Makeba, February 20, 2004. For efforts to smuggle albums by Max Roach and Abbey Lincoln into South Africa, see Maya Angelou, *The Heart of a Woman* (New York: Random House, 1981), p. 121; see also "No 'Freedom Now' in South Africa," *Down Beat*, June 21, 1962, p. 11.

68. For "the toast," see Masekela with Cheers, *Still Grazing*, pp. 150, 157; for her work with the African-American Institute, see "Benefit Performances," *New York Times*, November 28, 1965, p. 130; Robert Shelton, "Concert Benefits African Students: Miriam Makeba Stars—Institute Gains $15,000," *New York Times*, December 16, 1965, p. 62.

69. Harry Belafonte and Miriam Makeba, *An Evening with Belafonte/Makeba* (BMG Music, 1965); Shelton, "ABC's of Xhosa, Yoruba and Zulu," p. X19; for a critical review of the album, see O. B. Brummell, "An Evening with Harry Belafonte and Miriam Makeba," *High Fidelity*, September 1965, p. 124.

70. For "striking blend," see advertisement for *Miriam Makeba* (RCA, 1960), *New York Times*, October 16, 1960, p. 37.

71. Modisane, "Manhattan Brothers Mellow," p. 38.

72. For "artistry" alongside the primitive, see "Makeba Too Hip for Ciro's," *Billboard*, October 31, 1960, p. 52; for "simplicity," see "New Singer in Town," p. 60f; for "shy," see, for example, "With a Touch of Zulu," p. 84; for "soft-spoken," see "Xhosa Songstress," p. 32; for "bashful," see "Belafonte's Protégé," p. 109. In her two autobiographies, Makeba similarly places more emphasis on the maternal, and de-emphasizes issues of romance and sexuality, choosing, perhaps to keep all but her most public relationships private.

73. Makeba with Hall, *Makeba*, p. 86 (emphasis in original); see also Bernadine Morris, "Hair Stylist Is Honored by Blacks He Inspired," *New York Times*, June 25, 1980, p. C20.

74. For "sepia sensation," see Jackie Ormes, "Lena Horne Sets a New Box Office Record," *Chicago Defender*, October 21, 1944, p. 7; for "beguiling," see "Belafonte's Protégé," p. 109. John Pratt, fashion designer and collaborator/spouse of dancer Katherine Dunham designed Makeba's wardrobe for these

initial American performances; see Makeba in conversation with Mwamuka, *The Miriam Makeba Story*, pp. 60–63.

75. For "nut brown baby," see Makeba with Hall, *Makeba*, p. 48; Lynn Thomas, "Skin Lighteners in South Africa: Transnational Entanglements and Technologies of the Self," in Evelyn Nakano Glenn, ed., *Shades of Difference: Why Skin Color Matters* (Stanford, CA: Stanford University Press, 2009), pp. 188–209. For color consciousness and glamour in the United States and South Africa, see also Maxine Leeds Craig, "The Color of an Ideal Negro Beauty Queen: Miss Bronze, 1961–1968," in Evelyn Nakano Glenn, *Shades of Difference: Why Skin Color Matters* (Stanford, CA: Stanford University Press, 2009), pp. 81–94; Lynn Thomas, "Race, Skin, and Transnational Commerce" (unpublished manuscript, 2011).

76. For "chic gown," see "Crescendo, L.A.," p. 53; for "short and woolly," see Makeba with Hall, *Makeba*, p. 86.

77. Maxine Leeds Craig, *Ain't I a Beauty Queen: Black Women, Beauty and the Politics of Race* (New York: Oxford University Press, 2002), pp. 62–63, 78.

78. Judy Klemesrud, "Her Hairdo Started the 'Afro' Trend," *New York Times*, October 8, 1966, p. 38.

79. Lee McDaniel, quoted in Klemesrud, "Her Hairdo Started the 'Afro' Trend," p. 38.

80. "Good to My Ear," *Time*, February 1, 1960, p. 52.

81. Hal Halverstadt, liner notes, *Pata Pata* (Reprise, 1967). "Pata Pata" dated back to 1956; Makeba wrote the dance song whose title meant "touch, touch" in Zulu and Xhosa when she was in South Africa. It was "one of my most *insignificant* songs," Makeba later said. Fans in 1967 disagreed; it went to the top five on the charts in the United States, and translated versions and accompanying dances were popular around the world. Following up on the success of "Pata Pata," Makeba toured independently in the United States, South America and England early in 1967. See Makeba with Hall, *Makeba*, p. 140; "Makeba Clicks at Philharmonic," *New York Times*, January 7, 1967, p. 18. For Makeba and the complexities of "world music" in the 1980s and 1990s, see Sizemore-Barber, "The Voice of (Which) Africa"; see also Veit Erlmann, "The Aesthetics of the Global Imagination: Reflections on World Music in the 1990s," *Public Culture* 8 (1996): 467–487.

82. "Crescendo, L.A.," p. 53.

83. "Meet Miriam Makeba," unpaged.

84. For changes in SNCC, and for the Black Panther Party and developments in other organizations after passage of federal civil rights legislation in 1964 and 1965 that were relevant to this flux, see Joseph, *Waiting 'Til the Midnight Hour*; Hampton and Fayer, *Voices of Freedom*, pp. 349–356; Robert Self, *American Babylon: Race and the Struggle for Postwar Oakland* (Princeton, NJ: Princeton University Press, 2005).

85. Meriwether, *Proudly We Can Be Africans*; Kelley, *Africa Speaks, America Answers*; Irwin, *Gordian Knot*. For Carmichael on Vietnam, see, for example, speech at Garfield High School, Seattle, Washington, April 19, 1967, http://www.aavw

.org/special_features/speeches_speech_carmichael01.html; Gerome Ragni and James Rado, *Hair* (1967); for these as Carmichael's remarks, see Maurice Kelman, "On Prosecuting Sedition: A Reply to Dean O'Meara," *American Bar Association Journal* 54 (February 1968): 164–167.

86. Melani McAlister, *Epic Encounters: Culture, Media and U.S. Interests in the Middle East, 1945–2000* (Berkeley: University of California Press, 2001), pp. 84–124; Irwin, *Gordian Knot*, pp. 7–12.

87. Makeba with Hall, *Makeba*, pp. 142–145, 160. For Belafonte's sense of how Makeba changed in this period and into the '70s (he does not discuss this incident specifically), see Belafonte with Shnayerson, *My Song*, pp. 340–342.

88. For SNCC activists in Washington, D.C., see Borstelmann, *The Cold War and the Color Line*, p. 199; for New York, see "SNCC Members Arrested in Protests of Racist Government in South Africa," Memo by Cleveland Sellers, SNCC Papers, Subgroup A, Series 7, Reel 14, #3; for General Motors, see H. Rapp Brown to Oliver Tambo, August 27, 1967, SNCC Press Release, in SNCC Papers, Subgroup A, Series 7 Reel 14, #3.

89. For fans at a benefit performance disappointed by the appearance of Belafonte and not Aretha Franklin, see "Cleve. Benefit a Lotta Discord for Belafonte, His Sponsors, Aretha's Fans," *Variety*, October 25, 1967, p. 47; for Belafonte as "discredited" in years associated with black power, see Brian Ward, *Just My Soul Responding: Rhythm and Blues, Black Consciousness, and Race Relations* (Berkeley: University of California Press, 1998), pp. 315–325.

90. Carmichael with Thelwell, *Ready for Revolution*, p. 214; Makeba with Hall, *Makeba*, p. 147.

91. "Miriam Makeba Engaged to Stokely Carmichael," p. 34, for "the beginning of stronger ties," see "Stokely Takes a Bride," p. 137.

92. Makeba with Hall, *Makeba*, pp. 147, 154–155; Makeba in conversation with Mwamuka, *The Miriam Makeba Story*, p. 118; for Carmichael's sense that "this attractive, apparently so gentle, mature woman was a very political creature, in fact an uncompromising militant where her people's freedom was concerned," see Carmichael with Thelwell, *Ready for Revolution*, p. 619.

93. For "sold out," see Carmichael with Thelwell, *Ready for Revolution*, p. 673; for "going bourgeois," see C. Gerald Fraser, "S.N.C.C. in Decline After 8 Years in Lead," *New York Times*, October 7, 1968, p. 51; for reports of buying a house, see "Carmichael Purchasing Home Here," *Washington Post*, May 28, 1968, p. B1; for Carmichael's suggestions that these inaccurate stories were planted by the FBI, see Carmichael with Thelwell, *Ready for Revolution*, p. 673; for his wardrobe, see Makeba with Hall, *Makeba*, pp. 155–156; for "the image of," see A. B. Spellman, liner notes to *Makeba!* (Reprise, 1968). This album was, according to these liner notes, the "most African of her recent releases."

94. For "major difference" and "whenever possible," see Carmichael with Thelwell, *Ready for Revolution*, p. 651; for "don't ever," see Bernard Weinraub, "The Brilliancy

of Black," *Esquire*, January 1967, n.p., "Carmichael," SCBCCF, v. I; see also Craig, *Ain't I a Beauty Queen*, pp. 82–83, 114–128.

95. "Cocoanut Grove, L.A.," p. 65. For her professional difficulties, see also Makeba with Hall, *Makeba*, pp. 154–166; Makeba in conversation with Mwamuka, *The Miriam Makeba Story*, pp. 110–119.

96. "Mister Kelly's, Chi," p. 96.

97. Stephen Gayle, "Makeba at Fifty," *Essence*, July 1982, pp. 62–64, 135, quotes pp. 64, 135; for performances in Paris in 1969, see "One-Man Shows: Miriam Makeba," *Variety*, April 2, 1969, p. 66.

98. For the political dimensions of Carmichael's decision, see Joseph, *Waiting 'Til the Midnight Hour*, p. 240; for "the voice of Africa," see *Newsweek*, January 25, 1960, p. 84; for Makeba in Guinea, see Belafonte, *My Song*, pp. 340–342.

99. "Miriam Makeba: High Voltage Star," *Sepia*, October 1967, p. 81.

100. See especially Salamishah Tillet, "Hush and Listen: Mama Africa and Nina Simone's Global Civil Rights Sound," paper presented at the American Studies Association conference, San Juan, Puerto Rico, November 2012.

101. Robert Shelton, "Two Folk Singers Present Concert," *New York Times*, May 22, 1961, p. 37; Makeba in conversation with Mwamuka, *The Miriam Makeba Story*, p. 86.

CHAPTER 3

1. Phyl Garland, *The Sound of Soul: The Story of Black Music* (Chicago: NTC/Contemporary, 1969), p. 176; Nina Simone with Stephen Cleary, *I Put a Spell on You: The Autobiography of Nina Simone* (New York: Da Capo Press, 1993; orig. pub. 1991), pp. 89–90.

2. Nina Simone, "Mississippi Goddam," *In Concert* (Philips, 1964). For a brilliant discussion of versions of this song as a window into "the politics and poetics of counter-hegemonic, black feminist popular music 'crossover,'" see Daphne Brooks, "Nina Simone's Triple Play," *Callaloo* 34 (2011): 176–197, quote p. 179.

3. For "sing," "get a guitar," and the two new songs, see Lena Horne with Richard Schickel, *Lena* (New York: Signet, 1965), pp. 216–217; Betty Comden and Adolph Green, "Now," performed by Lena Horne, *Here's Lena NOW!* (20th Century-Fox Records, 1963); Yip Harburg, "Silent Spring," performed by Lena Horne, *Here's Lena NOW!*; for Horne at the March on Washington, see Norman Gorin, director, *CBS News Special Report, March on Washington*, August 28, 1963, The Paley Center for Media, New York, New York, T77:0163 and T77:0167; for Lena Horne leading marchers in the song "We Shall Overcome" after the murder of Evers, see Bernard Lefkowitz, "'We Shall Overcome': The Anthem of Struggle," *New York Post*, March 17, 1965, n.p., in Schomburg Center on Black Culture Clipping File, Volume I, 1925–1974, "Lena Horne" (hereafter "Horne," SCBCCF, v. I). For controversies over "Now" on the radio, see James Gavin, *Stormy Weather: The Life of Lena Horne* (New York: Simon and Schuster, 2009), pp. 332–333.

4. Nina Simone, *High Priestess of Soul* (Philips, 1967); for "one of the best," see Maurice Cullaz, "Une Divine Nina," *Jazz Hot*, May 1969, p. 7; for her connections to audiences, see, for example, John S. Wilson, "Recital Victory for Nina Simone," *New York Times*, December 30, 1968, p. 25, Schomburg Center for Black Culture Clipping File, Volume I, 1925–1974, "Nina Simone" (hereafter, "Simone," SCBCCF, v. I). In addition to the songs discussed, see also Jackie Alper, Ron Vander Groef, and Nina Simone, "Old Jim Crow," *In Concert*; Abbey Lincoln and Nina Simone, "Blues for Mama," [1966], *Simone Sings the Blues* (RCA, 1967); Langston Hughes and Nina Simone, "Backlash Blues," *Simone Sings the Blues*; William Taylor and Richard Carroll Lamb, "I Wish I Knew How It Would Feel to Be Free," performed by Nina Simone, *Silk and Soul* (RCA, 1967). In contrast to Simone, see accounts that Nat Cole was a "nonparticipant" in black activism and his subsequent financial pledge: "Singers Pledge Money for Civil-Rights Struggle," *Down Beat*, August 15, 1963, p. 11.

5. For this range of perspectives, see Peniel Joseph, ed., *The Black Power Movement: Rethinking the Civil Rights-Black Power Era* (New York: Routledge, 2006); Manning Marable, ed., *The New Black History: Revisiting the Second Reconstruction* (New York: Palgrave, 2011).

6. For Lewis, see Taylor Branch, *Parting the Waters: America in the King Years, 1954–1963* (New York: Simon and Schuster, 1988), pp. 874–881; for Williams, see Timothy Tyson, *Radio Free Dixie: Robert W. Williams and the Roots of Black Power* (Chapel Hill: University of North Carolina Press, 1999); for Murray, see Glenda Gilmore, *Defying Dixie: The Radical Roots of Civil Rights 1919–1950* (New York: Norton, 2008); for Simone's friendship with Hansberry, see Simone with Cleary, *I Put a Spell on You*, pp. 86–88; for the censuring of Abbey Lincoln, see Ingrid Monson, "Abbey Lincoln's *Straight Ahead*: Jazz in the Era of the Civil Rights Movement," in Richard G. Fox and Orin Starn, eds., *Between Resistance and Revolution: Cultural Politics and Social Protest* (New Brunswick, NJ: Rutgers University Press, 1997), pp. 171–94. For this subculture, see Robin D. G. Kelley, "Nap Time: Historicizing the Afro," *Fashion Theory* 1 (December 1997): 330–351; Simone with Cleary, *I Put a Spell on You*, pp. 66–72; see also chapter 1 in this volume.

7. For "recent discovery" and "rose to prominence," see "Nina Simone," *Down Beat*, May 12, 1960, p. 44; for "I was a sensation," see Simone with Cleary, *I Put a Spell on You*, p. 67. Other useful accounts include Nadine Cohodas, *Princess Noire: The Tumultuous Reign of Nina Simone* (New York: Pantheon Books, 2010); David Nathan, *The Soulful Divas* (New York: Billboard Books, 1999), pp. 42–65; Nick Spitzer interview with Nina Simone, "All Things Considered," *National Public Radio*, July 15, 2001.

8. For "excitement and spiraling intensity," see P. W., "Nina Simone: Nina's Choice," *Down Beat* June 20, 1963, p. 30; for "she is," see John S. Wilson, "Newport, the Music," *Down Beat*, August 18, 1960, p. 18. For the political significance of her musical versatility, see Brooks, "Nina Simone's Triple Play."

9. "The Rareness of Nina Simone," *Metronome*, June 1960, p. 30.

10. Ingrid Monson, "The Problem with White Hipness: Race, Gender, and Cultural Conceptions in Jazz Historical Discourse," *Journal of the American Musicological Society* 48 (Autumn 1995): 396–422; see also chapter 1 in this volume.

11. As Farah Jasmine Griffin has noted, "even" when a white-dominated musical establishment conceded that African American musicians like Charlie Parker might be "geniuses," there was an assumption that this genius had come "naturally," or, in the case of a woman like Billie Holiday especially, was "undisciplined." See Farah Jasmine Griffin, *If You Can't Be Free, Be a Mystery: In Search of Billie Holiday* (New York: Free Press, 2001), p. 15.

12. For "triple threat," see Joan Crosby, "As the Lyrics Go, So Go the Songs," *Nashville Tennessean*, February 15, 1965, n.p., "Simone," SCBCCF, v. I; for "artistic rarity," see "Annual Nina Simone Concert Due at Carnegie Hall," *News Release from Anne Fulchino* (New York: Stroud Productions and Enterprises), "Simone," SCBCCF, v. I; "because of," David Nathan, phone interview with author, November 2001; see also Sylvia Hampton, *Nina Simone: Break Down and Let It All Out* (London: Sanctuary, 2004), pp. 21–24; Brooks, "Nina Simone's Triple Play."

13. For black women blues singers, see Angela Davis, *Blues Legacies and Black Feminism: Gertrude "Ma" Rainey, Bessie Smith, and Billie Holiday* (New York: Vintage, 1998); Hazel Carby, "'It Jus Be's Dat Way Sometime': The Sexual Politics of Women's Blues," (1986), in Vicki Ruiz and Ellen Dubois, eds., *Unequal Sisters: A Multicultural Reader in U.S. Women's History* (New York: Routledge, 1994; orig. pub. 1990); for "unlike," see Simone with Cleary, *I Put a Spell on You*, p. 65.

14. For "undoubtedly," see "Nina Simone: Angry Woman of Jazz," *Sepia*, March 1967, p. 64; for "regardless" and "inner trappings," see Garland, "Nina Simone: High Priestess of Soul," p. 176; see also "Nina Simone," *Jazz Hot*, September 1969, p. 14. For the rural South and the church as repositories for blues and other African American music, see Marybeth Hamilton, "Sexuality, Authenticity, and the Making of the Blues Tradition," *Past and Present* 169 (November 2000): 132–160.

15. Langston Hughes, "Nina Simone," *New York Post*, June 29, 1962, n.p., "Simone," SCBCCF, v. I, emphasis in original; see also *Chicago Defender*, March 21, 1964, n.p., and the compilation of reviews that the International Talent Associates, Inc., assembled to represent Simone, both in "Simone," SCBCCF, v. I.

16. Assumptions that she was French-born, from Nathan interview; for "blues atmosphere," see Cullaz and Dellorme, "Nina Simone," p. 28; for "the nightmare," see Jean-Pierre Binchet, "Antibes 65: Soirees des 24 et 25 juillet (Nina Simone)," *Jazz Magazine*, September 1965, pp. 18–23; for conversations in French with audiences, see Nina Simone, "Four Women," at Antibes, 1965, http://www.youtube.come/watch?v=qCwME6Jpn3s (accessed July 1, 2011); for "take a predominantly white," see Michael Smith, "The Other (More Serious) Side of Nina," *Melody Maker*, December 7, 1968, p. 7.

17. For "difficult to work with," see "Nina Simone Pregnant; Settles Suit Secretly," *New York Amsterdam News*, March 17, 1962, p. 1; for "sufficiently respectful," see Smith, "The Other (More Serious) Side of Nina," p. 7; for "found out," see Simone with Cleary, *I Put a Spell on You*, p. 74; for "boisterous" and "stormy petrel," see "Nina Simone Pregnant," p. 1; for "deep-felt desire," "social graces," and "one must be," see Robert Lucas, "Nina Simone: A Girl with Guts," *Negro Digest*, February 1962, pp. 23–24. See also accounts of her opposition to bootlegging in "Trend May Be Set by Nina's Suit," *New York Amsterdam News*, February 20, 1965, p. 13. According to recent biographers, Simone's volatile behavior was the result of mental illness; at the time, those terms and serious discussions of mental illness were not part of the public conversation. See especially Cohodas, *Princess Noire*.

18. Scott DeVeaux, *The Birth of Bebop: A Social and Musical History* (Berkeley: University of California Press, 1999), pp. 8–10; Bernard Gendron, "A Short Stay in the Sun: The Reception of Bebop (1944–1950)," *Library Chronicle* 24 (1994): 136–139; for "rudeness," see Ralph Ellison, "On Bird, Bird-Watching, and Jazz," in Ellison, *Shadow and Act* (New York: Vintage, 1995; orig. pub. 1962), p. 225; also quoted in DeVeaux, *The Birth of Bebop*, p. 24.

19. For "temperamental," see "Simmering Down," September 30, 1963, unsourced, n.p., "Simone," SCBCCF, v. I; see also Nat Shapiro, liner notes, *In Concert*. For "mean," see "Simmering Down"; for "angry," see "Nina Simone: Angry Woman of Jazz"; for "unstable," see Raymond Robinson, "Nina Simone Thrills, Oscar Brown Chills," *New York Amsterdam News*, December 3, 1966, p. 10; for "inner fires," see John S. Wilson, "Nina Simone Sings Stirring Program: She Makes Everything Add to the Emotional Climate," *New York Times*, April 16, 1965, p. 33; see also "Snarls at Apollo Audience," *New York Citizen-Call*, February 18, 1961, p. 15.

20. Monson, "The Problem with White Hipness."

21. See especially Brooks, "Nina Simone's Triple Play," p. 179.

22. For SNCC, see "SNCC Backers," *New York Amsterdam News*, July 6, 1963, p. 5; "Sponsors of Carnegie Hall, February 1st [1963] Benefit for SNCC" (undated), Student Nonviolent Coordinating Committee Papers (hereafter SNCC), microfilm reel 45: B1–13, #1094, Widener Library, Harvard University. For CORE, see Jesse H. Walker, "Theatricals," *New York Amsterdam News*, July 20, 1963, p. 15; for the NAACP, see advertisement, "Mammoth Benefit to Fight Segregation and Brutality, New York State Conference of NAACP Presents the Amazing Nina Simone," *New York Amsterdam News*, May 25, 1963, p. 14; for the YMCA, see "Nina Sings for YMCA on Sunday," *New York Amsterdam News*, February 27, 1965, p. 16.

23. For "involved," "spurring," and "driven," see Simone with Cleary, *I Put a Spell on You*, pp. 90–91; for "take a stand" and the pressure that Simone faced from activist/singers in the SNCC Freedom Singers, see Ingrid Monson, *Freedom Sounds: Civil Rights Call Out to Jazz and Africa* (New York: Oxford University Press, 2007), pp. 216–223, quote p. 216.

24. For Carnegie Hall, see Julia Prettyman to Nina Simone, May 5, 1964, SNCC Papers, microfilm reel 45: B-I-12, #1053; Julia Prettyman to Andrew Stroud, June 17, 1964, SNCC Papers, microfilm reel 45: B-I-12, #1058; for CORE, see Andrew Stroud to Jim McDonald, April 26, 1965, The Papers of the Congress on Racial Equality—Addendum, 1944–1968 (hereafter Core-ADD), microfilm reel 12: E-II-44, #0892, Widener Library, Harvard University; Alan Gartner to Andrew Stroud, August 20, 1965, Core-ADD, microfilm reel 12: E-II-44, #0892; telegram from Jesse Smallwood to Allen Gardner [*sic*], August 23, 1965, Core-ADD, microfilm reel 12: E-II-44, #0895; for $2,000, see "Fund Raising Department Report," October, 1965, Core-ADD, Reel 8: B-I-13, #0735; Simone with Cleary, *I Put a Spell on You*, p. 108. Other concerts at which jazz musicians played in 1963 and 1964 to support the civil rights movement raised $984.10 and $1354.65. See "Caught in the Act," *Down Beat*, August 30, 1963, p. 37; "Hollywood Benefit Raises $1354 for Civil-Rights Campaign," *Down Beat*, November 5, 1964, p. 9. For jazz and benefit concerts for civil rights organizations, see especially Ingrid Monson, "Monk Meets SNCC," *Black Music Research Journal* 19 (Autumn 1999): 187–200, and Monson, *Freedom Sounds*.

25. For "ever-arresting," see *New York Amsterdam News*, August 10, 1963, p. 42; for "unprecedented," see "Fund Raisers for Freedom: Celebrities Rally to Civil Rights Call by Helping to Raise Thousands in Cash," *Ebony*, October 1963, pp. 120–126; for this event, see Brian Ward, *Just My Soul Responding: Rhythm and Blues, Black Consciousness, and Race Relations* (Berkeley: University of California Press, 1998), p. 302; Simone with Cleary, *I Put a Spell on You*, pp. 101–103; Bob Hunter, "Singer Gloria Lynne in her Glory," *Chicago Defender*, February 16–22, 1963, p. 22. For an audience of 15,000, see Monson, *Freedom Sounds*, p. 219.

26. Letter from Lorraine Hansberry and Leonard Nemiroff to Lena Horne, quoted in Rebeccah Welch, "Black Art and Activism in Postwar New York, 1950–1965" (Ph.D. diss., New York University, 2002), p. 253.

27. Ward, *Just My Soul Responding*, pp. 289–293; Monson, *Freedom Sounds*, p. 219; for the willingness of deejays to boycott controversial songs, see *Variety*, October 3, 1965, p. 63.

28. See, for example, "Sponsors of Carnegie Hall, February 1st [1963] Benefit for SNCC"; Charles McDew to Mr. Max Roach and Miss Abby [*sic*] Lincoln, December 22, 1962, SNCC Papers, microfilm reel 27: #40–0816; see also Monson, *Freedom Sounds*.

29. Abbey Lincoln, *Straight Ahead* (Candid Records, 1961); Ira Gitler, "Review: Abbey Lincoln, *Straight Ahead*," *Down Beat*, November 9, 1961, pp. 35–36; Monson, "Abbey Lincoln's *Straight Ahead*"; for more on Lincoln and this incident, see also chapter 4 in this volume.

30. For efforts among SNCC workers, see Charles McDew to Max Roach and Abby [*sic*] Lincoln, December 22, 1962; Jimmy [Forman] to Betty Garman, December 10, 1964, SNCC Papers, microfilm reel 27: 40, #0823; for "I would," see Julia

Prettyman to Nina Simone, May 5, 1964, SNCC Papers, microfilm reel 45: B-I-12, #1053.

31. For other albums from this period that included explicitly political lyrics, see chapter 1 in this volume; see also Robin D. G. Kelley, *Africa Speaks, America Answers: Modern Jazz in Revolutionary Times* (Cambridge, MA: Harvard University Press, 2012); Monson, *Freedom Sounds*; Ward, *Just My Soul Responding*.

32. With regard to her audience, Simone had at once a "tense relationship" and "interactive drama." See Brooks, "Nina Simone's Triple Play," p. 184.

33. As noted, Simone made related moves in other songs and on other albums. For a more musicological focus on Simone's politics, see Tammy Kernodle, "'I Wish I Knew How It Would Feel to Be Free': Nina Simone and the Redefining of the Freedom Song of the 1960s," *Journal of the Society for American Music* 2 (2008): 295–317; for Simone's commitment to Africa from her very first album, see especially Salamishah Tillet, "The World Nina Simone Made: The Story of a Sonic Radical" (unpublished manuscript in progress, 2012).

34. Bertolt Brecht and Kurt Weill, "Pirate Jenny," performed by Nina Simone, *In Concert*; this alliance, according to Michael Denning, "permanently altered the shape of American music." See Michael Denning, *The Cultural Front: The Laboring of American Culture in the Twentieth Century* (New York: Verso, 1997), p. 324. For German left-wing modernism and American protest music, and for Brecht and Simone, see Russell Berman, "Sounds Familiar? Nina Simone's Performances of Brecht/Weill Songs," in Nora M. Alter and L. Koepnick, eds., *Sound Matters: Essays on Acoustics of Modern German Culture* (New York: Berghahn Books, 2005), pp. 171–182. For the long civil rights movement and activism across decades, see introduction, in this volume.

35. For "perhaps," see Shapiro, liner notes, *In Concert*. For the white spectators in the song and in the audience, see Brooks, "Nina Simone's Triple Play," pp. 181–183.

36. See, for example, Robert Cantwell, *When We Were Good: The Folk Revival* (Cambridge, MA: Harvard University Press, 1996); Kerran L. Sanger, *"When the Spirit Says Sing!": The Role of Freedom Songs in the Civil Rights Movement* (New York: Garland, 1995); Matthew Frye Jacobson, "Take This Hammer: Odetta, Coffeehouse Publics, and the Tributaries of the Left, 1953–1962," paper presented at the American Studies Association Conference, Washington, D.C., November 2009.

37. Simone does not name the race of the woman or of the man with whom she becomes involved. As will become clear, this lack of clarity is part of the point.

38. For anger and Abbey Lincoln's songs, see Eric Porter, *What Is This Thing Called Jazz? African American Musicians as Artists, Critics, and Activists* (Berkeley: University of California Press, 2002); Griffin, *If You Can't Be Free, Be a Mystery*.

39. Nina Simone and Alex Comfort, "Go Limp," performed by Nina Simone, *In Concert*; for gender and the politics of respectability, see especially Evelyn Brooks

Higginbotham, *Righteous Discontent: The Woman's Movement in the Black Bap-tist Church, 1880–1920* (Cambridge, MA: Harvard University Press, 1993). For respectability and the civil rights movement, see, for example, William Chafe, *Civilities and Civil Rights: Greensboro, North Carolina, and the Black Struggle for Freedom* (New York: Oxford University Press, 1980); Marisa Chappell, Jenny Hutchinson, and Brian Ward, "'Dress Modestly, Neatly . . . As If You Were Go-ing to Church': Respectability, Class, and Gender in the Montgomery Bus Boy-cott and the Early Civil Rights Movement," in Peter J. Ling, ed., *Gender in the Civil Rights Movement* (New York: Routledge, 1999), pp. 69–100.

40. The literature on black power, the black arts movement, and black cultural na-tionalism is large. In addition to works cited in other chapters, for black cultural nationalism, see William Van Deburg, *New Day in Babylon: The Black Power Movement and American Culture, 1965–1975* (Chicago: University of Chicago, 1993); for community organizing and urban politics, see Paul Alkebulan, *Sur-vival Pending Revolution: The History of the Black Panther Party* (Tuscaloosa: Uni-versity of Alabama Press, 2007); Alondra Nelson, *Body and Soul: The Black Pan-ther Party and the Fight Against Medical Discrimination* (Minneapolis: University of Minnesota Press, 2011); for anticolonialism and transnationalism, see Laura Pulido, *Black, Brown, Yellow and Left: Radical Activism in Los Angeles* (Berkeley: University of California Press, 2006); Cynthia Young, *Soul Power: Culture, Radi-calism, and the Making of a U.S. Third World Left* (Durham, NC: Duke University Press, 2006). See also Manning Marable, *Malcolm X: A Life of Reinvention* (New York: Viking, 2011); Bill Mullen and James Smethurst, eds., *Left of the Color Line: Race, Radicalism and Twentieth Century Literature of the United States* (Chapel Hill: University of North Carolina Press, 2006).

41. A useful selection on women and black power includes Elaine Brown, *A Taste of Power: A Black Woman's Story* (New York: Pantheon, 1992); Kathleen Cleaver and George Katsiaficas, eds., *Liberation, Imagination and the Black Panther Party* (New York: Routledge, 2001); Nikki Giovanni, *The Selected Poems of Nikki Giovanni* (New York: Morrow, 1995); Sonia Sanchez, *We a BadddDD People* (De-troit: Broadside, 1970); Dayo Gore et al., eds., *Want to Start a Revolution? Radical Black Women in the Freedom Struggle* (New York: New York University Press, 2009); Sharon Harley, "'Chronicle of a Death Foretold': Gloria Richardson, the Cambridge Movement, and the Radical Black Activist Tradition," in Bettye Collier-Thomas and V. P. Franklin, eds., *Sisters in the Struggle: African American Women in the Civil Rights-Black Power Movement* (New York: New York Univer-sity Press, 2001), pp. 174–196; Regina Jennings, "Why I Joined the Party: An African Womanist Reflection," and Angela D. LeBlanc-Ernest, "'The Most Qual-ified Person to Handle the Job': Black Panther Party Women, 1966–1982," both in Charles Jones, ed., *The Black Panther Party Reconsidered* (Baltimore: Black Classic Press, 1998), pp. 257–265 and pp. 305–334, respectively; Anne Valk, *Radical Sisters: Second Wave Feminism and Black Liberation in Washington, D.C.*

(Champaign: University of Illinois Press, 2010), pp. 110–134. For an important discussion of why and how black power's complex history, including the central roles women played, has tended not to be seen, see especially Peniel Joseph, "The Black Power Movement: A State of the Field," *Journal of American History* 96 (December 2009): 751–776.

42. Wahneema Lubiano, "Black Nationalism and Black Common Sense: Policing Ourselves and Others," in Lubiano, ed., *The House That Race Built: Black Americans, U.S. Terrain* (New York: Vintage, 1998), pp. 232–252; Joy James, "Introduction," in James, ed., *The Angela Y. Davis Reader* (Malden, MA: Blackwell, 1998), pp. 6–10; Tracye Matthews, "'No One Ever Asks What a Man's Role in the Revolution Is': Gender Politics and Leadership in the Black Panther Party, 1966–1971," in Collier-Thomas and Franklin, eds., *Sisters in Struggle*, pp. 230–256; Jane Rhodes, *Framing the Black Panthers: The Spectacular Rise of a Black Power Icon* (New York: New Press, 2007).

43. "Nina Simone: Angry Woman of Jazz," p. 60. For the impact of "Mississippi Goddam," see Wilson, "Recital Victory for Nina Simone."

44. Lee Dembart, "Nina Simone: Soul on Voice," *New York Post*, March 15, 1969, sec. 3, p. 1, "Simone," SCBCCF, v. I; "Nina Simone: Angry Woman of Jazz," pp. 61–62. For references to Simone and censorship, see Cordell Thompson, "'Young, Gifted and Black' Tune May Have Nixed Nina's TV Showing," *Jet*, May 14, 1970, pp. 60–61.

45. Simone with Cleary, *I Put a Spell on You*, pp. 87, 98. For an early example of black male sexual aggression as related to liberatory black politics, see Leroi Jones, "Dutchman" (1964), in Amiri Baraka with William J. Harris, eds., *The Leroi Jones/Amiri Baraka Reader* (New York: Basic Books, 1991), pp. 76–99; for later examples, see Amiri Baraka, "T. T. Jackson Sings," in Baraka with Harris, eds., *The Leroi Jones/Amiri Baraka Reader*, p. 216; Larry Neal, "The Baroness and the Black Musician," in Amiri Baraka and Larry Neal, eds., *Black Fire: An Anthology of Afro-American Writing* (New York: William Morrow, 1968), p. 309.

46. Clearly, "Go Limp" could be interpreted in various ways, at the time and subsequently. The multiplicity of meanings, and the ambiguity about the race of the characters especially, is itself significant because it invites the audience into the meaning-making process.

47. Simone with Cleary, *I Put a Spell on You*, pp. 89–90.

48. Baraka, "Black Art," in Harris, ed., *The Leroi Jones/Amiri Baraka Reader*, p. 219. For the Black Arts Movement nationally, see Daniel Widener, *Black Arts West: Culture and Struggle in Postwar Los Angeles* (Durham, NC: Duke University Press, 2010); James Smethurst, *The Black Arts Movement: Literary Nationalism in the 1960s and 1970s* (Chapel Hill: University of North Carolina Press, 2005).

49. See Kevin Gaines, "From Center to Margin: Internationalism and the Origins of Black Feminism," in Russ Castronovo and Dana Nelson, *Materializing Democracy: Toward a Revitalized Cultural Politics* (Durham, NC: Duke University

Press, 2002), pp. 294–313; Danielle McGuire, *At the Dark End of the Street: Black Women, Rape and Resistance—A New History of the Civil Rights Movement, from Rosa Parks to the Rise of Black Power* (New York: Knopf, 2010); E. Frances White, "Africa on My Mind: Gender, Counterdiscourse, and African American Nationalism," in White, ed., *Dark Continent of Our Bodies: Black Feminism and the Politics of Respectability* (Philadelphia: Temple University Press, 2001), pp. 117–150.

50. "33 Americans Going to Negro Art Fete," *New York Times*, December 3, 1961, p. 87; Morris Kaplan, "U.S. Negro Artists Go to Africa to Join in Cultural Exchange," *New York Times*, December 14, 1961, p. 54; both in Schomburg Center on Black Culture Clipping File, Volume I, 1925–1974, "American Society of African Culture" (hereafter, "AMSAC," SCBCCF, v. I). For AMSAC, see also "AMSAC Annual Report, 1960–61," pp. 1–7, in "AMSAC," SCBCCF, v. I; for accounts of the trip, see "African-American Cultural Exchange: Nigerian and U.S. Negro Artists Blend Talents at AMSAC Festival in Lagos," *Ebony*, March 1962, pp. 87–94; Francesca Pereira, "AMSAC Festival was a Pleasure," *Daily Times*, December 30, 1961, n.p., "AMSAC," SCBCCF, v. I. For this trip and the negative coverage it received in Lagos, see Robin D. G. Kelley, *Africa Speaks, America Answers* (Cambridge, MA: Harvard University Press, 2012), pp. 66–70; for Langston Hughes's experience, see Arnold Rampersad, *The Life of Langston Hughes* (New York: Oxford University Press, 1986), p. 348; see also Tillet, "The World Nina Simone Made."

51. Simone with Cleary, *I Put a Spell on You*, pp. 80–81; Simone also noted that she had been "seduced by the Africa in my mind, my mythical home," and that Makeba, who hosted her in Liberia, understood her perspective (p. 138).

52. "Mammoth Benefit to Fight Segregation and Brutality," p. 14; "The Rareness of Nina Simone," p. 30; Philharmonic Hall Concert Program, November 22, 1966, "Simone," SCBCCF, v. I; for "I loved," see Simone with Cleary, *I Put a Spell on You*, p. 98; for "two incandescent," see Robert Shelton, "Two Folk Singers Present Concert," *New York Times*, May 22, 1961, p. 37.

53. Robinson, "Nina Simone Thrills, Oscar Brown Chills," p. 10.

54. Cullaz, "Nina Simone," p. 14. For other reactions to her performances abroad, see Philippe Carles, "Antibes 65: Entretien avec Nina Simone," *Jazz Magazine*, September 1965, pp. 46–48; "Nina Simone," *Jazz Hot*, September 1969, p. 14.

55. For Baker, see Matthew Pratt Guterl, "Josephine Baker's Colonial Pastiche," *Black Camera* 1 (Summer 2010): 25–37; for Holiday, see Griffin, *If You Can't be Free, Be a Mystery*, 99–103; for "looking almost," see Walsh and Hutton, "Antibes Jazz Festival Report," p. 6.

56. For "'Mississippi' is one," see Cullaz and Dellorme, "Nina Simone," pp. 27–31; for "attacks 'Strange Fruit,'" see Jacques Creuzevault, "Antibes," *Jazz Hot*, September 1965, pp. 16–27; for "a perfect world," see Jean-Pierre Binchet, "Antibes 65: Soirees des 24 et 25 juillet (Nina Simone)," *Jazz Magazine*, September 1965, pp. 18–23; for "larger public" see Cullaz, "Une Divine Nina"; "darling," from Nathan interview.

57. Nathan, interview; Nathan, *Soulful Divas*, p. 53.

58. Cullaz and Dellorme, "Nina Simone," p. 7.

59. For the "ever-increasing number of jazzmen making their homes in Europe," see "Americans in Europe, A Discussion," *Down Beat*, July 2, 1964, pp. 64–73, quote p. 64; see also Joachim Berendt, "Americans in Europe, A Dissident View," *Down Beat*, September 10, 1965, p. 19; for "glamour couple," see "Meet the Real Lena Horne," *Ebony*, November 1947, pp. 9–14, quote p. 12; for Horne's positive account of Paris, see Lena Horne, "My Life with Lennie," *Ebony*, November 1965, pp. 174–186, esp. pp. 182–184; for the racism they encountered there amidst her success, see James Gavin, *Stormy Weather: The Life of Lena Horne* (New York: Atria Books, 2009), pp. 230–231.

60. Smith, "The Other (More Serious) Side of Nina," p. 7.

61. Griffin, *If You Can't Be Free, Be a Mystery*, p. 106; Tillet, "The World Nina Simone Made."

62. "All the black people," from Nathan interview; for "the Negro revolution," see Smith, "The Other (More Serious) Side of Nina," p. 7; for "Revolution" and the "racial problem," see Royston Eldridge, "Nina's the Medium for the Message," *Melody Maker*, April 19, 1969, p. 5. In conversation with Eldridge, Simone was also more positive in assessments of race relations in Europe. For similar declarations on American stages, see Jennifer Gilmore, "Nina Simone," *Salon* (2000) http://www.salon.com/people/bc/2000/06/20/simone/index/html; Nina Simone, "To Be Young Gifted and Black" (1968), on *Forever Young, Gifted and Black: Songs of Freedom* (RCA, 2005).

63. For "the role of black women," see Third World Women's Alliance, "Statement" (1968), in Rosalyn Baxandall and Linda Gordon, eds., *Dear Sisters: Dispatches from the Women's Liberation Movement* (New York: Basic Books, 2000), p. 65. For these developments in literature, see especially Mary Helen Washington, "Alice Childress, Lorraine Hansberry, and Claudia Jones: Black Women Write the Popular Front," in Mullen and Smethurst, eds., *Left of the Color Line*, pp. 183–204; for organizations, see Rosalyn Baxandall, "Re-Visioning the Women's Liberation Movement's Narrative: Early Second Wave African American Feminists," *Feminist Studies* 27 (Spring 2001): 225–245; Premilla Nadasen, *Welfare Warriors: The Welfare Rights Movement in the United States* (New York: Routledge, 2004); Lisa Levenstein, *A Movement Without Marches: African American Women and the Politics of Poverty in Postwar Philadelphia* (Chapel Hill: University of North Carolina Press, 2010).

64. Toni Cade, ed., *The Black Woman: An Anthology* (New York: New American Library, 1970); for a reprint of Beale's essay, "Double Jeopardy: To Be Black and Female" (1969), see pp. 90–100.

65. Simone with Cleary, *I Put a Spell on You*, pp. 86–87.

66. Nina Simone and Weldon Irvine Junior, "To Be Young, Gifted and Black" (1968), *Platinum Series Nina Simone* (D3 Entertainment, 2000); Nathan, liner

notes, *The Very Best of Nina Simone*; Simone with Cleary, *I Put a Spell on You*, pp. 86–87.

67. Nina Simone, "Four Women," *Wild Is the Wind* (Philips, 1966).

68. "Nina Simone Pulls SRO $11,000 in Swinging Bash at Carnegie Hall, N.Y.," *Variety*, January 10, 1968, p. 51. For the rare critique of Simone, see Martin Williams, "Mostly About Pianists," *Saturday Review*, March 12, 1966, p. 130.

69. Garland, *Sounds of Soul*, p. 178; for skin color, see especially Maxine Leeds Craig, *Ain't I Beauty Queen: Black Women, Beauty, and the Politics of Race* (New York: Oxford University Press, 2002), pp. 23–44. The relationship between Simone and color consciousness came to the fore again, in 2012, when debates about Zoe Saldaña playing Nina Simone on screen proliferated. See Spectra, "In Honor of Nina Simone: Why Black Women Must Re-Frame the Conversation about Women in Hollywood," *Spectra Speaks*, September 18, 2012, http://www .spectraspeaks.com/2012/09/black-women-responses-nina-simone-zoe-sal-dana-biopic-media-diversity-solutions/; Mark Lamont Hill, host, "Fifty Shades of Black," *HuffPost Live*, September 14, 2012, http://live.huffingtonpost.come/r/ segment/why-does-hollywood/5051eal302a7600fa9000034.

70. Simone with Cleary, *I Put a Spell on You*, p. 117.

71. Otis Redding, "Respect," performed by Aretha Franklin, *I Never Loved a Man the Way I Loved You* (Atlantic Records, 1967); Carole King and Gerry Goffin, "You Make Me Feel Like a Natural Woman," performed by Aretha Franklin, *Lady Soul* (Atlantic Records, 1967), and by Carole King, *Tapestry* (A&M Recording Studios, 1971). For women, music, and sexuality in the 1960s and '70s, see especially Alice Echols, *Scars of Sweet Paradise: The Life and Times of Janis Joplin* (New York: Henry Holt, 1999).

72. For "brought the most reaction," see Robinson, "Nina Simone Thrills, Oscar Brown Chills"; for "biggest hit," see Bill McLarney, "Caught in the Act," *Down Beat*, January 23, 1969, pp. 34–35; for "overtones," see "Nina Simone Pulls SRO $11,000 in Swinging Bash at Carnegie Hall, N.Y.," p. 51; for "more fully" see McLarney, "Caught in the Act," pp. 34–35, emphasis in orig.

73. Garland, "High Priestess of Soul," p. 158.

74. For sex and women blues singers, see Carby, "'It Jus Be's Dat Way Sometime'; for sex and second-wave feminism, see Jane Gerhard, *Desiring Revolution: Second-Wave Feminism and the Rewriting of American Sexual Thought* (New York: Columbia University Press, 2001).

75. Simone with Cleary, *I Put a Spell on You*, p. 117.

76. Gaines, "From Center to Margin," p. 20. See also, Daphne Brooks, "Planet Earth(a): Sonic Cosmopolitanism and Black Feminist Theory," in Wilfried Raussert, ed., *Cornbread and Cuchifritos: Ethnic Identity Politics, Transnationalization, and Transculturation in American Urban Popular Music* (Tempe, AZ: Bilingual Review Press, 2011), pp. 111–126; Salamishah Tillet, "Hush and Listen: Mama Africa and

Nina Simone's Global Civil Rights Sound," paper presented at the American Studies Association conference, November 2012, San Juan, Puerto Rico.

77. For Simone as the ultimate freedom singer, see Dave Marsh, "Introduction," in Simone with Cleary, *I Put a Spell on You* (New York: Da Capo Press, 2003; orig. pub. 1991), n.p.; see also Kernodle, "I Wish I Knew How It Would Feel to Be Free." Because Simone was not a "traditional" jazz singer, she also tends not to play a big part in valuable studies of jazz and civil rights.

78. For "sung to," see Guy and Candie Carawan, eds., *Sing for Freedom: The Story of the Civil Rights Movement Through Its Songs* (Bethlehem, PA: Sing Out Corporation, 1990), p. 12; see also Bernice Johnson Reagon, "The Song Culture of the Civil Rights Movement," liner notes, *Voices of the Civil Rights Movement: Black American Freedom Songs, 1960–1966* (Smithsonian Folkways Recordings, 1997). Carawan's anthology was originally published as *We Shall Overcome: Songs of the Freedom Movement* (1963) and *Freedom is a Constant Struggle: Songs of the Freedom Movement.* (1968) "Mississippi Goddam" was included in the second volume. For the work SNCC did, see for example, the brochure, "Freedom Gifts: Posters, Books, Holiday Seals, Calendar," (undated), SNCC Papers, microfilm reel 27, #39: 0748–50; Dinky Romilly to Irwin Silver, February 25, 1964, SNCC Papers, microfilm reel 27, #34: 0122.

79. For descriptions of freedom songs, see Carawan, *Sing for Freedom*, "Introduction"; C. T. Vivian, quoted in Carawan, ed., *Sing for Freedom*, p. 4; *Black Music Research Journal* (1987), quoted in Carawan, ed., *Sing for Freedom*, p. 5; Reagon, "The Song Culture of the Civil Rights Movement"; for Highlander, see Benjamin Filene, *Romancing the Folk: Public Memory and American Roots Music* (Chapel Hill: University of North Carolina Press, 2000), p. 3; Joe Street, *The Culture War in the Civil Rights Movement* (Gainesville: University Press of Florida, 2007), pp. 163–67.

80. For freedom songs in contrast to "entertainment," see R. Serge Denisoff, "Protest Songs: Those on the Top Forty and Those of the Streets," *American Quarterly*, 22 (Winter 1970): 807–823. For the significance of Rosa Parks to memories of civil rights and to this process of canon formation, see Jeanne Theoharis, *The Rebellious Life of Mrs. Rosa Parks* (Boston, MA: Beacon Press, 2013).

81. Simone with Cleary, *I Put a Spell on You*, p. 98; Mark Anthony Neal, "Nina Simone: She Cast a Spell and Made a Choice," June 4, 2003, seeingblack.com, http://seeingblack.com/2003/x060403/nina/simone.shtml (accessed July 1, 2011).

82. Simone with Cleary, *I Put a Spell on You*, pp. 114–115; Gene Taylor, "Why? (The King of Love Is Dead)," performed by Nina Simone, *'Nuff Said* (RCA, 1968).

83. "Singers: More than an Entertainer," *Time*, February 21, 1969, n.p., "Simone," SCBCCF, v. I; see also Bill McLarney, "Caught in the Act," *Down Beat*, January 23, 1969, p. 34, for praise that "her music comes from a particular point of view."

CHAPTER 4

1. Daniel Mann, director, *For Love of Ivy* (Palomar, 1968); Hal Kanter, director, *Julia* (20th Century-Fox, 1968); Louis Pelegrine, "No Racial Slant in 'Love of Ivy': Mann," *Film Daily*, March 8, 1968, n.p., Margaret Herrick Library, Academy of Motion Pictures and Sciences, Los Angeles, CA, Special Collections, "Abbey Lincoln" (hereafter, "Lincoln," Herrick Library); Angela Nelson, "The Objectification of Julia: Texts, Textures and Contexts for Black Women in American Television Comedies," in Devoney Looser and E. Ann Kaplan, eds., *Generations: Academic Feminists in Dialogue* (Minneapolis: University of Minnesota Press, 1997), pp. 237–249.

2. Albert Johnson, "The Negro in American Films: Some Recent Works," *Film Quarterly* 18 (Summer 1965): 14–30, see p. 15.

3. For this trend, and for these and other films and television shows, see Donald Bogle, *Toms, Coons, Mulattoes, Mammies, and Bucks: An Interpretive History of Blacks in American Films* (New York: Continuum, 2001; orig. pub. 1973), pp. 194–229; Christopher Sieving, *Soul Searching: Black-Themed Cinema from the March on Washington to the Rise of Blaxploitation* (Middletown, CT: Wesleyan University Press, 2011); Christine Acham, *Revolution Televised: Prime Time and the Struggle for Black Power* (Minneapolis: University of Minnesota Press, 2004), see especially, p. 19; Aniko Bodroghkozy, *Equal Time: Television and the Civil Rights Movement* (Champaign: University of Illinois Press, 2012); Gene Handsaker, "The Negro Finds a Place in TV," *Los Angeles Herald-Examiner*, May 23, 1968, p. D7; for "Summer of the Negro," see *Newsweek*, quoted in Aram Goudsouzian, *Sidney Poitier: Man, Actor, Icon* (Chapel Hill: University of North Carolina Press, 2003), p. 295.

4. Edward Lipton, "Review of New Film: '*For Love of Ivy*,'" *Film TV Daily*, July 10, 1968, n.p., Margaret Herrick Library, Academy of Motion Pictures and Sciences, Los Angeles, CA, Special Collections, "*For Love of Ivy*" (hereafter, "*For Love of Ivy*," Herrick Library); Digby Diehl, "Diahann Carroll: Bid for a Historical Niche," *Los Angeles Times*, December 28, 1967, Part IV, p. 12. See also, "Diahann Carroll 1st Negress Lead in a TV Series," *Variety*, October 20, 1967, n.p., Margaret Herrick Library, Academy of Motion Pictures and Sciences, Los Angeles, CA, Special Collections, "Diahann Carroll" (hereafter "Carroll," Herrick Library); Frank J. Prial, "Will New TV Series About a Negro Open Eyes of Some Whites?," *Wall Street Journal*, April 18, 1968, p. 1.

5. "New: Sidney Poitier," *Cue*, July 20, 1968, n.p., "*For Love of Ivy*," Herrick Library. For *Julia*, class, and race, see, for example, Prial, "Will New TV Series About a Negro Open Eyes of Some Whites?"

6. Martin Luther King Jr., "Beyond Vietnam," April 4, 1967, http://www.americanrhetoric.com/speeches/mlkatimetobreaksilence.htm; U.S. Riot Commission Report, *Report of the National Advisory Commission on Civil Disorders* (New York:

Bantam Books, 1968); Peniel Joseph, *Waiting 'Til the Midnight Hour: A Narrative History of Black Power in America* (New York: Henry Holt, 2006).

7. Joseph, *Waiting 'Til the Midnight Hour*, pp. 178–188, 206–210, 226–228; Kevin Gaines, "The Crisis of Historical Memory: Harold Cruse, Julian Mayfield and African American Expatriates in Nkrumah's Ghana, 1957–1966," in Jerry G. Watts, ed., *Harold Cruse's The Crisis of the Negro Intellectual Reconsidered* (New York: Routledge, 2004), pp. 183–102; see esp. pp. 194–195; for Karenga, see Scot Brown, *Fighting for US: Maulana Karenga, the US Organization and Black Cultural Nationalism* (New York: New York University Press, 2005); for Newark, see Komozi Woodard, *A Nation Within a Nation: Amiri Baraka (LeRoi Jones) and Black Power Politics* (Chapel Hill: University of North Carolina Press, 1999); for black power organizing in other cities, see Matthew Countryman, *Up South: Civil Rights and Black Power in Philadelphia* (Philadelphia: University of Pennsylvania Press, 2007); for the Olympics, see Amy Bass, *Not the Triumph but the Struggle: 1968 Olympics and the Making of the Black Athlete* (Minneapolis: University of Minnesota Press, 2004).

8. For "would not recognize," see "Programs: Wonderful World of Color," *Time*, December 13, 1968, p. 70, "Carroll," Herrick Library; for "bourgeois," see Penelope Gilliatt, "The Current Cinema," *New Yorker*, July 27, 1968, p. 82; see also Joseph Morgenstern, "Maid in U.S.A.," *Newsweek*, July 29, 1968 n.p., "*For Love of Ivy*" Herrick Library.

9. Although scholarship about Lincoln tends not to focus on this film, invaluable analyses of Lincoln as singer and intellectual include Farah Jasmine Griffin, *If You Can't Be Free, Be a Mystery: In Search of Billie Holiday* (New York: Free Press, 2001), pp. 161–192; for her reading of Ivy as "path breaking," see p. 177; Eric Porter, *What Is This Thing Called Jazz: African American Musicians as Artists, Critics, and Activists* (Berkeley: University of California Press, 2002), pp. 149–190; for Ivy as a "coda," to Lincoln's other work, see p. 189. *For Love of Ivy* also tends not to be the focus in studies of Poitier, which emphasize *Guess Who's Coming to Dinner*, *In the Heat of the Night*, and *To Sir with Love* (all released in 1967), or earlier films like *Lilies of the Field* (1963) and *The Defiant Ones* (1958). Work on Carroll and *Julia* includes Aniko Bodroghkozy, *Groove Tube: Sixties Television and the Youth Rebellion* (Durham, NC: Duke University Press, 2001); Aniko Bodroghkozy, "'Is This What You Mean by Color TV?' Race, Gender, and Contested Meanings in NBC's *Julia*," in Lynn Spiegel and Denise Mann, eds., *Private Screenings: Television and the Female Consumer* (Minneapolis: University of Minnesota Press, 1992), pp. 143–168.

10. Adam Green, *Selling the Race: Culture, Community, and Black Chicago, 1940–1955* (Chicago: University of Chicago Press, 2007), p. 12.

11. Diahann Carroll with Ross Firestone, *Diahann! An Autobiography* (New York: Little, Brown, 1986), pp. 164–165.

12. For "chic chanteuse," see Richard Warren Lewis, "Rodgers and Carroll," *Show Business Illustrated*, April 1962, p. 45, "Carroll," Herrick Library.

13. For fuller accounts of Carroll's career, see Carroll with Firestone, *Diahann!*; Diahann Carroll, *The Legs Are the Last to Go: Aging, Acting, Marrying and Other Things I Learned the Hard Way* (New York: Amistad, 2008).

14. For Carroll's relationship with SNCC and other organizations, see "SNCC Backers," *New York Amsterdam News*, July 6, 1963, p. 5; "Sponsors of Carnegie Hall, February 1st [1963] Benefit for SNCC" (undated), Student Nonviolent Coordinating Committee Papers (hereafter SNCC Papers), microfilm reel 45: B1–13, #1094, Widener Library, Harvard University; letter from James Forman to Miss Diahann Carroll, February 13, 1963, SNCC Papers, reel 5-A-TV-69; for her congressional testimony, see Carroll with Firestone, *Diahann!*, p. 136; for *King*, see Sidney Lumet, director, *King: A Filmed Record . . . Montgomery to Memphis* (Commonwealth United Entertainment, 1970); Robert Greenspun, "Screen: The Pilgrimage of Martin Luther King, Jr.," *New York Times*, March 24, 1970, p. 40; Goudsouzian, *Sidney Poitier*, p. 309. (Lumet was Lena Horne's son-in-law at the time that he made this film.) For "long fingernails," see Carroll with Firestone, *Diahann!*, pp. 173, 161; for "alluring," see "Hands at the Heart of Song," *Life*, December 7, 1959, pp. 56–58, "Carroll," Herrick Library; for "sleek as a cheetah" and "clothes like a thoroughbred," see "Diahann Carroll: Show Stopper," *Look*, May 22, 1962, n.p., "Carroll," Herrick Library.

15. Hal Kanter, *So Far, So Funny: My Life in Show Business* (Jefferson, NC: McFarland and Company, 1999), p. 254, emphasis in original; Acham, *Revolution Televised*, pp. 114–115; Kwakiutl L. Dreher, *Dancing on the White Page: Black Women Entertainers Writing Autobiography* (Albany, NY: SUNY Press, 2008), p. 127. According to some accounts, Kanter worried that Carroll might be too chic to be Julia.

16. Aniko Bodroghkozy, "Julia; U.S. Domestic Comedy," http://www.museum.tv/archives/etv/J/htmlJ/julia/julia.htm, (accessed March 24, 2009); for "new kind of glamour," see "Diahann Carroll: A New Kind of Glamour," *Look*, October 29, 1968, pp. 66–69. Harry Belafonte was among those who urged Carroll not to take the part; see Carroll with Firestone, *Diahann!*, pp. 170–172; for parallels between Carroll and Julia, see Nelson, "The Objectification of *Julia*," pp. 241–242; for Carroll's resistance to Kanter's efforts to make the show seem color blind, see Dreher, *Dancing on the White Page*; Bodroghkozy, "Is This What You Mean by Color TV?"; Acham, *Revolution Televised*, pp. 110–142.

17. Nat Hentoff, liner notes, Max Roach, *We Insist! Max Roach's Freedom Now Suite* (Candid Records, 1960); also quoted in Griffin, *If You Can't Be Free, Be a Mystery*, p. 173.

18. "Music," *Time*, July 14, 1956, p. 45; Griffin, *If You Can't Be Free, Be a Mystery*, pp. 163–165.

19. "The New Abbey Lincoln: A Voice of Protest," *Pittsburgh Courier*, May 27, 1961, p. 20.

20. For "deserted" and "I'm a black woman," see "Abbey Lincoln Changes Act, Now Jazz Singer," *Jet*, December 4, 1958, p. 61; also quoted in Griffin, *If You Can't Be*

Free, Be a Mystery, p. 170; for "metamorphosis," see Barbara Gardner, "Metamorphosis," *Down Beat,* September 14, 1961, pp. 18–20.

21. Nat Hentoff, "How Wonderful to Be a Black Woman," *New York Times,* January 14, 1968, p. D-11.

22. For the review and this controversy, see Ira Gitler, "Review: Abbey Lincoln, *Straight Ahead," Down Beat,* November 9, 1961, pp. 35–36; Ingrid Monson, "Abbey Lincoln's *Straight Ahead:* Jazz in the Era of the Civil Rights Movement," in Richard G. Fox and Orin Starn, eds., *Between Resistance and Revolution: Cultural Politics and Social Protest* (New Brunswick, NJ: Rutgers University Press, 1997), pp. 171–194; for performances after this incident, see, for example, "Ye Little Club, L.A.," *Variety,* October 26, 1966, p. 57; David Bittan, "Newport Jazz Festival Clicks on All Fronts in 11th Annual Outing," *Variety,* July 8, 1964, pp. 45, 57; "Europe's Festival Schedule Heavy," *Down Beat,* July 14, 1966, p. 15; for essays, see Abbey Lincoln, "Who Will Revere the Black Woman?," *Negro Digest,* September 1966, pp. 16–20; Abbey Lincoln, "The Negro Woman in American Literature," *Freedomways* 6, no. 1 (1966): 11–13; for "among the most vocal," see Porter, *What Is This Thing Called Jazz?,* p. 148. For Lincoln's transformations and reactions to her, see also Jacqueline Castledine, "Gender, Jazz and Justice in Cold War Freedom Movements," in Danielle McGuire and John Dittmer, eds., *Freedom Rights: New Perspectives on the Civil Rights Movement* (Lexington: University Press of Kentucky, 2011), pp. 223–246.

23. Ira Gitler, Abbey Lincoln, et al., "Racial Prejudice in Jazz, Part I," *Down Beat,* March 20, 1962, pp. 20–26; "Racial Prejudice in Jazz, Part II," *Down Beat,* March 29, 1962, pp. 22–25; see also Monson, "Abbey Lincoln's *Straight Ahead."* Two years later, in France, both Roach and Lincoln said that participating in the debate was a "mistake," because *Down Beat* was a "Jim Crow journal." See Jean Wagner, "12 heures avec Abbey Lincoln," *Jazz Magazine,* March 1964, pp. 24–30.

24. Michael Roemer, director, *Nothing But a Man* (Cinema V, 1964); Judith Smith, "Close Up: Civil Rights, Labor, and Sexual Politics on Screen in *Nothing But a Man* (1964)," *Black Camera* 3 (Spring 2012): 164–193.

25. "*Nothing But a Man*: Triumph on a Budget," *Ebony,* April 1965, p. 199.

26. Abe Greenberg, "A Star Is Born in '*For Love of Ivy,*'" *Citizen News,* July 19, 1968, n.p., "*For Love of Ivy,*" Herrick Library; Renata Adler, "'Ivy,' or One Step at a Time," *New York Times,* August 18, 1968, p. D1.

27. For accounts of Poitier "secluding himself" for three weeks to write, see Jay Weston, "Care and Watering of Poitier 'Ivy,' 'Daring' to Have All-Black Romance," *Variety,* January 8, 1969, p. 40. For "first picture," "proud to announce," and "but a start," see undated press release from Leonard H. Goldenson, President of American Broadcasting Company, Inc., and Samuel H. Clark, Group Vice President of ABC, Inc., "*For Love of Ivy,*" Herrick Library; for the crisis in

Hollywood and films losing money, see Goudsouzian, *Sidney Poitier*, p. 332; for "curious," see John Mahoney, "Palomar-Cinerama '*Ivy*' Most Profitable for All," *Hollywood Reporter*, July 1, 1968, p. 3; for changes in the film and television industries, see also "Producer Edgar J. Scherick," December 3, 2002, http://www .lukeford.net/profiles/profiles/edgar_scherick.htm, (accessed July 14, 2009); Leonard Sloane, "Hidden Assets Build ABC Merger Appeal," *New York Times*, July 7, 1968, p. F1. For how a sense of a crisis in Hollywood affected the development of "blaxploitation" films, see chapter 5 in this volume.

28. Diahann Carroll, "From *Julia* to *Cosby* to *Oprah*: Tuning into 60 Years of TV," *Ebony*, November 2005, p. 101; also quoted in Dreher, *Dancing on the White Page*, p. 119.

29. For "lighthearted," "loads," and "turgid," see Ronald Gold, "While He's Sole U.S. Negro Star Seen Regularly, Sidney Poitier Expects to Play Only Heroes," *Variety*, October 4, 1967, n.p., "*For Love of Ivy*," Herrick Library; for "race is only brought in," see Edward Lipton, "Negro Stereotype—In a Lost World: Poitier," *Film Daily*, September 28, 1967, p. 3; for "sheer entertainment value" and "his answer," see Gold, "While He's Sole U.S. Negro Star Seen Regularly, Sidney Poitier Expect to Play Only Heroes" (though Poitier did answer that question "not exactly"); for "No Racial Slant," see Pelegrine, "No Racial Slant in '*Love of Ivy*.'"

30. Kanter, *So Far, So Funny*, p. 255. Similarly, in the Broadway show, *No Strings*, Carroll played the part of a model in an interracial romance in which race does not play any direct part.

31. For "except," see Stanley Kauffmann, "Stanley Kauffmann on Films: Hit and Myth," *New Republic*, August 10, 1968, p. 14; for "marks a first," see "*For Love of Ivy*: Abbey Lincoln Teams Up with Poitier in Romantic Comedy Film," *Ebony*, October 1968, p. 52.

32. For "the ultimate," see Mahoney, "Palomar-Cinerama 'Ivy' Most Profitable for All," p. 3; for "white America's," see Kauffmann, "Stanley Kauffmann on Films"; for "quite obviously," see Charles Champlin, "Two Films in the Romantic Tradition," *Los Angeles Times*, July 14, 1968, pp. 1, 19; quote p. 19.

33. "No Better, No Worse," letter by Robert Teal, *Newsweek*, August 12, 1968, n.p., "*For Love of Ivy*," Herrick Library.

34. "*For Love of Ivy*: Abbey Lincoln Teams Up with Poitier in Romantic Comedy Film," quote pp. 52, 53. For a similar perspective ("*For Love of Ivy* dares present the shocking truth that Negroes and whites, when they appear together, are not all cause-waving stereotypes. It even goes so far as to dare suggest that Negroes are really people not symbols manufactured for specific occasions"), see Harold Stern, "Is the World Ready for 'Ivy'?," *After Dark*, June 1968, p. 22; see also, Greenberg, "A Star Is Born in 'For Love of Ivy'"; Richard Mallett, "Cinema," *Punch*, July 24, 1968, pp. 132–133. For the depoliticization of leisure as a liberal political project, see Uta Poiger, *Jazz, Rock, and Rebels: Cold War Politics and American Culture in a Divided Germany* (Berkeley: University of California Press, 1999).

35. Kanter, *So Far, So Funny*, p. 254.
36. *Variety*, September 13, 1967, quoted in Goudsouzian, *Sidney Poitier*, p. 271.
37. For competing reactions to Poitier, see Goudsouzian, *Sidney Poitier*, p. 269; for "one star," see Harold Cruse, *The Crisis of the Negro Intellectual*, introduction by Stanley Crouch (New York: New York Review of Books, 2005; 1967), p. 111; for "idealized," see *San Francisco Examiner*, August 22, 1967, quoted in Goudsouzian, *Sidney Poitier*, p. 272; for "Uncle Tom refurbished," see Catherine Sugy, "Black Men or Good Niggers," *Take One*, quoted in Goudsouzian, *Sidney Poitier*, p. 273; for "antiseptic," see Clifford Mason, "Why Does White America Love Sidney Poitier So Much?," *New York Times*, September 10, 1967, sec. II, p. 1.
38. For "good little symbol," see Lena Horne with Richard Schickel, *Lena* (Garden City, NY: Limelight, 1986; orig. pub. 1965), p. 203; for "all sorts," "I'm the only," and "overcome," see Gold, "While He's Sole U.S. Negro Star Seen Regularly, Sidney Poitier Expects to Play Only Heroes"; for "middle-class aspect," see Carroll with Firestone, *Diahann!*, p. 171, emphasis in original; for "this is fairyland," see "Diahann Carroll: A New Kind of Glamour on TV," p. 68; for "show it like it is," see Robert Lewis Shayon, "'Julia' Symposium: An Opportunity Lost," *Saturday Review*, May 25, 1968, p. 36; for "overcome" and "all those," see Gold, "While He's Sole U.S. Negro Star Seen Regularly, Sidney Poitier Expects to Play Only Heroes."
39. For "Saint Sidney," see Morgenstern, "Maid in U.S.A."; Morgenstern went on to bemoan the lack of "honest-to-God sexuality" in the black characters. For "never on the screen," see *Playboy*, September 1968, n.p., "*For Love of Ivy*," Herrick Library; for "Jack and Ivy," see Richard Mallett, "Cinema," *Punch*, July 24, 1968, p 132–133, quote p. 133.
40. For "be one of the best," see Hentoff, "How Wonderful to Be a Black Woman," p. D-11; for domestic race relations and cold war foreign policy, see especially Mary Dudziak, *Cold War, Civil Rights: Race and the Image of American Democracy* (Princeton, NJ: Princeton University Press, 2003).
41. For breaking records in five cities, see "Winners' Corner," *Film/TV Daily*, July 19, 1968, n.p., "*For Love of Ivy*," Herrick Library; for "delightful," and "charming," see M.B., "For Love of Ivy," *Daily Cinema*, July 19, 1968, p. 14; see also John Russell Taylor, "For Love of Ivy," *London Times*, July 18, 1968, p. 7; Mallet, "Cinema." For awards, see IMDB, "*For Love of Ivy*," http://www.imdb.com/title/tt0062985/awards, (accessed July 1, 2011).
42. Lipton, "Negro Stereotype—In a Lost World: Poitier."
43. Important exceptions include a scene between Ivy and Jack in a Village restaurant, and the scenes in his very sophisticated Manhattan apartment.
44. Sydney Pollack, director, *They Shoot Horses Don't They?* (Palomar Pictures, 1969); "ABC's 5 Years of Film Production Profits & Losses," *Variety*, May 31, 1973, p. 3; Mahoney, "Palomar-Cinerama 'Ivy' Most Profitable for All," p. 3.
45. For questions about the white director, see Hollis Alpert, *Saturday Review*, August 3, 1968, p. 35; for "coyness," see Taylor, "For Love of Ivy," p. 6; for "Negro

culture," see Adler, "'Ivy,' or One Step at a Time," p. D1; for "black decorations" and "a whole black world," see Morgenstern, "Maid in U.S.A."

46. For "was trying to tell us," see "Movie Mailbag: 'Ivy' Misunderstood?," Letter by Ruth Ziony, *New York Times*, August 25, 1968, p. D10 (emphasis in original); for "brief respite," see Kauffmann, "Stanley Kauffmann on Films"; for "sadly dishonest," see "Movie Mailbag," letter by Loren Montes, *New York Times*, January 12, 1969, p. D11; for "I am certain," see Dennis Hunt, "For the Love of Ivy," *Film Quarterly* 22, no. 2 (Winter 1968–1969): 56–57; see also letter by Robert Teal, "No Better, No Worse," *Newsweek*, August 12, 1968, n.p., "*For Love of Ivy*," Herrick Library.

47. Lipton, "Negro Stereotype—In a Lost World: Poitier," p. 3; see also Stern, "Is the World Ready for 'Ivy'?," p. 22.

48. Lincoln quoted in Tusher [no first name], "Mann States 'Ivy' Breakthrough," *Film-TV Daily*, July 16, 1968, n.p., "*For Love of Ivy*," Herrick Library.

49. For "this country," see Don Alpert, "Abbey Lincoln's Brand of Domestic Tranquility," *Los Angeles Times*, Calendar, July 14, 1968, p. 14; for "still involved" and her answers, see Hentoff, "How Wonderful to Be a Black Woman."

50. Nina Simone with Stephen Cleary, *I Put a Spell on You: The Autobiography of Nina Simone* (New York: Da Capo Press, 2003; orig. pub. 1991), p. 115.

51. Porter, *What Is This Thing Called Jazz*, p. 180; Dave Hepburn, "No Nationalist, Says Abbey, She Just Wants Dignity . . .," *New York Amsterdam News*, June 30, 1962, p. 18; see also her discussion of "propaganda," in "Abbey Lincoln at Wells," *New York Amsterdam News*, September 18, 1965, p. 18.

52. For 300 women and the audition process, see "Bruin Theater Gets 'For Love of Ivy,'" *Citizen News*, June 26, 1968, n.p., "*For Love of Ivy*," Herrick Library; Mann quoted in Hentoff, "How Wonderful to Be a Black Woman"; see also see also Weston, "Care and Watering of Poitier 'Ivy,' 'Daring' to Have All-Black Romance," p. 49; Lipton, "Negro Stereotype—In a Lost World: Poitier."

53. Winfred Blevins, "'Ivy' Star Proud of 'Very Real People,'" *San Francisco Herald-Examiner*, July 16, 1968, n.p., "*For Love of Ivy*," Herrick Library.

54. For "the female Sidney Poitier," see "Last to Audition Got the Part," *Ebony*, October 1968, p. 56; for "going to eclipse," see Lipton, "Negro Stereotype—In a Lost World"; for "life reached," see Francis Davis, "Leading Lady," *High Fidelity*, May 1986, pp. 65–66, 79; quote p. 66, in Abbey Lincoln Collection (MC 101), Institute of Jazz Studies, Rutgers University Libraries; for Lincoln and *Lady Sings the Blues*, see Griffin, *If You Can't Be Free, Be a Mystery*, p. 181. While the story was resold to Berry Gordy who cast Diana Ross as the lead in the 1972 film, according to Jay Weston, producer of *Ivy* and one of the producers for *Lady Sings the Blues*, he "offered Ms. Lincoln the lead in the Holiday film . . . but she had to decline." See "Abbey Lincoln; Playing Holiday," Letter by Jay Weston, *New York Times*, March 17, 2002, n.p., in Abbey Lincoln Collection (MC 101), Institute of Jazz Studies, Rutgers University Libraries.

55. Carroll with Firestone, *Diahann!*, p. 172; Kanter, *So Far, So Funny*, p. 257.

56. For critics who raised these issues, see for example Gilliatt, "The Current Cinema," p. 81; "For Love of Ivy," *Time*, August 2, 1968, p. 64.

57. Frances Beale, "Double Jeopardy: to Be Black and Female," in Toni Cade, ed., *The Black Woman: An Anthology* (New York: New American Library, 1970), pp. 90–100, quotes p. 98; Pat Robinson and Group, "Poor Black Women's Study Papers by Poor Black Women of Mount Vernon, New York," in Cade, ed., *The Black Woman*, pp. 189-197, quote p. 194; Benita Roth, *Separate Roads to Feminism: Black, Chicana and White Feminist Movements in America's Second Wave* (New York: Cambridge University Press, 2003), pp. 87–88.

58. For critics who raised these points, see, for example, Taylor, "For Love of Ivy," p. 6.

59. For "in her honor," and "not that kind of maid," see Gold, "While He's Sole U.S. Negro Star Seen Regularly, Sidney Poitier Expects to Play Only Heroes."

60. Lipton, "Negro Stereotype—In a Lost World: Poitier," p. 3. For other references to Lincoln as domestic, see Blevins, "'Ivy' Star Proud of 'Very Real People'"; "Two New Stars," in *"For Love of Ivy*, Pressbook" (Cinerama Releasing Corp., 1968), *"For Love of Ivy*," Herrick Library.

61. Alpert, "Abbey Lincoln's Brand of Domestic Tranquility."

62. For Lincoln's connections to other black women performers, see especially, Griffin, *If You Can't Be Free, Be a Mystery*; Porter, *What Is This Thing Called Jazz?*, pp. 161–167.

63. Clarissa Start, "All She Seeks Is 'Human Dignity,'" *St. Louis Dispatch*, September 27, 1949, n.p., Schomburg Center on Black Culture Clipping File, Volume I, 1925–1974, "Lena Horne." For Horne's insight that there was no "sound image" to represent a black woman who was neither respectable servant nor whore, see Horne with Schickel, *Lena*, p. 10.

64. Roth, *Separate Roads to Feminism*; Glenda Gilmore, *Defying Dixie: The Radical Roots of Civil Rights, 1919–1950* (New York: Norton, 2008), pp. 247–399; Duchess Harris, *Black Feminist Politics from Kennedy to Obama* (New York: Palgrave, 2009).

65. Alice Childress, *Like One of the Family: Conversations from a Domestic's Life* (Boston: Beacon Press, 1986; orig. pub. 1956); Jill Watts, *Hattie McDaniel: Black Ambition, White Hollywood* (New York: HarperCollins, 2005); Ruth Feldstein, *Motherhood in Black and White: Race and Sex in American Liberalism, 1930–1965* (Ithaca, NY: Cornell University Press, 2000), pp. 12–39; Trudier Harris, *From Mammies to Militants: Domestics in Black American Literature* (Philadelphia: Temple University Press, 1982). Nor, of course, was Lincoln the last black woman to remake meanings of domestic work by portraying a maid on screen. See, for example, Tate Taylor, director, *The Help* (Dreamworks, 2011).

66. Porter, *What Is This Thing Called Jazz?*, p. 159; Griffin, *If You Can't Be Free, Be a Mystery*, pp. 179–180; Cobi Narita and James Briggs Murray, interviewers, *Oral History Interview with Abbey Lincoln/Animutu Moseka* (September 18, 1996),

Schomburg Center for Research on Black Culture, Louis Armstrong Jazz Oral History Project, New York, New York.

67. Griffin, *If You Can't Be Free, Be a Mystery*, p. 170.

68. Alpert, "Abbey Lincoln's Brand of Domestic Tranquility," p. 14; for her later comments about marriage, see Chester Higgins Sr., "Abbey Lincoln Talks of Breakup with Max Roach," *Jet*, May 25, 1972, pp. 16–17.

69. Alpert, "Abbey Lincoln's Brand of Domestic Tranquility," p. 14; Blevins, "'Ivy' Star Proud of 'Very Real People.'"

70. "*For Love of Ivy*: Abbey Lincoln Teams Up with Poitier in Romantic Comedy Film," *Ebony*, October 1968, pp. 52–54, 56, quote p. 52. By contrast, a few years earlier, Carroll appeared in advertisements for Wig City, "New York's largest wig salon," according to one ad, a shop that offered Carroll "instant glamour." See "Wig City," advertisement, *New York Amsterdam News*, June 22, 1963, p. 4, "Diahann Carroll," Schomburg Center on Black Culture Clipping File, Volume I, 1925–1974.

71. "She Yearns to Play an African Tribeswoman," *Ebony*, October 1968, p. 58.

72. Maxine Leeds Craig, *Ain't I a Beauty Queen: Black Women, Beauty, and the Politics of Race* (New York: Oxford University Press, 2002), pp. 16, 56, 73, 82.

73. Alpert, "Abbey Lincoln's Brand of Domestic Tranquility."

74. Griffin, *If You Can't Be Free, Be a Mystery*, p. 179; Pauline Rivelli, "Abbey Lincoln: Proud and Confident," *Jazz* 4 (1965): 8–12, quotes pp. 8, 10, 12, emphasis in original.

75. Alpert, "Abbey Lincoln's Brand of Domestic Tranquility."

76. For a consideration of these issues, see Gaines, "The Crisis of Historical Memory," p. 195.

77. Amiri Baraka with William J. Harris, ed., *The LeRoi Jones/Amiri Baraka Reader* (New York: Basic Books, 1999; orig. pub. 1991), p. 369; James Smethurst, *The Black Arts Movement: Literary Nationalism in the 1960s and 1970s* (Chapel Hill: University of North Carolina Press, 2005), pp. 12–27.

78. Craig, *Ain't I a Beauty Queen*, p. 91.

79. Carroll with Firestone, *Diahann!*, p. 192.

CHAPTER 5

1. Marvin Chomsky, et al., directors, *Roots*, Episode One (David L. Wolper Productions, Warner Brothers, 1977); Tyson appeared at other points in this episode after giving birth to Kunta Kinte, but she was available for just three days of shooting and her part was small. See David Wolper with Quincy Troupe, *The Inside Story of T.V.'s "Roots"* (New York: Warner Books, 1978), p. 82.

2. Alex Haley, *Roots: The Saga of an American Family* (New York: Doubleday 1977); for African Americans in television and film in the 1970s, see Christine Acham, *Revolution Televised: Prime Time and the Struggle for Black Power* (Minneapolis: University of Minnesota Press, 2004); Christopher Sieving, *Soul Searching: Black-Themed*

Cinema from the March on Washington to the Rise of Blaxploitation (Middletown, CT: Wesleyan University Press, 2011); see also chapter 4 in this volume. Haley's book was published in October 1976; executive producer David Wolper signed with Haley in 1974. See Wolper with Troupe, *The Inside Story of T.V.'s "Roots,"* p. 45.

3. For "middle brow," see Richard Schickel, quoted in Wolper with Troupe, *The Inside Story of T.V.'s "Roots,"* preface, n.p.; for "120 million," see Wolper with Troupe, *The Inside Story of T.V.'s "Roots,"* preface, n.p. The finale remains the third-highest-rated television program in the United States.

4. For "with whom," see Wolper with Troupe, *The Inside Story of T.V.'s "Roots,"* p. 57; for "first great black heroine," see Bart Mills, "Cicely Tyson: Success Is a Big Bowl of Cherries," *San Francisco Sunday Examiner and Chronicle Datebook,* August 13, 1978, n.p., Schomburg Center on Black Culture Clipping File, Volume I, 1925–1974, "Cicely Tyson" (hereafter, "Tyson," SCBCCF, v. I); for "sublime achievement," and "so special," see Daniel Bright, "An Emmy Award for Cicely?," *Sepia,* April, 1974, pp. 16–20; for awards, see "Awards for Cicely Tyson," IMDB, http://www.imdb.com/name/nm0001807/awards, (accessed July 1, 2011). Martin Ritt, director, *Sounder* (Radnitz/Mattell Productions, Twentieth Century-Fox, 1972); John Korty, director, *The Autobiography of Miss Jane Pittman* (Tomorrow Broadcasting, CBS, 1974). Ed Asner and O. J. Simpson, in their respective roles as slave ship captain and tribal leader, were other cast members who the producers felt would appeal to white audiences.

5. *Roots*—as book, television miniseries, and combined blockbuster "event"—generated a virtual avalanche of positive media coverage at the time; subsequent scholarship has considered Haley's historical accuracy, his relationship to white-authored accounts of slavery, and the adaptation from book to television screen, as well as charges of plagiarism. In addition to work cited, see also Leslie Fielder, *The Inadvertent Epic: From Uncle Tom's Cabin to Roots* (CBS Merchandising, 1979); Helen Taylor, "'The Griot from Tennessee': The Saga of Alex Haley's *Roots,*" *Critical Quarterly* 37 (Spring 1993): 46–62; Lauren R. Tucker and Hemant Shah, "Race and the Transformation of Culture: The Making of the Television Miniseries *Roots,*" *Cultural Studies in Mass Communication* 9 (1992): 325–336; and for useful statistics, see David Gerber, "Haley's *Roots* and Our Own: An Inquiry into the Nature of a Popular Phenomenon," *Journal of Ethnic Studies* 5 (Fall 1977): 87–111.

6. Matthew Frye Jacobson, *Roots Too: White Ethnic Revival in Post-Civil Rights America* (Cambridge, MA: Harvard University Press 2002); Natasha Zaretsky, *No Direction Home: The American Family and the Fear of National Decline, 1968–1980* (Chapel Hill: University of North Carolina Press, 2007). Other historically oriented programming from this period includes *Mandingo* (1975), *Lady Sings the Blues* (1972), and other television specials in which Tyson starred.

7. I mean to be self-conscious about "remembering," and the selective and/or manufactured "memories" popular culture could produce for audiences who were

not actually remembering their own experiences. See Renee Romano and Leigh Raiford, eds., *The Civil Rights Movement in American Memory* (Athens: University of Georgia Press, 2006); Renee Romano, "A Really Long 'Long Civil Rights Movement'? Memory Work and the Struggle for Racial Equality," Southern Oral History Program Conference, "The Long Civil Rights Movement: Histories, Politics, Memories," Chapel Hill, North Carolina, April 2009, https://lcrm.lib.unc .edu/blog/index.php/tag/commemoration; Paul Grainge, ed., *Memory and Popular Film* (Manchester, England: Manchester University Press, 2003). After *Roots*, Tyson portrayed Harriet Tubman, Coretta Scott King, and a celebrated teacher named Marva Collins in other historically oriented television specials. Important work on black activism in the 1970s includes, Peniel Joseph, *Waiting 'Til the Midnight Hour: A Narrative History of Black Power in America* (New York: Henry Holt, 2006); Premilla Nadasen, *Welfare Warriors: The Welfare Rights Movement in the United States* (New York: Routledge, 2005); Laura Pulido, *Black, Brown, Yellow and Left: Radical Activism in Los Angeles* (Berkeley: University of California Press, 2006); Robert O. Self, *American Babylon: Race and the Struggle for Postwar Oakland* (Princeton, NJ: Princeton University Press, 2003), see especially pp. 256–325; James Smethurst, *The Black Arts Movement: Literary Nationalism in the 1960s and 1970s* (Chapel Hill: University of North Carolina Press, 2005); Daniel Widener, *Black Arts West: Culture and Struggle in Postwar Los Angeles* (Durham, NC: Duke University Press, 2010).

8. For "enthralled," see Muriel Davidson, "What Makes Miss Tyson Run . . . Even at 3 A.M.?," *TV Guide*, January 26, 1974, pp. 14–16, quote p. 16; for "top New York," see Bright, "An Emmy for Cicely Tyson?," pp. 17–18, quote p. 17; see also Robert Windeler, "Cicely Tyson, From the Typing Pool to an Emmy," *People*, June 3, 1974, pp. 36–40. For "started as a fluke," see "Cicely Was Once Too Shy to Act," *New York Amsterdam News*, September 23, 1972, p. D-2; for comparisons to Lana Turner, see Shaun Considine, "Cicely Tyson: A Rare Avis Who Never Wings It," *After Dark*, July 1976, pp. 56–58, quote p. 57; for "too nervous," see Louie Robinson, "Cicely Tyson, a Very Unlikely Movie Star," *Ebony*, May 1974, pp. 33–40, quote p. 34; for "too shy," see "Cicely Was Once Too Shy to Act"; for "kept her out," see George Perry, "The Belle of New York," 1979, unsourced, p. 24, Margaret Herrick Library, Academy of Motion Pictures and Sciences, Special Collections, "Cicely Tyson clipping file" (hereafter "Tyson," Herrick Library).

9. For "had church," see Alan Ebert, "Inside Cecily" [*sic*], *Essence*, February, 1973, pp. 41, 73–74, quote p. 74; for "felt exposure," and "all our friends," see Bright, "An Emmy Award for Cicely?," p. 17; for "her mother," see Phyl Garland, "Her Mother Made Her a Star," *Good Housekeeping*, October 1974, pp. 37–40, 44, 46; for "on relief" and "hemmed in," see Lloyd Shearer, "Cicely Tyson—from Slum to Stardom," *Parade*, December 3, 1972, cover photo, n.p., "Tyson," Herrick Library; for "was grateful," see Windeler, "Cicely Tyson," p. 40; see also Robinson, "Cicely Tyson: A Very Unlikely Movie Star," p. 35; George Simor, "Destination:

Stardom," *Sepia*, March 1967, p. 26. As with Nina Simone, a religious mother who disapproved of show business figured largely in Tyson's biographical narrative; that Tyson grew up in Harlem made that figure even more significant and helped confirm Tyson's apparent authenticity as a representative of blackness on screen.

10. For the report and reactions to it, see Daniel Patrick Moynihan, "The Negro Family: The Case for National Action" (1965), reprinted in Lee Rainwater and William Yancey, *The Moynihan Report and the Politics of Controversy* (Cambridge, MA: MIT Press, 1967); James T. Patterson, *Freedom Is Not Enough: The Moynihan Report and America's Struggle Over Black Family Life—from LBJ to Obama* (New York: Basic Books, 2010).

11. Annelise Orleck, *Storming Caesar's Palace: How Black Mothers Fought Their Own War on Poverty* (Boston: Beacon Press, 2005); Julian Zelizer and Bruce Schulman, eds., *Rightward Bound: Making America Conservative in the 1970s* (Cambridge, MA: Harvard University Press, 2008).

12. For these myths and their relationship to policy, see Robin D. G. Kelley, *Yo' Mama's Disfunktional!: Fighting the Culture Wars in Urban America* (Boston: Beacon Press, 1998); for Drake's song, see Nadasen, *Welfare Warriors*, p. 196; for Nixon and Cash, see Orleck, *Storming Caesar's Palace*, p. 171; see also Susan J. Douglas and Meredith Michaels, *The Mommy Myth: The Idealization of Motherhood and How It Has Undermined All Women* (New York: Free Press, 2005), p 186.

13. For "at long last," see Ellen Holly, "At Long Last, the Super Sound of 'Sounder,'" *New York Times*, October 15, 1972, p. D15; for "I'm proud," see Eve Sharbutt, "Cicely Star of a 'Classic,'" *New Orleans Times-Picayune*, February 18, 1973, sec. 2, p. 12; for the observation that "beneath her rags in 'Sounder,' for instance, is pride and passion that translates into beauty," see Ray Loynd, "Cicely Tyson: 'Sounder' Roots on New York's Upper East Side," *Los Angeles Herald Examiner*, undated, pp. F-1, F-6, "Tyson," Herrick Library; Toni Morrison, *The Bluest Eye* (New York: Vintage Books, 1970).

14. Sharbutt, "Cicely Star of a 'Classic'"; Pauline Kael, "The Current Cinema: Cicely Tyson Goes to the Fountain," *New Yorker*, January 28, 1974, p. 74.

15. Shearer, "From Slum to Stardom," pp. 14–15; for expressions of reassurance, see also Mary Daniels, "Cicely Rides the Crest . . .," *Chicago Tribune*, June 9, 1974, pp. 6–7; Liz Gant, "Beauty Talk with the Stars," *Essence*, January 1974, pp. 38–39, 90–91.

16. Bright, "An Emmy for Cicely Tyson?," p. 120; Daniels, "Cicely Rides the Crest . . .," pp. 6–7.

17. For "typecast" and "play different types," see Edwin Miller, "From the Heart: Cicely Tyson," *Seventeen Magazine*, February 1973, pp. 107, 154, quotes p. 154; for "pride, dignity, and strength," see "Cicely Tyson, Star-Fire," *Vogue*, December 1972, n.p., "Tyson," Herrick Library; for "concern," see Cecil Smith, "Neither Butterfly nor Barbie Doll," *Los Angeles Times*, February 22, 1973, n.p., "Tyson,"

Herrick Library. Accounts of the serious-minded nature of Tyson's career prior
to *Sounder* also include Miller, "From the Heart"; Shearer, "From Slum to Stardom"; Ida Peters, "What's Happening," *Baltimore Afro-American*, November 25,
1972, p. 13.

18. For "seemed to," see Joel Dreyfuss, "A Woman Called Cicely," *Redbook*, October
    1979, pp. 31, 97–98, 103, quote p. 98; for "broke," see Ebert, "Inside Cecily [sic],"
    p. 41; for "four long years," and "increasingly discriminating," see Yvonne, "The
    Importance of Cicely Tyson," *Ms.*, August 1974, p. 78; for the "soul which is,"
    see Ebert, "Inside Cecily [sic]," p. 73. According to many accounts, Tyson had
    considered quitting show business, but her friend Sidney Poitier convinced her
    to persevere. See Dreyfuss, "A Woman Called Cicely," p. 97.

19. Ebert, "Inside Cecily [sic]"; Windeler, "Cicely Tyson," p. 38; Robinson, "Cicely
    Tyson," p. 40; Dreyfuss, "A Woman Called Cicely," p. 98; Maya Angelou, "Cicely
    Tyson: Reflections on a Lone Black Rose," *Ladies' Home Journal*, February 1977,
    pp. 40–46, see especially p. 46; see also Richard Cook, *It's About Time: Miles
    Davis On and Off Record* (New York: Oxford University Press, 2005), p. 179;
    Miles Davis, *Miles: The Autobiography* (New York: Simon and Schuster, 1989),
    p. 228. In 1981, Tyson and Davis married (at the home of Bill Cosby, where Andrew Young officiated); they divorced in 1988. For Tyson's photo on the cover of
    Davis's celebrated album, see Miles Davis, *Sorcerer* (Columbia, 1967).

20. Tyson, with relatively little publicity, worked with Arthur Mitchell to found the
    Dance Theater of Harlem in 1969; see Considine, "Cicely Tyson," p. 58.

21. For accounts in the 1970s of her hair in the late 1950s and early 1960s, see,
    for example, Yvonne, "The Importance of Cicely Tyson," p. 46; Peters, "What's
    Happening," p. 12; Windeler, "Cicely Tyson: From the Typing Pool to an Emmy,"
    p. 37; for "revolutionary glamour," see Angela Davis, "Afro Images: Politics,
    Fashion, and Nostalgia," in Joy James, ed., *The Angela Y. Davis Reader* (Malden,
    MA: Blackwell, 1998), pp. 273–278, quote p. 274; James Brown, *Say It Loud—
    I'm Black and I'm Proud* (Polygram, 1996, 1969).

22. For "then daring step," see Windeler, "Cicely Tyson: From the Typing Pool to
    the Emmy," p. 36; for "set off a national furor," see Robinson, "Cicely Tyson: An
    Unlikely Movie Star," p. 38; for "I had to make a choice," see "*Ebony* Interview:
    Cicely Tyson," *Ebony*, February 1981, p. 124; for "discreet," "during," and "style,"
    see Yvonne, "The Importance of Cicely Tyson," p. 46. Other perspectives on Tyson's hair were evident. Ida Peters, an African American critic for the *Baltimore
    Afro-American*, observed that in the early 1960s, Tyson was "an unwitting midwife to the painful/joyful birth of a new phase of Black awareness and pride";
    see Peters, "What's Happening," p. 12. For Tyson's argument that to straighten
    one's hair was simply a matter of "choice" and personal style, see Gant, "Beauty
    Talk with the Stars," p. 39; see also Leslie Bennetts, "How Cicely Got to Teach in
    Wales," *New York Times*, August 22, 1983, p. C14.

23. Loynd, "Cicely Tyson: 'Sounder' Roots on New York's Upper East Side," p. F-6.

24. For Ritt, see "Martin Ritt: Human Relationships and Moral Choices Fuel His Movies," *New York Times*, January 12, 1986, p. H23; for his background and for a "white backlash" to his earlier efforts to depict race relations in films, see "Ritt Sees White Backlash on 'Great White Hope' Pic," *Hollywood Reporter*, June 4, 1971, n.p., Margaret Herrick Library, Academy of Motion Pictures and Sciences, "*Sounder* Microfiche Collection, Production File" (hereafter "*Sounder*," Herrick Library); for the collaboration, see "Radnitz-Mattel Slate 8 Family Pix Over 3 Years," *Variety*, July 14, 1971, n.p., "*Sounder*," Herrick Library; "Letters," letter from Robert Radnitz and Martin Ritt to the editor, *Hollywood Reporter*, August 24, 1972, n.p., "*Sounder*," Herrick Library; for "as meaningful," see Mel Gussow, "Lonne Elder, 69, Pioneering Playwright, Dies," *New York Times*, June 13, 1996, p. D24. For evidence of friction in this team, see letter from Lonne Elder to Charles Champlin, Entertainment Editor, *Los Angeles Times*, as it appeared in *Variety*, March 20, 1973, n.p., "*Sounder*," Herrick Library; and "Letter to the Editor," *Variety*, March 23, 1973, n.p., "*Sounder*," Herrick Library.

25. See "*Sounder* Pressbook," "*Sounder*," Herrick Library.

26. Vivian Robinson, "A Beautiful Black Movie," *New York Amsterdam News*, September 23, 1972, p. D-4; for "like most classics," see Donia Mills, *Washington Star News*, quoted in "*Sounder* Pressbook," "*Sounder*," Herrick Library; "Soviet Leaders Weep at 'Sounder' Screening," *Variety*, February 14, 1973, n.p., "*Sounder*," Herrick Library; for the Oscar nominations, see Gertrude Gipson, "Academy Award Nominees," *Los Angeles Sentinel*, February 15, 1973, p. 1; for "wild horses," see Hazel Garland, "Video Vignettes," *Tri-State Defender*, March 24, 1973, p. 13. It was a "historically significant year" for blacks, as Gipson (and many others) noted, because African American performers and films focusing on race relations earned a total of nine awards. Tyson and Diana Ross (for *Lady Sings the Blues*) were among the nominees for best actress. Tyson won the best actress award at the Atlanta International Film Festival and from the National Society of Film Critics. For lukewarm reviews of *Sounder*, see Roger Greenspun, "Screen: 'Sounder' Opens," *New York Times*, September 25, 1972, p. 45; Lindsay Patterson, "'Sounder'—a Hollywood Fantasy?," *New York Times*, November 12, 1972, p. D11.

27. For Tyson and Coretta Scott King, see *Baltimore Afro-American*, September 30, 1972, p. 12; for "Cicely Tyson Day at Harvard," see Luix Overbea, "Cicily [*sic*] Tyson: 'Hey, Ma, Look Where I Am,'" *Los Angeles Herald-Examiner*, September 16, 1974, p. B-5, "Tyson," Herrick Library; for "beyond mere entertainment," see "The Motion Picture Sounder," *Senate Congressional Record*, March 8, 1973, Volume 119, Part 6, 93rd Congress, First Session, p. 6904; for "personal resolution" and "highly recommend," see "Motion Picture, 'Sounder,'" *House Congressional Record*, March 15, 1973, Volume 119, Part 7, 93rd Congress, First Session, p. 8020; see also "'Sounder' Wins High Accolades on Capitol Hill," *Variety*, March 7, 1973, n.p., "*Sounder*," Herrick Library.

28. "*Sounder* Pressbook," "*Sounder*," Herrick Library; Roscoe C. Brown Jr., "Study Guide: A Teacher's Guide for 'Sounder,'" in "*Sounder* Pressbook," "*Sounder*," Herrick Library.

29. For "rare" and "much needed," see Joy Gould Boyum, "The Lost Kingdom of Boyhood," *Wall Street Journal*, October 6, 1972, p. 8, Schomburg Center on Black Culture Clipping File, Volume I, 1925–1974, "*Sounder*, Moving Pictures" (hereafter "*Sounder*," SCBCCF, v. I); for "at last," see "First Step," *Time*, October 9, 1972, n.p., "*Sounder*," SCBCCF, v. I; for "I have," see Roy Innis quoted in "Film *Sounder* Praised," *Los Angeles Sentinel*, September 21, 1972, p. B2-A.

30. Kael, "The Current Cinema: Cicely Tyson Goes to the Fountain," pp. 73, 75; see also Wes Rehberg, "'Sounder'—Heart-Rending but Safe Film," *The Home News*, October 27, 1972, n.p., "*Sounder*," SCBCCF, v. I.

31. Paul Warshow, "Film Review: *Sounder*," *Film Quarterly* 26 (Spring 1973): 61–64, quote p. 62; see also, Rehberg, "'Sounder'—heart rending but safe film." For a backlash in the 1970s, see Eric Porter, "Affirming and Disaffirming Actions: Remaking Race in the 1970s," in Beth Bailey and David Farber, eds., *America in the 1970s* (Lawrence: University Press of Kansas, 2004), p. 64; for the Nixon administration and race relations, see Bruce Schulman, *The Seventies: The Great Shift in American Culture, Society and Politics* (New York: Da Capo Press, 2002; 2001), pp. 35–42.

32. Toni Morrison, "MS. On the Arts: Film Find: A Really Good Movie About Blacks," *Ms.*, December 1972, n.p., "*Sounder*—Moving Pictures," SCBCCF, v. I.

33. For "stoic," see Smith, "Neither Butterfly Nor Barbie Doll"; for "quiet strength," see Loynd, "Cicely Tyson: 'Sounder' Roots on New York's Upper East Side"; for "suffers in quiet," see Boyum, "The Lost Kingdom of Boyhood"; for "THE strong black woman," see Sharbutt, "Cicely: Star of a Classic," emphasis in original; for "rip-cord," see Paul Zimmerman, "Black Nightmare," *Newsweek*, October 2, 1972 n.p., "*Sounder*," SCBCCF, v. 1; also quoted in "*Sounder* Pressbook," "*Sounder*," Herrick Library.

34. Yvonne, "The Importance of Cicely Tyson."

35. For "the first," see *London Times*, February 20, 1973, n.p., "Tyson," Herrick Library; for "significant" and "never ever," see Judy Klemesrud, "Cicely, the Looker from 'Sounder,'" *New York Times*, October 1, 1972, p. D-13; for "if it weren't," see Miller, "Cicely Tyson: From the Heart," p. 107. For Tyson on black men having endured more in slavery than women ("Our whole history is that the black man was the one who would be lynched, tarred, castrated. The worst that could happen to a black woman was that she was taken behind a shack and raped"), see Loynd, "Cicely Tyson."

36. Margaret Hinxman, "Films," *London Sunday Telegraph*, February 18, 1973, n.p., in "*Sounder*," Herrick Library; Pauline Kael, "Soul Food," *New Yorker*, September 30, 1972, n.p., in "*Sounder*," Herrick Library. Positive reactions to this scene in the African American press include Earl Calloway, "Cinema Happenings: 'Sounder'

Premieres at Todd Theater," *Chicago Defender*, November 25–December 1, 1972, p. 19; Clarence B. Jones, "'Sounder' a Classic of Our Era," *New York Amsterdam News*, September 23, 1972, p. 1.

37. Margaret Tarratt, "Sounder," *Films and Filming* 19 (February 1973): 54; Frances Taylor, "Winfield Lauds 'Sounder' Accuracy," *Sunday Star Ledger*, March 11, 1975, n.p., "*Sounder*," SCBCCF, v. I.

38. In the award-winning novel, the nameless characters are types ("the boy," for example), and both father and dog die in the final pages. See William H. Armstrong, *Sounder* (New York: HarperCollins, 1969). According to Lonne Elder, the film was "different in every way" from the novel, which he regarded as having "certain racist characteristics and overtones." He sought to "make something meaningful out of it" by developing the perspectives of the black characters in ways that the white author had not. Yet, Elder did not like Nathan's kick because he felt that this moment of overt resistance was forced and unrealistic. See "Says Lonne Elder: 'Sounder' Movie Is Not Like the Book," *New York Amsterdam News*, September 23, 1972, p. 2; Rochelle Reed, "Interview with '*Sounder*' Screenplay Writer, Lonne Elder, III, Seminar," *Dialogue on Film* 2 (May 1973): 2–12. To the extent that a black power ideology infused the film through that scene, it was not because of the African American writer who came of age in the black arts movement; this is worth noting because debates about the film's representations of blackness and "authenticity" were always taking shape in a context in which "authenticity" could not be determined in some essentialist way based only on the race of the cultural workers. For a consideration of these issues, see Linda Williams, *Playing the Race Card: Melodramas of Black and White from Uncle Tom to O. J. Simpson* (Princeton, NJ: Princeton University Press, 2001), p. 239.

39. In another instance, the school that David Lee attends is explicitly pro-black and not just all black; the teacher encourages them to stand up for themselves and she reads to David Lee about Crispus Attucks, Harriet Tubman, and W. E. B. Dubois (he's "very much alive," she tells David Lee).

40. Daniels, "Cicely Tyson: Riding the Crest of Her Triumph," *Chicago Tribune*, June 9, 1974, p. 7; for another response to this scene, see Gerard Burke, "*Sounder*," *Baltimore Afro-American*, November 18, 1972, p. 11. According to some accounts, Ritt based this scene on the finale in King Vidor's 1925 film *The Big Parade*. See Steve Vineberg, "A Child Actor Grows Up to Retell a Tale of Poverty and Hope," *New York Times*, January 19, 2003, p. AR34.

41. For the circulation of *Sounder* abroad, see *Variety* (no headline), April 26, 1973, n.p., "Tyson," Herrick Library; for Tyson's efforts to promote the film internationally, see Perry, "The Bell of New York."

42. For the NWRO, see Nadasen, *Welfare Warriors*; for up to 100,000, see p. xiv; for higher benefits, see pp. 79–101; for strategies of activism connected to liberal reform and radicalism, see also pp. 231–235. For antipoverty and welfare

rights organizing in Las Vegas, see Orleck, *Storming Caesar's Palace*; for the discourse against black women and resistance to it, see Kelley, *Yo' Mama's Disfunktional*.

43. For "instilled," see Yvonne, "Cicely Tyson," p. 39; for "I felt," see Ebert, "Inside Cecily [*sic*]," p. 74.

44. Toni Cade, ed., *The Black Woman: An Anthology* (New York: New American Library, 1970). For black women's organizations and their work, see especially Kimberly Springer, *Living for the Revolution: Black Feminist Organizations, 1968–1980* (Durham, NC: Duke University Press, 2005); Anne Valk, *Radical Sisters: Second-Wave Feminism and Black Liberation in Washington, D.C.* (Urbana: University of Illinois Press, 2010); for the influential "womanist" framework, see Alice Walker, *In Search of Our Mother's Gardens: Womanist Prose* (New York: Harcourt, Brace, Jovanovich, 1983).

45. For "Don't let," see Hazel Garland, "Video Vignettes," *Tri-State Defender*, February 2, 1974, p. 11; for "what Americans are talking about," see "Here's What America Is Talking About Today" (CBS advertisement), *New York Times*, February 1, 1974, p. 60.

46. Vashti McKenzie, "The McKenzie Report," *Baltimore Afro-American*, May 21–25, 1974, p. 11; "Miss Jane Pittman Is Alive and Well at LCA" (advertisement for the Learning Corporation of America), *Literature/Film Quarterly* 3 (Spring 1975): 194; "Emmy Vote Is Led by 'Jane Pittman,'" *New York Times*, April 26, 1974, p. 74; Kael, "The Current Cinema: Cicely Tyson Goes to the Fountain." For *The Autobiography of Miss Jane Pittman* as a "smash success" at the Cannes Film Festival but "disallowed as an official entry because it was made for television," see Windeler, "Cicely Tyson: From the Typing Pool to an Emmy," p. 39.

47. Jeannette Smyth, "Of History, Past and Present," *Washington Post*, January 23, 1974, p. B-3.

48. John J. O'Connor, "TV: Splendid 'Jane Pittman' Relates Black History," *New York Times*, January 21, 1974, p. 67; see also John Carmody, "'Miss Jane Pittman,' Holding on, Keeping On, Moving On," *Washington Post*, January 31, 1974, pp. B-1, 11. For the novel, see Ernest Gaines, *The Autobiography of Miss Jane Pittman* (New York: Bantam Press, 1971); for the television film in relation to the novel, see Irwin Silber, "A Reformist View of Black History," *Guardian*, November 20, 1974, n.p., in Schomburg Center on Black Culture Clipping File, Volume I, 1925–1974, "*The Autobiography of Miss Jane Pittman*" (hereafter, "*Autobiography*," SCBCCF, v. I).

49. Leroy Thomas, "Jane Pittman's Autobiography Is a Drama to Watch," *Chicago Defender*, January 30, 1974, p. 10.

50. O'Connor, "TV: Splendid 'Jane Pittman' Relates Black History," p. 67.

51. When the white landowner demands interest, Jane gives him her wedding ring "for our freedom." Once they are in Texas, Joe Pittman feels that he must prove himself with horses because Jane is barren.

52. See O'Connor, "TV: Splendid 'Jane Pittman'"; Thomas, "Jane Pittman's Autobiography Is a Drama to Watch"; Nikki Giovanni, "'Jane Pittman' Fulfilled My Deepest Expectations," *New York Times*, March 3, 1974, p. 115.

53. Joseph, *Waiting 'Til the Midnight Hour*, pp. 276–283, *Washington Post* quote p. 283.

54. Frances Njubi Nesbitt, *Race for Sanctions: African Americans Against Apartheid, 1946–1994* (Bloomington: Indiana University Press, 2004), pp. 77–78, 82–96; Joseph, *Waiting 'Til the Midnight Hour*, pp. 283–286; Robin D. G. Kelley, *Africa Speaks, America Answers: Modern Jazz in Revolutionary Times* (Cambridge, MA: Harvard University Press, 2012).

55. Untitled photo spread, in *Baltimore Afro-American*, January 26, 1974, p. 11; Giovanni, "'Jane Pittman' Fulfilled My Deepest Expectations," p. 115; see also "Cicely Tyson in 'Autobiography of Jane Pittman,'" *Tri-State Defender*, January 26, 1974, p. 10; "Scenes from 'The Autobiography of Jane Pittman,'" *New York Amsterdam News*, February 2, 1974, p. D-11; Thomas, "Jane Pittman's Autobiography Is a Drama to Watch"; Lawrence Laurent, "91 Years as Jane Pittman," *Washington Post*, January 27, 1974, pp. TV-5, 7.

56. For awards from the NCNW, see *Hollywood Reporter*, November 29, 1972, n.p., "Tyson," Herrick Library; for CORE, see "Cicely Tyson Is Presented Best Actress Award," *Box Office*, March 1 (no year), n.p., "Tyson," Herrick Library; for NAACP, see "NAACP Image Awards Presented," *Los Angeles Sentinel*, November 3, 1972, p. B-1; for the SCLC, see "Baltimore," *Box Office*, September 2, 1974, n.p., "Tyson," Herrick Library; for three honorary doctorates, see "Cicely Tyson Presented with Three Doctorates," *Los Angeles Times*, May 31, 1974, n.p., "Tyson," Herrick Library.

57. Vilma Raskin Potter, "*The Autobiography of Miss Jane Pittman*: How to Make a White Film from a Black Novel," *Literature/Film Quarterly* 3, no. 4 (Fall 1975): 371–375, quotes p. 371; Stephanie Harrington, "Did 'Jane Pittman' Really Show Us Black History?" *New York Times*, February 10, 1974, p. 123; for responses, see Giovanni, "'Jane Pittman' Fulfilled My Deepest Expectations"; see also, Stephen Farber, "Where Has All the Protest Gone? To Television," *New York Times*, March 31, 1974, p. 127. For a critique similar to Harrington's, see also Dorothy Gilliam, "A Giant Step, but Still a Long Road Ahead," *Washington Post*, February 1, 1974, p. D1, D6.

58. See "Miss Jane's Ratings," *Washington Post*, February 2, 1974, p. B7; for "too good," see Jeannette Smyth, "Of History, Past and Present," *Washington Post*, January 23, 1974, p. B-3.

59. See Larry Neal, "Any Day Now: Black Art and Black Liberation," *Ebony*, August 1969, pp. 54–58, 62; for this sensibility in different arena, see Smethurst, *The Black Arts Movement*; Amy Ongiri, *Spectacular Blackness: The Cultural Politics of the Black Power Movement and the Search for a Black Aesthetic* (Charlottesville: University Press of Virginia, 2009); Van Deburg, *New Day in Babylon*.

60. William Styron, *The Confessions of Nat Turner* (New York: Vintage, 1992; orig. pub. 1967); C. Vann Woodward quoted in Daryl Michael Scott, *Contempt and Pity: Social Policy and the Image of the Damaged Black Psyche, 1880–1996* (Chapel Hill: University of North Carolina Press, 1997), p. 174; for Franklin and other enthusiastic responses, see Kenneth S. Greenberg, "Epilogue: Nat Turner in Hollywood," in Kenneth Greenberg, ed., *Nat Turner: A Slave Rebellion in History and Memory* (New York: Oxford University Press, 2003), pp. 242–249. James Baldwin was among the black intellectuals who offered Styron support. For Styron on Baldwin's role, see William Styron, "Jimmy in the House," *New York Times,* December 20, 1987, reprinted in Quincy Troupe, ed., *Baldwin: The Legacy* (New York: Simon and Schuster, 1989), pp. 43–46.

61. John Henrik Clarke, ed., "Introduction," *William Styron's Nat Turner: Ten Black Writers Respond* (Boston: Beacon Press, 1968), p. vii.

62. For "because its lesson is," see Charles Hamilton, "Our Nat Turner and William Styron's Creation," in Clarke, *William Styron's Nat Turner,* p. 74; for "virile" and "impotent," see Lerone Bennett Jr., "Nat's Last White Man," in Clarke, *William Styron's Nat Turner,* pp. 4–5; for "pining," see Alvin Poussaint, "The Confessions of Nat Turner and the Dilemma of William Styron," in Clarke, *William Styron's Nat Turner,* p. 20; for "more than anger," and "scholarship," see Ossie Davis, "Nat Turner: Hero Reclaimed," *Freedomways* 8 (Summer 1968): 230.

63. Greenberg, "Epilogue"; for Meriwether's letter to King and for brochures on campuses, see letter from Louise Meriwether to Martin Luther King Jr., March 19, 1968, in The Martin Luther King Center of Nonviolent Social Change, Digital Archive, http://www.thekingcenter.org/archive/document/letter-louise-m-merriwether-mlk; for "for a black actor," see Greenberg, "Epilogue," p. 245. For more on this controversy, see also Wolper with Troupe, *The Inside Story of T.V.'s "Roots,"* pp. 27–28, 34; Steven Roberts, "Storm Over 'Nat Turner' Film Wanes," *New York Times,* March 31, 1969, p. 28; Christopher Sieving, "The Concessions of Nat Turner," *The Velvet Light Trap* 61 (Spring 2008): 38–50; Sieving, *Soul Searching,* pp. 83–118. Meriwether is most well known for her novel, *Daddy Was a Number Runner* (1970).

64. For "pasted to a pillar," see Lena Horne with Richard Schickel, *Lena* (Garden City, NY: Limelight, 1986; orig. pub. 1965), p. 109; for "misconceptions," "as simple," and "heads," see Ramona Lewis, "'Cabin' Picture Called Insult," *New York Amsterdam News,* June 12, 1943, p. 17; for "follows the same" and "in its present form," see Marc Connelly to Walter White, November 17, 1942, in NAACP Papers, Part 18: Special Subjects, 1940–1955, reel 15, #00069, Widener Library, Harvard University; for an ongoing conversation about the film among members and leaders in the NAACP, see Walter White to A. P. Tureaud, July 15, 1943, in NAACP Papers, Part 18: Special Subjects, 1940–1955, reel 15, #00071. Critiques of *Cabin in the Sky* appeared in the *Pittsburgh Courier,* the *Baltimore Afro-American* and in the *New Yorker; Variety* was among the other publications that praised the film.

65. Horne with Schickel, *Lena*, p. 120. For black consumers as a growing segment of the "movie-conscious" population (one estimate suggested that the "Negro audience" for films was thirteen million strong), see "Negro Movie-Conscious; Support Film Houses," *Motion Picture Herald*, January 24, 1942, n.p., from NAACP Papers, Part 18: Special Subjects, 1940–1955; Series B: General Office Files, Abolition of Government Agencies-Jews, reel 17, #00341. For *Cabin in the Sky* as a box office success, see Thomas Cripps, *Slow Fade to Black: The Negro in American Film, 1900–1942* (New York: Oxford University Press, 1977), p. 82; Arthur Knight, *Disintegrating the Musical: Black Performance and American Musical Film* (Durham, NC: Duke University Press, 2002), p. 150; Lauren Sklaroff, *Black Culture and the New Deal: The Quest for Civil Rights in the Roosevelt Era* (Chapel Hill: University of North Carolina Press, 2009), pp. 218–220.

66. Greenberg, "Epilogue," pp. 244–246; Wolper with Troupe, *The Inside Story of T.V.'s "Roots,"* pp. 27–28; Stevens, "Storm Over 'Nat Turner' Screenplay Subsides." Earlier, Wolper had also hired black playwright Louis Peterson to work on the script. See Sieving, "The Concessions of Nat Turner."

67. Greenberg, "Epilogue," p. 246; Wolper with Troupe, *The Inside Story of T.V.'s "Roots,"* pp. 27–28; Scot French, "Mau-Mauing the Filmmakers: Should Black Power Take the Rap for Killing Nat Turner, the Movie?," in Brian Ward, ed., *Media, Culture, and the Modern African American Freedom Struggle* (Gainesville: University Press of Florida, 2001), pp. 233–254.

68. Greenberg, "Epilogue," p. 244.

69. Gordon Parks, director, *Shaft* (MGM, 1971); Melvin Van Peebles, director, *Sweet Sweetback's Baadasssss Song* (Yeah, Cinemation Industries, 1971).

70. Vincent Canby, "'Shaft'—at Last, a Good Saturday Night Movie; About 'Shaft,'" *New York Times*, June 11, 1971, p. D1.

71. For "decolonization," see Derrick Morrison, "Film: Sweet Sweetback's Baadasssss Song," *Militant*, May 28, 1971, n.p., "Blaxploitation," SCBCCF, v. I; for "the need for unity," see Huey Newton, "He Won't Bleed Me: A Revolutionary Analysis of 'Sweet Sweetback's Baadasssss Song,'" *Black Panther* 6 (June 19, 1971), n.p., in Schomburg Center for Black Culture Clipping File, Volume I, 1925–1974, "Blaxploitation" (hereafter "Blaxploitation," SCBCCF, v. I); for the film as "personal cinema at its best—one man telling it like he sees it, his dream of liberation unadulterated by studio pressures or commercial considerations," see "Stud on the Run," *Newsweek*, May 10, 1971, n.p., "Blaxploitation," SCBCCF, v. I; see also Melvin Van Peebles letter to Danny Cook, undated, "Blaxploitation," SCBCCF, v. I.

72. Cicely Tyson was among those who made this point; see Smith, "Neither Butterfly nor Barbie Doll."

73. Kael, "Soul Food"; Loften Mitchell, "Harlem Author Loften Mitchell How He Grooved on 'Sounder,'" *New York Amsterdam News*, September 23, 1972, p. D3; for *Sounder* as inauthentic, see Lindsay Patterson, "'Sounder'—a Hollywood

Fantasy?" *New York Times*, November 12, 1972, p. D11. For a critique of this critique, see "Movie Mailbag," letter from Omar Hendrix, "I Cried During 'Sounder,'" *New York Times*, November 26, 1972, p. D12.

74. Lerone Bennett, "The Emancipation Orgasm: Sweetback in Wonderland," *Ebony*, September 1971, pp. 106–111.

75. Klemesrud, "Cicely, the Looker from 'Sounder,'" p. D13.

76. For "take your clothes off," see Ebert, "Inside Cecily [sic]"; for "kind of Barbie Doll," see Smith, "Neither Butterfly nor Barbie Doll"; for "the black woman has never," see Klemesrud, "Cicely, the Looker from 'Sounder'"; for "I have pride" and "I couldn't portray," see Ebert, "Inside Cecily [sic]," p. 41; see also Daniels, "Cicely Rides the Crest . . .," p. 6; Windeler, "Cicely Tyson, From the Typing Pool to an Emmy."

77. John Berry, director, *Claudine* (Third World Cinema, Twentieth Century-Fox, 1974).

78. Davis quoted in Mark Krasovic, "*Claudine* in the Model City," Conference Paper, Organization of American Historians, Washington, D.C., April 2010, p. 17; I am indebted to Mark Krasovic for sharing his work and thoughts on *Claudine*. See also *Los Angeles Sentinel*, November 23, 1972, p. B1; Vincent Canby, "Cheers for 'Claudine,'" *New York Times*, May 5, 1974, sec. II, p. 8.

79. See, for example, Herbert Gans, "Gans on Film: Black Poverty as Comedy," *Social Policy* 5 (October 1974): 59–60.

80. Jon Landau, "Films: The Peeper Principle," *Rolling Stone*, May 23, 1974, p. 82.

81. Krasovic, "*Claudine* in the Model City."

82. For "unlike the worst," see Landau, "Films: The Peeper Principle," p. 82; for "the super-jive," see "'Claudine' Links Garbage Collector, Unwed Mother," *Chicago Defender*, April 27, 1974, p. A-12; for "like 'Sounder,'" see "Claudine," *Variety*, April 10, 1974, p. 17.

83. For "unlike *Sounder*," see Landau, "Films: The Peeper Principle"; see also Canby, "Cheers for 'Claudine,'" p. 1; Buckley, "Claudine," p. 372. For "uplift," see Anne Blair, "Movie 'Claudine' Tugs at Your Heartstrings," *Chicago Defender*, May 11, 1974, p. 35.

84. For "promoted as," see Richard Schickel, "Fried Chicken Romance," *Time*, May 20, 1974, n.p., http://www.time.com/time/magazine/article/0,9171,944841,00.html, (accessed July 1, 2011). See also Gary Arnold, "'Claudine': 'A Fitfully Effective Comedy,'" *Washington Post*, May 17, 1974, p. D10; Molly Haskell, "Boiled Away in the Melting Pot," *Village Voice*, May 16, 1974, p. 101; "'Claudine' Links Garbage Collector, Unwed Mother"; Gans, "Gans on Film," p. 59; Pauline Kael, "Current Cinema: Bouncing Back," *New Yorker*, April 29, 1974, pp. 115, 119.

85. "From Our Readers—Improve Films," letter from Sylvia Harris, *Chicago Defender*, June 5, 1974, p. 13; see also Earl Calloway, "Fox's 'Claudine' Moves with Swift Comic Action," *Chicago Defender*, May 6, 1974, p. 9.

86. For "deglamorized," see Michael Buckley, "Claudine," *Films in Review* 25 (June–July 1974): 372–373, quote p. 372; for "even without," see Gans, "Gans on Film,"

p. 60; for "gap," see Haskell, "Boiled Away in the Melting Pot"; for "slumming expedition," see Schickel, "Fried Chicken Romance."

87. For "sheltered life," and "presume," see Vernon Scott, "Suicides Puzzle Diahann," *Chicago Defender*, June 27, 1974, p. 12; for Carroll as unconvincing because she had inherited the part from Diana Sands after Sands's death, see Arnold, "*Claudine*"; for Third World Cinema after *Claudine*, see Krasovic, "Claudine in the Model City," pp. 21–22; for "floundering," see Diahann Carroll with Ross Firestone, *Diahann! An Autobiography* (New York: Little, Brown, 1986), p. 253.

88. "Says Lonne Elder: 'Sounder' Movie Is Not Like the Book."

89. Ebert, "Inside Cecily [*sic*]," p. 74.

90. Linda Williams, *Playing the Race Card: Melodramas of Black and White from Uncle Tom to O. J. Simpson* (Princeton, NJ: Princeton University Press, 2001), p. 221.

91. *Washington Post*, February 7, 1977; also quoted in *Crisis* 84 (May 1977): 165.

EPILOGUE

1. For the "new star" (Makeba), see "New Singer in Town," *Look*, February 2, 1960, p. 60D; for the "greatest singer" (Simone), see Sidney Lazard, *Chicago Sun-Times*, quoted in Phyl Garland, *The Sound of Soul* (Chicago: H. Regnery, 1969), p. 175; for the "hottest new thing," and "arrival" (Lincoln), see Dom Cerulli, "The Arrival of Abbey," *Down Beat*, June 12, 1958, p. 19; for the "entertainer of the year" (Carroll), see "The Entertainer of the Year," *Cue: The Complete Entertainment Guide for New York and Suburbs*, December 30, 1961, n.p., in Schomburg Center for Black Culture, Clipping File, Volume 1, 1925–1974, "Diahann Carroll" (hereafter "Carroll," SCBCCF, v. I); for "rising star" (Tyson), see George Simor, "Destination: Stardom," *Sepia*, March 1967, p. 26.

2. For "Broadway perfectionist," see Diahann Carroll with Ross Firestone, *Diahann! An Autobiography* (New York: Little, Brown, 1986), p. 81. For relationships to jazz and musical styles, see Miriam Makeba with James Hall, *Makeba: My Story* (New York: New American Library, 1987), p. 85; Louie Robinson, "Cicely Tyson: A Very Unlikely Movie Star," *Ebony*, May 1974, pp. 33–36, 38–40; Farah Jasmine Griffin, *If You Can't Be Free, Be a Mystery: In Search of Billie Holiday* (New York: Free Press, 2001); *Down Beat*, August 18, 1960, p. 18; Daphne Brooks, "Nina Simone's Triple Play," *Callaloo* 34 (2011): 176–197.

3. See, for example, Harry Belafonte and Lena Horne, *Porgy and Bess* (RCA Victor, 1959); Martin Ritt, director, *Paris Blues* (United Artists, 1961); Daniel Mann, director, *For Love of Ivy* (Palomar, 1968). Lena Horne recorded "Brown Baby" on the album *Harry and Lena* (1970), Simone recorded "Brown Baby" on the album *Nina Simone at the Village Gate* (1962), and Carroll performed the song at the Persian Room; see Diahann Carroll with Bob Morris *The Legs Are the Last to Go: Aging, Acting, Marrying, and Other Things I Learned the Hard Way* (New York: HarperCollins, 2008), p. 148; for Simone and Makeba, see Robert

Shelton, "Two Folk Singers Present Concert," *New York Times*, May 22, 1961, p. 37; for Simone and Lincoln, see Abbey Lincoln, "Blues for Mama," recorded by Nina Simone, *Nina Simone Sings the Blues* (RCA, 1967). This is an incomplete list of overlapping personal and professional relationships and collaborations.

4. Sherrie Tucker, "Bordering on Community: Improvising Women Improvising Women-in-Jazz," in Daniel Fischlin and Ajay Heble, eds., *The Other Side of Nowhere: Jazz, Improvisation, and Communities in Dialogue* (Middletown, CT: Wesleyan University Press, 2004), pp. 244–267, quote p. 263.

5. For "tantalizing singer" and "siren," see "The Horne of Plenty," *New York Herald Tribune*, September 3, 1947, n.p., in Schomburg Center on Black Culture Clipping File, Volume I, 1925–1974, "Lena Horne" (hereafter, "Horne," SCBC-CF, v. I); for "sepia sensation," see Jackie Ormes, "Lena Horne Sets a New Box Office Record," *Chicago Defender*, October 21, 1944, p. 7; for "voluptuous," see "The Horne of Plenty"; for "simple white gown," "quality," and "complete poise," see John Wm. Riley, "Theatre Talk: Lena Horne Captures Oval Room Audience on her Opening Night," *Boston Globe*, May 4, 1950, n.p., "Horne," SCBCCF, v. I.

6. For "tawny," see *New York Post*, November 24, 1959, n.p., in "Carroll," SCBCCF, v. I; for "the sophisticated lady," see "Nightclubs: Bottom of the Top," *Time*, December 7, 1959, n.p., "Carroll," SCBCCF, v. I; for "Diahann Carroll has been called," see Joseph Weshba, "A Subwayman's Daughter Heads for the Heights on Broadway," *New York Post*, December 14, 1962, p. 41. For both women being praised for their light skin, and facing challenges on that basis, see the discussion of "Oriental make up" in Richard Warren Lewis, "Rodgers and Carroll," *Show Business Illustrated*, April 1962, p. 46; Lena Horne with Richard Schickel, *Lena* (Garden City, NY: Limelight, 1986; orig. pub. 1965), pp. 106–107; for Horne's ongoing influence, and comparisons between her and Abbey Lincoln, see Morton Cooper, "Lena Horne Bids Farewell to Night Clubs," *Chicago Defender*, March 2–8, 1963, n.p., in "Horne," SCBCCF, v. I; for Horne resenting Carroll, see James Gavin, *Stormy Weather: The Life of Lena Horne* (New York: Simon and Schuster, 2009), pp. 306–307, 431–432.

7. For television news, see Christine Acham, *Revolution Televised: Prime Time and the Struggle for Black Power* (Minneapolis: University of Minnesota Press, 2004), pp. 24–53; for variety shows, see Donald Bogle, *Primetime Blues: African Americans on Network Television* (New York: Farrar, Straus and Giroux, 2002); for news, drama, and comedy, see Aniko Bodroghkozy, *Equal Time: Television and the Civil Rights Movement* (Urbana: University of Illinois Press, 2012). Tyson also was cast in the soap opera *The Guiding Light*.

8. "The New Abbey Lincoln," *Jet*, May 1959, p. 58; Abbey Lincoln, *It's Magic*, (Riverside, 1958); Griffin, *If You Can't Be Free, Be a Mystery*.

9. Makeba with Hall, *Makeba*, p. 86. See also Bernadine Morris, "Hair Stylist Is Honored by Blacks He Inspired," *New York Times*, June 25, 1980, p. C20.

10. Robin D. G. Kelley, "Nap Time: Historicizing the Afro," *Fashion Theory* 1 (December 1997): 330–351.

11. For "her hairdo," see Judy Klemesrud, "Her Hairdo Started the 'Afro' Trend," *New York Times*, October 8, 1966, p. 38; for "wore an afro," see Chester Higgins, "Abbey Lincoln Talk of Breakup with Max Roach," *Jet*, May 1972, pp. 16–17; for "short African cut," see George Simor, "Destination: Stardom," *Sepia*, March 1967, p. 27; for "the mother," see "Ebony Interview: Cicely Tyson," *Ebony*, February 1981, pp. 124–130, 132, quote p. 128.

12. For a focus on women collectively versus individually, see also Carol A. Muller, "Musical Echoes: Composing a Past in/for South African Jazz," in Grant Olwage, ed., *Composing Apartheid: Music For and Against Apartheid* (Johannesburg, South Africa: Wits University Press, 2008), p. 140; and especially Salamishah Tillet, "Hush and Listen: Mama Africa and Nina Simone's Global Civil Rights Sound," paper presented at the American Studies Association conference, November 2012, San Juan, Puerto Rico.

13. See "Swingin' Lena Horne Backed by Fans," *New York Post*, February 17, 1960, n.p., "Horne," SCBCCF, v. I; as with other episodes, details of this incident vary slightly from one account to the next, but all focus on Horne's rage. See, for example, *Time*, February 29, 1960, n.p., in "Horne," SCBCCF, v. I; "Lena Horne in Dispute: Singer Throws Lamp at Diner Over Racial Remarks" *New York Times*, February 17, 1960, p. 30; "Lena Horne's Experience" (caption under photograph), *Chicago Defender*, July 2, 1960, p. 18; "Lena Horne, Foe Tell of Café Row," *Los Angeles Examiner*, February 17, 1960, p. 2; Chester Washington, "'No Intention of Apologizing,' Lena Horne Says," *Pittsburgh Courier*, February 27, 1960, p. 2; Horne with Schickel, *Lena*, pp. 204–206.

14. Horne with Schickel, *Lena*, p. 205. For Horne's militance, see Gavin, *Stormy Weather*, pp. 328–331.

15. See Ray Allen and Lois Wilcken, eds., *Island Sounds in the Global City: Caribbean Popular Music in New York* (Urbana: University of Illinois Press, 2001); Shane Vogel, "*Jamaica* on Broadway: The Popular Caribbean and Mock Transnational Performance," *Theater Journal* 62 (March 2010): 1–21, quote p. 17.

16. Horne with Schickel, *Lena*, pp. 199–200; Vogel, "*Jamaica* on Broadway."

17. Horne with Schickel, *Lena*, p. 205.

18. Horne with Schickel, *Lena*, p. 203.

19. Lena Horne and Jeanne Noble, "The Three-Horned Dilemma Facing Negro Women," *Ebony*, August 1966, pp. 118–124.

20. Halle Berry, "2002 Oscar Acceptance Address for Best Leading Actress," March 24, 2002, Hollywood, CA, http://www.americanrhetoric.com/speeches/halleberryoscarspeech.htm; Denzel Washington, "2002 Oscar Acceptance Speech for Best Leading Actor," March 24, 2002, Hollywood, CA, http://www.americanrhetoric.com/speeches//denzelwashingtonoscar.htm, (accessed June 20, 2011).

21. Makeba with Hall, *Makeba: My Story*; Alan Cowell, "Miriam Makeba, 76, Singer and Activist, Dies," *New York Times*, November 10, 2008, http://www.nytimes .com/2008/11/11/world/afrcia/11makeba.html; Nina Simone with Stephen Cleary, *I Put a Spell on You: The Autobiography of Nina Simone* (New York: Da Capo Press, 1993; orig. pub. 1991), pp. 137–139; Miriam Makeba in conversation with Nomsa Mwamuka, *The Miriam Makeba Story* (Johannesburg, South Africa: STE, 2004), pp. 140–143, 171, 211; Cobi Narita and James Briggs Murray, interviewers, *Oral History Interview with Abbey Lincoln/Animata Moseka* (September 18, 1996), Schomburg Center for Research on Black Culture, Louis Armstrong Jazz Oral History Project, New York, New York; Miriam Makeba, *Eyes on Tomorrow* (Gallo, 1991). For Harry Belafonte's critical perspective on Makeba's years in Guinea, see Harry Belafonte with Michael Shnayerson, *My Song: A Memoir* (New York: Knopf, 2011), pp. 340–343; for exile as an experience that Simone, Makeba, and Lincoln shared, see Jacqueline Castledine, "Gender, Jazz and Justice in Cold War Freedom Movements," in Danielle McGuire and John Dittmer, eds., *Freedom Rights: New Perspectives on the Civil Rights Movement* (Lexington: University Press of Kentucky, 2011), pp. 223–246; for Makeba and Simone's collaborations, see Tillet, "Hush and Listen."

22. For her range of performances and activism, see Makeba in conversation with Mwamuka, *The Miriam Makeba Story*; Dais Risasi, "Makeba Makes Whirlwind Visit to NY," *New York Amsterdam News*, May 25, 2000, p. 25; for "I'm not a political singer," see Makeba quoted in Robin Denselow, "The Long Goodbye: Robin Denselow Talks to African Superstar and Activist Miriam Makeba," *Guardian*, May 16, 2008, p. 15; Makeba's later film roles include Darrel Roodt, director, *Sarafina!* (BBC, 1992); Lee Hirsch, director, *Amandla! A Revolution in Four Part Harmony* (ATO Pictures, 2002).

23. Makeba in conversation with Mwamuka, *The Miriam Makeba Story*, p. 239.

24. For her difficulties and travels, see David Nathan, *The Soulful Divas* (New York: Billboard Books, 1999), pp. 60–63; "Nina Simone Ends Voluntary Exile From U.S.," *Jet*, April 22, 1985, pp. 54–55; for "if ever," see Simone with Cleary, *I Put a Spell on You*, p. 137; for tours in the United States, see Ann Powers, "Jazz Festival Reviews: A Diva Who Holds Fans in the Palm of Her Hand," *New York Times*, July 2, 2001, sec. E, p. 5; Somini Sengupta, "The Voice of Misfit Girls Like Me," *New York Times*, June 24, 2001, sec. 2, p. 28; for Simone's move to Liberia as an expression of her long interest in Africa and, especially, for Simone and Makeba's collaborations as having both social and political dimensions, see Salamishah Tillet, "The World Nina Simone Made: The Story of a Sonic Radical" (unpublished manuscript); Tillet, "Hush and Listen." For Simone's long-term struggles with mental illness, see especially Nadine Cohodas, *Princess Noire: The Tumultuous Reign of Nina Simone* (New York: Pantheon, 2010).

25. Accounts of Simone's career and obituaries include John Fordham, "Nina Simone: Soul-Jazz Diva Whose Music Spoke of Love, Respect, and Their

Opposites—Particularly in Relation to Race," *Guardian Leader*, April 22, 2003, p. 23; Richard Harrington, "Nina Simone, A Voice to Be Reckoned With," *Washington Post*, April 22, 2003, sec. C, p. 1; "Singer, Nina Simone, 70, Dies in France," *Jet*, May 5, 3003, pp. 50–53; for "condolences," see Susan Bell, "Friends and Family Pay Their Tributes to Jazz Legend's Political Courage at Packed Funeral," *Scotsman*, April 26, 2003, p. 17; for "sister," see Makeba in conversation with Mwamuka, *The Miriam Makeba Story*, p. 250; for "terrifying reputation," see Martin Gayford, "Difficult? She Just Hates Showbiz," *Daily Telegraph London*, December 14, 1998, quoted in "The Nina Simone Web-Guardian's Interview," *The Nina Simone Webpage*, http://www.boscarol.com/nina/htm/articles/telegraph.html, (accessed July 23, 2001). For attention to her political work, see, for example, Craig Seymour, "An Appreciation: Nina Simone's Voice Fused Art, Politics," *Atlanta Journal and Constitution*, April 23, 2003, p. 1E. For Simone as an increasingly visible touchstone since her death, see for example, Beyonce's comments about Simone in Beyonce Knowles and Ed Burke, directors, *Beyonce: Life Is but a Dream* (New York: Parkwood Entertainment, 2013).

26. Matt Schudel, "Jazz Singer, Actress Abbey Lincoln Dies at 80," *Washington Post*, August 15, 2010, p. C-06; Griffin, *If You Can't Be Free, Be a Mystery*, pp. 185–190.

27. Larry Blumenfeld, "Abbey Lincoln in Command," *Wall Street Journal*, July 18, 2007, p. D10; see also Nate Chinen, "Abbey Lincoln's Emancipation Proclamation," *New York Times*, May 20, 2007, p. 25; Tony Gieske, "Lincoln Recalls Her Years of Tomorrows," *Hollywood Reporter*, October 31, 2000; John Leland, "You Gotta Pay Respect," *Newsweek*, January 6, 1992, pp. 50–51; Hilton Als, "Body and Soul," *Village Voice*, March 23, 1993, pp. 65–66.

28. For "unshakable integrity," see Schudel, "Jazz Singer, Actress Abbey Lincoln Dies at 80"; for "one of a kind," see Martin Johnson, "An Appreciation of Abbey Lincoln," *The Root*, August 15, 2010, http://www.theroot.com/views/appreciation-abbey-lincoln; for "singular figure," see Nate Chinen, "Abbey Lincoln, Bold and Introspective Jazz Singer, Dies at 80," *New York Times*, August 14, 2010, http://www.nytimes.come/2010/08/14/arts/music/15/lincoln/html; for "guiding conscience," see Schudel, "Jazz Singer, Actress Abbey Lincoln Dies at 80."

29. For "militant" see "Jazz Singer Abbey Lincoln Dead at 80," *The Root*, August 14, 2010, http://www.theroot.com/buzz/jazz-singer-abbey-lincoln-dead-80; for "glamorous ingénue" see Johnson, "An Appreciation of Abbey Lincoln"; for "in the forefront," see Vetalie Fusilier, "For the Love of Abbey," *Ebony*, http://ebony/jet.com/Templates/DetailsView.aspx?id=17474; for "silky chanteuse," see Schudel, "Jazz Singer, Actress Abbey Lincoln Dies at 80"; for *We Insist*, see Gwen Ansell, "South Africa: Jazz," *Business Day* (Johannesburg, South Africa), August 19, 2010, http://allafrica.com/stories/201008190890.html; see also Charles Gans, "Jazz Singer Abbey Lincoln Dies at Age 80 in NY," *Chicago Defender*, August 16, 2010, http://www.chicagodefender.com/

article-8521-jazz-singer-abbey-lincoln-dies-at-age-80-in-ny.html/; for "retreated," see John Fordham, "Abbey Lincoln Obituary," *Guardian*, August 15, 2010,
http://www.guardian.co.uk/music/2010/aug/15/abbey/lincoln/obituary.

30. See Diahann Carroll with Ross Firestone, *Diahann! An Autobiography* (New York:
Ivy Books, 1986), pp. 268–290; for her successful stint on Broadway in *Agnes of
God* before *Dynasty*, see pp. 276–281; for "first black bitch," see p. 281; for "void,"
"done incest," "wealthy and ruthless," "a blow," "the only black actress," and
"pioneering," see Scott Haller, "Diahann Carroll Dresses Up 'Dynasty': "As the
Show's New Shrew, She's Making Trouble and Breaking Boundaries on Prime
Time—Again," *People Magazine*, May 14, 1984, p. 122; Susan Faludi, *Backlash:
The Undeclared War Against American Women* (New York: Crown, 1991). On
October 27, 1988, the short-lived satirical television comedy *D.C. Follies* aired an
episode in which "Reagan" auditions for a part on *Dynasty*.

31. Yolanda Sangweni, "Red Carpet: 21st Annual NAACP Theatre Awards," *Essence*,
August 30, 2011, http://www.essence.com/2011/08/30/21st-annual-naacp-
theatre-awards-red-carpet/. Over the years, both Lena Horne and Cicely Tyson
received the NAACP Spingarn Medal for African Achievement (Horne in 1983
and Tyson in 2009); Horne received the NAACP Image Award in 1999. More
recently, Carroll wrote a second memoir, had guest roles on television series like
Grey's Anatomy and *White Collar*, and became active in breast cancer awareness
and education campaigns. See Diahann Carroll with Bob Morris, *The Legs Are
the Last to Go: Aging, Acting, Marrying and Other Things I Learned the Hard Way*
(New York: HarperCollins, 2008).

32. For "incomparable Cicely Tyson," see L. Lamar Wilson, "'The Help': Missed Opportunities," *The Root*, August 13, 2011, http://www.theroot.com/views/helps-
missed-opportunities; Willow Smith, "21st Century Girl," http://www.youtube
.com/watch?v=AfuHSJqqAo, (accessed May 1, 2011); Tate Taylor, director, *The
Help* (Dreamworks, 2011); "Cicely Tyson Wins Tony for 'The Trip to Bountiful,'"
Harlem World, June 10, 2013, http://harlemworldmag.com/2013/06/10/cicely-
tyson-wins-tony-for-the-trip-to-bountiful/; for Tyson as 79-year-old, see Ruth
Manuel-Logan, "Cicely Tyson Wins First Tony Award At Age 79!," *NewsOne for
Black America*, June 10, 2013, http://newsone.com/2569853/cicely-tyson-tony-
award/.

33. For "body of work" and "speaks," see Karu F. Daniels, "Cicely Tyson Breaks Barriers on Broadway," *Jet*, July 1, 2013, http://jetmag.com/insidejet/cicely-tyson-
breaks-barriers-on-broadway/; for Tyson on C-SPAN as Sojourner Truth, see
"Tribute to Sojourner Truth," April 28, 2009, C-SPAN Video Library, http://
www.c-spanvideo.org/program/285528-1, (accessed May 20, 2011). Tyson received a Freedom Award from the National Civil Rights Museum in Memphis.
See Michael Lollar, "National Civil Rights Museum Set for Big Gala," *Memphis Commercial Appeal*, August 10, 2011, http://www.commercialappeal.com/
news/2011/aug/10/cicely-tyson-danny-glover-bill-russell-among-freed/.

34. Gavin, *Stormy Weather*, pp. 373–374; for "Turning Point," see Nina Simone, *Silk and Soul* (RCA: 1967, music and lyrics by Billy Taylor and Martha Holmes).

35. Steven Holden, "Lena Horne: The Lady and Her Music," *Rolling Stone*, November 26, 1981; see also Frank Rich, "Theater: 'Lena Horne: The Lady and Her Music,'" *New York Times*, May 13, 1981, p. C27; for the show as a performance of authenticity, see the comments by Arthur Laurents, quoted in Gavin, *Stormy Weather*, p. 430; for her retirement prior to her Broadway show, see "Jazz Singer, Actress Lena Horne Dead at 92," *Agence France-Presse*, Monday, May 10, 2010, http://www.google.com/hostednews/afp/article/ALeqM5iyFJol8tsrjZ GtaolkDo74c71qeQ.

36. Michiko Kakutani, "Lena Horne: Aloofness Hid the Pain Until Time Cooled Her Anger," *New York Times*, May 3, 1981, p. D1; Arthur Bell, "Lena Horne: All Storms Weathered," *Village Voice*, May 12, 1981, n.p., Schomburg Center on Black Culture Clipping File, Volume II, 1974–1981, "Lena Horne"; for how she represented herself and her past in the aftermath of her hit show, see also Gavin, *Stormy Weather*, pp. 427–431; for her own counternarrative that emphasized African Americans' anger, see Brian Lanker, *I Dream a World: Portraits of Black Women Who Changed America* (New York: Stewart Tabori and Chang, 1989), pp. 80–82.

37. For "worked tirelessly," see Barack Obama, quoted in Frank James, "Obama on Lena Horne: She Forged Progress," *National Public Radio*, May 10, 2010, http:// www.npr.org/blogs/the two-way/2010/05/obama_on_lena_horne_she_forged .html; see also Aljean Harmetz, "Lena Horne, Singer and Actress Dies at 92," *New York Times*, May 10, 2010, http://www.nytimes.com/2010/05/10/arts/music/ 10horne.html; Joel Dreyfuss, "Lena Horne Dead at 92," *The Root*, May 10, 2010, http://www.theroot.com/views/lena-horne-dead-92; Michele Gielan, "Remembering Lena Horne, CBS Video," http://www.cbsnews.com/video/ watch/?id=6470779n; "Jazz Singer, Actress Lena Horne Dead at 92," *Agence France-Presse*, Monday, May 10, 2010; Dennis McLellan and Valerie J. Nelson, "Lena Horne Dies at 92; Singer and Civil Rights Activist Who Broke Barriers," *Los Angeles Times*, May 10, 2010, http://articles.latimes.com/2010/may/10/ local/la-me-horne-20100510.

38. Stanley Crouch, "Lena Horne and the Hollywood Shuffle," *The Root*, May 13, 2010, http://www.theroot.com//views/lena-horne-and-hollywood-shuffle.

39. See for example, Brother Ali, "Uncle Sam, Goddam," *The Undisputed Truth* (Rhymesayers Entertainment, 2007); Melissa Block, interview with Meshell Ndegeocello, "Meshell Ndegeocello Honors Simone's 'Sovereign Soul,'" *National Public Radio*, *All Things Considered*, November 26, 2012, http://www.npr.org/2012/11/26/165920219/ meshell-ndegeocello-honor-nina-sovereighn-soul; Prudence Chauke, "Miriam's 'Pata Pata' Featured on the New 2010 Honda Accord Crosstour Commercial," January, 25, 2010, Jamati.com, http://www.jamati.com/online/music/miriams-pata-pata-featured-on-the-new-2010-honda-accord-crosstour-commercial/.

40. Cynthia Mort, director, *Nina* (forthcoming, 2013); for responses to the casting, see, for example, Spectra, "In Honor of Nina Simone: Why Black Women Must Re-Frame the Conversation About Black Women in Hollywood," *Spectra Speaks*, September 18, 2012, http://www.spectraspeaks.com/2012/09/black-women-responses-nina-sione-zoe-saldana-biopic-media-diversity-solutions/; "Fifty Shades of Black: Why Does Hollywood 'Lightwash' Blacks?" *Huffington Post Live*, September 24, 2012, http://videos/huffingtonpost.come/entertainment/fifty-shades-of-black-517479706; Karen Grigsby Bates, "Controversial Casting for a Nina Simone Biopic," National Public Radio, November 26, 2012, http://www.npr.org/2012/11/20/165346202/controversial-casting-for-a-nina-simone-biopic.

41. Gloria Hull, et al., eds., *All the Women Are White, All the Blacks Are Men, but Some of Us Are Brave: Black Women's Studies* (New York: Feminist Press, 1982).

42. William Taylor and Richard Carroll Lamb, "I Wish I Knew How It Would Feel to Be Free," performed by Nina Simone, *Silk and Soul* (RCA, 1967).

Index